Working with Microsoft Forms and Customer Voice

Efficiently gather and manage customer feedback, insights, and experiences

Welly Lee

BIRMINGHAM—MUMBAI

Working with Microsoft Forms and Customer Voice

Associate Group Product Manager: Pavan Ramchandani
Publishing Product Manager: Bhavya Rao
Senior Editor: Sofi Rogers
Content Development Editor: Feza Shaikh
Technical Editor: Deepesh Patel
Copy Editor: Safis Editing
Project Coordinator: Manthan Patel
Proofreader: Safis Editing
Indexer: Manju Arasan
Production Designer: Vijay Kamble

First published: May 2021
Production reference: 2260521

Published by Packt Publishing Ltd.
Livery Place
35 Livery Street
Birmingham
B3 2PB, UK.

ISBN 978-1-80107-017-1

www.packt.com

Written during the pandemic with special thanks to my wife, Anna, for her support, and to my parents, Inge and Aris, for their cheers.

– Welly Lee

Foreword

2020 has been a difficult year on so many levels. The challenge, however, drove human creativity and accelerated invention and transformation in healthcare, communications, education, commerce, and many other fields. We still have a long way to go, but many of those innovations will change the way we do things well beyond the end of the pandemic. For businesses of all kinds, the accelerated adoption of e-commerce is surely one of those permanent shifts. To create great e-commerce experiences, organizations must learn from data gathered from a dramatically expanded set of sources. The transactions captured in application software provide important context but are only the tip of the data iceberg. Signals gathered about what a prospective customer looks at on the web, how and when they shop, and the data that lets one customer be grouped with a population of similar customers provide an important backdrop for the transaction data. Health, economic, and demographic trends affecting the area where the customers live help businesses look forward to understand what is coming. Software like the family of business applications from Microsoft harnesses this broad collection of data to help businesses deliver the best personalized experiences for every customer with every interaction.

The breadth and depth of available data is amazing, but sometimes, the best way to understand a customer's point of view is just to ask them. In the digital world, that happens through surveys, and surveys are the role of Dynamics 365 Customer Voice. Customer Voice enables business users – without a requirement for coders – to create personalized, branded surveys that can be delivered at any point in the customer journey. The right survey, delivered at the right time, lets a customer feel heard – increasing satisfaction whether the experience being surveyed was positive or negative. The wrong survey at the wrong time becomes an annoyance. Customer Voice lets business users create the right personalized survey and control the orchestration to deliver it to the right customers at the right time.

Other survey applications isolate survey data in another data silo. Since Customer Voice is built on Microsoft Dataverse, it is straightforward to connect surveys with customer transactions and the broader connection of data signals to provide a complete, contextualized picture. Personalized surveys are an essential component of a modern e-commerce strategy, and Dynamics 365 Customer Voice gives organizations the tools to build modern, personalized surveys, the orchestration to deliver those surveys to the right customers at the right time, and the data and intelligence platform to create powerful insights from the combination of survey data, transaction data, and the universe of other available data sources.

James Phillips

President, Digital Transformation Platform Group at Microsoft

As the world adapts to always-on, all-encompassing digital interactivity, cutting through noise and authentically connecting with a customer becomes exponentially more important, and equally, more challenging. Customers expect timely and personalized interactions, and for their favorite brands to act swiftly and proactively to their needs and wants. They want to be able to give feedback in the moment and then expect immediate action or situational awareness during the next interaction.

Likewise, business leaders across industries are searching for the most impactful way to instill a customer-centric culture within their organization. They are challenged with amplifying customer insights across their business, and across their customer's journey: from initial marketing touchpoints with prospects, through the sales cycle, and ultimately once customers begin to use their products and services. Dynamics 365 Customer Voice empowers businesses to collect deep prospect and customer insights and deliver them across each function of an organization, ensuring a seamless and delightful experience that results in customers for life and valued brand ambassadors.

Dynamics 365 Customer Voice converges with Microsoft's family of business applications to create a perfectly calibrated customer voice solution that transforms the end-to-end customer experience. With out-of-the-box templates, point-and-click usability, and AI-infused feedback management features, businesses waste no time with setup. Leaders can quickly deploy their surveys to listen to customers in the moment and across the life cycle to be armed with actionable insights in real time. This is exactly what's needed to foster a customer-centric culture, process, and discipline across an entire organization, where each business function is aligned to proactively address customer needs and deliver personalized experiences with every interaction across the customer journey.

This book provides the most comprehensive guidance to help you to implement a feedback management solution and program in your organization. The book not only includes the technical how-to instructions but also uses real-life examples to share survey best practices to help you create an end-to-end feedback management solution. Whether you want a simple pulse or NPS feedback template off the shelf or want to create more complex periodic surveys with branching, triggers, journey orchestration, and reporting, this book is for you.

Ray Smith

General Manager for Dynamics 365 Sales and Customer Voice

Contributors

About the author

Welly Lee is the head of product for Dynamics 365 Customer Voice. He has been with Microsoft for more than 14 years working on products such as SQL Server, SharePoint, and Dynamics 365. Prior to Microsoft, he was a professional consultant advising multi-national organizations on business process and technology implementation for more than 10 years.

He has a master's in engineering and a **Master of Business Administration** (**MBA**), as well as a bachelor's degree in psychology from the University of Washington.In his free time, he likes to travel around the world, having visited 79 countries, and plans to continue to travel as soon it becomes safe again from the pandemic.

About the reviewer

Megan V. Walker is a Microsoft Business Applications MVP and an independent consultant working under the business name of MVW Consulting Ltd. Her experience is wide and varied, covering most aspects of Dynamics and the Power Platform, with experience in web design, social media, and marketing.

She has built a reputation as one of the world's leading experts in Microsoft Forms and Dynamics 365 Customer Voice, with her videos, articles, and presentations being referenced and used as learning resources by Microsoft.

Megan is a passionate blogger, writing about tips, tricks, and ideas for non-developer geeks. She is also a podcast host with fellow Microsoft MVP and good friend, Lisa Crosbie on The UP Podcast.

Table of Contents

3

Creating a Survey with Microsoft Forms

Section 2: Implementing Common Feedback Solutions with Microsoft Forms and Dynamics 365 Customer Voice

4

Conducting a More Productive Meeting with Microsoft Forms and Microsoft Teams

5

Post-Training Assessment and Feedback

6

Conducting an Employee Survey with Dynamics 365 Customer Voice

7

Collecting Periodic Customer Feedback with Customer Voice

8

Automating Customer Support Surveys with Dynamics 365 Customer Voice

9

Closing a Feedback Loop with Customer Voice

Section 3:
Administering Microsoft Forms and Dynamics 365 Customer Voice

10
Administering Microsoft Forms and Dynamics 365 Customer Voice

11
Managing Usage with Dynamics 365 Customer Voice

Other Books You May Enjoy

Index

Preface

Microsoft Forms and Dynamics 365 Customer Voice enable organizations to collect and analyze feedback from employees and customers, helping developers to integrate customer and employee feedback, as well as business users who need to collect feedback to be able to develop customer-centric solutions. This book takes a hands-on approach to leverage Microsoft Forms and Dynamics 365 Customer Voice capabilities for common feedback scenarios and shows you best practices and tips and tricks that will have your solution up and running in no time.

You will begin by exploring common scenarios where organizations collect feedback from employees and customers and implement end-to-end solutions with Microsoft Forms and Dynamics 365 Customer Voice. Next, you'll discover how to create surveys and get to grips with different configuration options commonly used for each scenario. Throughout the book, you'll also find sample questions, along with step-by-step instructions for integrating the survey with related technology such as Microsoft Teams, Power Automate, and Power BI, for an end-to-end scenario.

By the end of this book, you'll be able to build and deploy your complete solution using Microsoft Forms and Dynamics 365 Customer Voice to your customers and employees, thus allowing you to listen to them, interpret their feedback, take timely follow-up action, and monitor results.

Who this book is for?

This book is for business users who want to increase customer and employee engagement and collect data for measuring user satisfaction and driving product and process improvements. Beginner-level knowledge of Microsoft products such as Office 365 (including Teams, Outlook, and Excel) is expected. The book also includes advanced topics for citizen developers to automate sending Customer Voice surveys, follow-up actions, and creating custom dashboards using Microsoft Power Platform applications like Power Automate and Power BI.

What this book covers?

Chapter 1, Introducing Microsoft Forms and Customer Voice, we will review the two products, including their key capabilities and licensing requirements.

Chapter 2, Best Practices for Collecting Feedback through Surveys, we will discuss some of the best practices for designing surveys to collect feedback from your customers and employees. At the end of this chapter, you will get to understand how to design survey questions and send surveys to maximize responses, as well as learning about common methods for analyzing survey results.

Chapter 3, Creating a Survey with Microsoft Forms, we will go through step-by-step instructions to create and send a survey. At the end of this chapter, you will understand how survey authoring works, including the different types of questions you can create with Microsoft Forms.

Chapter 4, Conducting a More Productive Meeting with Microsoft Forms and Microsoft Teams, we will review how you can use Microsoft Forms to send a survey to prepare for a meeting, conduct live polls during the meeting, and collect and share feedback after the meeting. By the end of this chapter, you will know how to use Microsoft Forms to make your meetings more productive.

Chapter 5, Post-Training Assessment and Feedback, we will look at quiz capabilities in Microsoft Forms to conduct a training assessment, including creating a quiz, scoring a quiz, and publishing grades. We will then go over how to use Microsoft Forms to collect training feedback, as well as the additional benefit of collecting feedback through Dynamics 365 Customer Voice.

Chapter 6, Conducting an Employee Survey with Dynamics 365 Customer Voice, we will review Customer Voice capabilities in the context of common employee feedback scenarios. By the end of this chapter, you will understand how to use Customer Voice to collect feedback from your employees.

Chapter 7, Collecting Periodic Customer Feedback with Customer Voice, we will use an example of a customer experience manager at a bank who sends monthly customer feedback surveys to a customer list provided by the bank operations team. We will start by creating a personalized survey based on your customer type, and then brand the survey, send the survey, and link the results to the customer records.

Chapter 8, Automating Customer Support Surveys with Dynamics 365 Customer Voice, we will look at how you can use and customize these templates. We will also discuss additional ways you can collect feedback as part of your customer support process, such as collecting feedback through text messages and chat.

Chapter 9, Closing a Feedback Loop with Customer Voice, we are going to show you how to implement follow-up actions using Customer Voice. We will start with an out-of-the-box follow-up action in Customer Voice, and then discuss how you customize the follow-up workflow, and we will conclude the chapter by showing you how you can also use Power Automate to create workflows for Office Forms responses.

Chapter 10, Administering Microsoft Forms and Dynamics 365 Customer Voice, we will review the administration settings for Forms and Customer Voice, walk through the process of setting up users in Dataverse for Customer Voice, and review functionalities to help you to move Customer Voice projects from development to test and production environments.

Chapter 11, Managing Usage with Dynamics 365 Customer Voice, we will review the Customer Voice license model and how you can get usage reports and discuss the departmental capacity management that is being previewed in Customer Voice.

To get the most out of this book

Microsoft Forms and Dynamics 365 Customer Voice use Microsoft Power Automate to automate sending surveys and follow-up actions. We will cover creating a workflow using Power Automate in this book. Although it is not required that you know Power Automate to read this book, I recommend you familiarize yourself with Power Automate. Microsoft provides free learning content for Power Automate that you can access at `https://docs.microsoft.com/en-us/learn/modules/get-started-flows/`

Software/Hardware covered in the book	OS Requirements
Microsoft Forms	Since they are all software as a service, they are accessible via browser and do not depend on a specific OS.
Dynamics 365 Customer Voice	
Microsoft Power Automate	
Microsoft Power BI	
Dynamics 365	

If you are using the digital version of this book, we advise you to type the code yourself or access the code via the GitHub repository (link available in the next section). Doing so will help you avoid any potential errors related to copy/pasting of code.

Download the example code files

You can download the example code files for this book from your account at www. packt.com. If you purchased this book elsewhere, you can visit www.packtpub.com/support and register to have the files emailed directly to you.

You can download the code files by following these steps:

1. Log in or register at www.packt.com.
2. Select the **Support** tab.
3. Click on **Code Downloads**.
4. Enter the name of the book in the **Search** box and follow the onscreen instructions.

Once the file is downloaded, please make sure that you unzip or extract the folder using the latest version of:

- WinRAR/7-Zip for Windows
- Zipeg/iZip/UnRarX for Mac
- 7-Zip/PeaZip for Linux

The code bundle for the book is also hosted on GitHub at https://github.com/PacktPublishing/Working-with-Microsoft-Forms-and-Customer-Voice. In case there's an update to the code, it will be updated on the existing GitHub repository.

We also have other code bundles from our rich catalog of books and videos available at https://github.com/PacktPublishing/. Check them out!

Download the color images

We also provide a PDF file that has color images of the screenshots/diagrams used in this book. You can download it here:

https://static.packt-cdn.com/downloads/9781801070171_ColorImages.pdf

Conventions used

There are a number of text conventions used throughout this book.

`Code in text`: Indicates code words in text, database table names, folder names, filenames, file extensions, pathnames, dummy URLs, user input, and Twitter handles. Here is an example: " Add new variables for general employee information you would like to include in your reporting—such as `Title`, `Department`, and `Location`"

A block of code is set as follows:

```
{
    "type": "object",
    "properties": {
        "EmbedContextParameters": {
            "type": "object",
            "properties": {
                "<Survey Variable>": {
                    "type": "string"
                },
            }
        }
    }
}
```

When we wish to draw your attention to a particular part of a code block, the relevant lines or items are set in bold:

```
{
    "type": "object",
    "properties": {
        "EmbedContextParameters": {
            "type": "object",
```

Bold: Indicates a new term, an important word, or words that you see onscreen. For example, words in menus or dialog boxes appear in the text like this. Here is an example: "Select **System info** from the **Administration** panel."

> **Tips or important notes**
> Appear like this.

Get in touch

Feedback from our readers is always welcome.

General feedback: If you have questions about any aspect of this book, mention the book title in the subject of your message and email us at customercare@packtpub.com.

Errata: Although we have taken every care to ensure the accuracy of our content, mistakes do happen. If you have found a mistake in this book, we would be grateful if you would report this to us. Please visit www.packtpub.com/support/errata, selecting your book, clicking on the Errata Submission Form link, and entering the details.

Piracy: If you come across any illegal copies of our works in any form on the Internet, we would be grateful if you would provide us with the location address or website name. Please contact us at copyright@packt.com with a link to the material.

If you are interested in becoming an author: If there is a topic that you have expertise in and you are interested in either writing or contributing to a book, please visit authors.packtpub.com.

Reviews

Please leave a review. Once you have read and used this book, why not leave a review on the site that you purchased it from? Potential readers can then see and use your unbiased opinion to make purchase decisions, we at Packt can understand what you think about our products, and our authors can see your feedback on their book. Thank you!

For more information about Packt, please visit packt.com.

Section 1: Working with Microsoft Forms and Customer Voice

In this section, you will learn the fundamentals of surveys and how to get started with Microsoft Forms and Dynamics 365 Customer Voice in order to collect feedback from customers and employees.

This section contains the following chapters:

- *Chapter 1, Introducing Microsoft Forms and Customer Voice*
- *Chapter 2, Best Practices for Collecting Feedback through Surveys*
- *Chapter 3, Creating a Survey with Microsoft Forms*

1

Introducing Microsoft Forms and Customer Voice

In September 2020, my team released **Dynamics 365 Customer Voice** as an upgrade for **Microsoft Forms Pro**. Soon after, we noticed that the **Net Promoter Score** (**NPS**) started to fall. From the user feedback, we learned that many users were not happy with the data export functionality in the new product. Along with the product upgrade, we switched the data export format from Excel to .csv format, to enable the exporting of larger datasets. Users hated the new .csv format, so based on the feedback, we quickly made a change to go back to exporting data to Excel format and only provided an option for .csv for larger datasets. After we introduced the change, we saw that the NPS score started to go up again.

That story is a real-life example of how collecting feedback can help you identify issues early, and then track your progress in solving them to make customers happy. Despite our best attempts to use data to drive decisions, many of our day-to-day decisions still rely on intuition. While product leaders use their experience to shape their intuition, occasionally the wrong decision is made, and having a feedback measurement system in place is critical to provide an early warning signal to correct your decision.

Our goal at Microsoft is to make it easy for you to collect feedback from your employees and your customers through two products: **Microsoft Forms** and **Dynamics 365 Customer Voice**. Microsoft Forms is a productivity tool targeted at collecting simple surveys and quizzes. Dynamics 365 Customer Voice is an enterprise feedback management system used to collect feedback from employees and customers and integrate the survey data with your existing business application systems. In this chapter, we will review the two products, including their key capabilities and licensing requirements. By the end of this chapter, you will understand the difference between the two products and when to use one over the other.

We will cover the following topics:

- What is Microsoft Forms?
- What is Dynamics 365 Customer Voice?
- Differences between Microsoft Forms and Dynamics 365 Customer Voice
- Licensing requirements

What is Microsoft Forms?

Microsoft Forms (`forms.microsoft.com`) is an application that enables you to collect simple data from people both inside and outside your organization. Without any training, a user can create a simple survey through an easy-to-use interface and share a direct link to the survey. It uses artificial intelligence throughout the experience to make it easy for anyone to get started. When you create a new survey and type in a survey name, Microsoft Forms provides suggestions of commonly used questions based on the survey title. For example, when creating a new survey with the title **Customer feedback survey**, you may get a question suggested such as **Overall, how satisfied are you with our company?** (as shown in *Figure 1.1*):

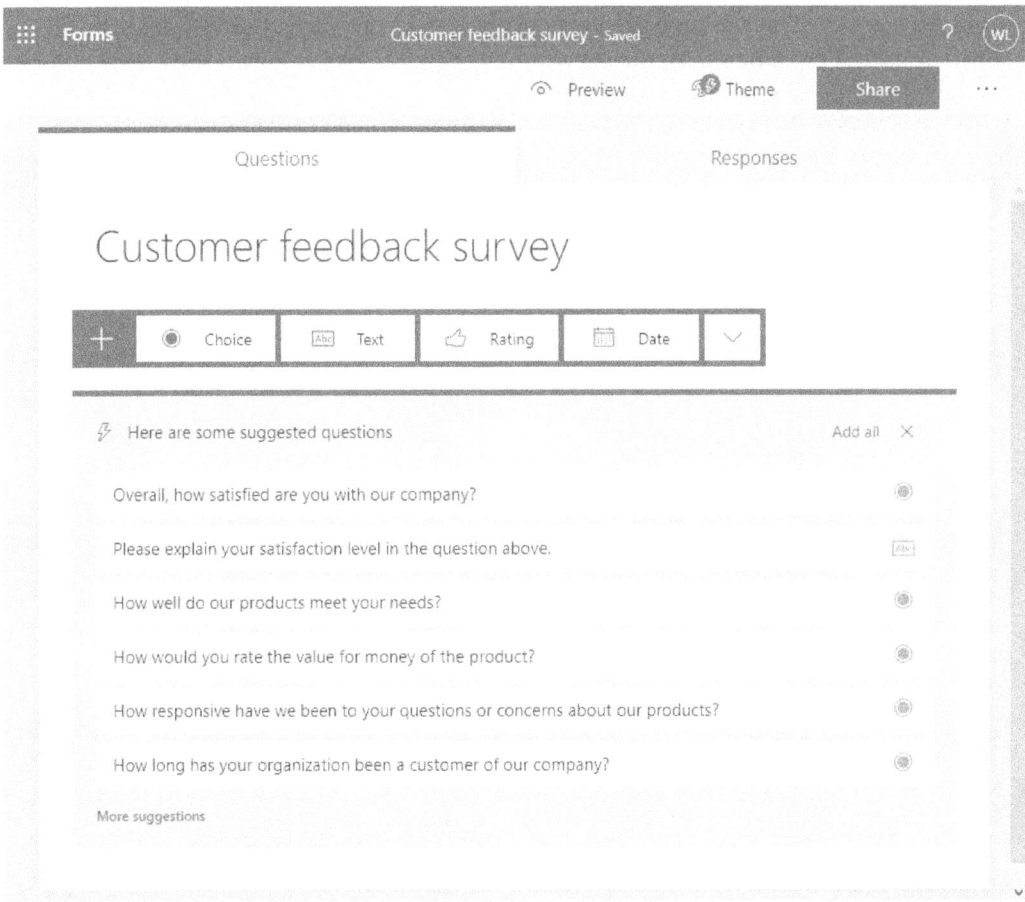

Figure 1.1 – Suggested questions for a customer feedback survey

You can select any or all of the suggested questions or use your own questions by first selecting a question type. Based on the survey questions, Microsoft Forms provides suggestions that may be relevant to your questions:

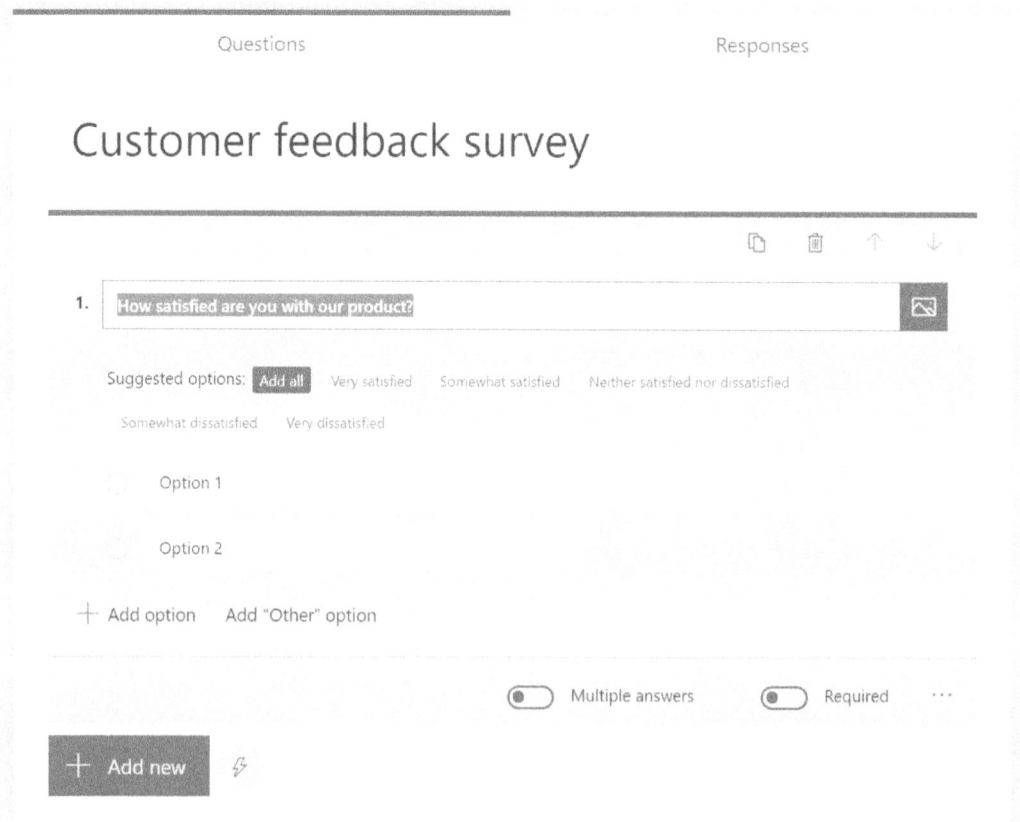

Figure 1.2 – Suggested options on a survey question

You can access a link to the survey and then share it with responders to collect their feedback. The collected information is shown through a built-in report as in the following figure:

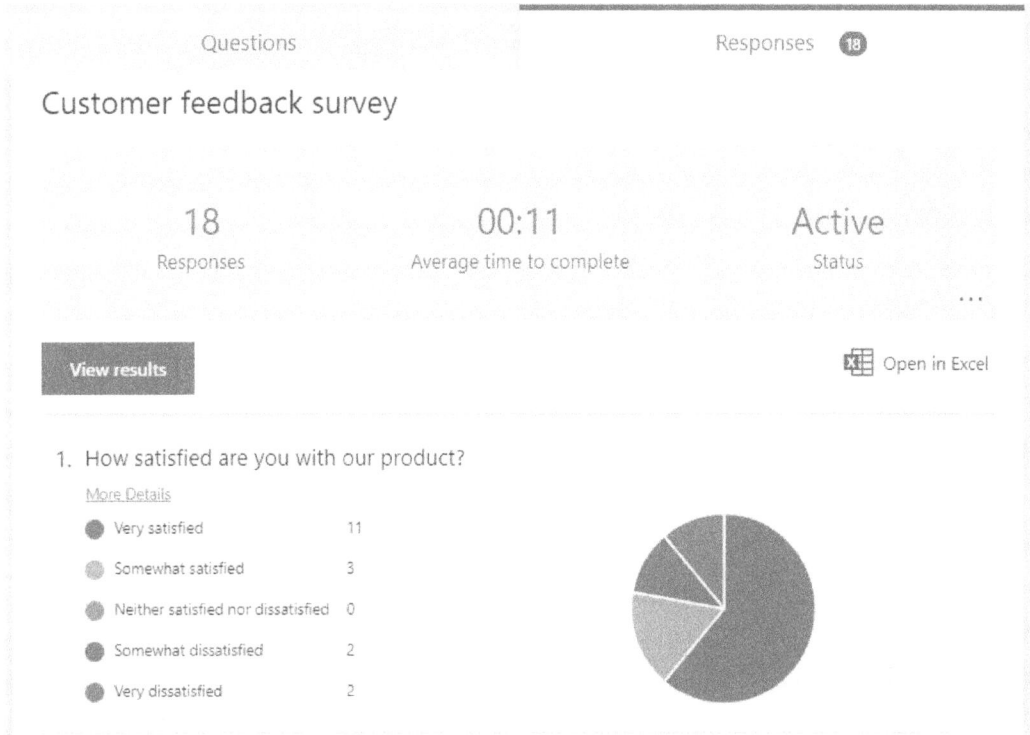

Figure 1.3 – Report summary

In addition to viewing the results from the report summary, you can export the data to Excel and then share the results with other people in your organization.

Microsoft Forms is integrated with other **Microsoft Office** applications (such as **Microsoft Teams**) to allow the collection of data as part of the application's experience. For example, you can create a poll to display in a Teams channel, and then have the results displayed instantly to all channel members:

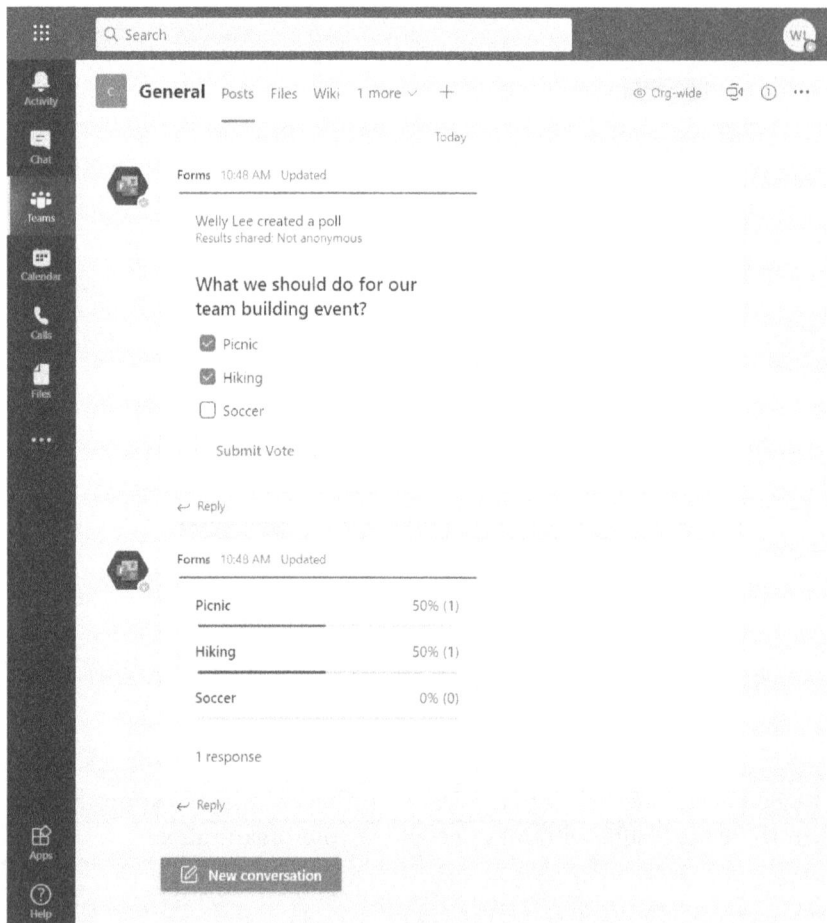

Figure 1.4 – Meeting poll in Teams

In addition to adding a poll to a channel, you can create polls prior to a Teams meeting, and then show the poll during the meeting. We will discuss creating a poll for a meeting in *Chapter 4, Conducting a More Productive Meeting with Microsoft Forms and Microsoft Teams*.

You can also use Microsoft Forms to create a quiz, making it a popular tool for the education sector. When creating a quiz, teachers can include mathematical formulas as part of a question or multiple-choice options to test the students' knowledge, as shown in *Figure 1.5*:

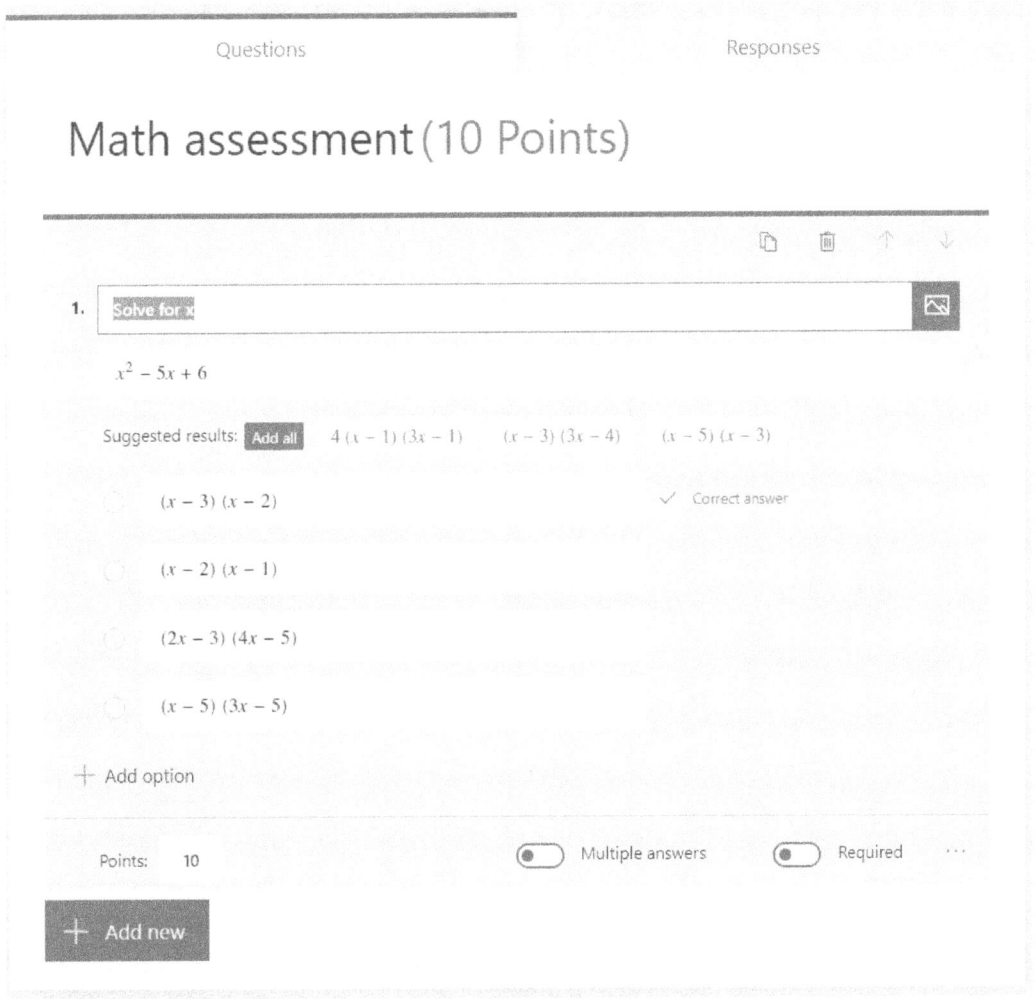

Figure 1.5 – Example of a quiz in Microsoft Forms

You can mark the correct option to the question and assign points for students who answer it correctly. We will discuss quiz capability in *Chapter 5, Post-Training Assessment and Feedback*.

With its easy-to-use interface and integration with Microsoft Office applications, Microsoft Forms has become a popular tool for business users and educators to easily collect data from colleagues and students. As Microsoft Forms is intended for simple data collection tool, it lacks more advanced functionalities. Dynamics 365 Customer Voice fills the gap and offer more capabilities for an enterprise feedback management solution.

What is Dynamics 365 Customer Voice?

Microsoft released Microsoft Forms Pro as an advanced version of Microsoft Forms in July 2019 and rebranded it as Dynamics 365 Customer Voice a year later. Customer Voice builds upon Microsoft Forms' simple survey authoring experience and adds the capabilities needed for an enterprise feedback management platform. Organizations using Dynamics 365 as a **Customer Relationship Management** (**CRM**) system can benefit from the built-in integration to send survey data directly to customer contacts and have survey results be automatically linked to customer records. Organizations using other CRM systems can integrate through **Power Automate** using its 300+ connectors to many popular non-Microsoft business applications.

You can get started with Customer Voice by going to `https://aka.ms/CustomerVoice` and starting a 30-day trial. After completing the sign-up process, you are presented with a list of survey project templates:

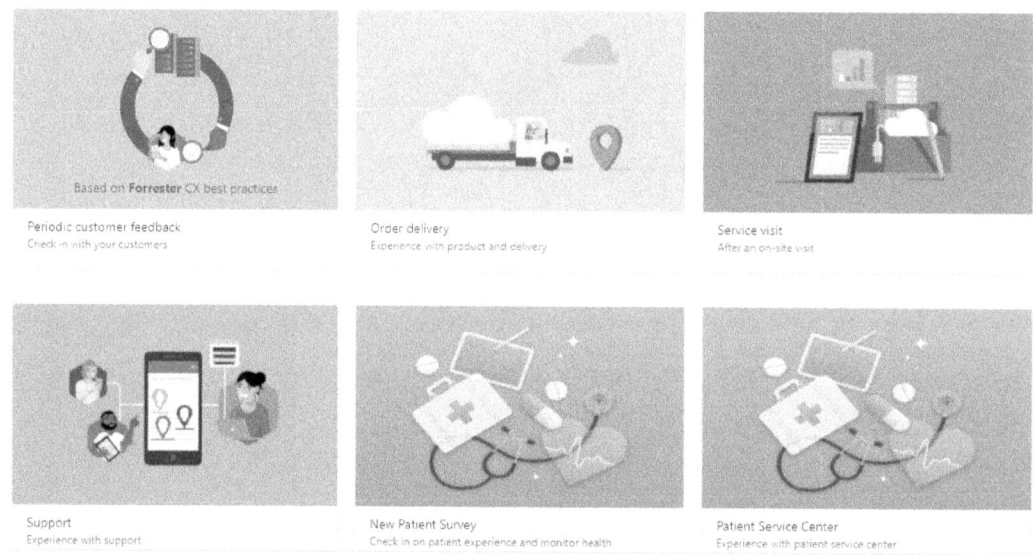

Figure 1.6 – Customer Voice project template gallery

The scenario-based templates include survey questions commonly used for periodic customer feedback, sending a survey after an order delivery or a service visit, and sending a survey after a customer support case is closed. We will go over the customer support template later in *Chapter 8, Automating Customer Support Surveys with Dynamics 365 Customer Voice* .

Some of the project templates include built-in workflows to automate sending the survey based on activities in Dynamics 365. If you are not using Dynamics 365 for your CRM system, you can customize the workflows to connect to your own application.

After you select a template, a survey is created with relevant questions. You can customize the questions by adding and removing them with a similarly easy-to-use authoring experience to that of Microsoft Forms. In addition to the simple survey authoring features, Customer Voice includes advanced survey authoring capabilities such as advanced branching rules (which enable you to skip ahead or dynamically control showing/hiding other questions based on survey responses), branding (styling), and personalizing the survey with variables:

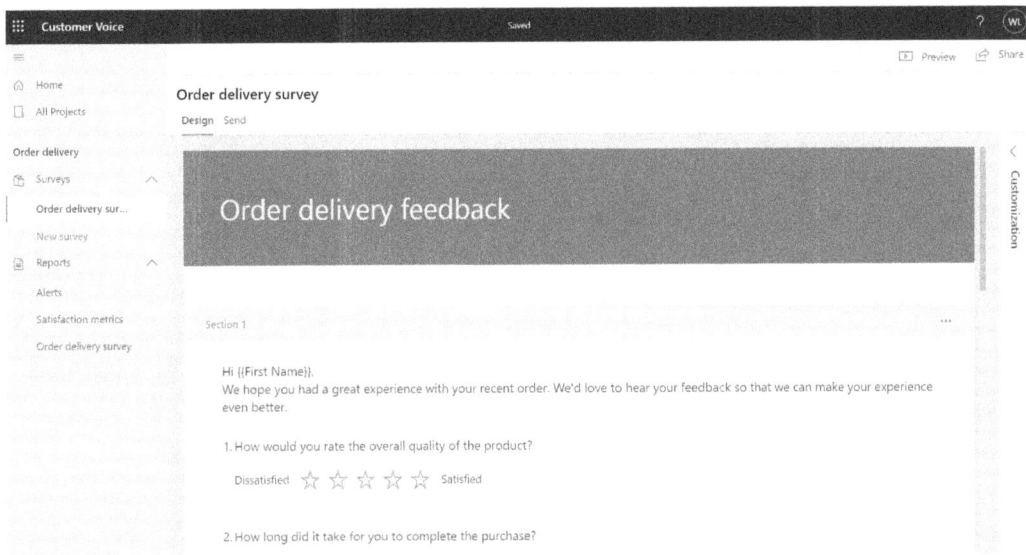

Figure 1.7 – Advanced survey authoring customization pane

The personalization options enable you to dynamically customize the survey questions based on an individual responder's data, such as what product the customer bought, and use the personalization data as additional context for the survey responses. For example, when collecting anonymous feedback for an employee pulse survey, you can include information such as roles or departments without capturing personally identifiable information. We will cover these options in *Chapter 6, Conducting an Employee Survey with Dynamics 365 Customer Voice.*

In addition to the advanced customization, Customer Voice also includes **Satisfaction metrics**:

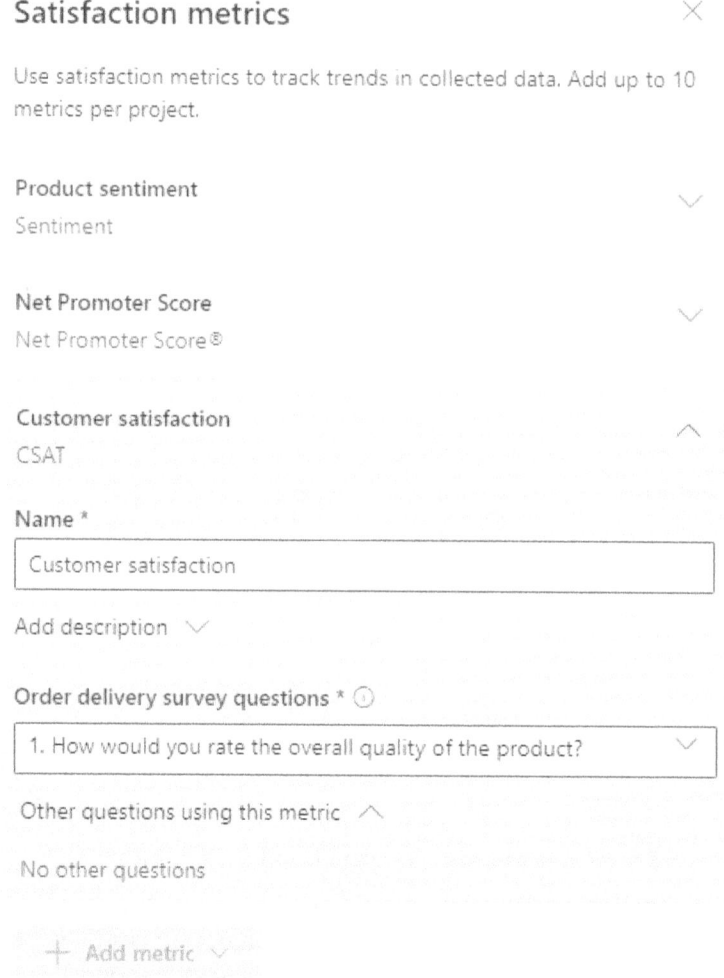

Figure 1.8 – Satisfaction metrics configuration panel

You can define one or more metrics to measure customer or employee satisfaction and map the metrics to questions in your survey. Customer Voice includes a dashboard to report the score for each metric and set alert notifications when the metric is triggered by specified conditions.

Customer Voice includes the ability to distribute surveys through an automated process or on-demand. You can upload a list of contacts to receive the survey invitation by uploading from a `.csv` file. Each of the recipients will receive a personalized survey invitation email and individualized survey link. The individualized survey link allows you to identify people outside your organization who respond to your survey without requiring them to log in. The email invitation also includes an unsubscribe functionality to enable your recipient to opt out, helping to comply with your organization's compliance and privacy policies.

After you send the survey invitations, you can track the progress by going to the **Send** tab from your survey. The survey invite report includes email tracking capability to monitor the number of recipients who read the email, start the survey, and complete the survey:

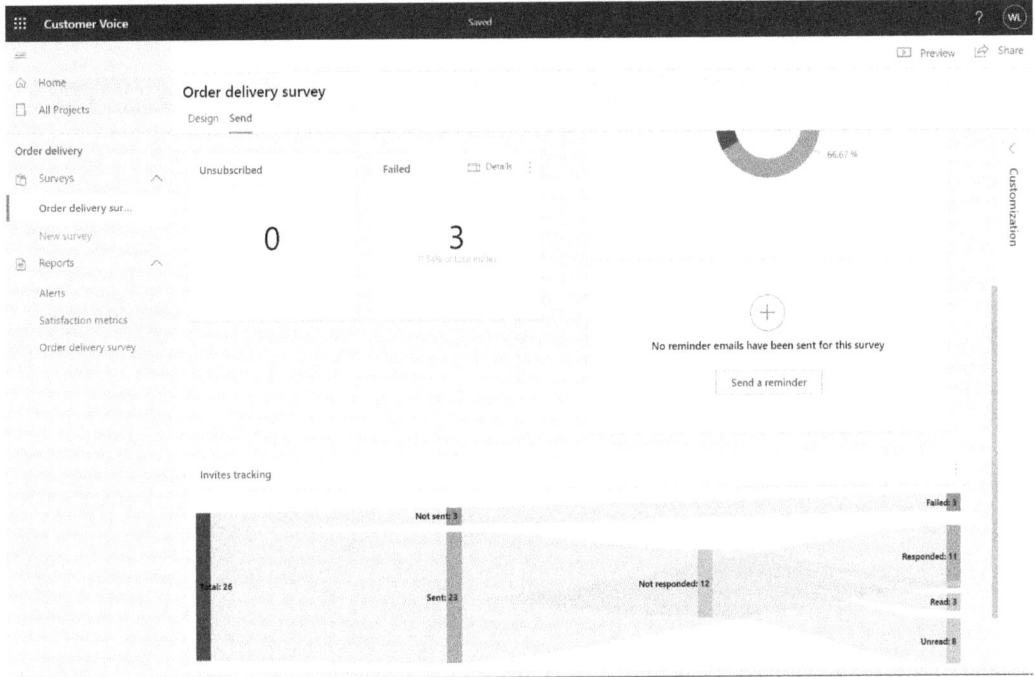

Figure 1.9 – Survey distribution report

In addition, you can automate sending survey invitations based on a customer activity, such as automatically sending a survey invite after a customer support call. You can use the out-of-the-box workflow templates to automate the process or customize your own workflows using Microsoft Power Automate. We will cover automation in detail in *Chapter 8, Automating Customer Support Surveys with Dynamics 365 Customer Voice*, and *Chapter 9, Closing a Feedback Loop with Customer Voice*.

While Forms provides a summary report from your survey results, it does not support filtering. Customer Voice provides a more robust report filtering based on dates, user responses or survey variables. In addition to the survey report, you can specify satisfaction metrics for your survey and track the metrics through satisfaction metrics dashboard under the **Reports** section. You can also define alerts on a metric to notify you when you receive feedback below the target so that you can follow up with your customers or employees in a timely manner:

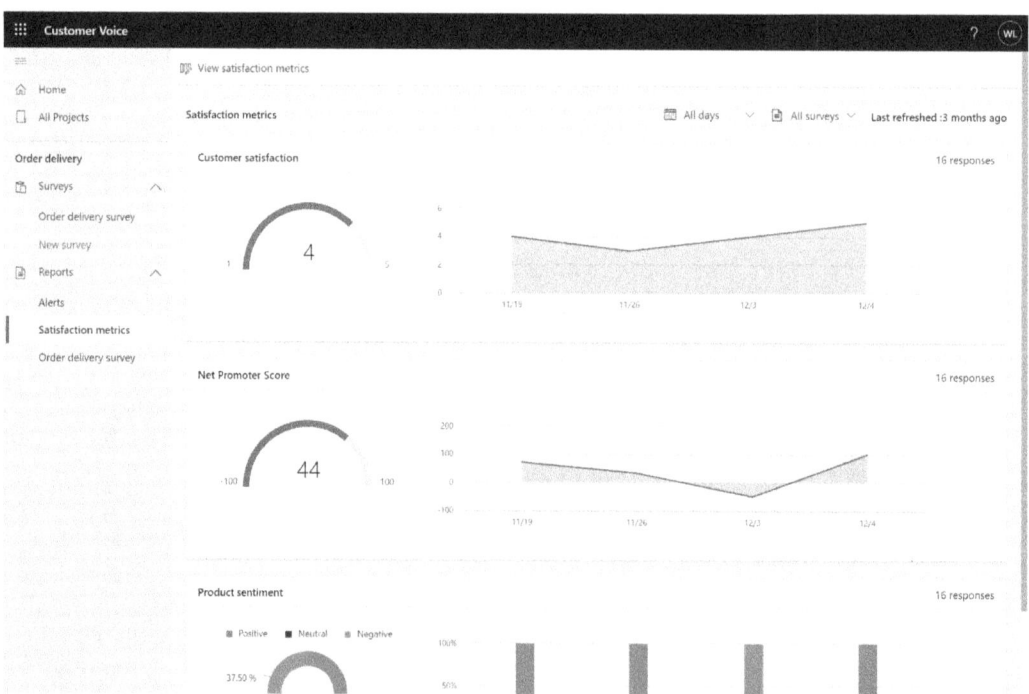

Figure 1.10 – Satisfaction metrics dashboard

Customer Voice writes the survey data directly to **Dataverse**, the online data storage part of your Microsoft 365 subscription. If you are using Dynamics 365 to manage your customer relationship, you can select the Dataverse instance for your environment so the survey responses are automatically linked to your customer records. This provides everyone who works with the customer the ability to view the latest customer feedback. The Dataverse integration enables other Microsoft business applications such as Dynamics 365 and the Power Platform to use the data being collected. For example, using Power BI, you can create a custom dashboard that shows customer sentiment in the context of a customer profile by reading data directly from Dataverse without the need to export data and import it into another data storage solution.

The integration with the Microsoft business application platform makes Customer Voice a powerful tool for you to collect customer and employee feedback as part of your business process, and having the information tie back to customer and employee records enables you to get the right insights and take timely actions.

Now that we have discussed Microsoft Forms and Customer Voice, what are the differences between the two products and when should we use one over the other?

Difference between Microsoft Forms and Customer Voice

Customer Voice is built on top of Microsoft Forms and includes most of Forms' functionalities. In addition to the easy survey-authoring experience from Microsoft Forms, Customer Voice adds what is needed for an end-to-end feedback management solution.

The following table summarizes the functionalities Forms and Customer Voice have in common and the additional capabilities that are unique to Customer Voice:

Survey Authoring	Forms	Customer Voice
Drag-and-drop survey authoring experience	●	●
Multi-language support	●	●
Advanced branching logic		●
Survey personalization		●
Custom header and styling		●
Satisfaction metrics definition		●
Multi-survey project management		●
Ready-to-use feedback project template		●
Survey Distribution		
Anonymous survey link	●	●
QR code	●	●
Send survey via email		●
Personalized email invitation		●
Variable-based survey links		●
Pause and resume survey		●
Survey reminders		●
Survey frequency management		●
Unsubscribe support		●
Automate sending survey via Power Automate		●
Embed survey in web / app with variable inputs		●
Survey Reporting		
Export results to Excel	●	●
Survey result summary	●	●
Survey result filtering		●
Satisfaction metrics score and trends		●
Link survey results to business application		●
Custom Power BI report dashboard support		●
Auto alert for low satisfaction metric score		●
Manage follow up for low satisfaction metric score		●

Figure 1.11 – Feature capability summary between Forms and Customer Voice

> **Important note**
>
> Megan Walker, Microsoft MVP and the technical reviewer for this book, published a detailed blog post to compare Microsoft Forms and Customer Voice features. You can find her blog post at `https://aka.ms/FormsVsCV`.

With the capability comparison in *Figure 1.11*, how do you decide when to use Microsoft Forms and when to use Customer Voice? It depends on your use case. Microsoft Forms is a great productivity tool designed for collecting ad hoc survey feedback, especially when you need to collect and share feedback through Microsoft office application suite such as Teams.

When you need to collect feedback on behalf of your organization from your customers or your employees, then you should consider using Customer Voice. Customer Voice is designed to deliver high-volume surveys and integrate data with your business systems so that you can link the feedback to customer and employee records. Customer Voice also includes closed-loop actions so you can define metrics and get notified when you receive a low metric score so you can get back to customers or employees in a timely manner.

In addition to the feature capability and use case scenarios, Microsoft Forms and Customer Voice have different license requirements to consider.

License requirements for Microsoft Forms and Customer Voice

Microsoft Forms is included in most Office 365 work/school account subscriptions and is also available as part of your free personal Microsoft account (such as for `outlook.com`). The Microsoft Forms that comes as part of your personal Microsoft account is similar to the one that comes as part of your work/school account but has a limit of 200 responses per survey and does not include the following features:

- Share to collaborate
- File upload question type
- Customization of theme color
- AI-based insights on report summary
- Email receipt
- Grading and post-quiz scores
- Office integration

The version included as part of your work/account Office subscription includes a limit of 200 surveys/user and 50,000 responses/survey.

Customer Voice requires a license and is not included as part of your Microsoft 365 subscription. The Customer Voice license is based on survey responses. You can distribute your survey to as many people as you need, and the usage is tracked when you receive survey responses. The Customer Voice base license starts at $200 for a 2,000 responses-per-month capacity for your entire organization. There is no additional user license for Customer Voice but anyone using Customer Voice will be linked to the same capacity. For example, if there are two users in your organization and each user receives 100 responses for a survey they create, you have 1,800 as your remaining response capacity.

Customer Voice tracks usage against capacity at the annual level to provide flexibility for organizations to send surveys periodically (such as quarterly or annual surveys), so you can use your annual capacity at once and not send a survey again until next year. *Chapter 11, Managing Usage with Dynamics 365 Customer Voice*, will cover how you can manage capacity, including how to distribute capacity to different department users and how to track usage against capacity.

Several Dynamics 365 applications include 2,000 survey responses/month as part of the license entitlement. These applications are listed here:

- Dynamics 365 Customer Insights
- Dynamics 365 Sales Enterprise and Sales Premium
- Dynamics 365 Customer Service Enterprise
- Dynamics 365 Marketing
- Dynamics 365 Project Service Automation
- Dynamics 365 Human Resources

Note that the 2000 responses included as part of your Dynamics 365 subscription is for your entire organization (not for each user). If you need additional responses, you can purchase an additional license at $100/1,000 responses per month.

Summary

In this chapter, you have learned about Microsoft Forms and Dynamics 365 Customer Voice and the difference between the two products. Microsoft Forms provides a basic survey capability and Customer Voice adds more feature-rich functionalities to support enterprise feedback management scenarios.

Now that you understand the tools you can use to create surveys and collect feedback, in *Chapter 2, Best Practices for Collecting Feedback through Surveys*, we will discuss how to design survey questions, distribute surveys, and analyze survey results.

2
Best Practices for Collecting Feedback through Surveys

Microsoft Forms and Customer Voice are tools designed to make it easier for you to collect feedback from your employees and customers. Customer Voice provides templates and uses artificial intelligence to guide you through the process, but you ultimately still need to customize, distribute, and analyze survey feedback based on your specific business requirements.

In this chapter, we will discuss some of the best practices for designing surveys to collect feedback from your customers and employees. At the end of this chapter, you will get to understand how to design survey questions and send surveys to maximize responses, as well as learning about common methods for analyzing survey results.

The chapter is organized as follows:

- Designing survey questionnaires
- Distributing surveys
- Analyzing survey results

Designing survey questionnaires

There is a popular belief that you should collect as much data as possible and worry about how to use the data later. In my experience, collecting too much data can backfire. Data must be collected with specific objectives in mind. Collecting feedback without a clear purpose tends to result in a lot of noise and makes it hard to get useful insights. This is especially important for collecting feedback through surveys when participation is often voluntary, and respondents must be persuaded to participate. The longer the survey, the less willing the respondents will be to complete it and the fewer responses you will collect. You just need to design your survey carefully so that you can get the most insight with minimal effort from your survey respondents.

A survey questionnaire usually comprises the following:

- **Key Performance Indicator** (**KPI**) questions
- Key driver questions
- Open-ended questions

Let's discuss each of these components.

KPI questions

KPI metrics are often needed to quantitatively measure satisfaction and compare your performance over time. Ask yourself, how do you know when your customers or employees are happy? What metrics would you use to measure a customer or employee's satisfaction? By collecting the same KPI metrics over time, you can compare the current period against the last period to track progress.

There are standard KPIs that I would recommend starting with to help determine satisfaction. These include **Net Promotor Score (NPS)**, **Customer Satisfaction Score (CSAT)**, and **Customer Effort Score (CES)**. Adopting standard metrics not only helps you to get started but also enables you to compare across products or compare your organization's performance against others in the industry.

Net Promotor Score (NPS)

NPS is a popular metric to measure customer satisfaction. The NPS question asks the likelihood of the respondent recommending your product and service to others. The question forces the respondent to think broadly about their overall satisfaction with your product/service. If the respondent is not happy with any aspect of the product, then they are less likely to recommend it to someone else. The broad nature of the question makes NPS a reliable long-term measurement of your product or service. The 11-scale rating defines responses with either 9 or 10 as a promoter and 0-6 as detractors. The NPS score is calculated based on the percentage of the number of promoters minus the percentage of detractors. *Figure 2.1* illustrates how an NPS score is calculated:

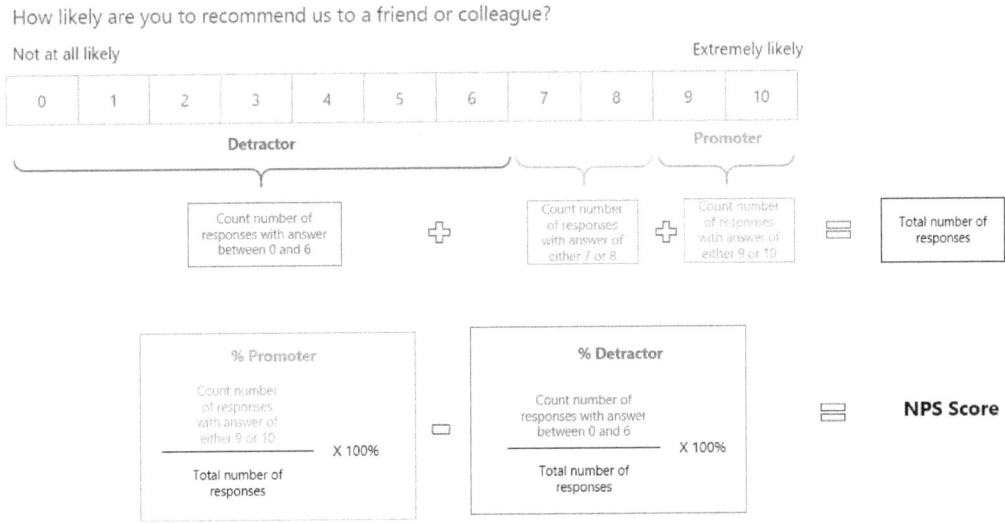

Figure 2.1 – NPS calculation

Note that although an NPS score of 7 or 8 is not used in the NPS score calculation, some organizations analyze customers giving scores in that range in order to identify ways to move them to the **Promoter** range.

Although NPS is typically used for customer feedback surveys, many organizations use the metric to measure employee satisfaction and loyalty by modifying a question slightly; for example:

- Original NPS question: "How likely are you to recommend us to a friend or colleague?"
- Modified NPS question: "How likely are you to recommend a friend to work here?"

Another popular KPI metric is **CSAT**.

Customer Satisfaction Score (CSAT)

CSAT is typically used to measure specific interactions and is asked right after an activity, such as at the end of customer service calls or at the end of an online purchase. CSAT can be asked and calculated in a variety of ways but it is frequently measured on a five point scale from dissatisfied to satisfied. The CSAT score is calculated based on the percentage of respondents giving 4 or 5 points. *Figure 2.2* illustrates how a CSAT score is calculated:

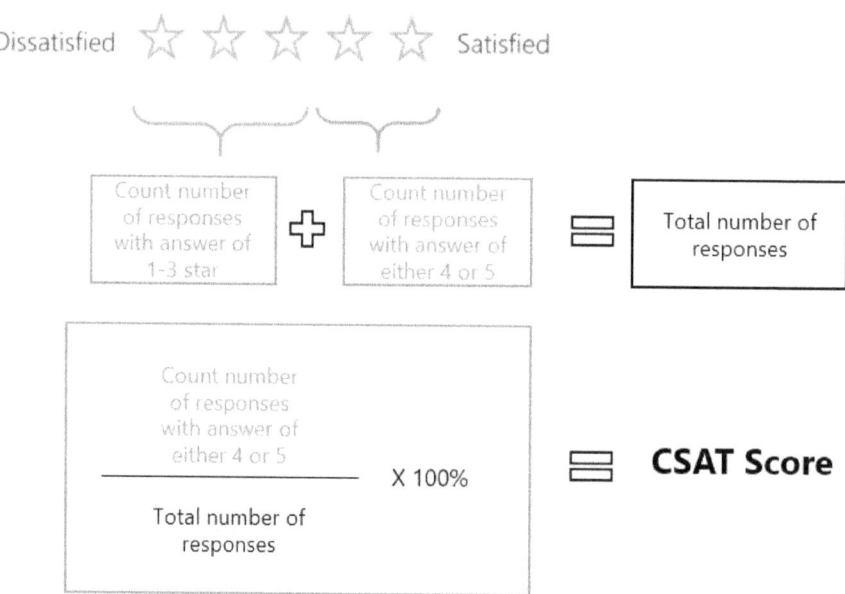

Figure 2.2 – CSAT calculation

Note that, although CSAT is commonly done on a rating scale of five, some organizations use a scale of 7 or 10. For those scales, the top two scales are still considered the CSAT score.

Another metric often used to measure customer satisfaction is **CES**.

Customer Effort Score (CES)

CES is based on how much effort a customer must make to complete a transaction, such as scheduling a visit, making payment, getting an issue resolved, and so on. CES metrics were introduced by **Corporate Executive Board (CEB)** after a customer service and loyalty study indicated that reducing customer pain points when using a product contributes more to customer loyalty than trying to make your customer happy.

> **Important note**
>
> For more information, see *Stop Trying to Delight Your Customers* by Matthew Dixon, Karen Freeman, and Nicholas Toman: `https://hbr.org/2010/07/stop-trying-to-delight-your-customers`.

Examples of CES questions:

- How much effort did you personally have to put forth to handle your request?

- Overall, how easy was it to ___? (Replace ___ with the activity or product functionality you are trying to measure.)

The CES question is based on a five-point scale question to ask how easy it is to accomplish a task, then calculate the score based on the percentage of respondents answering *easy* and the percentage of respondents answering *difficult*. *Figure 2.3* illustrates how a CES score is calculated:

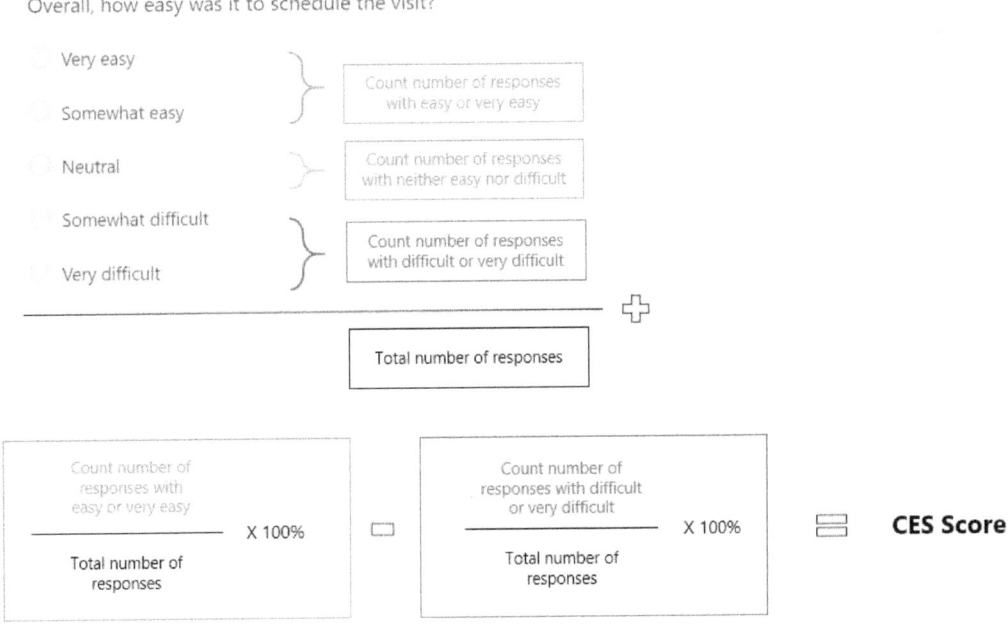

Figure 2.3 – CES calculation

CES is often used to identify potential customer experience issues throughout the customer journey.

While standard metrics such as NPS, CSAT, and CES are good metrics for many scenarios, you may have specific measurement requirements.

Custom metrics

In addition to the standard metrics, many organizations also create their own custom metrics. For example, Microsoft conducts an annual employee feedback survey and uses a composite metric called **Workgroup Health Index (WHI)** that aggregates results from several questions in the annual survey. **Forrester Research** also uses a custom index to measure employee experience as part of their organizational research study (see `https://www.forrester.com/report/Forresters+EX+Index+A+Deeper+Look+At+The+Data/-/E-RES157896`).

Custom metrics typically aggregate results from several questions. For example, the following question asks employees to rate several statements:

Thinking about your typical workday, how much do you agree with the following statements?

	Strongly disagree	Disagree	Neither disagree nor agree	Agree	Strongly agree	Does not apply
I am satisfied with my work	◯	◯	◯	◯	◉	◯
I am proud of the work I do	◯	◯	◯	◯	◉	◯
I can find new and interesting aspects in my work	◯	◯	◯	◉	◯	◯
I am working on my own growth and development to make me better at my job	◯	◯	◯	◉	◯	◯

Figure 2.4 – Example of questionnaires for custom score

The respondent's answer for each statement is converted to the following score:

- **Strongly disagree** = 1
- **Disagree** = 2
- **Neither disagree nor agree** = 3
- **Agree** = 4
- **Strongly agree** = 5
- **Does not apply** = 0

The score is then totaled, and the score is calculated based on the maximum possible points. In the example from *Figure 2.4*, the total score is 5 + 5 + 4 + 4 = 18 and the maximum possible score is 20, so the score is 90%. Many organizations use 10 or 100 base points to calculate the score, so the 90% is converted to 90 points for a 100-point score.

Now that you have collected surveys to measure overall KPIs, how do you determine what causes the number to be high or low? To answer that question, you may need to include key driver questions in your survey.

Key driver questions

Metric questions can be complemented with additional questions to give you more information about *why* the respondents gave you a poor score. One solution would be to add an open-ended question to ask your respondents to explain their score. While open-ended questions are useful, free-text comments are less often to be filled out and even when they are, analyzing them can be difficult. Instead, you can use closed or rating questions to ask about specific aspects of your survey to help explain your respondent's score. For example, for a bank, in addition to the NPS question to measure overall satisfaction, you can ask what your customer thinks about your rates, flexibility, and communication like question #2 in *Figure 2.5*:

1. How likely are you to recommend us to a friend or colleague?

0	1	2	3	4	5	6	7	8	9	10

Not at all likely   Extremely likely

2. How would you rate the following areas?

	Very dissatisfied	Dissatisfied	Neither satisfied or dissatisfied	Satisfied	Very satisfied	Not applicable
Rates and fees	◯	◯	◯	◯	◯	◯
Flexibility to meet your needs	◯	◯	◯	◯	◯	◯
Keeping you up-to-date	◯	◯	◯	◯	◯	◯

3. Please share additional feedback

Enter your answer

Figure 2.5 – A survey example with key driver questions

When you get the results, you may associate the overall NPS score with the result of question #2 in *Figure 2.5* to determine whether any of the services such as rates, flexibility, and communication explain the result of the high/low NPS score. These are referred to as **key driver questions**.

Key driver questions commonly accompany broad KPI questions like NPS. If the CSAT or CES is asking about a specific aspect of your product or service, then you may not need to ask additional key driver questions. However, for NPS questions, you want to list different aspects of your service to help you identify which of those aspects contributes to the NPS score.

Keep in mind that, as mentioned at the beginning of this chapter, it is important to keep your survey as short as possible to minimize the work for your respondents. So, you need to make sure that each question has a purpose. For every question you come up with, ask yourself *Why do I need to know this?* and *What actions can I take based on the answer?* If you cannot answer those questions, then you probably do not need the question.

Once you determine that the questions are necessary, you then need to make sure to ask the questions correctly to get accurate answers. There are several research studies on designing survey questions and I include references to those studies at the end of this chapter so you can do some further reading. Let's take a look at some common problems with survey feedback questions.

Ambiguous questions

Ambiguous terms lead to different interpretations. For example, when asking your customer *How was our service?*, you raise questions about which service (especially when the customer has multiple interactions), and how you define good/bad service. Instead, you could consider asking *How was our sales representative in answering you with your inquiry about X last week?*, which includes a specific transaction inquiry and time period.

Leading or loaded questions

You want to design your survey question to avoid leading or loaded questions. Leading questions give clues to your respondent about what "the right answer" is.

An example of a leading question is *How do you rate our award-winning customer service?* Instead, remove the leading terms in your question and be more specific: *How do you rate how our customer service solved your issue?*

In addition to leading questions, loaded questions can lead the respondent into an answer that does not reflect their experience. An example of a loaded question is *Based on recent research, most dentists prefer our brand. Do you agree?* Loaded questions often lead to *social desirability bias* where the respondents answer in a way that they believe is more correct and more socially acceptable.

Double-barreled questions

Your questions should avoid asking for more than one thing even though they may be similar. *Double-barreled* questions will make it harder for respondents to understand, and you will not be sure whether the answer you get is related to the first topic, the second topic, or both. For example, instead of asking *Please rate how our interest rates and fees compare to others*, you may want to split them into separate questions: *How do you rate our interest rates?* and *How do you rate our fees?*

Designing a rating scale

Key driver questions often use a rating scale to measure the respondent's experience. You want to use the following guidelines when designing rating questions:

- Try to use between a 5- and 7-point scale. Using less than 5 is too generic and more than 7 is too complicated for respondents.

- Provide a middle category for respondents who have a neutral opinion.

- The point scale should be labeled with clear directions (a 1-star rating is bad and a 5-star rating is good).

- Ordering the ratings from the lowest to the highest is typical of surveys and therefore often assumed by respondents. You can see an example of a Likert question, which uses a lowest-to-highest scale in *Figure 2.6*:

How would you rate your satisfaction with our customer service representative in terms of:

	Very dissatisfied	Dissatisfied	Neutral	Satisfied	Very satisfied
Timeliness of resolution	○	○	○	○	○
Courtesy and professionalism	○	○	○	○	○
Product knowledge and competence	○	○	○	○	○
Ability to resolve issue during the first interaction	○	○	○	○	○

Figure 2.6 – Example of a scale rating

Key driver questions can be created when you have some ideas about possible drivers for your KPIs and would like to measure them. However, sometimes you cannot include all possible drivers, or you may not know them at first. Hence, you should include an open-ended question to capture additional reasons for why your respondents are not happy.

Open-ended questions

An open-ended question is typically added right after NPS and key driver questions, such as the following example:

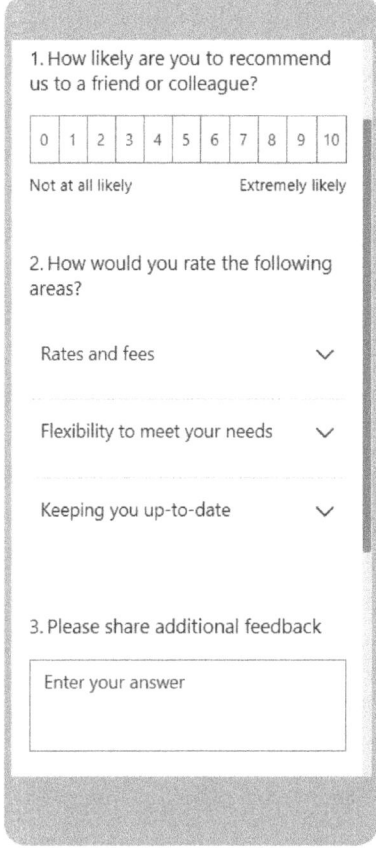

Figure 2.7 – Survey with an open-ended question

Open-ended questions require more effort from your respondents. To get better responses, you could make the question more engaging; you could consider making the question dynamic based on how the respondent answered the previous question(s).

For example, possible follow-up questions based on an NPS score include the following:

- Promoter NPS score: *Glad to hear it! Would you tell us why you feel that way?*

- Passive NPS score: *We appreciate your feedback. Would you like to tell us why you have scored us that way?*

- Detractor NPS score: *What would make you use our product/service again?*

Additional follow up questions for CSAT include the following:

- Satisfied score: *What is the most important reason for your score?*
- Dissatisfied score: *Can you share any specific feedback about _____?*

Open-ended question following a CES question:

- Easy score: *What would make your experience easier?*
- Difficult score: *We are sorry you had difficulty. Would you share how we can make it easier for you?*

In addition to designing survey questions to get accurate responses, you also need to design your survey to maximize the rate of responses.

Distributing surveys

To get the maximum number of responses, you need to think about the **return on investment** for your survey respondents. How much effort will your respondents think it will take to respond to your survey (**cost**) and what is in it for them (**benefit**)? In other words, you need to minimize the perceived cost and to make the benefit clear upfront. Otherwise, your survey respondent will be less motivated to answer your survey and you will get fewer survey responses.

There are several ways to minimize the cost of taking a survey.

Keep the survey as short as possible

The most direct way to reduce the cost for your survey respondent is to reduce the number of survey questions. At the beginning of the chapter, I talked about only collecting data for specific purposes. Your survey should have a goal and you need to make sure you ask just enough questions to meet your goal. Every additional question you add to your survey will add more effort for respondents and will risk the respondent giving up on completing your survey.

It is not only the actual effort to take the survey, but you should think about perceived effort. Using matrix-style questions like in *Figure 2.6* allows you to combine several questions together and will make your survey appear shorter than having a separate question for each statement.

Another popular technique to make the survey appear short is to embed the first question in your survey as part of an email invitation. For example, in *Figure 2.8*, the survey question *How would you rate the overall quality of the product?* is embedded directly in the survey invitation email.

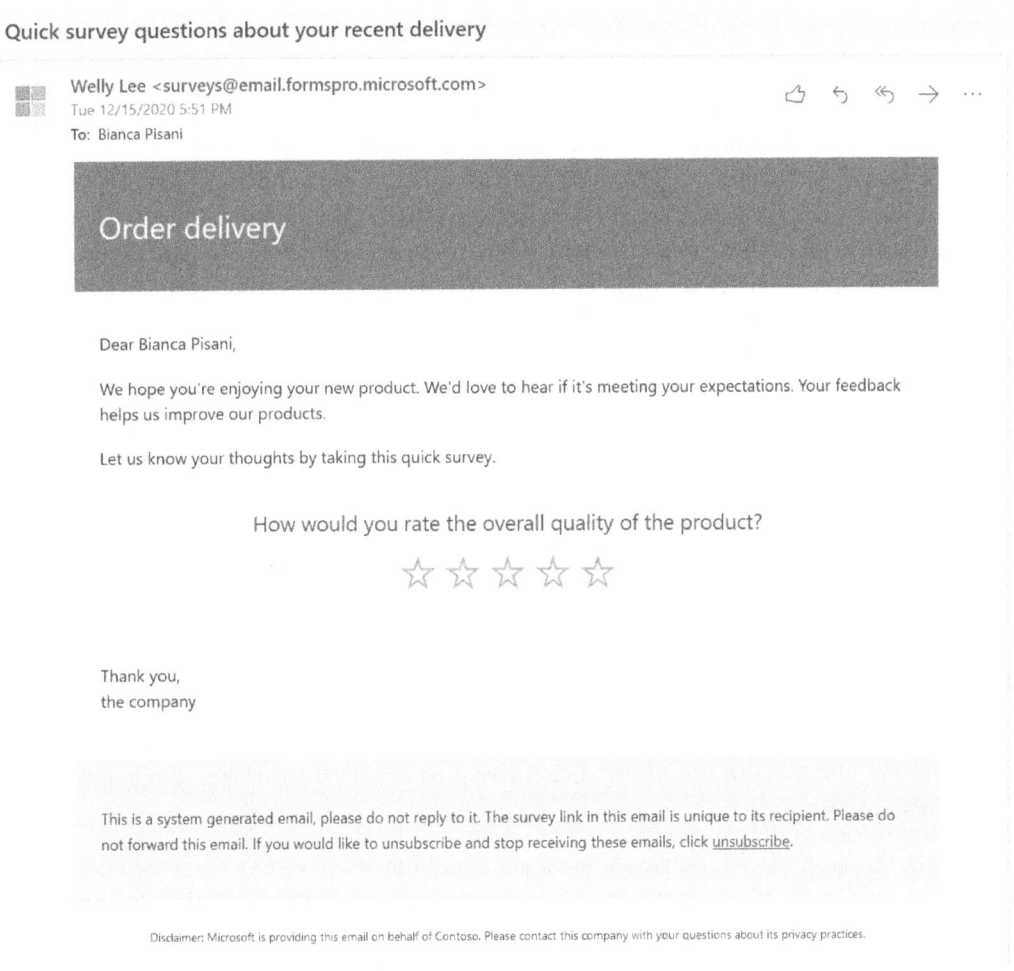

Figure 2.8 – Embedding a survey question in the email invitation

The first question being in the email makes it appear that the survey is easy to answer. Answering the question, by clicking a star in the email, will open a web page for the full survey with the first question already answered. Even though there are more questions on the survey, because the respondent has already made the effort to answer the first question, they will be more likely to continue to finish the survey. Last year, I worked with an organization that collects customer satisfaction feedback from their global customers every quarter. We started implementing embedding the first question in the survey email invitation and compared the response rate against the previous period when they did not embed the question in the email. The response rate was almost 50% higher compared to before they embedded the question in the invite.

Make it easy to take the survey

You should understand who your audiences are and how to make it easy for them to respond. One of the organizations I've worked with is **DAI** (www.dai.com). The organization works on social projects throughout the world. One of the projects was *Women for Health* in Nigeria. Nigeria is one of the countries with the highest maternal mortality in the world. DAI studied why women, especially in rural areas, have a high number of health issues. It turned out many women in rural villages were reluctant to seek medical help when they must see male doctors. So, DAI ran a project to recruit young women from local villages and to provide medical training to them. After they completed the training, these women were sent back to their villages to provide health care services to other women in those villages. DAI wanted to evaluate the effectiveness of their program and to report the impact to their sponsors through a survey. Since many of those women lived in rural areas, access to computers was limited, however, many of them used mobile phones. Hence, DAI sent surveys through **WhatsApp** to the students, as well as to leaders in the villages, to collect the feedback. Without mobile distribution to make it easy for the respondents to take the survey, DAI would not have been able to get the data they needed to evaluate the success of their program.

Make it safe to take the survey

Not only do you need to keep a survey short and make it convenient for respondents to take the survey, but you also need to reduce the cost by lowering the risk and make your respondents feel safe.

I spoke with the head of IT for a global hotel chain about the importance of branding. He shared that branding is important to give peace of mind. Customizing the look and feel of your survey is not only about making the survey look beautiful, but it is also about instilling trust in your respondents. If you are sending the survey to people outside your organizations, they may be suspicious when opening a survey that is not familiar and has a different look and feel compared to your website. At the time when you often hear about malicious attempts to steal information, respondents may be reluctant to answer a survey that does not look familiar.

Not only do you need to customize the look and feel of your survey, but when you send the survey via email, you will need to customize the email address to make sure it comes from your company domain. Receiving a survey invite from an unknown email address would reduce the likelihood of the email recipient opening and responding to your survey.

Another way to provide peace of mind to your respondents is to collect survey results anonymously. This is very common for employee feedback; employees need to feel safe that their feedback will not result in retaliation if they think their manager would not like their answers. If the employee is concerned about the risk of retaliation, they may not answer the survey truthfully and you will not get accurate results. Sending a survey anonymously also may improve accuracy and reduce social desirability bias. Survey respondents may provide answers that they think are more socially accepted when the result is not anonymous. When collecting feedback anonymously, make sure that you remind your respondents that their feedback will be anonymous, both within the invitation and at the start of the survey.

While an anonymous survey makes sense for employee-based feedback, sending non-anonymous surveys is more common for customer feedback to provide as much context as possible from the survey results.

Conveying the benefits

Not only do you need to reduce the actual and perceived cost of taking the survey, but you will also need to make it worthwhile for the survey respondent to take the survey. An introduction email to explain why you are collecting data and how the data can be used to improve the survey respondent experience is important to communicate the benefits. At Microsoft, after every annual employee feedback, each of the team leaders sends a report summarizing the feedback insights and define specific actions plan to address the feedback. The report helps the participation levels of the annual survey as the employees can see how their feedback helps to improve overall workplace conditions.

Personalizing your survey

Personalization is also proven to be effective in increasing response rates. When you send a personalized survey invite and survey question that specifically asks about the support call your customer made or a product they purchased, your respondents will feel that you have invested in them. Respondents will also be more likely to believe that their feedback will make an impact because it is not going to someone who does not know them, but will be tied to their specific transaction. This will increase the respondent's confidence that taking the survey will benefit them.

Sending a timely survey

Personalization will be significantly more effective when you also ask for feedback in a timely manner. Asking for feedback right after a rideshare (such as Uber) is completed will make it more likely for the customer to complete the feedback rather than receiving the feedback request a week or even a day later. Not only will you get a higher response rate when sending the survey right after the relevant transaction, but you will also get more accurate feedback. You would want the survey respondent to provide feedback when they still remember the transaction. One of the organizations I worked with sends customer feedback surveys right after a customer support calls and the survey link expires 7 days after they send the link. I spoke with the customer experience manager who explained that the longer the time it takes for the customer to provide the feedback, the less confident they are in the accuracy of the feedback.

Survey reward

Finally, what about a reward? Some surveys offer rewards to the survey respondents for completing a survey. While giving a direct reward is certainly an effective way to boost your response, it also depends on the value of the reward. Giving some small token such as 100 loyalty points or a $5 gift certificate at the end of a survey may be meaningful for the survey respondents, but it would increase the cost of you running your survey.

We worked with one of our customers to collect response data and measure the impact of surveys with rewards and without rewards offered. The result showed that there was no significant difference between the response rates. We spoke with some respondents who shared that they did not believe they were lucky enough to win and offering them a chance to win did not motivate them. Given the results, we did not continue with the preview feature and the survey reward was discontinued when Microsoft Forms Pro transitioned to Customer Voice.

Another approach to minimize cost is to offer a sweepstake where the survey respondent is given a chance to win a big prize when they complete the survey. This approach may not be possible in some places where sweepstakes are considered gambling and are prohibited. We also found that offering a chance to win a big prize is much less appealing than to directly get something even though it is smaller in value. In 2019, Customer Voice (when it was named Microsoft Forms Pro) offered a preview feature in the United States where any respondent completing a survey was entered into a monthly sweepstake to win a new **Microsoft Surface Laptop** and **Surface Headphones**.

After you distribute a survey and receive results, you need to analyze the survey results and get insights from them.

Analyzing survey results

Analyzing survey results involves evaluating the KPI score, identifying relevant key drivers for the KPI scores, and summarizing the text comments.

Analyzing KPIs

When analyzing survey results and KPI scores, how do you know whether the score is good? Ideally, you can compare your score with other organizations in your industry.

Forrester Research publishes an annual report of the NPS score for 250 brands across 14 industries (see `https://www.forrester.com/report/Net+Promoter+Benchmarks+2020+US/-/E-RES162297`). In addition, there are other organizations that are conducting surveys and compiling scores based on the same questions, so they can be benchmarked. In the United States, the American Customer Satisfaction Index (`theacsi.org`) compiles a customer satisfaction index across 50 industries and publishes the scores on their website.

For employee feedback, there are a few consortiums that share index scores among member organizations, among them the following:

- Mayflower Group (`mayflowergroup.org`), whose members are large, mainly Fortune 500 companies representing diverse industries

- ITSG (`itsg.org`), which includes leaders in the technology industries

As members of these organizations, you can use the same questions that other organization members used then compare the scores with each other.

However, benchmark data may not be available for your organizations or there may not be a benchmark as you are measuring a unique aspect of your product or service. In that case, you can use trend analysis to compare data from one period against the last period or a comparable period in the year, as shown in *Figure 2.9*:

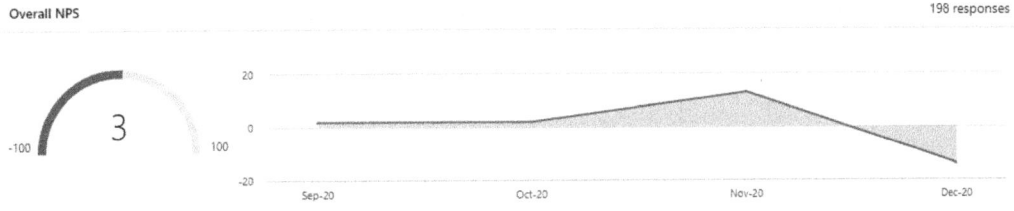

Figure 2.9 – NPS score and monthly trend

Comparing the NPS result against the previous month's would indicate whether the score this month is better and you are improving. One thing to note is that depending on the number of responses, you may have large swings between one period and another. If your sample is low, then you need to use bigger time periods to make sure you have enough samples in each period to collect an average, then compare the result from one period to another.

After you get the KPI results, you will want to understand them. As we discussed, key driver questions may give you clues.

Identifying relevant key drivers

Key driver analysis can give you insights into possible reasons for your KPI score. By finding correlations between the result of key drivers and the KPI score, you could derive a hypothesis about possible cause-and-effect relationships.

For example, *Figure 2.10*, shows a custom Power BI report (based on a template available from `https://github.com/PacktPublishing/Working-with-Microsoft-Forms-and-Customer-Voice/tree/main/Chapter02`) that shows NPS together with scores from key driver questions. The drop in the NPS is associated with a drop in **KEEPING YOU UP TO DATE** scores during the same period. This suggests that issues with customer communication may cause customer dissatisfaction and drive a lower NPS score:

Figure 2.10 – NPS score and key driver trend dashboard

Displaying a trend line between your KPI and key driver scores for visual correlation is one way to find a possible link. Another way is to perform statistical analysis between your KPIs and key drivers. In addition to providing a benchmarking service, the **American Customer Satisfaction Index (ACSI)** also provides a statistical model and shows the correlation between key drivers and their ACSI satisfaction score. *Figure 2.11* shows an example of an ACSI key driver analysis report (available from `aka.ms/ACSICustomerVoice`):

Retail Banking
Prediction Model

Figure 2.11 – Example of a key driver and satisfaction metric score report

In the report, ACSI calculates the statistical correlation strength between each key driver and the ACSI score. For example, *Branches & ATMs* shows the strongest correlation (88.7 out of 100) followed by *Mobile App* (82.5), then *Financial Products* (75).

Summarizing text comments

While you can use visual indicators and statistical analysis to identify key drivers to explain KPI scores, analyzing open-ended text comment questions is much more challenging, especially for a large volume of feedback.

Artificial Intelligence (**AI**) is commonly used to analyze text comments in a survey to determine the respondent's sentiment. Is the respondent happy with your product or service? Microsoft Azure Cognitive Services (`https://azure.microsoft.com/en-us/services/cognitive-services/`) provides an API that you can use to determine the sentiment of text comments. Customer Voice includes out-of-the-box sentiment analysis based on Azure Cognitive Services as part of its survey report.

In addition to text sentiment, many organizations use AI to automatically group similar comments through a clustering method. The AI model finds similar patterns in comments and groups related comments together in the same cluster, as shown in *Figure 2.12*.

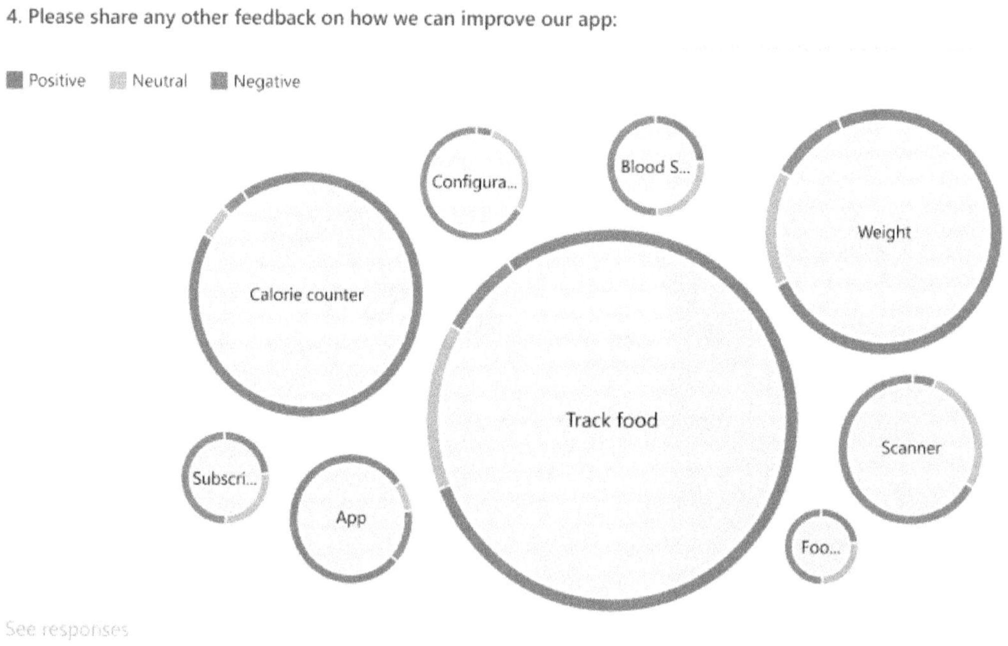

4. Please share any other feedback on how we can improve our app:

Figure 2.12 – Example of clustering analysis on text comments

Sentiment analysis is often applied to determine whether a group of comments are positive, neutral, or negative. In the previous example, the feedback comments are automatically grouped into several clusters with the size of the bubble representing the amount of feedback and the color representing the sentiment. Visualizing the text comments with this bubble chart makes it easier to identify issues.

In addition to automatically grouping related comments, AI can also be used to automatically classify your text into different categories. This approach typically involves manually tagging your sample comments then using the comments with manual labels to train an AI model on how to classify the text to the pre-defined tags. Then you can apply the AI model against your new text comments to automate classifying the comments with your tags.

Summary

In this chapter, we discussed best practices for creating, sending, and analyzing feedback surveys. It started with defining questions to measure your KPIs, key drivers, and open text comments to allow your respondent to add detail to their answers. The survey must be designed to be as easy as possible for your respondent to complete and when distributing the survey, you should convey the personal benefits to your respondents. Analyzing the survey involves comparing results between one period and another. The correlation between the KPI scores and key drivers may help explain the KPI scores. While open-ended questions provide good information to explain why a respondent has answered in a certain way, analyzing a large volume of text comments may be challenging and AI models such as sentiment, clustering, and classification techniques are often used to help analyze open text questions.

Having now familiarized yourself with how to design your survey, in the next chapter, we will use Microsoft Forms to create your first form.

Further reading

Here are some further reading suggestions based on the information provided in this chapter:

- Questionnaire Design Tip Sheet: `https://psr.iq.harvard.edu/book/questionnaire-design-tip-sheet`

- Question and Questionnaire Design: `https://web.stanford.edu/dept/communication/faculty/krosnick/docs/2009/2009_handbook_krosnick.pdf`

- Sudman, S., & Bradburn, N, *Asking questions: A practical guide to questionnaire design*, (San Francisco, CA: Jossey-Bass, 1982)

- Rossi, P., Wright, J., and Anderson, A. (eds.), *Handbook of Survey Research* (San Diego, CA: Academic Press, 1983)

3
Creating a Survey with Microsoft Forms

Microsoft Forms and Customer Voice share common interface to create a survey. Knowing how to create a simple survey in Microsoft Forms prepares you to create a more complex survey in Customer Voice.

In this chapter, we will go through step-by-step instructions to create and send a survey. At the end of this chapter, you will understand how survey authoring works, including the different types of questions you can create with Microsoft Forms.

The chapter is organized as follows:

- Creating survey questions
- Exploring question types
- Branding and styling a survey
- Previewing a survey
- Sending a survey
- Viewing survey results

Creating survey questions

To get started with Microsoft Forms, simply follow these steps:

1. Go to forms.office.com. If your organization has an Office 365 subscription, you can log on with your existing work or school account. Otherwise, you can sign up for a trial of Office 365 at office.com.

2. After you log on, you are presented with the option to create a new form:

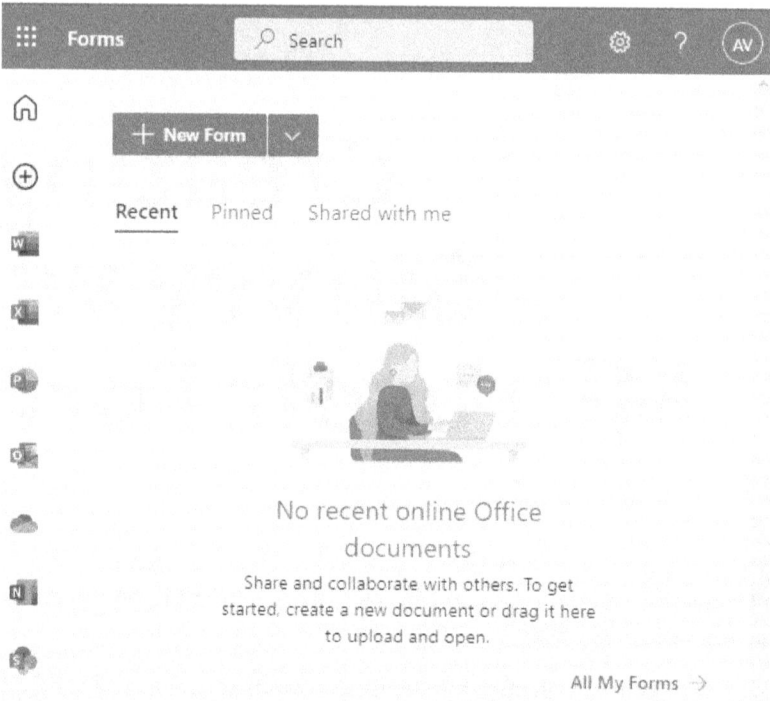

Figure 3.1 – Creating a new form

Microsoft Forms provides two options: **New Form** or **New Quiz**. A form lets you collect data or send a survey. A quiz is intended to be used as a simple assessment tool for a training or education setting.

> **Important note**
>
> A quiz includes most of Forms' authoring functionalities and additional functionalities to mark a correct answer, assign scores, and add math-type questions and equations. In addition to authoring functionalities, quiz response pages have additional functionality to manage quiz scores. We will talk more about quizzes in *Chapter 5, Post-Training Assessment and Feedback*.

3. Select **New Form** and specify a title. You can also add a description, which could be used to give an overview of the survey to your survey respondents:

Figure 3.2 – Adding a form title

You can have a maximum of 90 characters as the form title and 1,000 characters for the subtitle.

4. Based on the title of the form, Microsoft Forms provides some suggestions of commonly asked questions based on the survey title. For example, when you have your survey named **Employee Feedback**, Microsoft Forms shows suggested questions like the following:

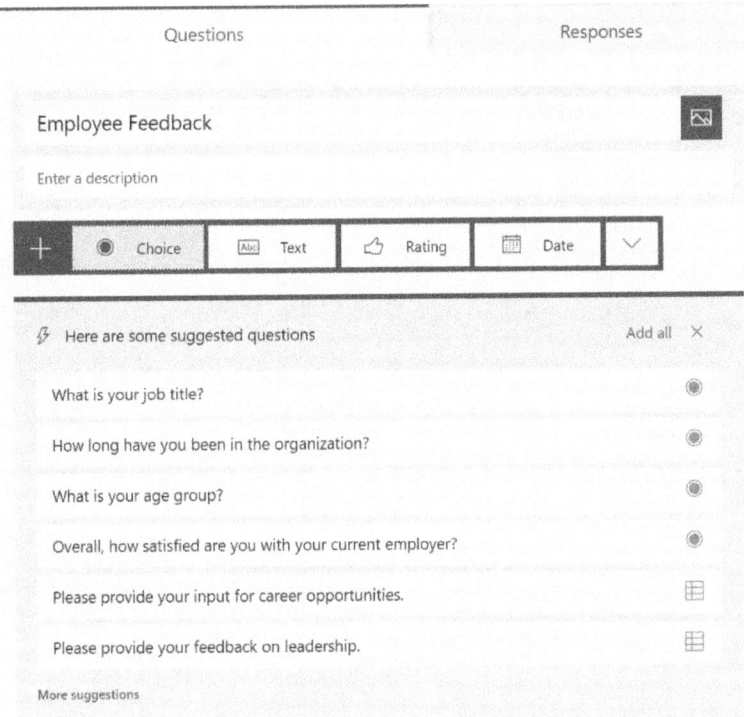

Figure 3.3 – Suggested questions for an employee feedback survey

The suggested questions also include information about the type of question that includes the **Choice**, **Text**, and **Likert** types. More on question types later.

5. Select the questions you would like to include by clicking the questions, then click the **Add selected** command text at the top of the **Here are some suggested questions** section. The selected questions will be added to your new form:

1. How long have you been in the organization?

   ○ Less than 1 year

   ○ 1-2 years

   ○ 2-3 years

   ○ 3-4 years

   ○ 4-5 years

   ○ More than 5 years

2. Please provide your feedback on leadership.

	Strongly agree	Agree	Neither agree nor disagree	Disagree	Strongly disagree
I have confidence in this company's senior leadership team.	○	○	○	○	○
I hear enough communication from the senior leadership team about what is happening at the company.	○	○	○	○	○
The senior leadership team has communicated a vision for the future that motivates me.	○	○	○	○	○

Figure 3.4 – Forms questions from the selected suggestion

6. Customize the question **How long you have been in the organization?** by clicking on the question to enter edit mode. This question is a **Choice** question type, which allows respondents to select a single answer or multiple answers. You can click the **Multiple answers** toggle at the bottom of the question to make it a multi-selection option. You can add up to 4,000 options or add the **Other** option, which adds a textbox for your survey respondent to enter an additional option that is not pre-listed:

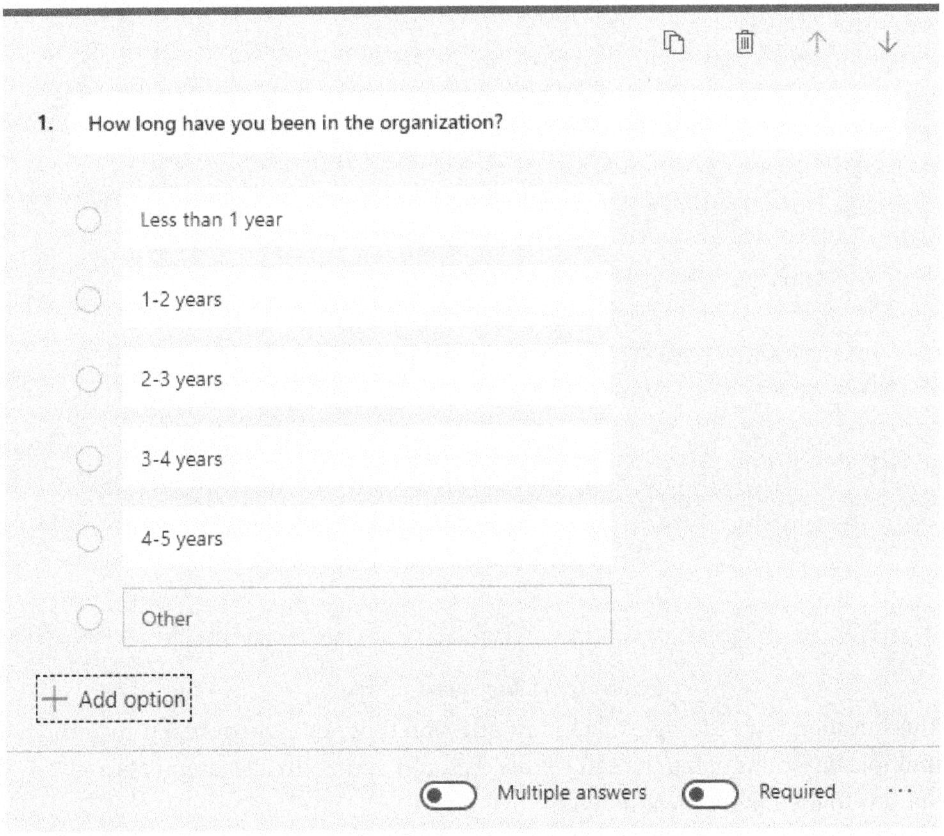

Figure 3.5 – Question with the Other option

> **Tip**
> You can create options by copying and pasting the list of options from an Excel or Word document into the option field.

7. Edit the question **Please provide your feedback on leadership**, and customize the question text, statement, or scale text (for example, **Strongly disagree**, **Disagree**, and so on):

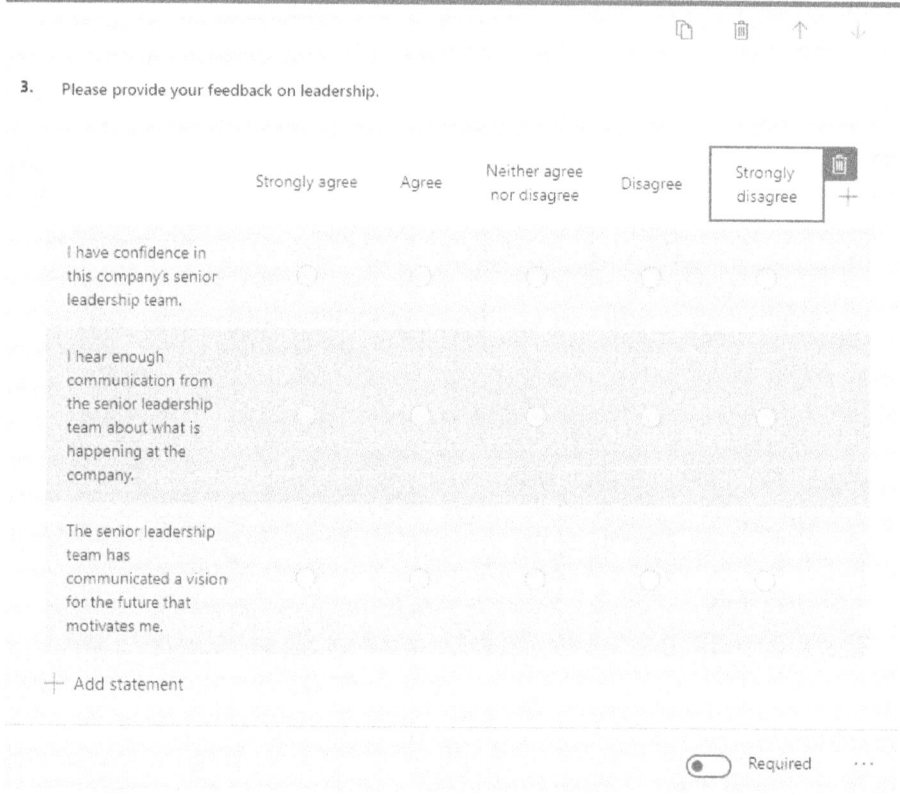

Figure 3.6 – Likert question type

This question is an example of a Likert question type, an approach to measure multiple questions using the same scale. You can add up to 20 statements and 7 options to the Likert question type.

8. Add a new question for your form by clicking the **Add new** button at the end of your form and select the **Rating** question type to add to the form.

9. Customize the rating question and update the question text. You can enter a question of up to 4,000 characters. You can also change the number of rating scales (up to 10 scales) and you can also change the rating display style to either the number rating or star rating style. The rating question includes the option to add a label to your rating. You can select the label option through the **...** setting at the bottom of the question:

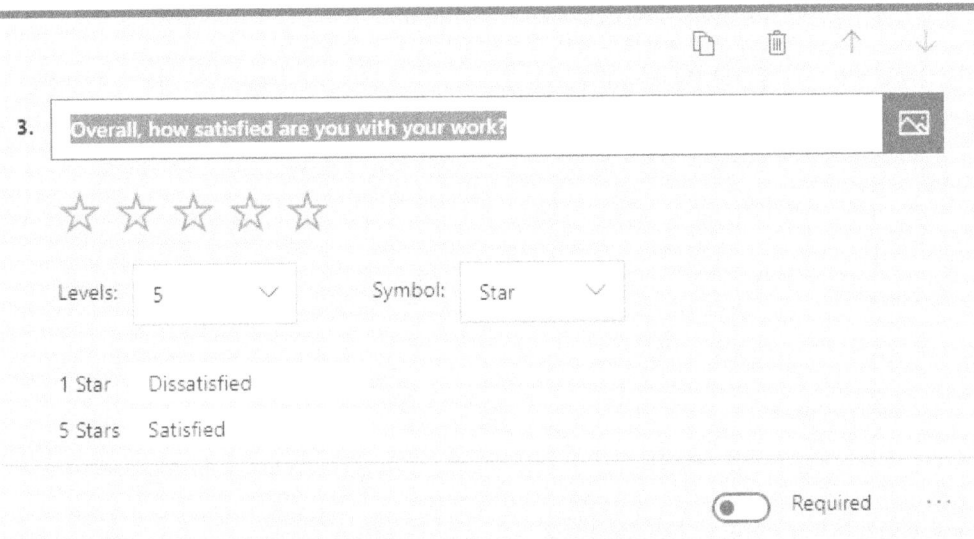

Figure 3.7 – Rating question with label

> **Tip**
> As discussed in *Chapter 2, Best Practices for Collecting Feedback through Surveys*, you should include labels in your rating question to remove any ambiguity for your survey respondents about the direction of the rating. In this example, you make it clear that five stars are better than one star.

10. Move the rating question up to be the second question on your form by clicking the up arrow on the question editor menu. The question editor menu enables you to copy, delete, or change the order of the questions:

Figure 3.8 – Question editor menu

After you move the question, your form should look like the following:

1. How long have you been in the organization?

   ○ Less than 1 year

   ○ 1-2 years

   ○ 2-3 years

   ○ 3-4 years

   ○ 4-5 years

   ○ More than 5 years

2. Overall, how satisfied are you with your work

   Dissatisfied ☆ ☆ ☆ ☆ ☆ Satisfied

3. Please provide your feedback on leadership.

	Strongly agree	Agree	Neither agree nor disagree	Disagree	Strongly disagree
I have confidence in this company's senior leadership team.	○	○	○	○	○

Figure 3.9 – Reordered survey questions

> **Tip**
> If you would like to insert a new question in between existing questions, you can edit the existing questions to show the **Add new** button and insert the new question.

11. Add branching logic to your survey to control how your survey respondent answers the survey. For example, you may only want to ask questions about leadership for employees who have been with the company longer than 1 year. To do so, edit the question you would like to add branching logic to and under the **...** option at the bottom of the question, select **Add branching**:

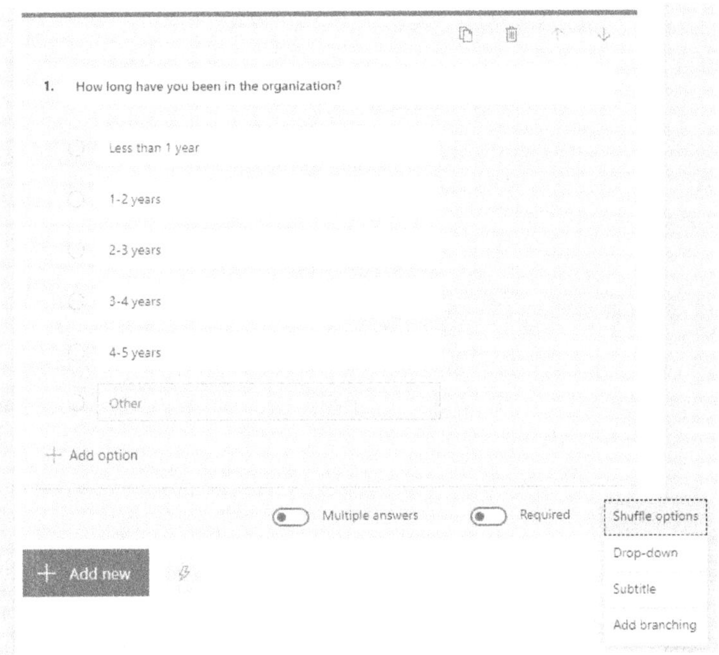

Figure 3.10 – Add branching option for a survey question

Update the **Go to** selection for each option:

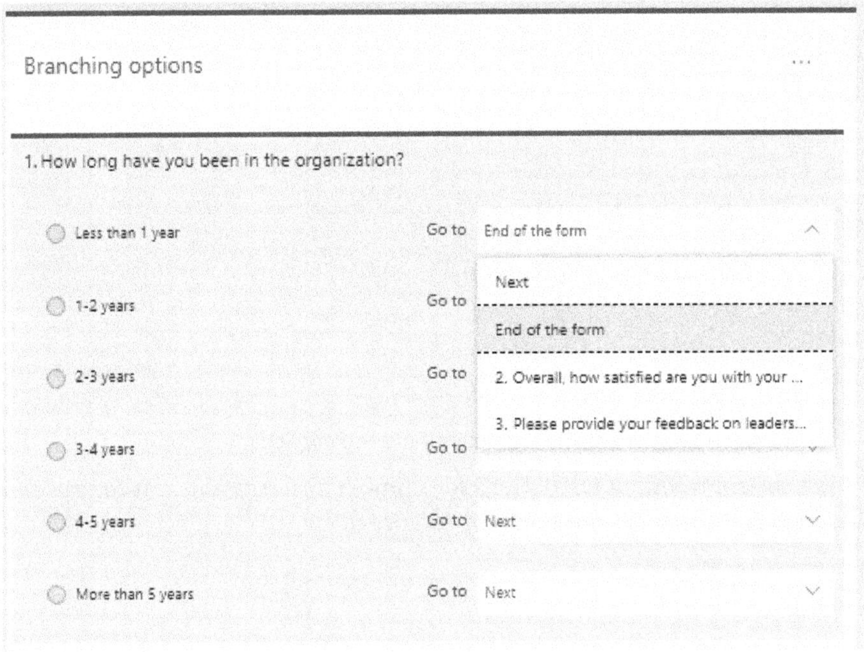

Figure 3.11 – Configuring branching logic

For example, with the branching rule defined in *Figure 3.11*, when a survey respondent selects the first option, **Less than 1 year**, the respondent will be taken directly to the **End of the form**.

You can continue to add more questions to your survey and use the different types of questions supported in Microsoft Forms. In the next section, we will look at some of these question types in more detail.

Exploring question types

In the previous section, we looked at how to create survey questions and started exploring some of the question types available, in the following section, we'll take a look at some of these question types in more detail.

Text

The text question type allows you to create a free text question on your survey. The survey respondent can enter up to 130 characters for short answers and you can turn on the option to increase the limit to 4,000 characters (with spaces) by enabling the **Long Answer** option. Note that there is a maximum of 16,000 characters for the entire survey and your respondent may not be able to submit a survey that exceeds the limit:

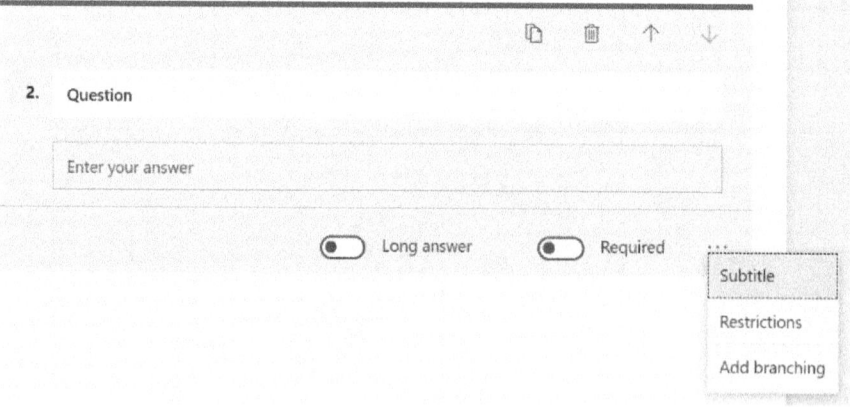

Figure 3.12 – Text question setting options

A text question supports adding restrictions for number answers, and you can specify the range of numbers that the survey respondent can provide:

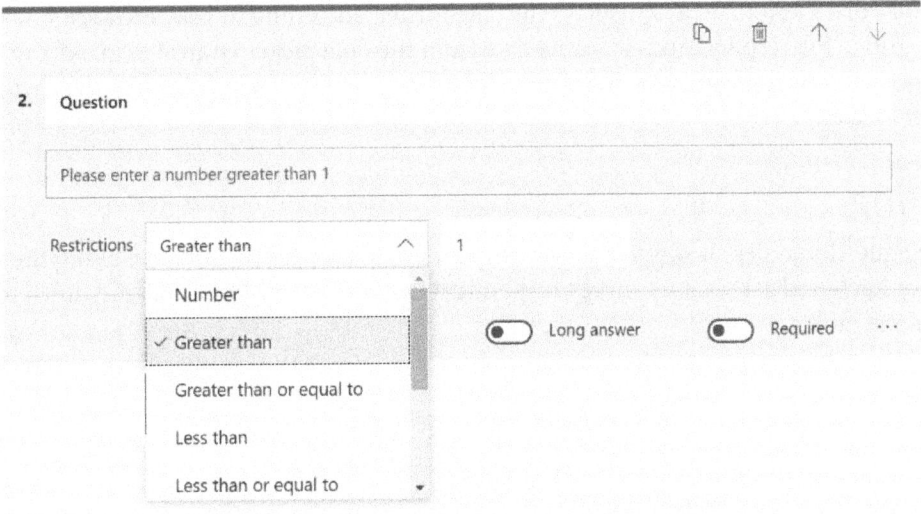

Figure 3.13 – Adding a restriction to a text question

When adding a restriction, the textbox will include default text to specify the valid range:

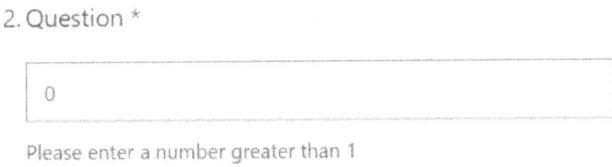

Figure 3.14 – Error message when the survey respondent enters a value outside the range

As shown, a message will show when the survey respondent enters a value outside the valid range.

Date

The rating question allows your survey respondent to enter dates:

Figure 3.15 – Date question type

Microsoft Forms automatically displays the date format according to your browser's locale setting. The respondent selects the date from the date picker control to avoid any ambiguity from selecting month and date in a different format when collecting data across different locales.

Ranking

Ranking question types allow your survey respondent to reorder the options. Using their mouse or keyboard arrows, the survey respondent can move the options up and down to indicate the ranking:

Figure 3.16 – Ranking the options

You can specify up to 10 options for ranking questions.

File upload

The file upload question type allows your survey respondents to upload files and attach them to the survey. The files are uploaded to a OneDrive for Business folder for the survey owner:

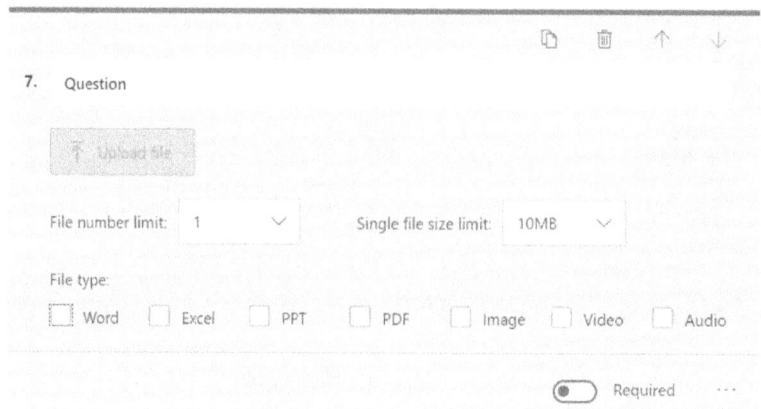

Figure 3.17 – File upload question type

You can specify the number of files that can be uploaded – up to 10 files per question – and the maximum size is up to 1 GB per question.

The following files type are supported for file uploads:

- Word file formats: `.doc`, `.dot`, `.wbk`, `.docx`, `.docm`, `.dotx`, `.dotm`, and `.docb`.
- Excel file formats: `.xls`, `.xlt`, `.xlm`, `.xlsx`, `.xlsm`, `.xltx`, and `.xltm`.
- PowerPoint file formats: `.ppt`, `.pot`, `.pps`, `.pptx`, `.pptm`, `.potx`, `.potm`, `.ppam`, `.ppsx`, `.ppsm`, `.sldx`, and `.sldm`.
- PDF file format: `.pdf`.
- Image file formats: `.jpg`, `.jpeg`, `.png`, `.gif`, `.bmp`, `.tiff`, `.psd`, `.thm`, `.yuv`, `.ai`, `.drw`, `.eps`, `.ps`, `.svg`, `.3dm`, and `.max`.
- Video file formats: `.avi`, `.mp4`, `.mov`, `.wmv`, `.asf`, `.3g2`, `.3gp`, `.asx`, `.flv`, `.mpg`, `.rm`, `.swf`, and, `.vob`.
- Audio file formats: `.mp3`, `.aif`, `.iff`, `.m3u`, `.m4a`, `.mid`, `.mpa`, `.ra`, `.wav`, and `.wma`.

The uploaded files can be found in the survey owner's OneDrive for Business folder with the survey name under **My files | Apps | Microsoft Forms**:

My files > Apps > **Microsoft Forms**

	Name	Modified	Modified By	File size	Sharing
	Employee Feedback	2 hours ago	Welly Lee	1 item	Private

Figure 3.18 – Microsoft Forms folder in OneDrive for Business

Inside the folder, you can find the folder named **Question** for each file upload question in your survey. When you have more than 1 file upload questions, you will have multiple folders with sequence numbers (such as **Question**, **Question 1**, **Question 2**, and so on):

My files > Apps > Microsoft Forms > **Employee Feedback**

	Name	Modified	Modified By	File size	Sharing
	Question	2 hours ago	Welly Lee	2 items	Private
	Question 1	A few seconds ago	Welly Lee	1 item	Private

Figure 3.19 – Question folders in the survey folder

Inside the question folder, the uploaded filename is appended with the name of the survey respondents:

My files > Apps > Microsoft Forms > Employee Feedback > **Question**

	Name ⌄	Modified ⌄	Modified By ⌄	File size ⌄	Sharing
▣	Book1_Lidia Holloway.xlsx	A few seconds ago	Lidia Holloway	8.85 KB	Private
▣	Document1_Lidia Holloway.docx	A few seconds ago	Lidia Holloway	12.3 KB	Private

Figure 3.20 – Filename under the question folder

Remember the following:

- You cannot rename the folder, otherwise, your survey respondent will get an error message when trying to upload the file.

- When you delete a question, the previously uploaded files are not deleted, and you must remove them manually.

- When respondents upload files for your form questions, you can find those files in your OneDrive for Business folder.

- The respondent's name is always recorded when you are using **file upload**, even if you change the survey setting to not record names (anonymous). Even though the respondent's name is changed to anonymous, the **modified by** column in OneDrive still records the respondent's name.

- Microsoft Forms supports file upload for surveys distributed to people inside an organization. To collect files from people outside an organization, you can create surveys with Customer Voice.

Net Promoter Score

Net Promoter Score (NPS) is a popular metric for customer feedback. NPS uses a specific formula to calculate the score, as discussed in *Chapter 2, Best Practices for Collecting Feedback through Surveys*.

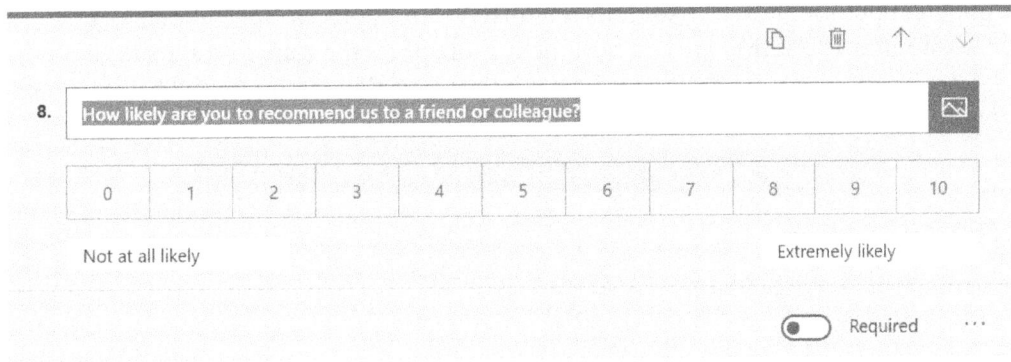

Figure 3.21 – NPS question type

You can add a label to the NPS scale to clarify that a higher number indicates a higher likelihood.

Section

Section allows the survey owner to break a survey down into multiple pages. Each section is displayed as a separate page to your survey respondents. Open the menu options from ... to manage sections, including copying, deleting, and moving sections to a different location in your survey:

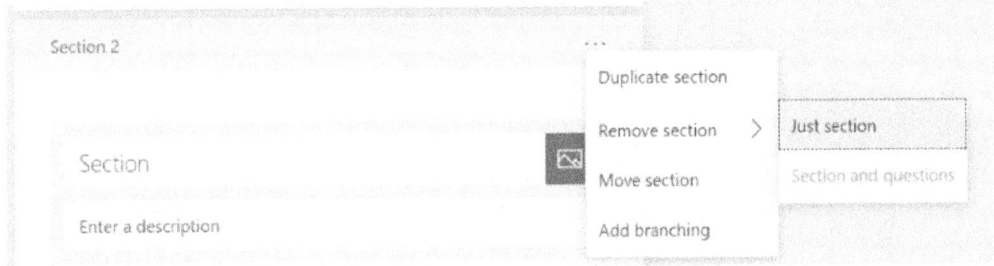

Figure 3.22 – Setting options for sections

One popular option when using sections is to display a progress bar to let the survey respondent know where they are and how many more pages there are to complete the survey. The progress bar is displayed next to the navigation button to enable the respondent to go to the previous or next page:

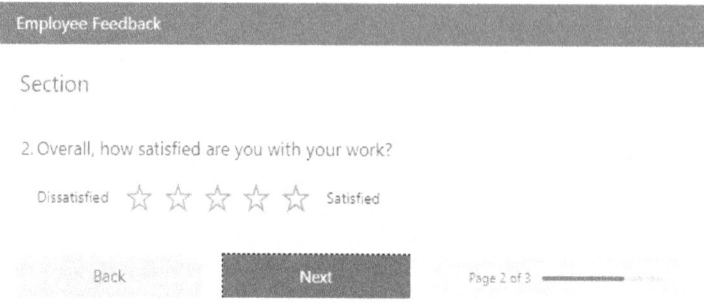

Figure 3.23 – Survey question with a section and progress bar

To enable the progress bar, you open the **Settings** pane by clicking **…** next to the **Share** button and check the **Show progress bar** option:

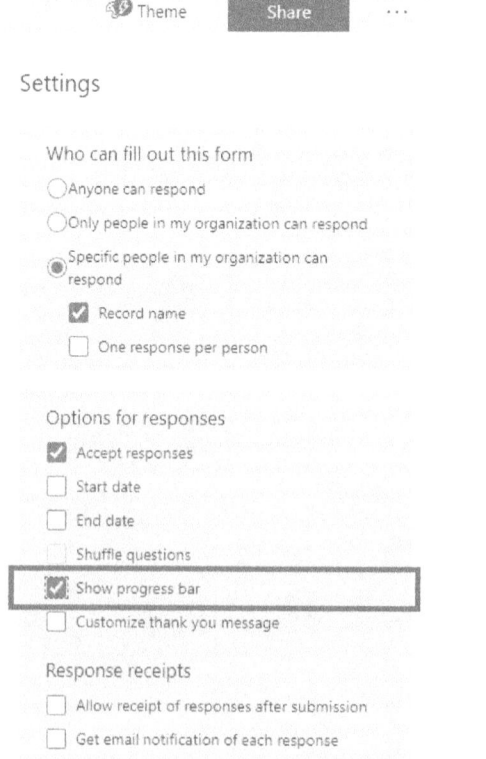

Figure 3.24 – Setting option to show the progress bar

Now that you are familiar with the types of questions you can use in your forms, let's review how you can customize the look and feel of your forms.

Branding and styling a survey

Microsoft Forms supports branding and styling your surveys by adding your company logo, theme color, and background images. You can add a logo by editing the survey title and clicking the image icon:

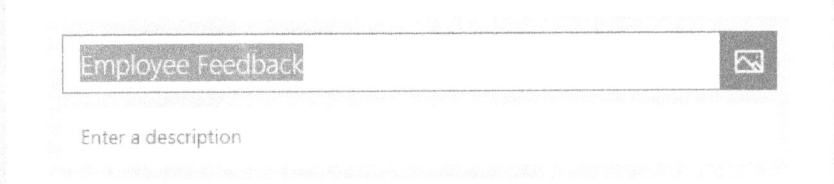

Figure 3.25 – Accessing the logo editor on your survey

You can search for an image using **Bing** or pick an image from your computer or from your **OneDrive** location:

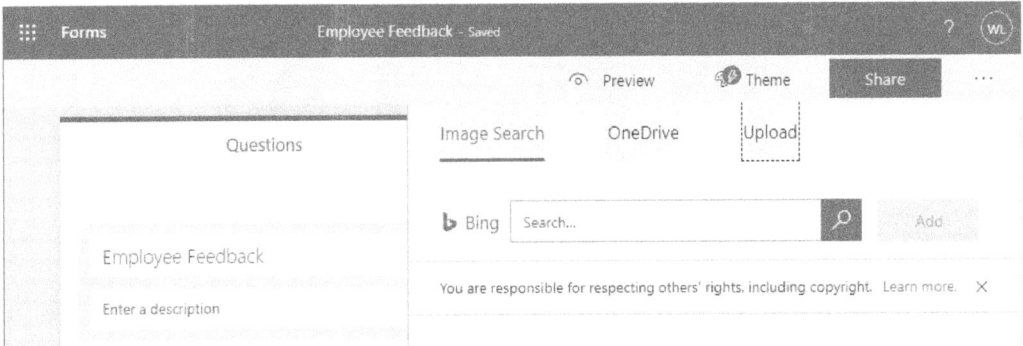

Figure 3.26 – Different options for uploading a logo

In addition to uploading a logo, you can also upload a background image and change the color theme for your survey. Edit the theme by clicking the **Theme** button on the command bar menu at the top:

Figure 3.27 – Customizing the survey theme

Click the + button to upload the background image or to enter a specific color theme. Microsoft Forms automatically calculates the color that matches the background image. You can override the theme color by specifying the HEX color value:

Figure 3.28 – Specifying a custom theme color

Using large image files may impact the loading of the survey. I recommend you to use file less than 1 MB in size and use an image file with the following format:

- Survey logo resolution: Less than 800x600 px and 1:1 aspect ratio
- Background image resolution: less than 4000x3000 px and 4:3 aspect ratio

In addition to adding a logo, image, and theme color, Customer Voice provides additional branding support such as uploading a custom image for your survey header, button style, custom font, and custom CSS.

After you've added your questions to your survey, you can test the survey by previewing it.

Previewing a survey

You can preview how your survey will look to your survey respondents by clicking the **Preview** button in the command bar at the top of the page:

Figure 3.29 – Preview button on the command bar

You can preview the survey in **Computer** or **Mobile** mode. Note that because we added a branching rule, Microsoft Forms will automatically hide other questions and only show them depending on the answer to the first question:

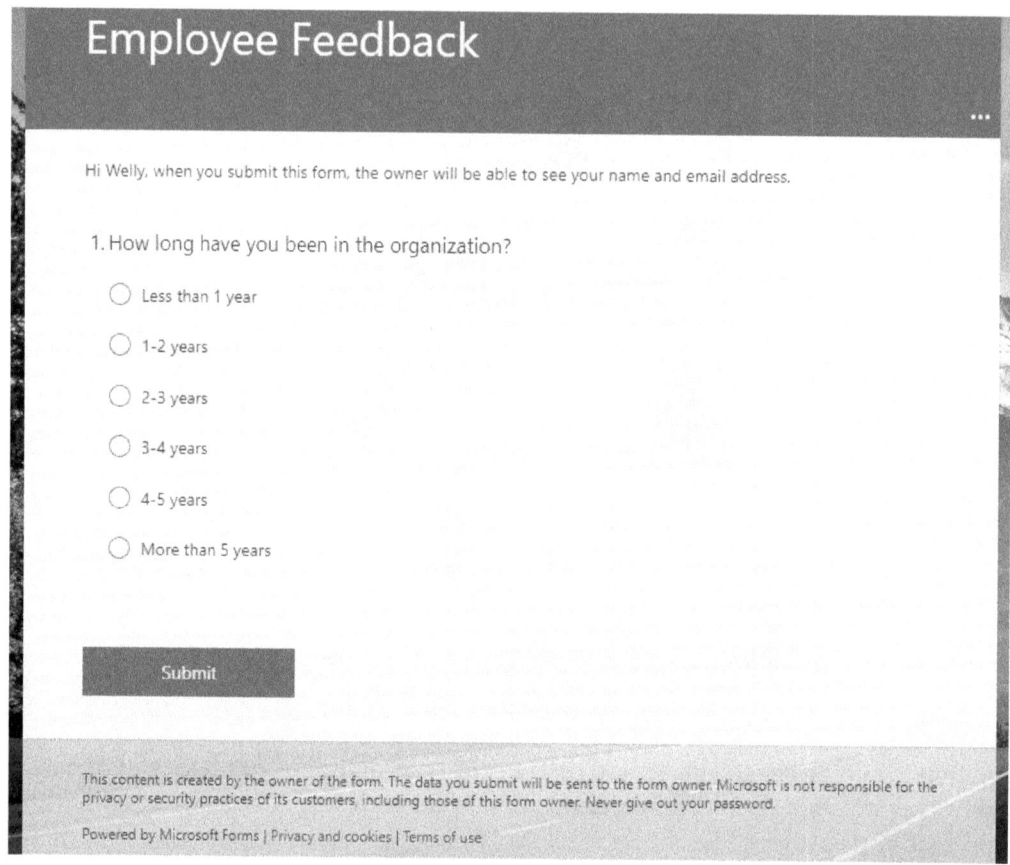

Figure 3.30 – Previewing the survey in computer mode

Based on how the survey respondent answers the question, the branching rule determines the next set of questions to show:

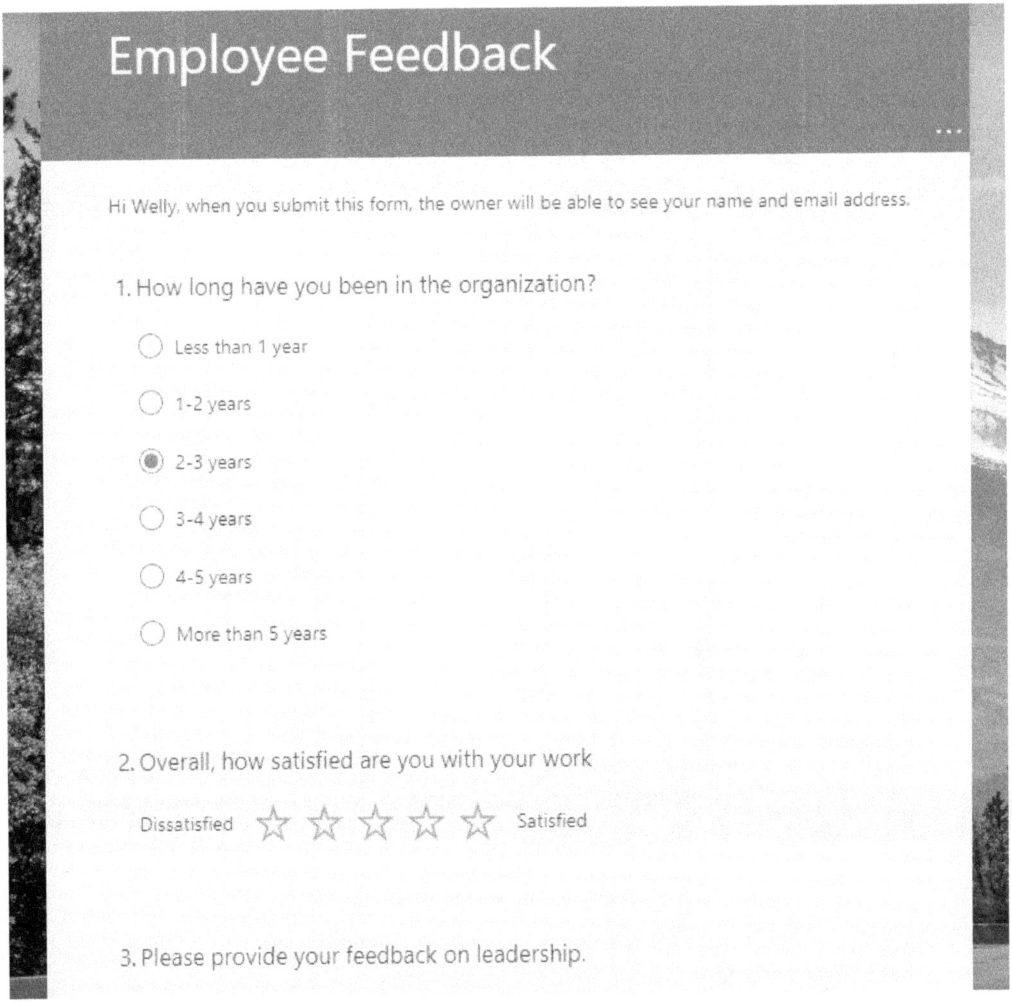

Employee Feedback

Hi Welly, when you submit this form, the owner will be able to see your name and email address.

1. How long have you been in the organization?

○ Less than 1 year

○ 1-2 years

◉ 2-3 years

○ 3-4 years

○ 4-5 years

○ More than 5 years

2. Overall, how satisfied are you with your work

Dissatisfied ☆ ☆ ☆ ☆ ☆ Satisfied

3. Please provide your feedback on leadership.

Figure 3.31 – Additional survey question that appeared based on how the previous question was answered

I am frequently asked about the ability to format the layout of a survey. Microsoft Forms does not support freeform layout as we automatically adjust the layout based on the screen size. The Likert question is an example where the question is displayed differently in the **Computer** and **Mobile** layouts:

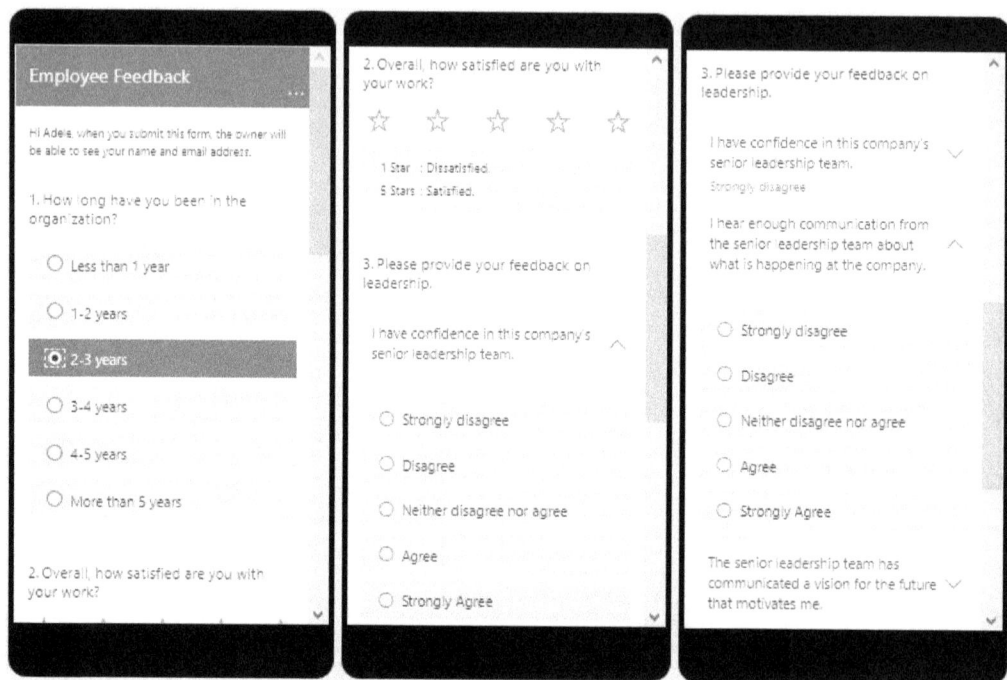

Figure 3.32 – Previewing the survey in mobile mode

On the mobile layout, the Likert question is turned from table format into multiple-choice questions where each statement is expanded one at a time while the other statements are automatically collapsed to make it easier to answer on a smaller mobile screen.

> **Important note**
>
> When previewing, you can submit the survey and the responses are included in the survey report. If you would like to exclude the test survey data during the preview, you will need to delete the response data before sending your survey.

When you are happy with the survey, you can start sending the survey.

Sending a survey

To send a survey, click the **Share** button and get the survey link:

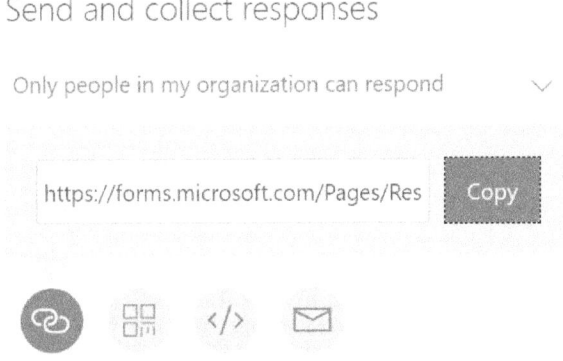

Figure 3.33 – Option for distributing your survey

Make sure to change the option to **Anyone with the link can respond** if you are sharing the link to people outside your organization:

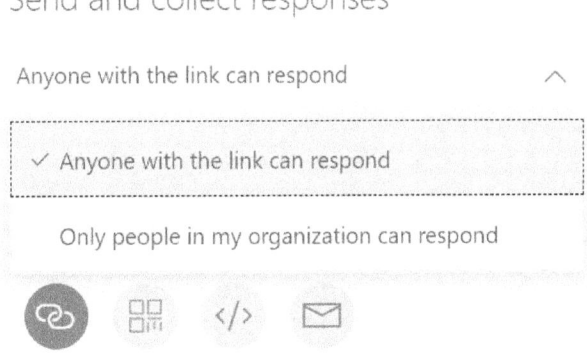

Figure 3.34 – Options for who can respond to your survey

You can then copy the link and share it with others by sending the link via email or by adding the link to your website. Once you receive responses, you can view the results on the response report.

Viewing survey results

You can view the results by opening the survey and opening the **Responses** tab. The **Responses** tab shows the result tally for each question. The top of the page includes a header section that summarizes the survey, including the number of survey responses received and the average time it took survey respondents to complete your survey. It also includes a **View results** button to see individual survey responses:

Figure 3.35 – Response tab header

The responses from each respondent are shown and you can move to the next respondents through the next and back arrow buttons on the header:

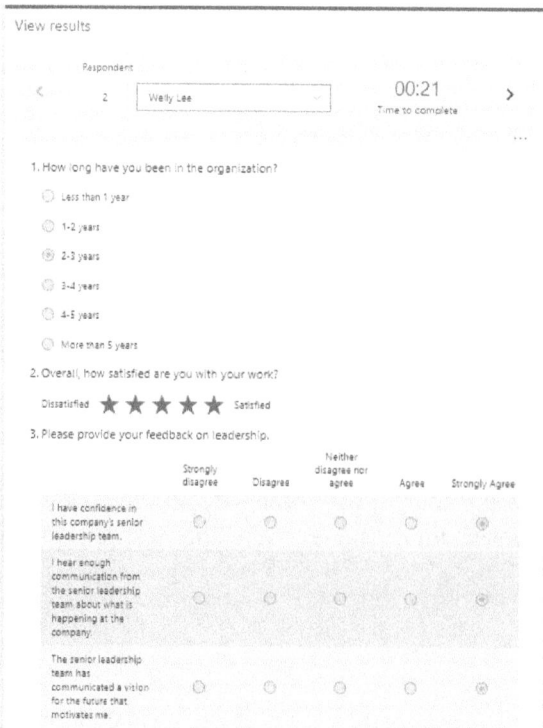

Figure 3.36 – Survey response details

The header also includes an additional menu option under **....** Opening the menu option shows you additional commands such as **delete** all responses to remove all responses. This option could be useful when you are testing your survey and would like to delete all the responses before you send the survey to the actual respondents.

You can invite other people in your organization as co-owners through the **Share** button on the command bar at the top of your survey:

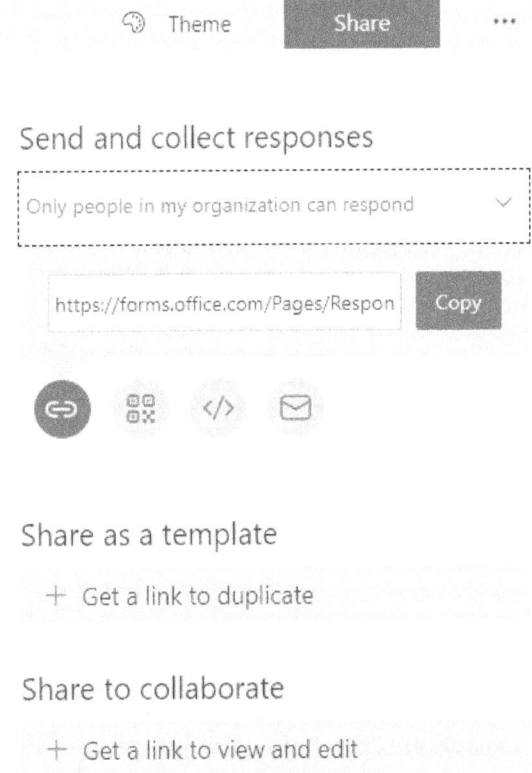

Figure 3.37 – Sharing survey options

If you would like others to copy your survey (without giving them co-owner access to your survey), then you can share the link using **Share as a template**. When your colleague clicks the link from **Share as a template**, a copy of the survey will be created. You can give full access to your survey using **Get a link to view and edit**. Anyone with this link will have full access to the survey, including viewing the results and modifying the survey questions.

If you would like to share only the survey report, you can get the link to the report summary from the response tab. Open the **…** menu and select **Create a summary link**:

Figure 3.38 – Creating a summary link to the survey report

Anyone with the link (even people outside your organization) can view the summary report (including the five most recent text comments) but will not be able to get a detailed response from each respondent and will not be able to delete survey responses:

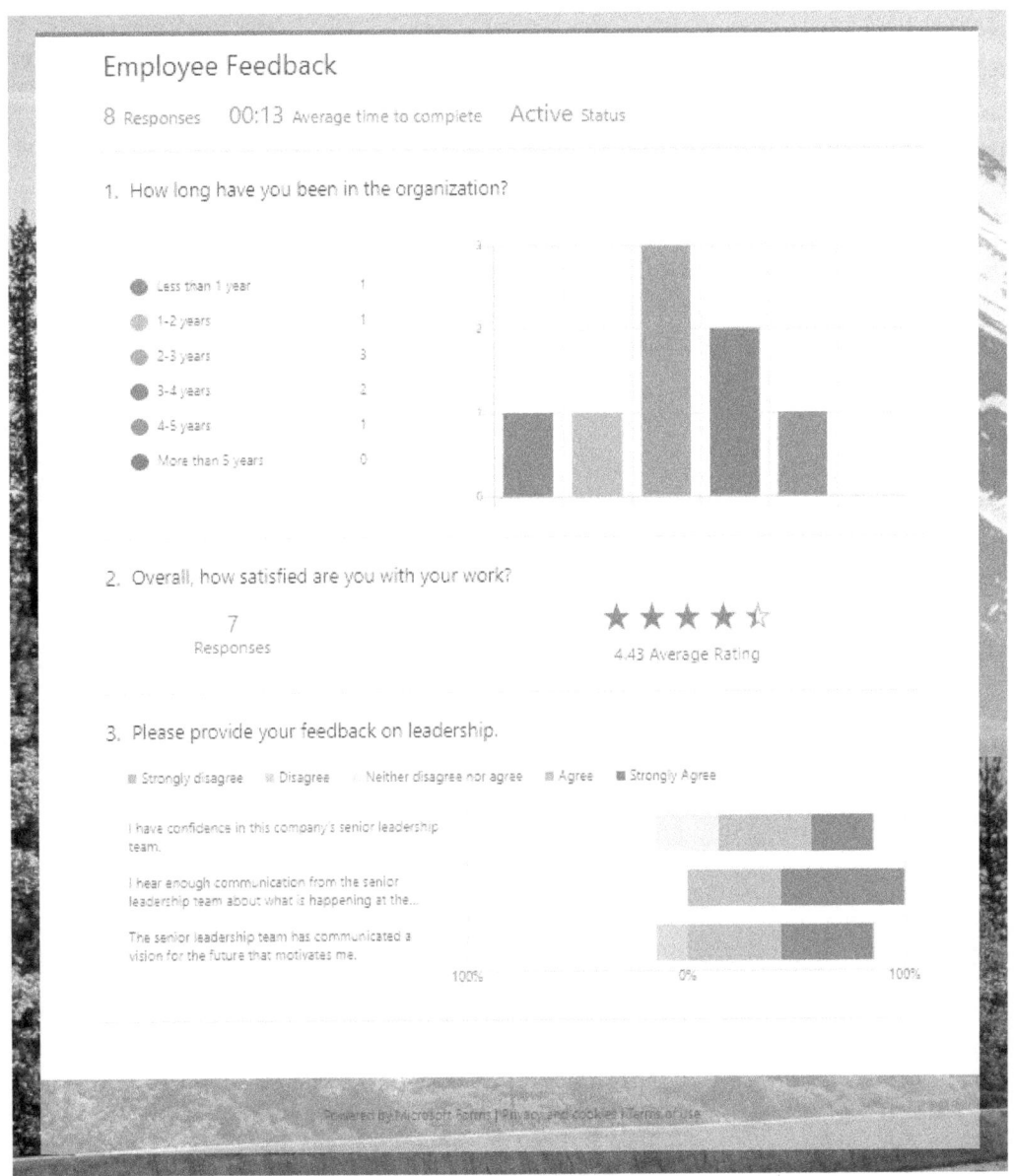

Figure 3.39 – Report summary view

With the survey responses summary, you can get insights and make data-driven decisions to follow up on the feedback from your colleagues and customers.

Summary

In this chapter, we walked through an example of creating a simple employee feedback survey with Microsoft Forms, from creating the survey questions to viewing the survey response report. With this basic step of creating a survey, you are now ready to use Microsoft Forms and Customer Voice to collect feedback from your colleagues and customers.

In the next few chapters, we will discuss using Microsoft Forms and Customer Voice for several common scenarios. We will start in the next chapter by discussing how you can use Microsoft Forms to collect feedback during a meeting.

Section 2:
Implementing Common Feedback Solutions with Microsoft Forms and Dynamics 365 Customer Voice

This section will go over common feedback scenarios and how to use Microsoft Forms or Dynamics 365 Customer Voice in each of the common feedback scenarios. Each chapter will focus on a specific capability area and provide practical implementation steps on building an end-to-end solution using Microsoft Forms and Dynamics 365 Customer Voice.

This section contains the following chapters:

- *Chapter 4, Conducting a More Productive Meeting with Microsoft Forms and Microsoft Teams*
- *Chapter 5, Post-Training Assessment and Feedback*
- *Chapter 6, Conducting an Employee Survey with Dynamics 365 Customer Voice*
- *Chapter 7, Collecting Periodic Customer Feedback with Customer Voice*
- *Chapter 8, Automating Customer Support Surveys with Dynamics 365 Customer Voice*
- *Chapter 9, Closing a Feedback Loop with Customer Voice*

4
Conducting a More Productive Meeting with Microsoft Forms and Microsoft Teams

According to a Harvard Business Review article, *executives spend an average of nearly 23 hours per week in meetings* (see `https://hbr.org/2017/07/stop-the-meeting-madness`). As we become more and more dependent on each other to get things done, the meeting will become a more and more important way to work together. As the COVID-19 pandemic has forced many businesses to adopt working remotely, online meetings have become the new normal. **Microsoft Teams** is now the tool of choice for many organizations conducting online meetings. Microsoft Forms has built-in integration with Microsoft Teams to collect feedback before and during the meeting, and results can be shared through Microsoft Teams.

In this chapter, we will review how you can use Microsoft Forms to send an anonymous survey to prepare for a meeting, conduct live polls during the meeting, and collect and share feedback after the meeting. By the end of this chapter, you will know how to use Microsoft Forms to make your meetings more productive.

The chapter is organized as follows:

- Sending an anonymous survey before a meeting
- Conducting a live poll during a meeting
- Collecting and sharing meeting feedback

Let's get right to it.

Sending an anonymous survey before a meeting

A meeting often includes a **Question-and-Answer (Q&A)** session. In a large meeting, sometimes you send out the questions ahead of time so that answers can be prepared in advance. Answers are often collected anonymously to allow your team to express their thoughts more freely.

The following are the steps required to create a simple anonymous survey to conduct a Q&A survey:

1. Go to `forms.office.com` and create a new form.

2. Add a title and create a text question on your new form.

3. Set the option for **Long answer** on your text question. Your form should look as shown in *Figure 4.1*:

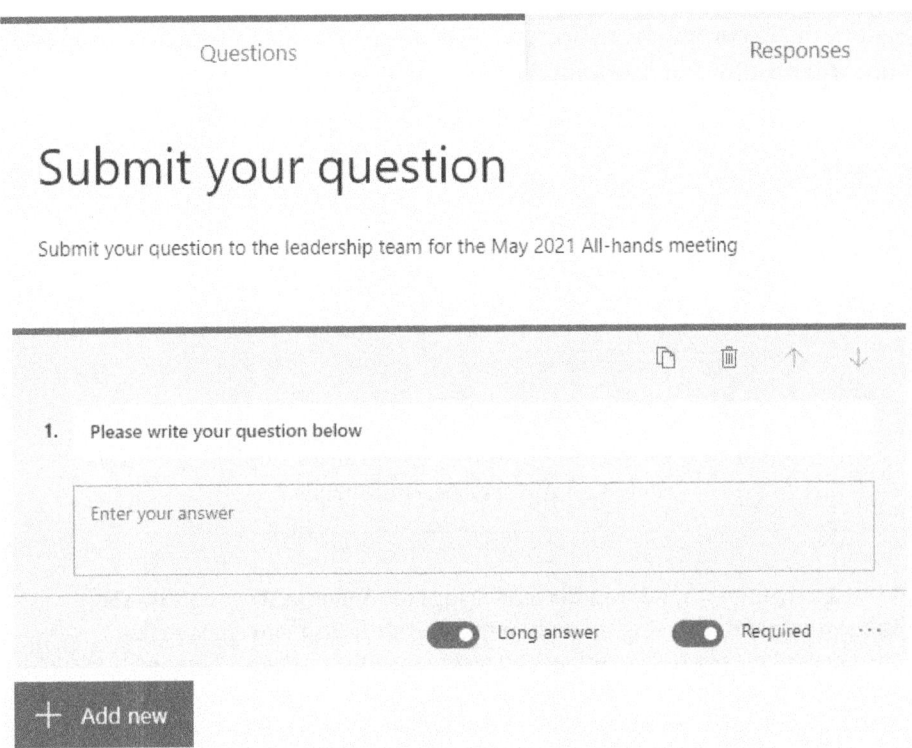

Figure 4.1 – An example of a form to set questions for a meeting

4. Open the **Settings** pane by clicking **...** next to the **Share** button in the command bar at the top (see *Figure 4.2*):

Figure 4.2 – Accessing the Settings pane in Microsoft Forms

5. Uncheck the **Record name** option under **Who can fill out this form** > **Only people in my organization can respond**, as shown in *Figure 4.3*:

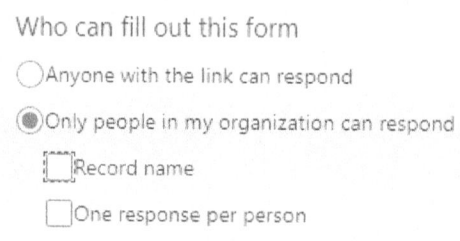

Figure 4.3 – Anonymous setting option

Tip

As an alternative to *Step 5*, you can also change the option to **Anyone with the link can respond**. Selecting this option makes your form anonymous so that the names of the responders will not be recorded in the response. With this option, however, anyone, including people outside your organization who have the link, can respond to your survey. When you select the **Only people in my organization can respond** option, Microsoft Forms authenticates the user who opens the link by prompting them to log in using a work or school account (if the user has not already done so). The **Record name** option determines whether the user information will be recorded as part of the response.

---

6. Edit the text question by adding a subtitle through the **...** menu (see *Figure 4.4*):

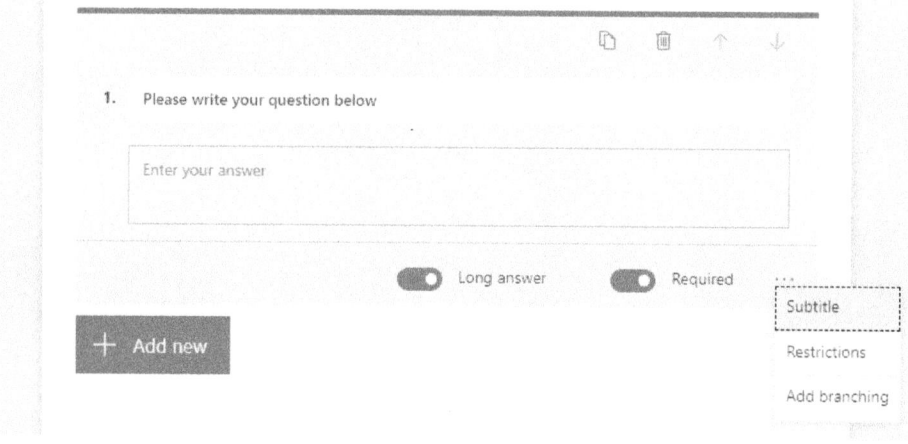

Figure 4.4 – Adding a subtitle to a question

7. Add a label to inform the user that their questions will be collected anonymously. This is important to give assurance to the user about their anonymity, as they may be prompted to log in (see the previous *Tip*). *Figure 4.5* shows an example of the completed form:

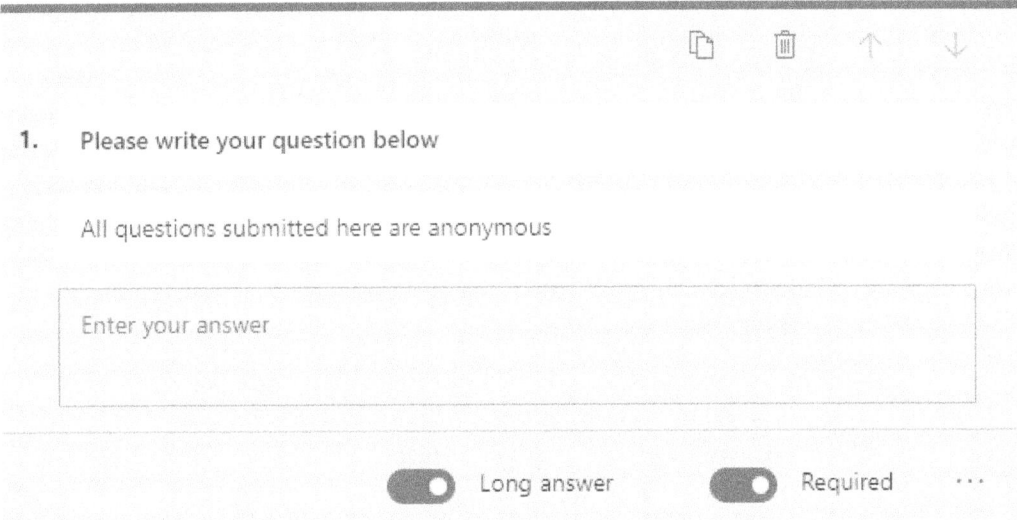

Figure 4.5 – Completed question collection form

8. Copy the survey link by clicking the **Share** button in the command bar:

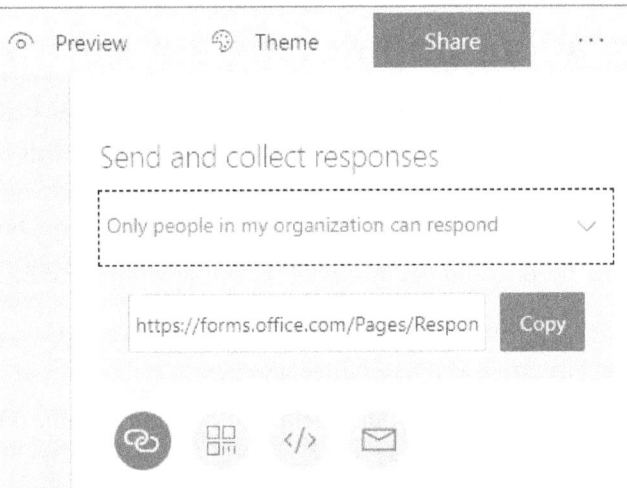

Figure 4.6 – Getting the survey link

After getting the link as shown in *Figure 4.6*, you can send a message to your team by including the link via either email or a Microsoft Teams chat, as shown in *Figure 4.7*:

Figure 4.7 – Sharing the link to the Q&A submission form through Teams

In addition to collecting information to prepare for a meeting, you can also use Microsoft Forms to conduct live polls during a meeting.

Conducting a live poll during a meeting

The Microsoft Forms app for Microsoft Teams enables you to conduct **live polls** during a Teams meeting.

Installing the Forms app

To use the app, you first need to add the Microsoft Forms app to your meeting by following these steps:

1. Edit your Teams meeting and open the **Details** tab.

2. Add the Microsoft Forms app to your meeting by clicking + in the tab header of the meeting tab, as shown in *Figure 4.8*:

Figure 4.8 – Adding an app to a Teams meeting

3. Search for and add the **Forms** app, as shown in *Figure 4.9*:

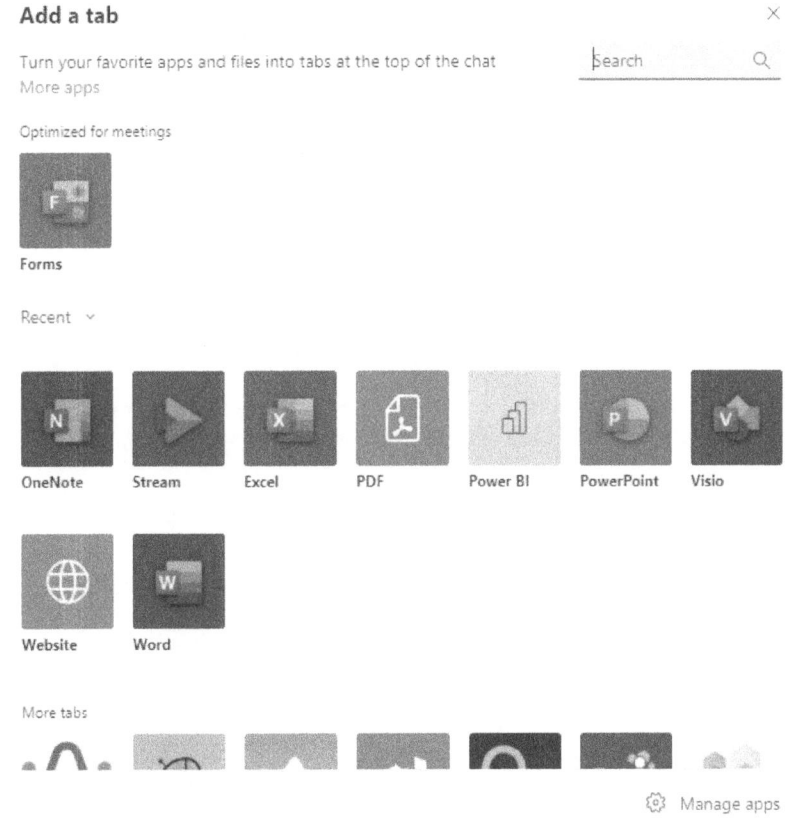

Figure 4.9 – Adding Forms to the Microsoft Teams tab

4. Review and agree to the terms of use by clicking on the **Add** button.

5. Click save to complete the installation.

Now that you have added the Microsoft Forms app to your meeting, you can use the app to create poll questions prior to the meeting.

Creating poll questions

Use the following steps to configure the poll questions:

1. Open your meeting, navigate to the **Polls** tab, and click on **Create New Poll**:

Figure 4.10 – Create a new poll for your Teams meeting

2. In the dialog window, specify the question and options for the poll question as shown in *Figure 4.11*:

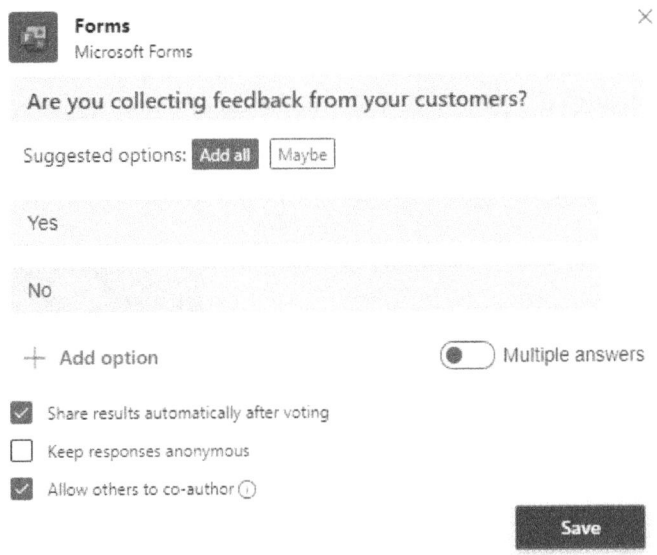

Figure 4.11 – An example of a poll question

3. You can add as many questions are needed for your meeting. All the poll questions are shown in the **Polls** tab, as in *Figure 4.12*:

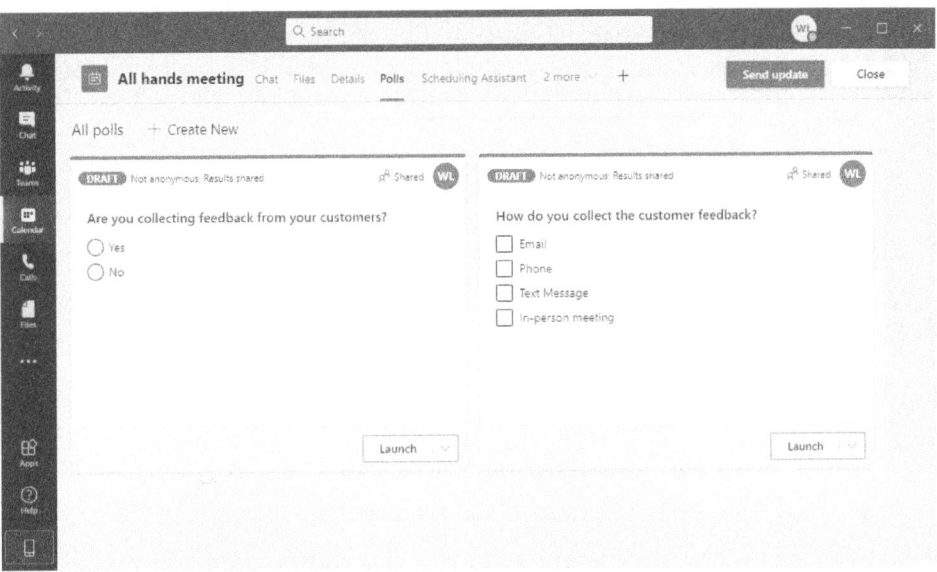

Figure 4.12 – List of all the poll questions for the meeting

You can set up all the poll questions before the meeting and launch the poll during the meeting at the appropriate time.

Launching poll questions

During the meeting, anyone with presenter access can view all the poll questions created for the meeting and launch the poll by clicking the **Launch** button for a question (see *Figure 4.12*).

All meeting participants should see the live polls through the chat window as shown in *Figure 4.13*:

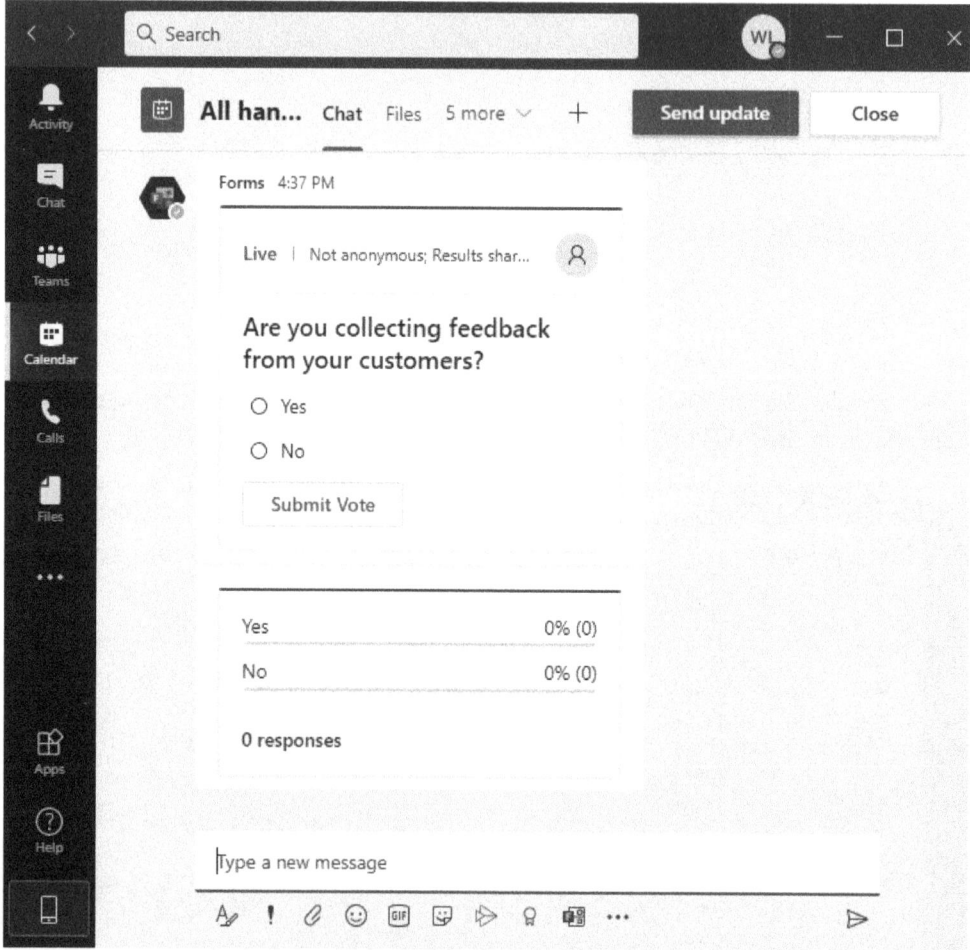

Figure 4.13 – Poll questions appearing in the chat conversation during the meeting

In addition to seeing the poll questions as part of the chat conversation, the meeting attendees can also see the launched poll questions under the **Polls** tab for the meeting:

After answering the poll, the answer is displayed live in the chat window as shown in *Figure 4.14*:

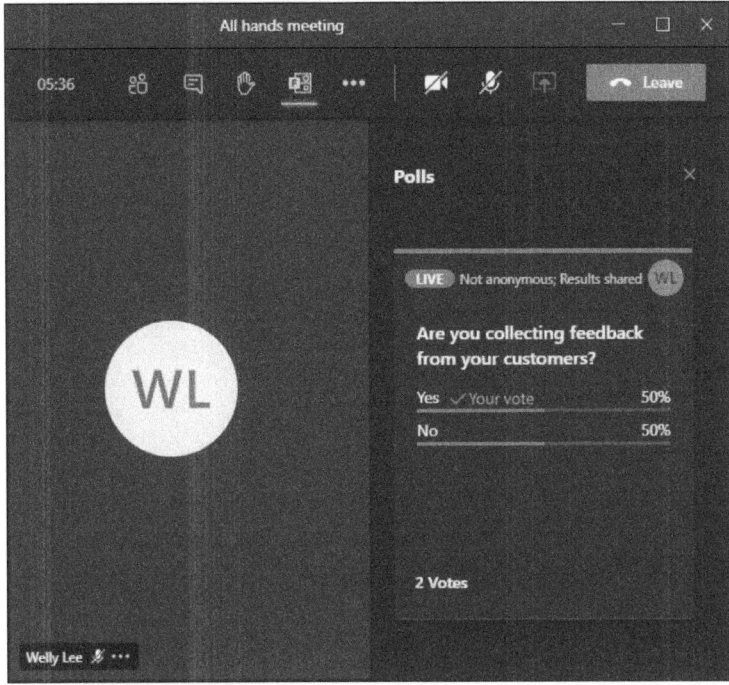

Figure 4.14 – Poll results as shown to the attendees

An attendee can change their answer to a live poll by closing and reopening the **Polls** pane if the presenter has not closed the poll through the **Polls** tab, as shown in *Figure 4.15*:

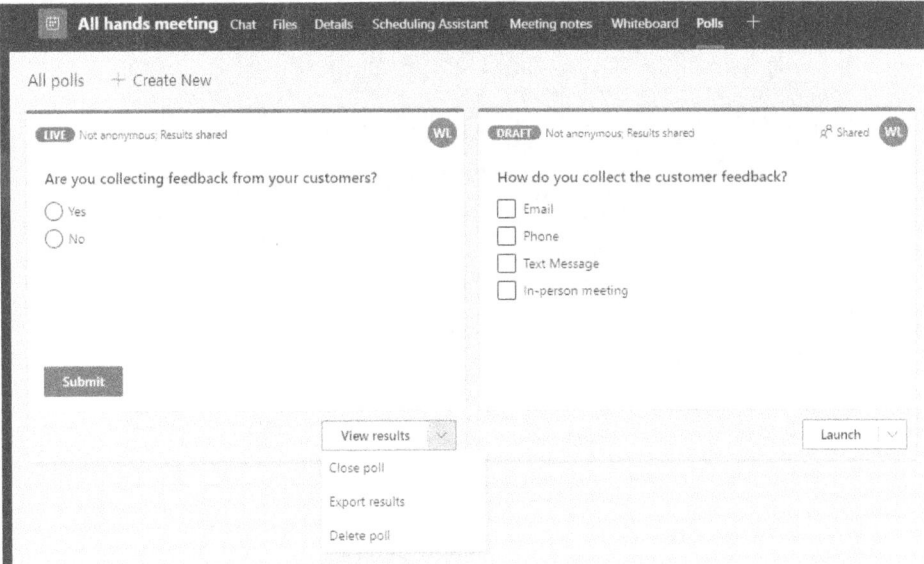

Figure 4.15 – The All polls view for the meeting presenter

A presenter can edit polls with a status of **draft** and change how the poll is to be presented; they can also change the **Share results automatically after voting** option, as shown in *Figure 4.16*:

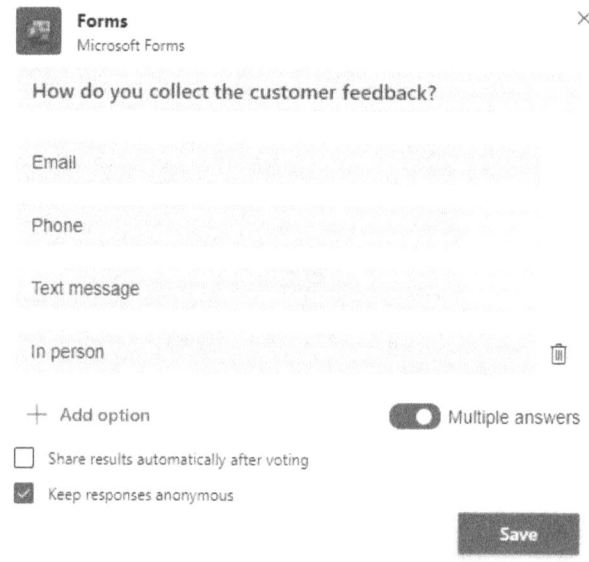

Figure 4.16 – Meeting poll options

When you uncheck **Share results automatically after voting**, the meeting attendees will not be able to see results from other attendees (see *Figure 4.17*):

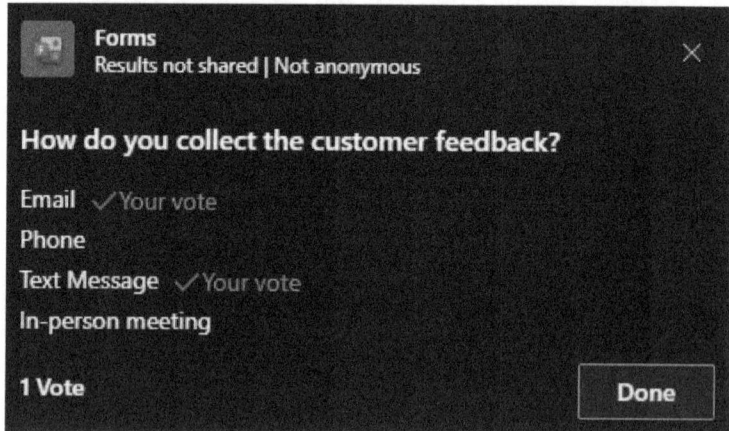

Figure 4.17 – An attendee's view of a polling result

A meeting presenter can manage the poll, using options to launch a draft poll, close a live poll, and reopen a closed poll, as shown in *Figure 4.18*:

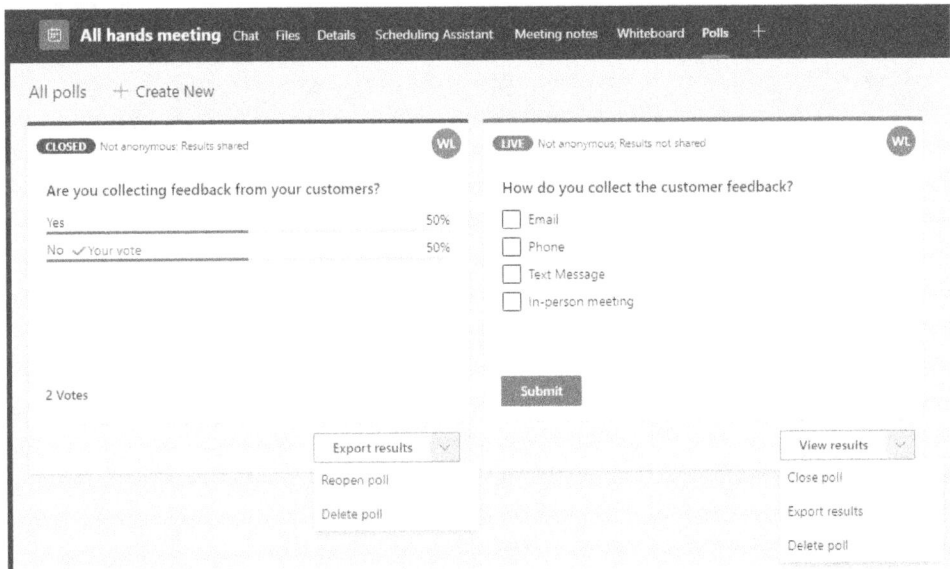

Figure 4.18 – The presenter can manage all polls for the meeting

When the poll is closed, the presenter can export the results to Excel, as shown in *Figure 4.19*:

A	B	C	D	E	F
ID	Start time	Completion time	Email	Name	Are you collecting feedback from your customers?
1	5/3/21 8:49:57	5/3/21 8:49:57	alland@mysurvey.onn	Allan DeYoung	Yes
2	5/3/21 8:50:17	5/3/21 8:50:17	welly@mysurvey.onm	Welly Lee	No

Figure 4.19 – Exported poll results for non-anonymous responses

If the pool option is set to **Keep responses anonymous,** the resulted export file will look as shown in *Figure 4.20*:

A	B	C	D	E	F
ID	Start time	Completion time	Email	Name	Are you collecting feedback from your customers?
1	5/3/21 8:49:57	5/3/21 8:49:57	anonymous		Yes
2	5/3/21 8:50:17	5/3/21 8:50:17	anonymous		No

Figure 4.20 – Exported poll results for anonymous responses

Each poll question is created as a separate quick poll in Microsoft Forms (see *Figure 4.21*). You can view the quick polls and view the results using the Microsoft Forms portal (`forms.microsoft.com`), but you cannot edit there. You must edit the quick poll while viewing the Microsoft Teams meeting details.

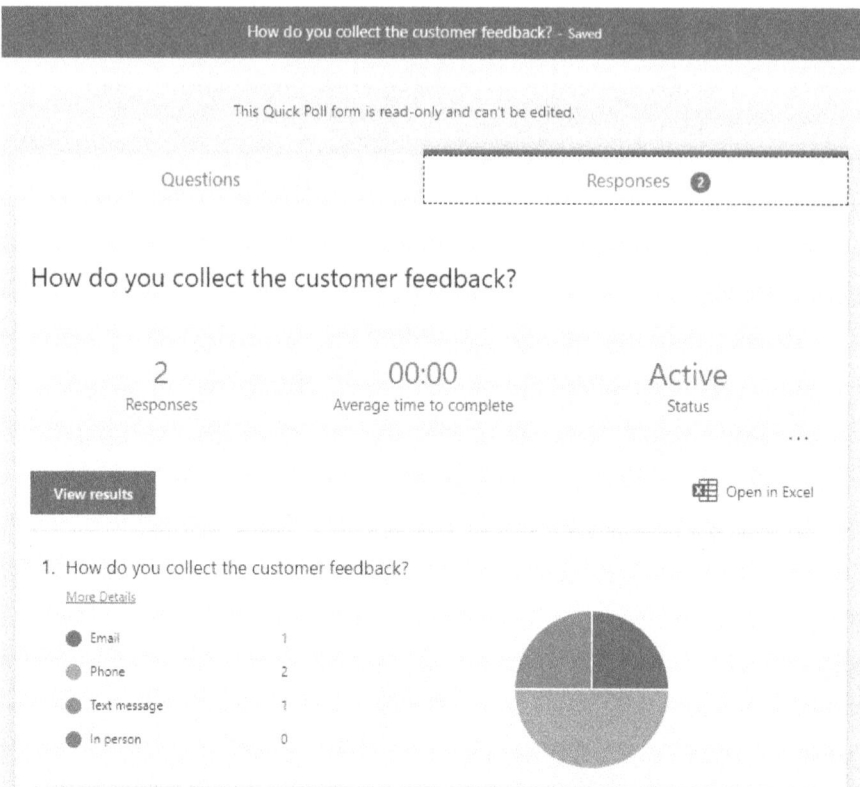

Figure 4.21 – Viewing poll results from the Microsoft Forms portal

Important note

Since each poll question appears as a separate form, each individual poll question counts toward the 200-surveys-per-user limit. If create a lot of meeting poll questions, you may exceed the limit and need to delete the previous polls. Be sure to permanently delete unused forms from the recycle bin to free up your limit.

After the meeting is over, you may want to send a follow-up survey to collect additional information, including feedback on how well the meeting went and suggestions to improve future meetings.

Collecting and sharing meeting feedback

Once the meeting is finished, you may want to collect feedback from those who attended your meeting; you first need to find out who attended the meeting.

Getting a meeting attendance list

Microsoft Teams keep track of attendance and provides an attendance report. After the meeting is completed, you can go to the **Details** tab and download the attendance list as shown in *Figure 4.22*:

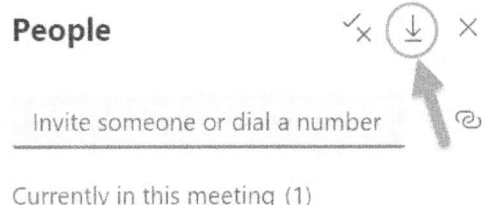

Figure 4.22 – Attendance list on Microsoft Teams

Important note

If you do not see the attendance link in the **Details** tab, check the meeting policy setting with your administrators and follow the instructions at `https://docs.microsoft.com/en-us/microsoftteams/ meeting-policies-in-teams` to enable the feature.

Downloading the report gives you the list of attendees and the times at which they joined and left the meeting as shown in *Figure 4.23*:

	A	B	C	D	E	F
1	Meeting Summary					
2	Total Number of Participants	5				
3	Meeting Title	All hands meeting				
4	Meeting Start Time	5/3/2021, 8:30:30 AM				
5	Meeting End Time	5/3/2021, 9:27:47 AM				
6						
7	Full Name	Join Time	Leave Time	Duration	Email	Role
8	Allan DeYoung	5/3/2021, 8:30:40 AM	5/3/2021, 9:27:43 AM	57m 3s	alland@mysurvey.	Attendee
9	Adele Vance	5/3/2021, 8:31:12 AM	5/3/2021, 9:27:43 AM	56m 31s	adelev@mysurvey	Attendee
10	Bianca Pisani	5/3/2021, 8:30:37 AM	5/3/2021, 9:27:44 AM	57m 6s	biancap@mysurve	Attendee
11	Cameron White	5/3/2021, 8:30:41 AM	5/3/2021, 9:09:32 AM	38m 51s	cameronw@mysur	Attendee
12	Welly Lee	5/3/2021, 8:30:30 AM	5/3/2021, 8:27:42 AM	57m 12s	welly@mysurvey.c	Organizer
13						

Figure 4.23 – Attendance list

Once you have the list of meeting attendees, you can send meeting feedback surveys to collect feedback.

Meeting feedback surveys

As we discussed in *Chapter 2, Best Practices for Collecting Feedback through Surveys*, you need to define the key metrics you would like to measure with your meeting feedback. After you have defined your key metrics, then you can add key driver questions that may explain the responders' answers and free-form text questions for additional suggestions. *Figure 4.24* shows an example of a meeting feedback survey:

Meeting Feedback

1. Was the meeting useful?

Not useful ☆ ☆ ☆ ☆ ☆ Very useful

2. How much do you agree with the following statements?

	Strongly disagree	Disagree	Neutral	Agree	Strongly agree
I found the information discussed to be actionable	○	○	○	○	○
I have my questions answered	○	○	○	○	○
I learned new things from the discussion	○	○	○	○	○

3. Please share your suggestions to improve the meeting

Enter your answer

Figure 4.24 – An example of a meeting feedback survey

The survey in *Figure 4.24* uses a "meeting's usefulness" metric and has three key driver questions, including questions about the clarity of direction, whether the meeting answered the attendee's questions, and whether the attendee learned new things. You should customize the key metrics and key driver questions based on the nature and the objective of your meeting.

After you have created the survey, you can get the link through the **Share** button to distribute the survey. There are a few options for you to get the survey link to the attendees:

- Send the link using email.
- Show the survey on a Microsoft Teams channel.
- Display a QR code at the end of the meeting.

Sending the link using email

Copy the email addresses from the attendee list (see the relevant column in *Figure 4.23*) and paste them to an Outlook email's **To** field. If you are sending to people in the organization, Outlook will automatically convert the email address to the names of the recipients, as shown in *Figure 4.25*:

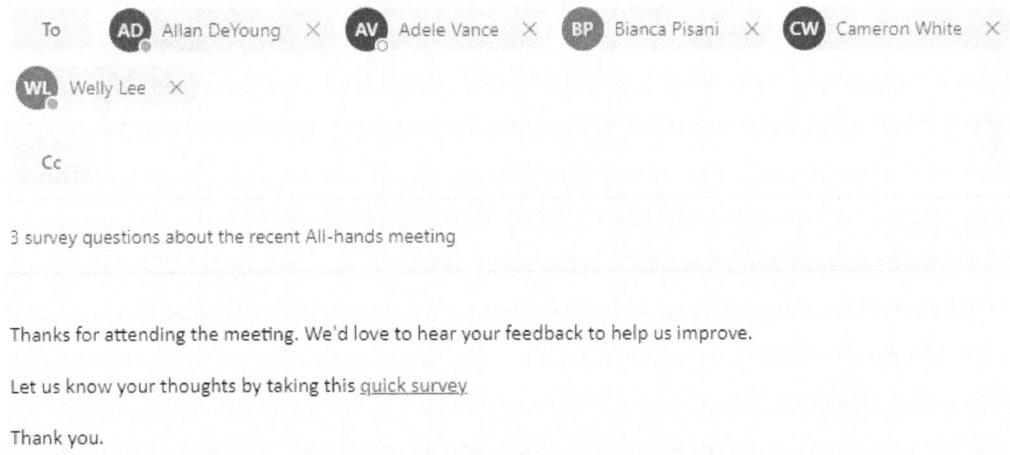

Figure 4.25 – An example of a meeting feedback survey invitation

Add the link to the survey in the body of the email along with the invitation text. The email recipient can then click on the link to open the online survey for the meeting feedback.

Showing the survey on a Microsoft Teams channel

As an alternative to email distribution, you can also embed the survey in a Microsoft Teams channel with the following steps:

1. Open a Microsoft Teams channel and add a new tab by clicking **+**, as shown in *Figure 4.26*:

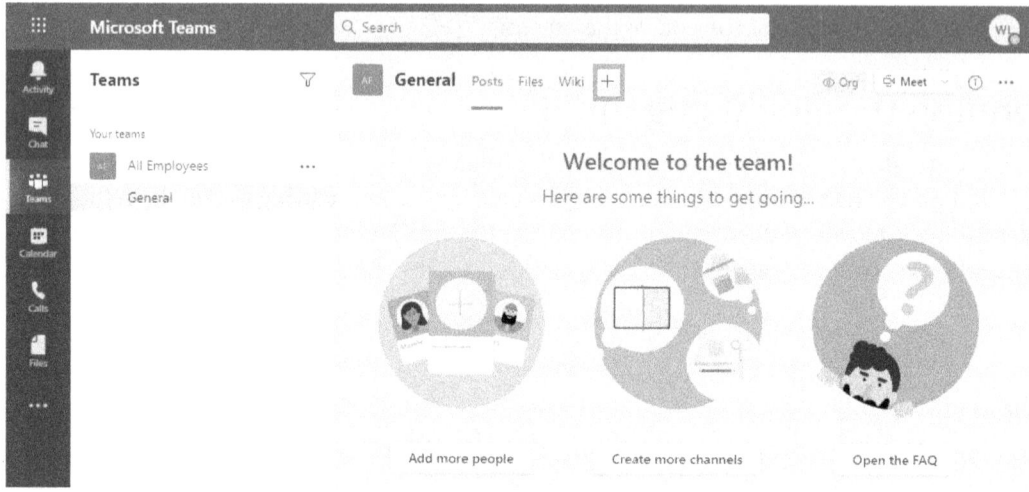

Figure 4.26 – Adding a new tab to a Microsoft Teams channel

2. Select the **Forms** app from the list of applications.

3. Select **Add an existing form**, choose the survey you created for the meeting feedback (see *Figure 4.27*), and click **Save**:

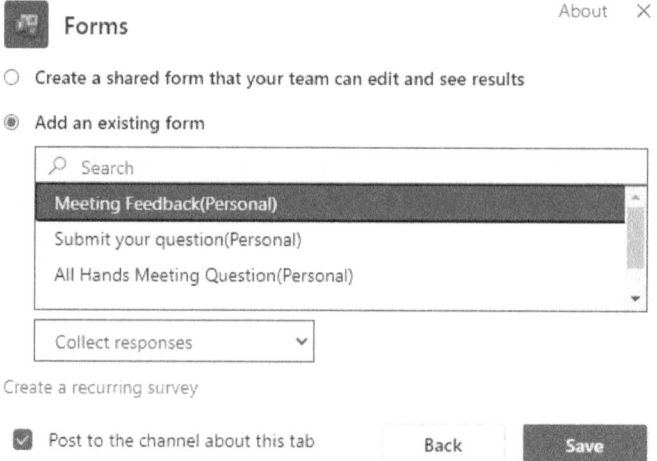

Figure 4.27 – Form selection screen

The meeting feedback survey will be added as a separate tab on your Microsoft Teams channel as shown in *Figure 4.28*:

Figure 4.28 – Embedded meeting feedback survey on a Microsoft Teams channel

> **Tip**
>
> Showing a survey in a Teams channel is usually done for continuous and long-running feedback collection. For short-term feedback collection, you may add the survey to the channel and remove the channel when the feedback has been collected.

Displaying a QR code at the end of the meeting

In addition to distributing the survey through email and Teams, you can also display a **QR code** at the end of your meeting so that participants can scan the code to take the survey right away.

You can download the QR code as follows:

1. Open the meeting feedback survey on `forms.microsoft.com`.

2. Click the **Send** button and select the **QR code** option under **Send and collect responses**:

Figure 4.29 – Getting the QR code for your survey

3. Download the image containing the QR code (see *Figure 4.29*).

A `.png` file is downloaded of the QR code, and you can display the image on a slide at the end of the meeting. Your meeting attendees can use their mobile phones and scan the QR code to open the meeting feedback survey link.

After your meeting attendees have provided their feedback, you can share the results with your team.

Sharing meeting feedback

You can share survey results through different options in Microsoft Forms:

*   Share a link to the survey response summary page.
*   Share the results through Teams.
*   Share the results through Excel.

Let's take a look at each of these options.

Sharing a link to the survey response summary page

As discussed in *Chapter 3, Creating a Survey with Microsoft Forms,* you can view the survey responses in the **Responses** tab on your form (see *Figure 4.30*):

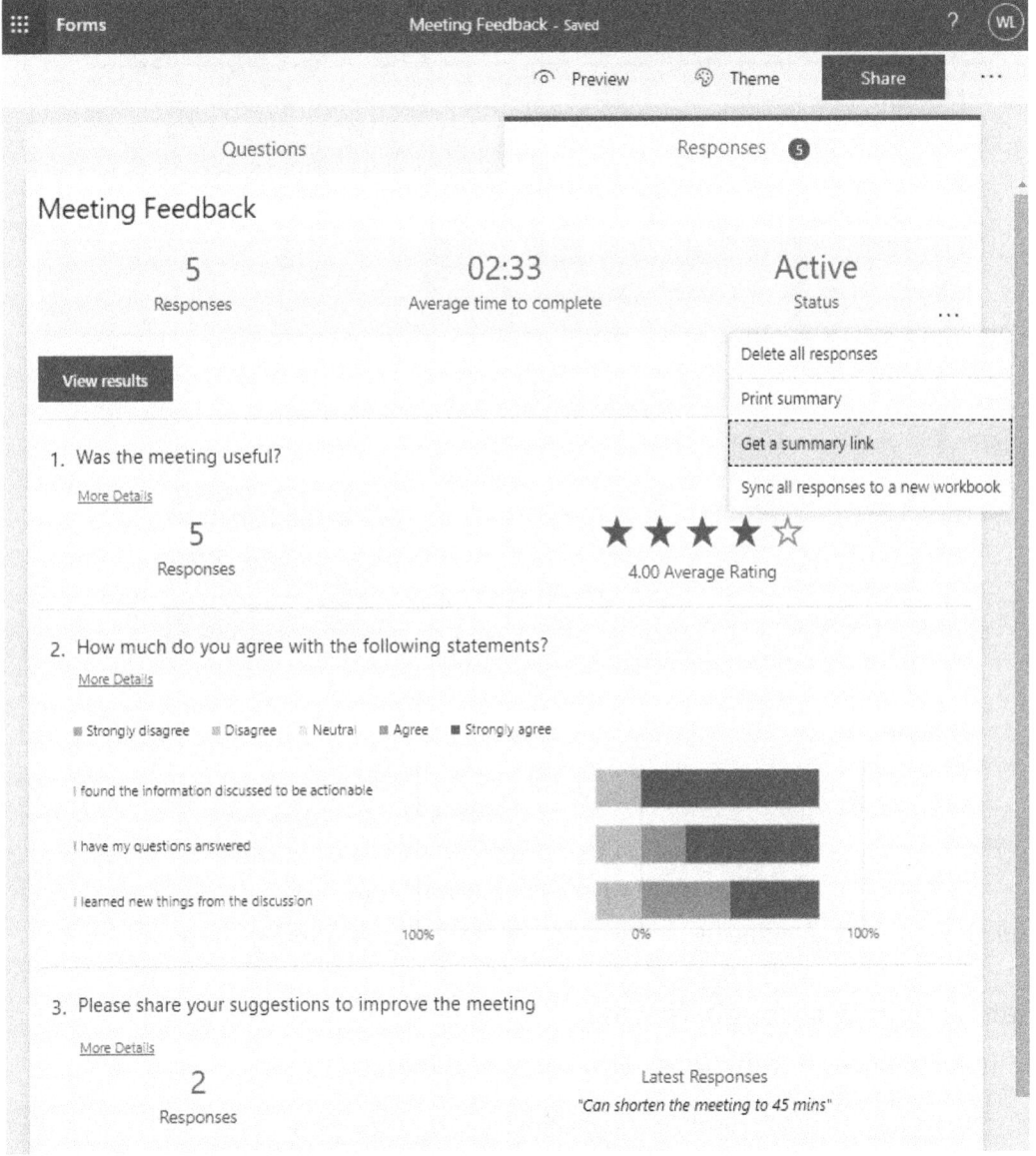

Figure 4.30 – Meeting feedback survey results

The survey responses report is available to the survey owner and anyone you share the survey with using the **Share to collaborate** link. If you would like to share the summary report without giving the ability to change the survey questions (or delete survey responses), you can use the **Create a summary link** option to share a summary with others via a link. The summary link opens a summary report in read-only mode, as shown in *Figure 4.31*:

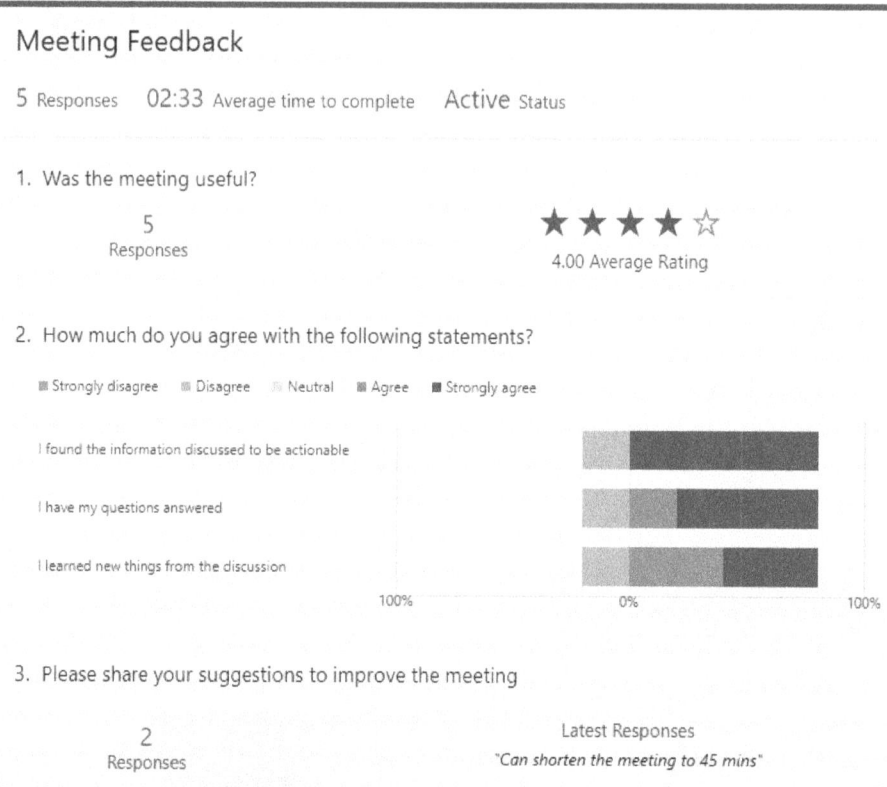

Figure 4.31 – Read-only summary report

In addition to sharing online reports, you can also share results through Teams.

Sharing results through Teams

Use the following steps to display survey results using Teams:

1. Navigate to your Microsoft Teams channel to show the report.

2. Add a new tab and select the **Forms** app.

3. After selecting the right form, choose the **Show results** option from the dropdown (see *Figure 4.32*):

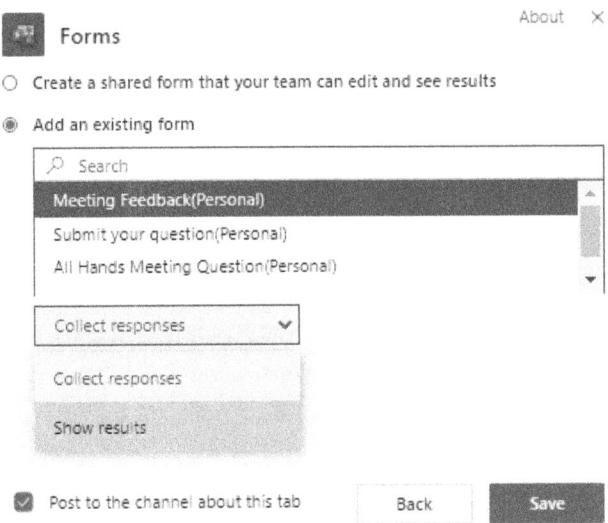

Figure 4.32 – The Show results option when adding a form to a Microsoft Teams channel

Members of the team will be able to see the survey results by opening the Teams channel tab, as shown in *Figure 4.33*:

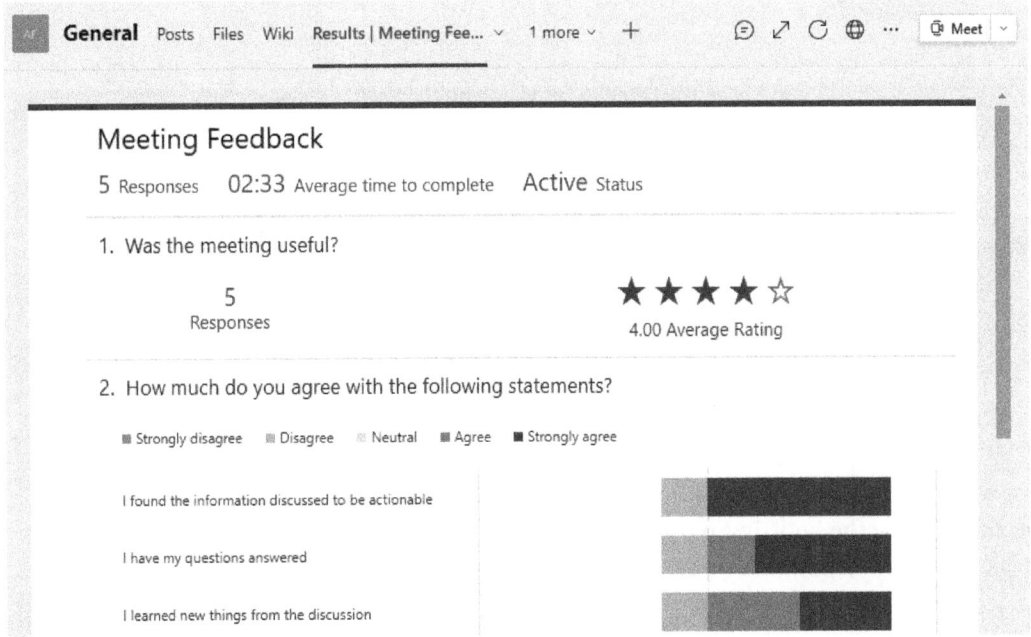

Figure 4.33 – Survey results on a Teams channel

While getting access to a summary is sufficient for most cases, in some situations, you may need to share the raw data through Excel.

Sharing results through Excel

You can get the raw data by downloading the response in Excel using the **Open in Excel** link on the **Responses** page, as shown in *Figure 4.34*:

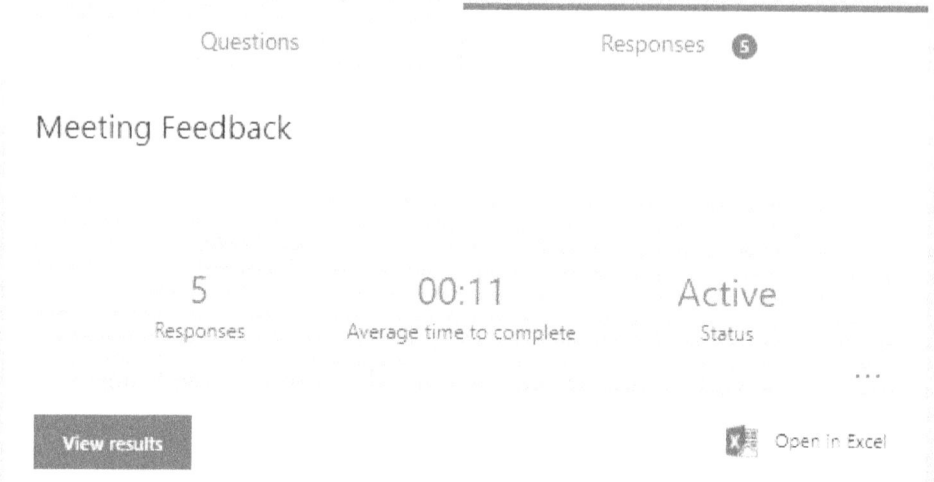

Figure 4.34 – The Open in Excel link on the Responses page

The Excel file shows each response as a separate row and each question as a separate column, as shown in *Figure 4.35*:

Figure 4.35 – An example of survey results in Excel

Whenever there is a new response, you can refresh Excel Online to get the latest response. You can also use the built-in **Share** functionality in Excel to share the report with other people in your organization.

The Excel file is stored in your OneDrive for Business storage, and you can also locate the file in your **OneDrive for Business** > **My Files** folder and share it directly from that location (see *Figure 4.36*).

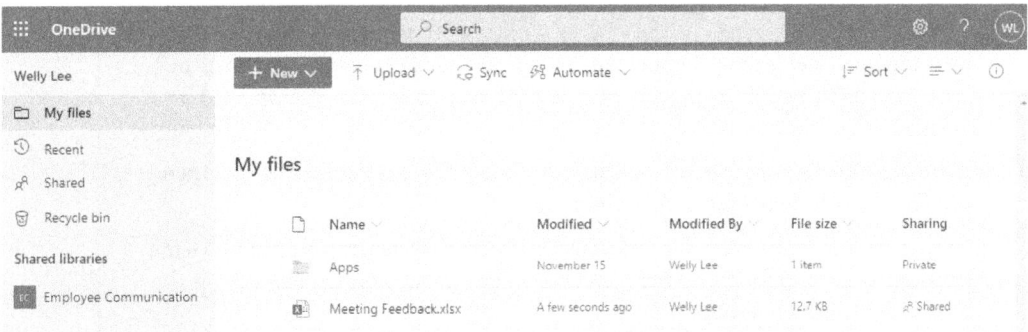

Figure 4.36 – Survey result file on OneDrive for Business

If you would like to have the survey results stored on an existing **SharePoint** team site, you can create your survey directly using SharePoint. To do so, navigate to your SharePoint team site's document library and create a new form (see *Figure 4.37*):

Figure 4.37 – The Forms for Excel option in the SharePoint document library

A new form will be created with an associated Excel file on the SharePoint site. When there is a new response, the Excel file will be automatically updated.

> **Important note**
>
> **Forms for Excel** is only supported on modern SharePoint team sites with an associated Office 365 group. The **Forms for Excel** option is not supported on classic SharePoint team sites.
>
> The Excel file is not created by default; you must first explicitly click on **Open in Excel** to create the file in SharePoint.
>
> If you have already created a survey as your personal survey, you can move the survey to a group form and the Excel file will be created on the SharePoint site associated with the group.

Summary

In this chapter, we discussed how to use Microsoft Forms to collect anonymous questions before a meeting, conduct live polls during a meeting, and send a feedback survey after the meeting. In some cases, you may want to assess attendees' knowledge after a meeting and discuss a new process or a new product. In the next chapter, we will discuss how you can use quizzes in Microsoft Forms to check how much attendees understood of the topics discussed during a meeting.

5
Post-Training Assessment and Feedback

In addition to creating a simple survey, you can create a simple quiz using Microsoft Forms. Quizzes are commonly used in schools and training organizations, but they are also used by business organizations to do assessments after internal training sessions. In addition to conducting assessments, collecting feedback following a training session is often done to help the instructor to improve and for the organizers to plan for future training.

In this chapter, we will look at quiz capabilities in Microsoft Forms to conduct a training assessment, including creating a quiz, scoring a quiz, and publishing grades. We will then go over how to use Microsoft Forms to collect training feedback, as well as the additional benefit of collecting feedback through Dynamics 365 Customer Voice.

By the end of this chapter, you will understand the tools available to you for collecting information following a training session.

The chapter is organized as follows:

- Creating a quiz with Microsoft Forms
- Grading and posting quiz results

- Collecting training feedback with Microsoft Forms
- Using Customer Voice to collect multi-course training feedback

We will start with creating a new quiz.

Creating a quiz with Microsoft Forms

Creating a new quiz in Microsoft Forms is very similar to creating a new form, whereby you have all the question types and options available in Forms, but you also have the ability to mark the correct answer, add comments, and assign points to a question.

To create a new quiz in Microsoft Forms, follow these steps:

1. Go to https://forms.microsoft.com.
2. Click the dropdown next to the **New Form** button and select **New Quiz**.
3. Add a quiz title, as shown in the following screenshot:

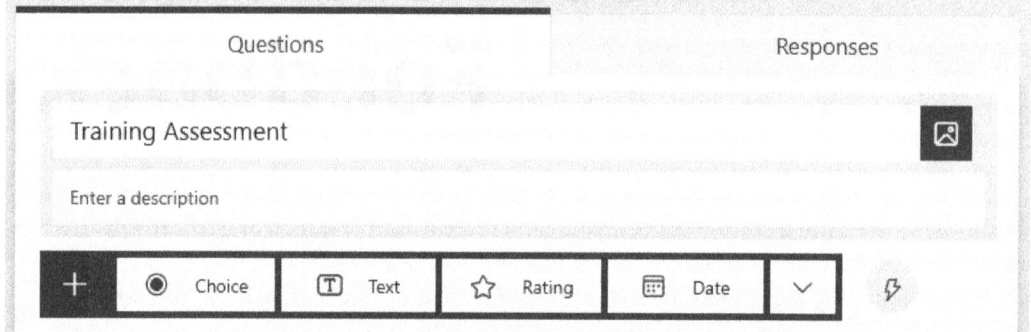

Figure 5.1 – Creating a new quiz

4. Click the + button to show the question-type options and select the **Choice** question type.

> **Tip**
> In a quiz, you can enter a math formula through the ... menu in your question editor to show a formula editor pane to enable you to write a math equation. When adding a math formula to a question, Microsoft Forms automatically adds suggested choices that include incorrect answers, to help you with your test creation, as shown in *Figure 5.2*.

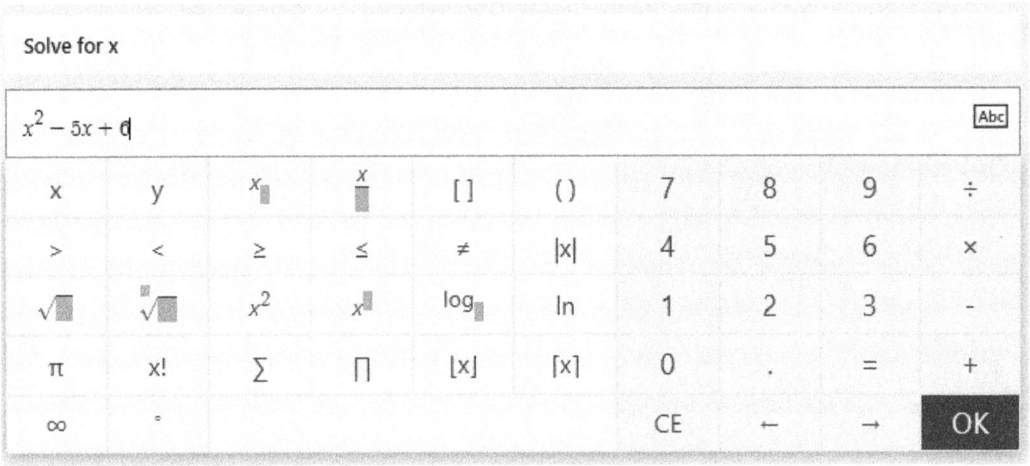

Solve for x

$$x^2 - 5x + d$$

x	y	$x_{\blacksquare}$	$\frac{x}{\blacksquare}$	[ ]	( )	7	8	9	÷
>	<	≥	≤	≠	|x|	4	5	6	×
$\sqrt{\blacksquare}$	$\sqrt[\blacksquare]{\blacksquare}$	x^2	$x^{\blacksquare}$	$\log_{\blacksquare}$	ln	1	2	3	-
π	x!	Σ	∏	⌊x⌋	⌈x⌉	0	.	=	+
∞	°					CE	←	→	OK

Figure 5.2 – Formula editor screen in Microsoft Forms

5. Mark the correct answer by selecting an option, then click on the checkmark icon that appears next to the option, as shown in the following screenshot. Repeat this step for all the correct options if there are multiple answers:

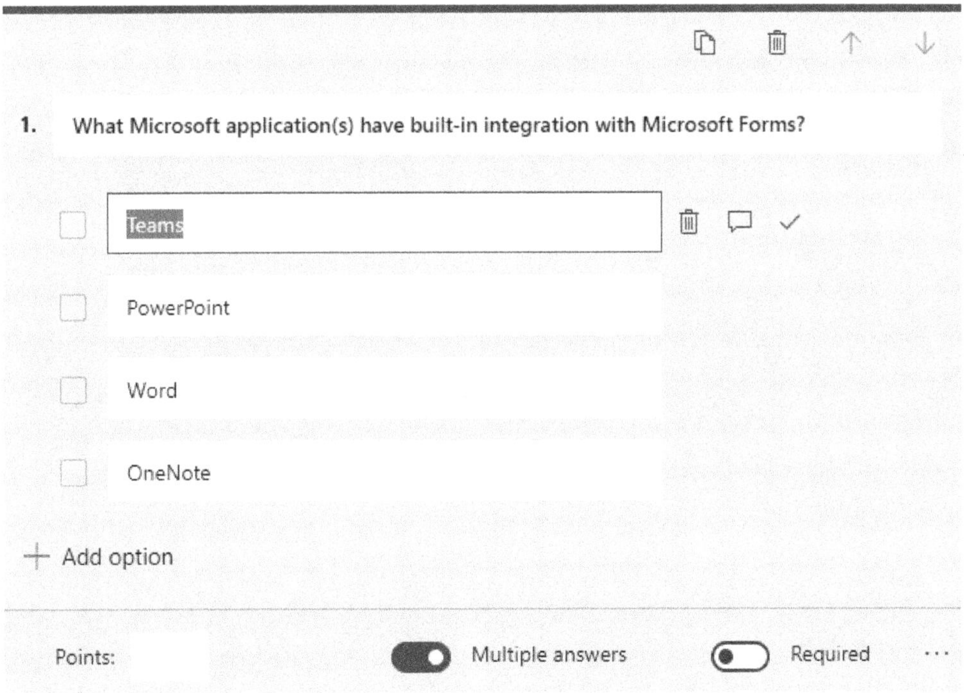

1. What Microsoft application(s) have built-in integration with Microsoft Forms?

☐ Teams

☐ PowerPoint

☐ Word

☐ OneNote

+ Add option

Points: ⬤ Multiple answers   ⬤ Required   ...

Figure 5.3 – Marking the correct answer by selecting the checkmark icon on the selected option

6. Add an optional message to explain to the user why the answer is correct or incorrect. Clicking the message icon would show a textbox to specify the message, as shown in the following screenshot:

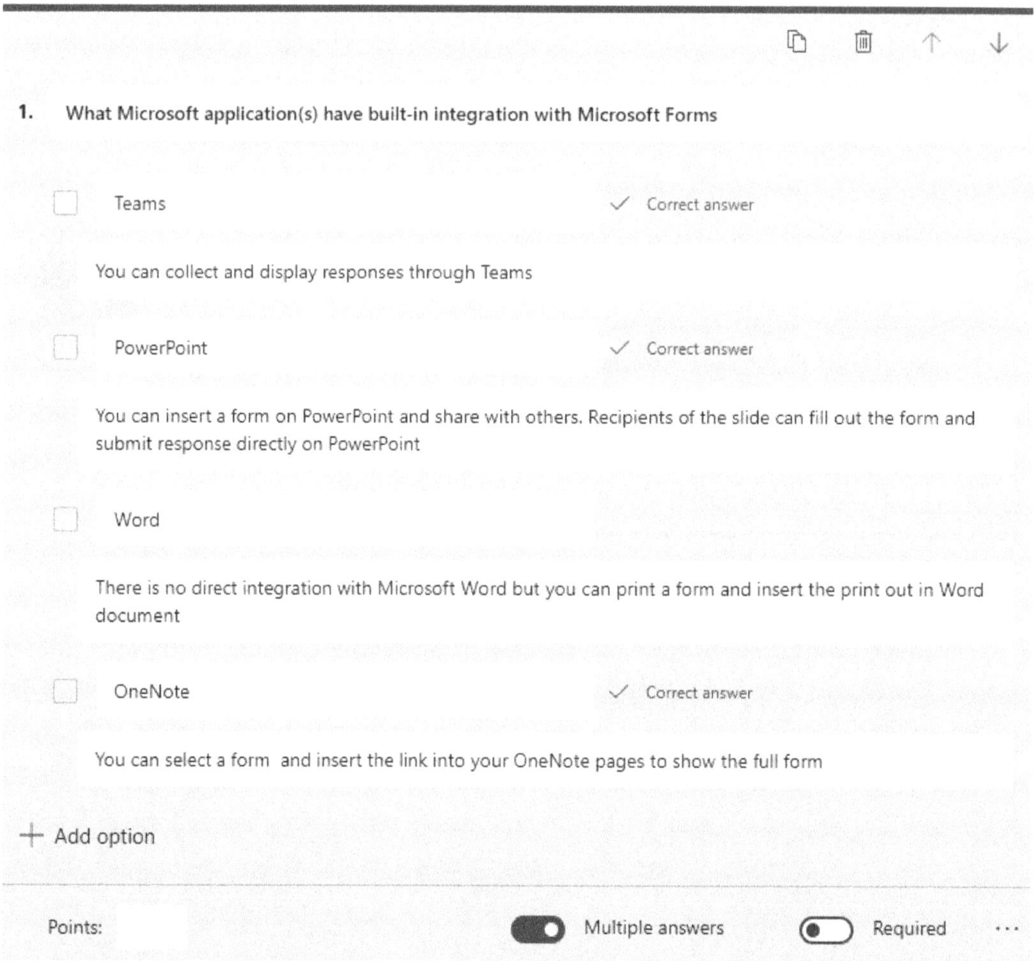

1.   What Microsoft application(s) have built-in integration with Microsoft Forms

☐   Teams   ✓ Correct answer

You can collect and display responses through Teams

☐   PowerPoint   ✓ Correct answer

You can insert a form on PowerPoint and share with others. Recipients of the slide can fill out the form and submit response directly on PowerPoint

☐   Word

There is no direct integration with Microsoft Word but you can print a form and insert the print out in Word document

☐   OneNote   ✓ Correct answer

You can select a form and insert the link into your OneNote pages to show the full form

＋ Add option

Points: Multiple answers   Required   · · ·

Figure 5.4 – A quiz question with correct answer and message display

The message appears at the end after the trainee has submitted the quiz, along with the correct answer(s), as shown in the following screenshot:

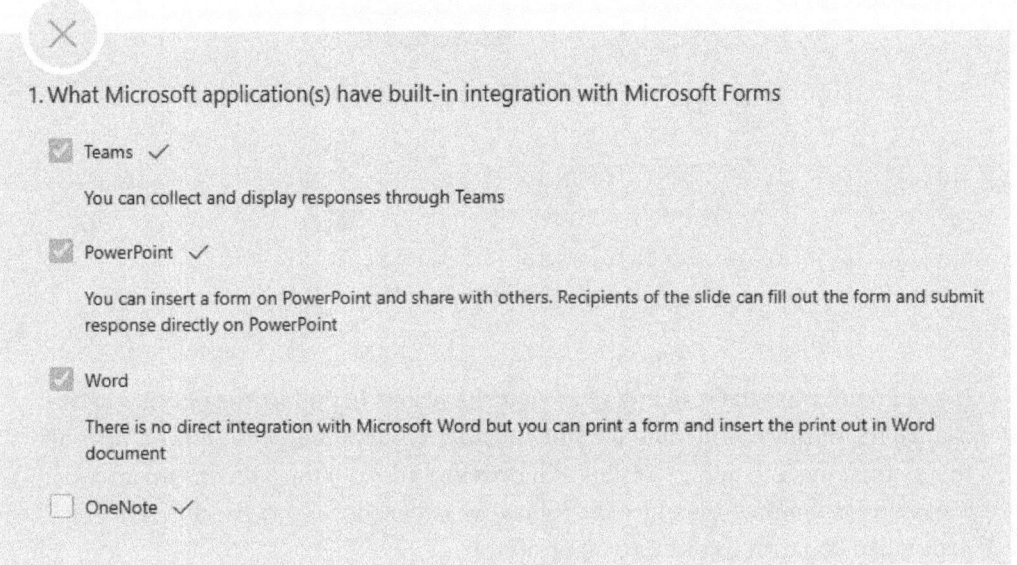

Figure 5.5 – Quiz result shown after the trainee has submitted the quiz

7. Add points to each of the questions that are answered correctly. Note that for a question with multiple answers, Microsoft Forms does not support partial credit; the trainee must get all the answers correct to get points or will get zero points otherwise.

> **Important note**
>
> By default, Microsoft Forms calculates the points based on the percentage of questions correctly answered. For example, if you have two questions and answer only one question correctly, then you get 50%.
>
> You can either leave all questions without a score or you must assign scores to all questions. If you only assign scores to some questions, then the trainee will not get any points when correctly answering questions that do not have any scores assigned.

8. Adjust the settings for the quiz to show results at the end of the quiz, as illustrated in the following screenshot:

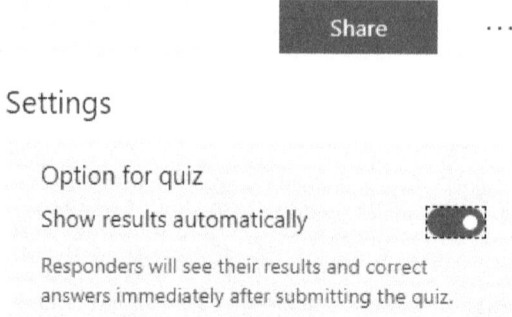

Figure 5.6 – Settings option for quiz

If you do not want the respondent to view the results including the point, you can change the settings by turning off **Show results automatically**. When you turn off this setting, the link to view results will be removed from the page shown after the trainee has submitted the quiz. The following screenshot shows the difference on the page when you turn this setting on or off:

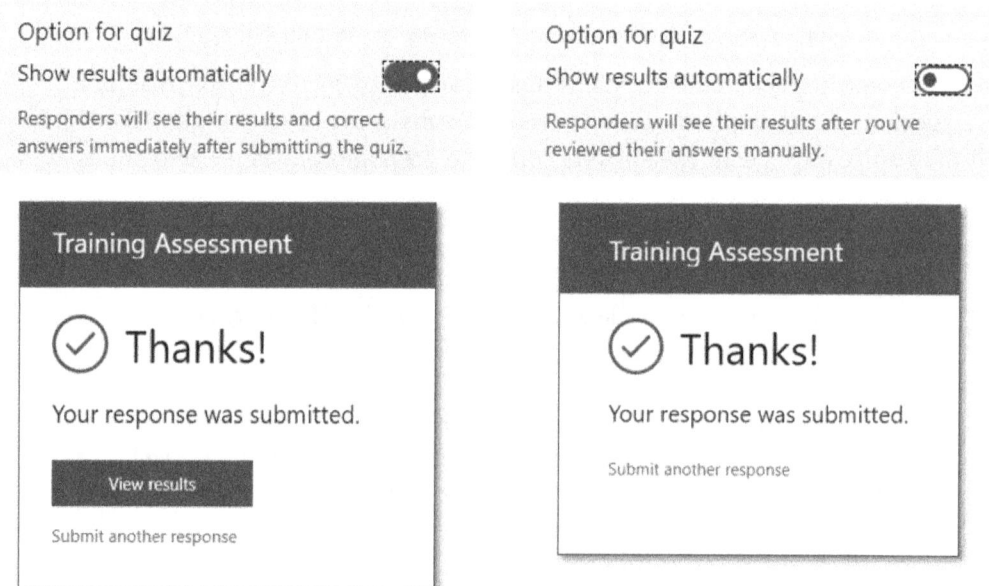

Figure 5.7 – Difference in the page shown after the quiz submission, based on the option setting

9. Set the shuffle setting for the question, as shown in the following screenshot. When you turn on **Shuffle options**, the options are randomly reordered to make it harder for the respondent to copy the answer:

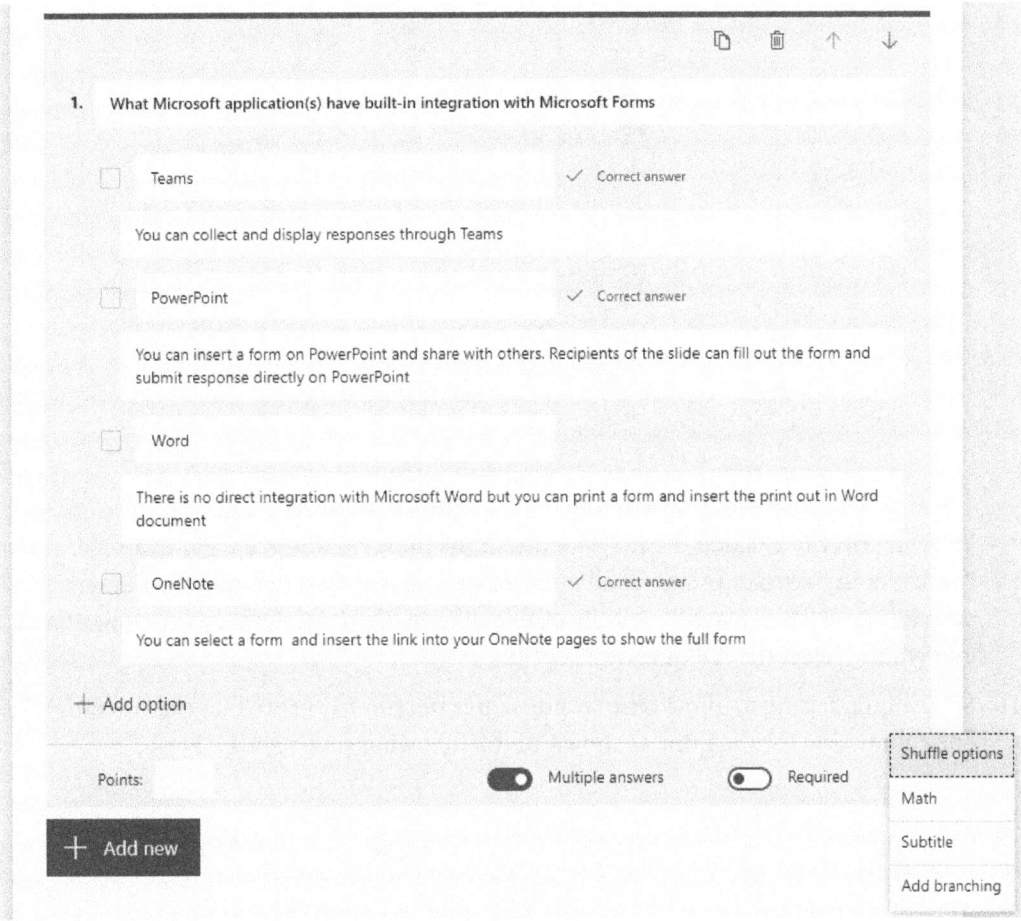

Figure 5.8 – Shuffling option on the question

10. Set the option to shuffle questions for the quiz by opening the **Settings** pane from ... on the command bar at the top of the quiz and select the option for **Shuffle questions**, as shown in the following screenshot:

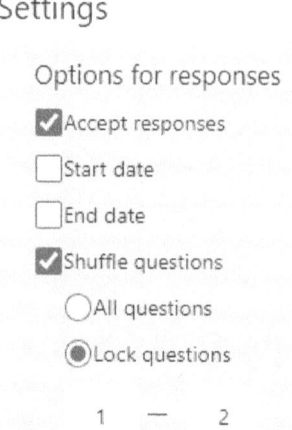

Figure 5.9 – Setting the option to shuffle questions

You can select to exclude the range of questions to be randomized. For example, if you would like to only shuffle all questions except the first two questions, then you can select the range of **Lock questions** between 1 and 2. Otherwise, to shuffle everything, select the **All questions** option.

11. Set the quiz setting to allow **One response per person** to ensure that there is only one submission for the quiz, as shown in the following screenshot:

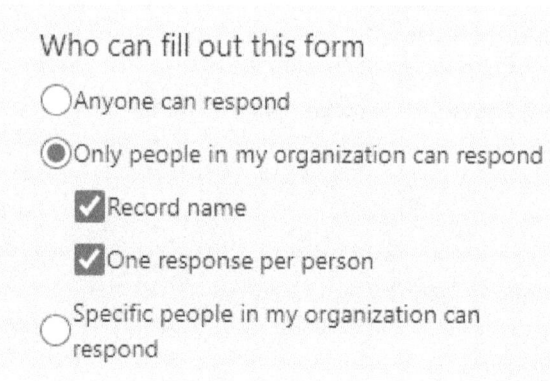

Figure 5.10 – Setting the option to allow only one response per person

By default, you can only restrict one response per person when you distribute a quiz to people in your organization. When a trainee opens a link to a quiz, Microsoft Forms will prompt the trainee to authenticate with their work or school account (if the trainee has not previously logged on to other Microsoft websites). This credential will be used to check if the trainee has previously submitted a response for the same quiz. If the trainee has previously submitted a response, the trainee will be shown the message displayed in the following screenshot:

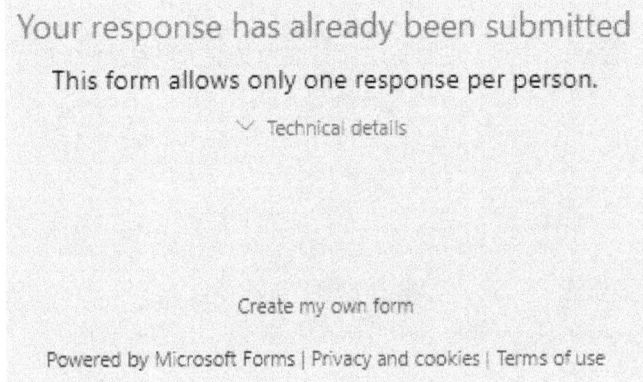

Figure 5.11 – Message shown when a trainee tries to open a quiz again

12. Optionally, set the date range during which a quiz is open by opening the quiz settings, and set the **Start date** and **End date** under **Options for responses**, as illustrated in the following screenshot:

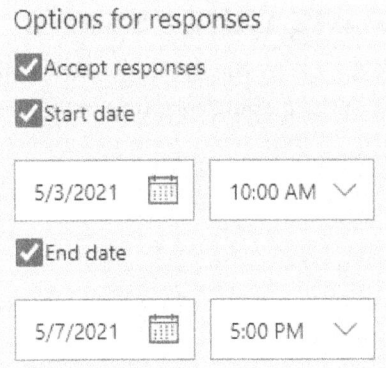

Figure 5.12 – Setting the option to specify the date and time a quiz can be taken

> **Important note**
> The time is based on the quiz author's local time zone. If a quiz author in
> Pacific Standard Time (UTC-8) set the time for the quiz to start at 10 A.M.,
> then the quiz will open at 1 P.M. Eastern Standard Time (UTC-5).

When a recipient opens a link to a quiz outside the date-time range, a message will
be shown to inform the trainee that the quiz is no longer accepting responses, as
illustrated in the following screenshot:

Figure 5.13 – Message shown when a trainee opens a quiz link outside the date-time range

Now that you have created the quiz questions and set the options, you can distribute the
quiz by sharing a link with the trainees. After you receive their responses, you can start
grading and posting the results.

Grading and posting quiz results

Viewing responses in quizzes is similar to viewing responses in forms. The following
screenshot shows the difference in the response reports for forms and quizzes:

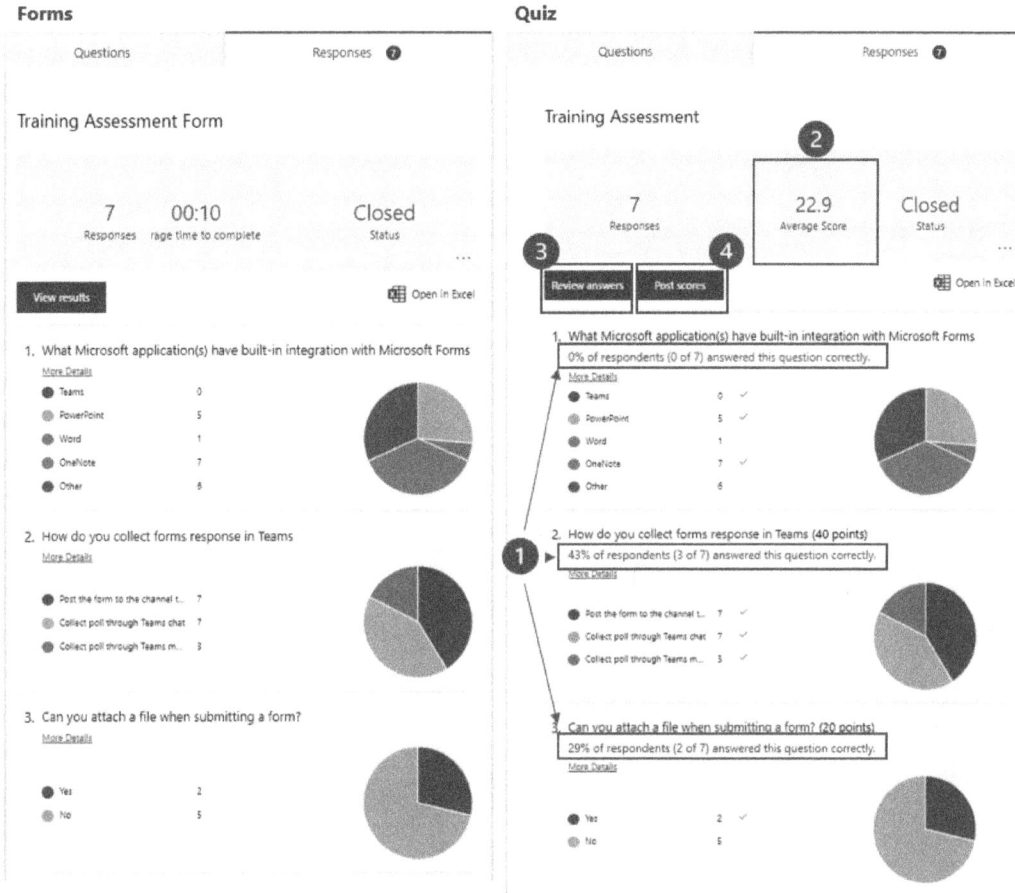

Figure 5.14 – Difference between forms and quiz response reports

The key differences between forms and quiz reporting are outlined here:

1. Each question summary includes the percentage of respondents answering the question correctly

2. The average score for the quiz is displayed instead of the average time it took to complete the form

3. A **Review answers** button is displayed instead of **View results**

4. A **Post scores** button is added

We will now discuss the **Review answers** and **Post scores** functionalities.

Review answers

Clicking the **Review answers** button on quiz reports shows how each trainee has answered the question and gives a score for each question, as shown in the following screenshot:

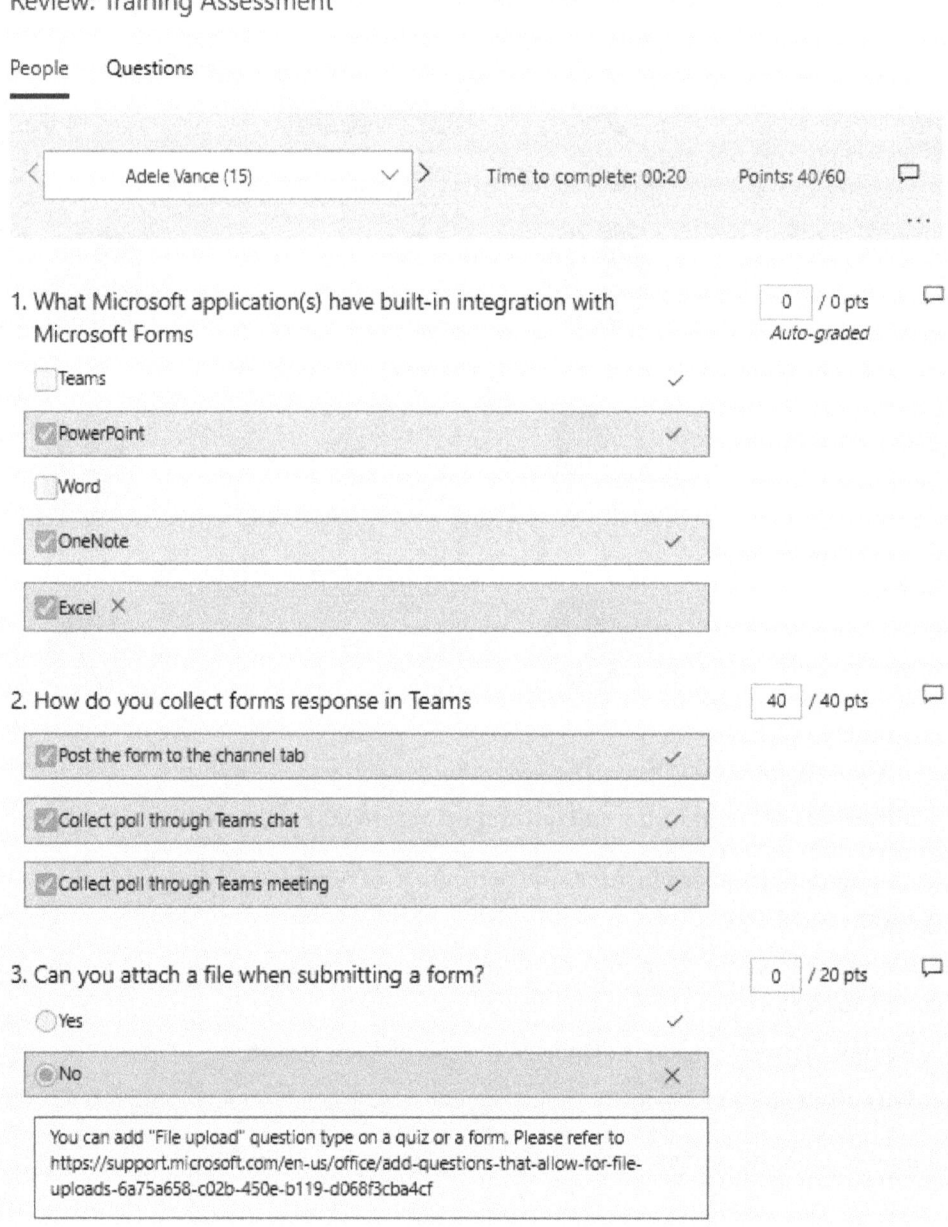

Figure 5.15 – Reviewing each trainee response

When reviewing the answer, you can also add feedback to the trainee's answer by clicking the feedback icon next to the points.

Clicking **...** in the lower-right corner of the header shows an option to delete the response, print the response, or post scores, as illustrated in the following screenshot:

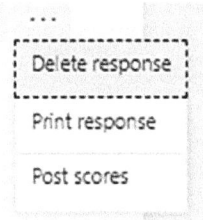

Figure 5.16 – Options for each response

You can also give feedback at the question level on the review response report by going to the **Questions** tab, as illustrated in the following screenshot:

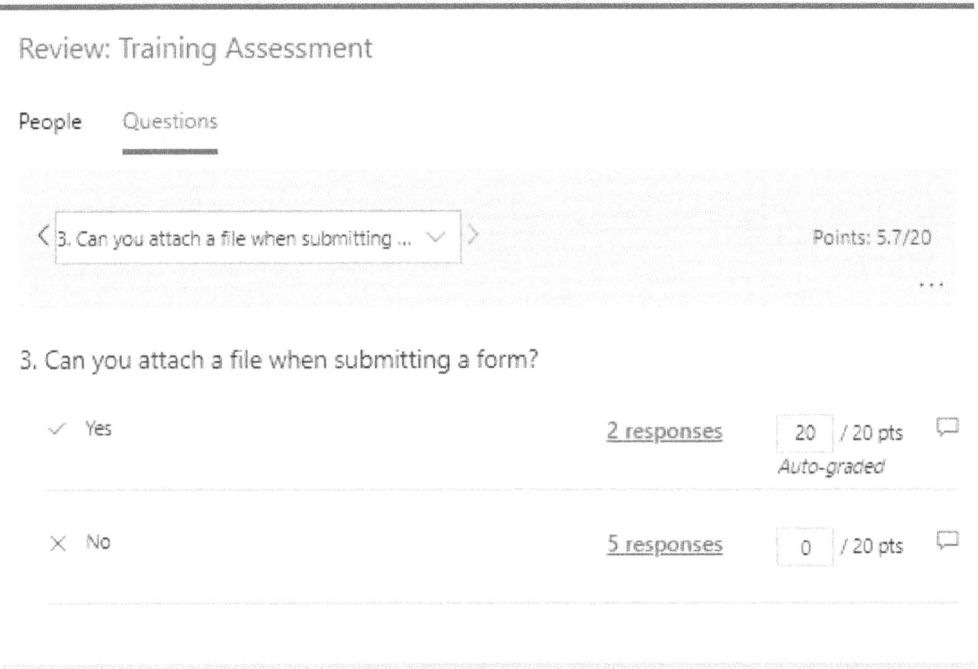

Figure 5.17 – Reviewing results by question

On this report, you can view who selected each option on the question. You can also give feedback to all trainees who select the same option, as illustrated in the following screenshot:

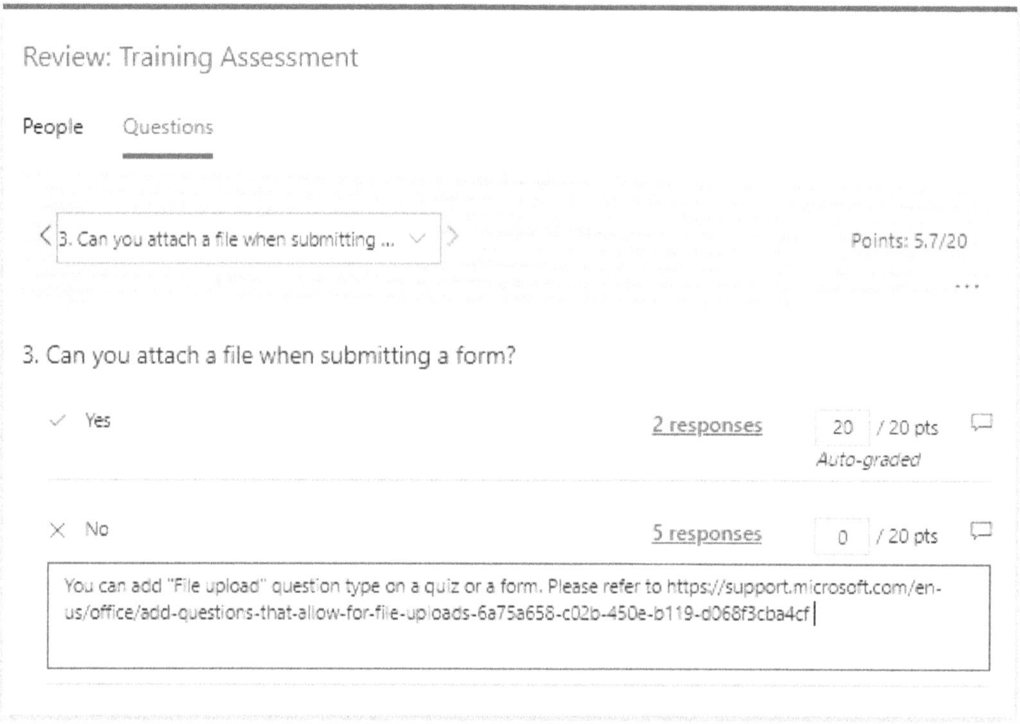

Figure 5.18 – Posting feedback message to all trainees

The last action on the ... menu in *Figure 5.19* is to post the scores to the trainees. Posting scores gives trainees access to quiz results and feedback. Trainees can see the posted scores by opening the original quiz link.

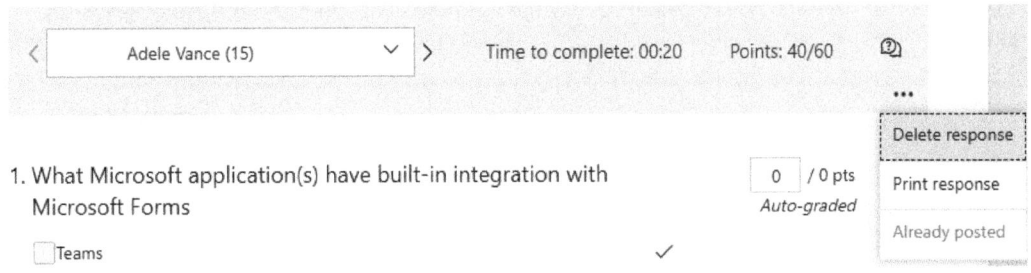

Figure 5.19 – Posting results to the trainee

Note that you cannot undo posting the score; when opening the ... menu again, it says that the score has already been posted, as illustrated in the following screenshot:

Figure 5.20 – Posting a score message is disabled after it has already been posted

However, even after you post a message, you can continue to update an existing feedback form and add new feedback. You can post scores individually or post them to multiple trainees through the **Post scores** button on the main response page.

Post scores

The **Post scores** page shows you a list of all trainees and the status of the scores. From this report, you can review points and rank participants based on the highest or lowest scores, as well as multi-select quiz takers to post the scores, as illustrated in the following screenshot:

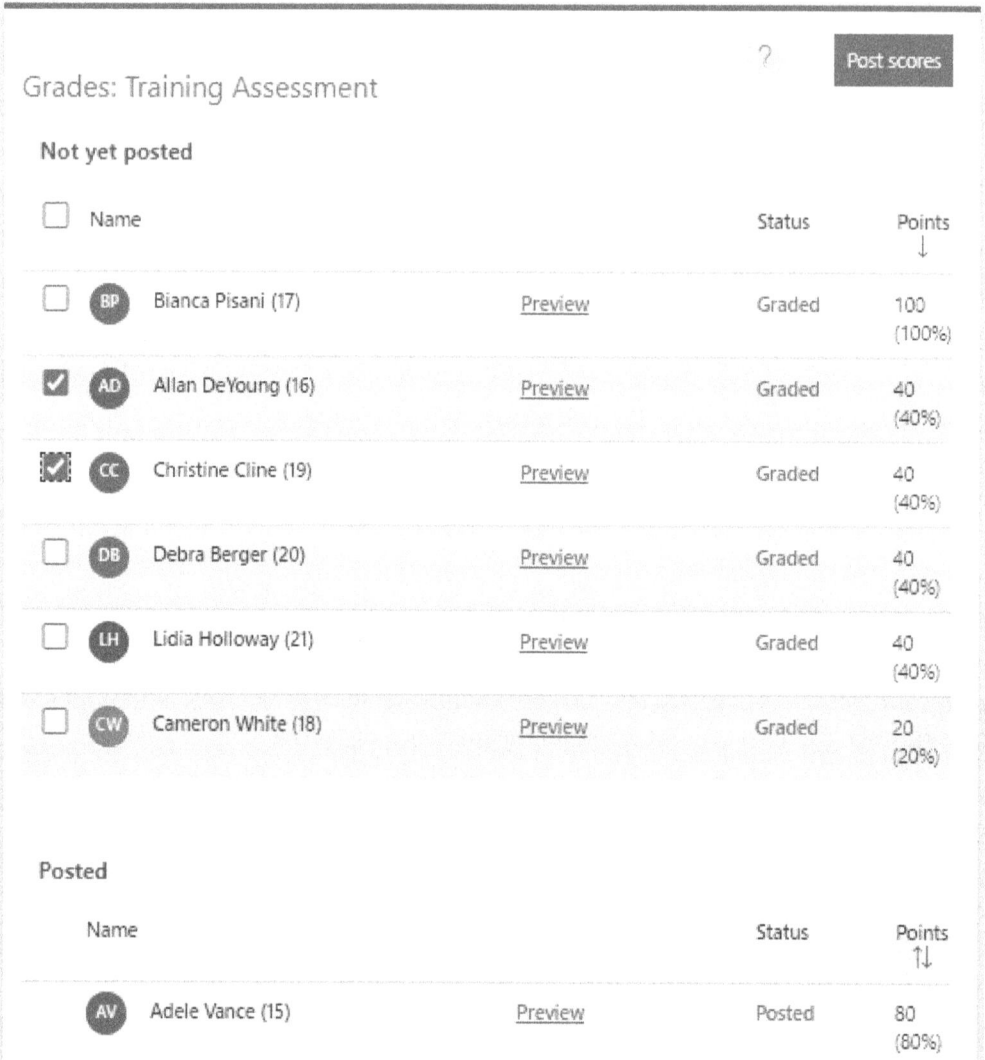

Figure 5.21 – Post scores report

After completion of a course, you may want to collect feedback on the course to help you improve, and you can create a form to do this.

Collecting training feedback with Microsoft Forms

To create a new form, go to `https://forms.microsoft.com` and click the **New Form** button. Add questions to the form, such as those shown in the following screenshot:

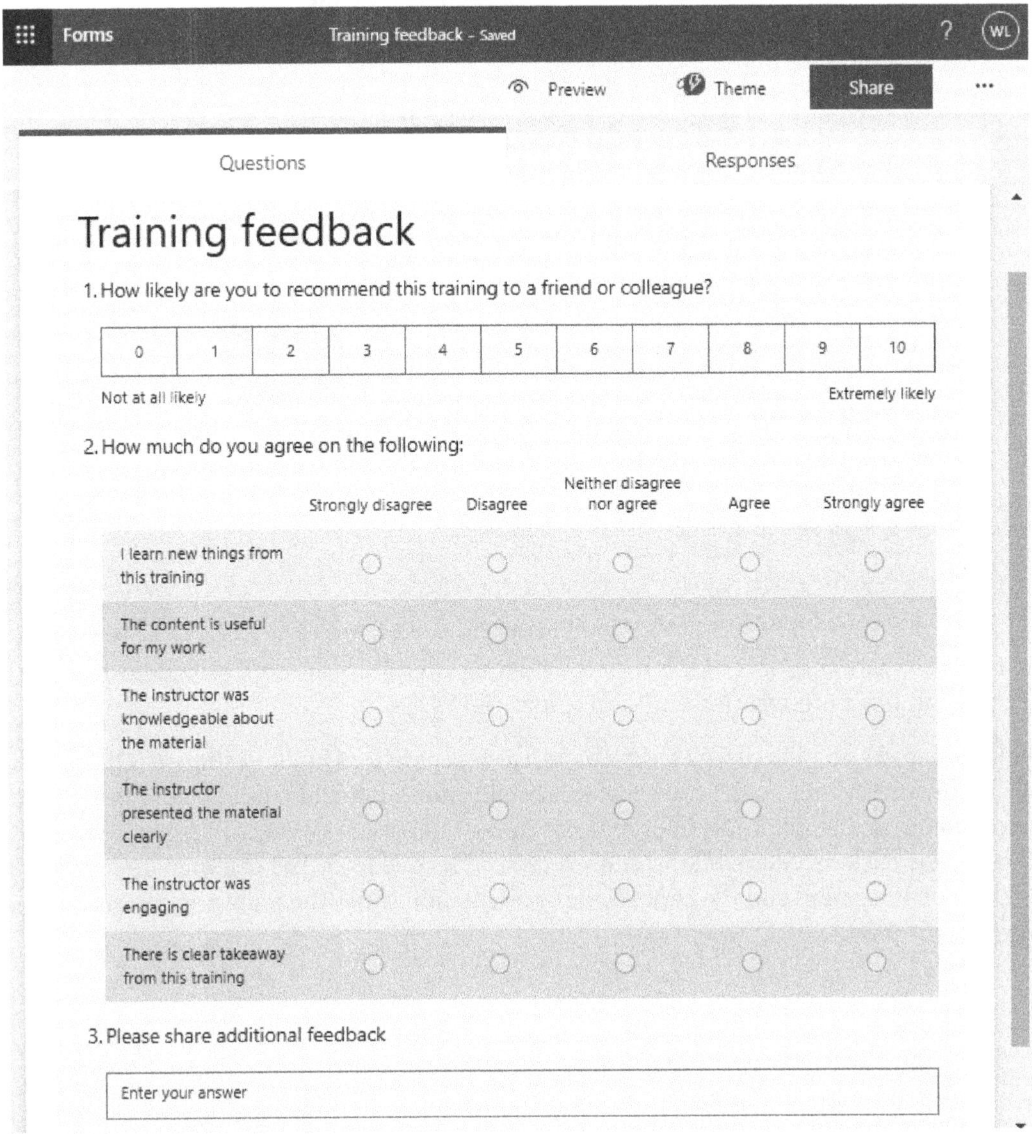

Figure 5.22 – An example of a training feedback form

After you have added all the questions, get the survey link by clicking the **Share** button and copy the survey **Uniform Resource Locator** (**URL**), as illustrated in the following screenshot:

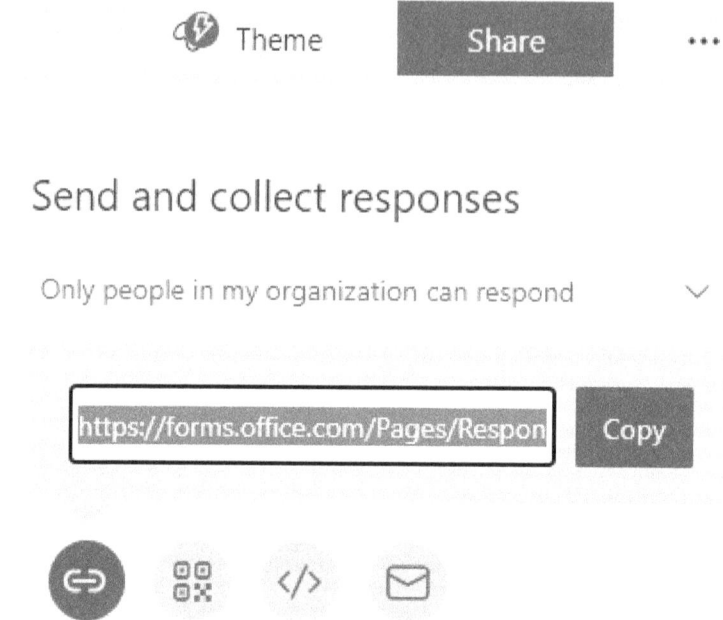

Figure 5.23 – Getting a survey link to the feedback form

You can then share the survey URL with the training attendees via email or include it as part of the training presentation and course material.

In addition to sharing the survey URL, you can also generate a **Quick Response** (**QR**) code for the survey link. A QR code enables mobile phone and tablet users to use the device camera to scan the code, in order to open the online survey page. To generate a QR code, you click the **Share** button and select the QR code icon. You can then download the QR code image and add the code to your presentation slide. The following screenshot illustrates the process:

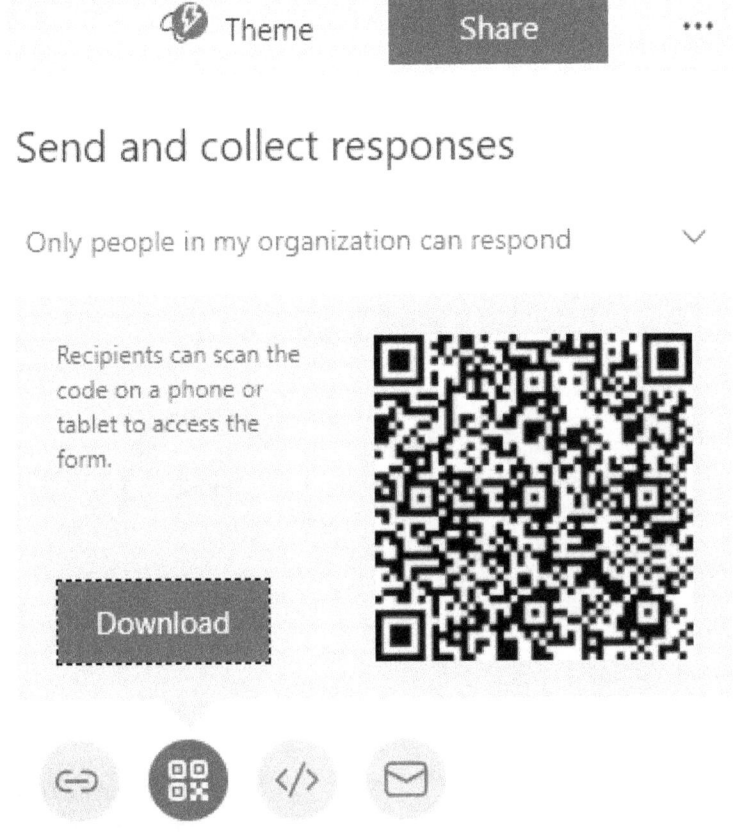

Figure 5.24 – Getting a QR code for the feedback form link

After you receive the response, you can view the feedback from the **Responses** tab, as shown in the following screenshot:

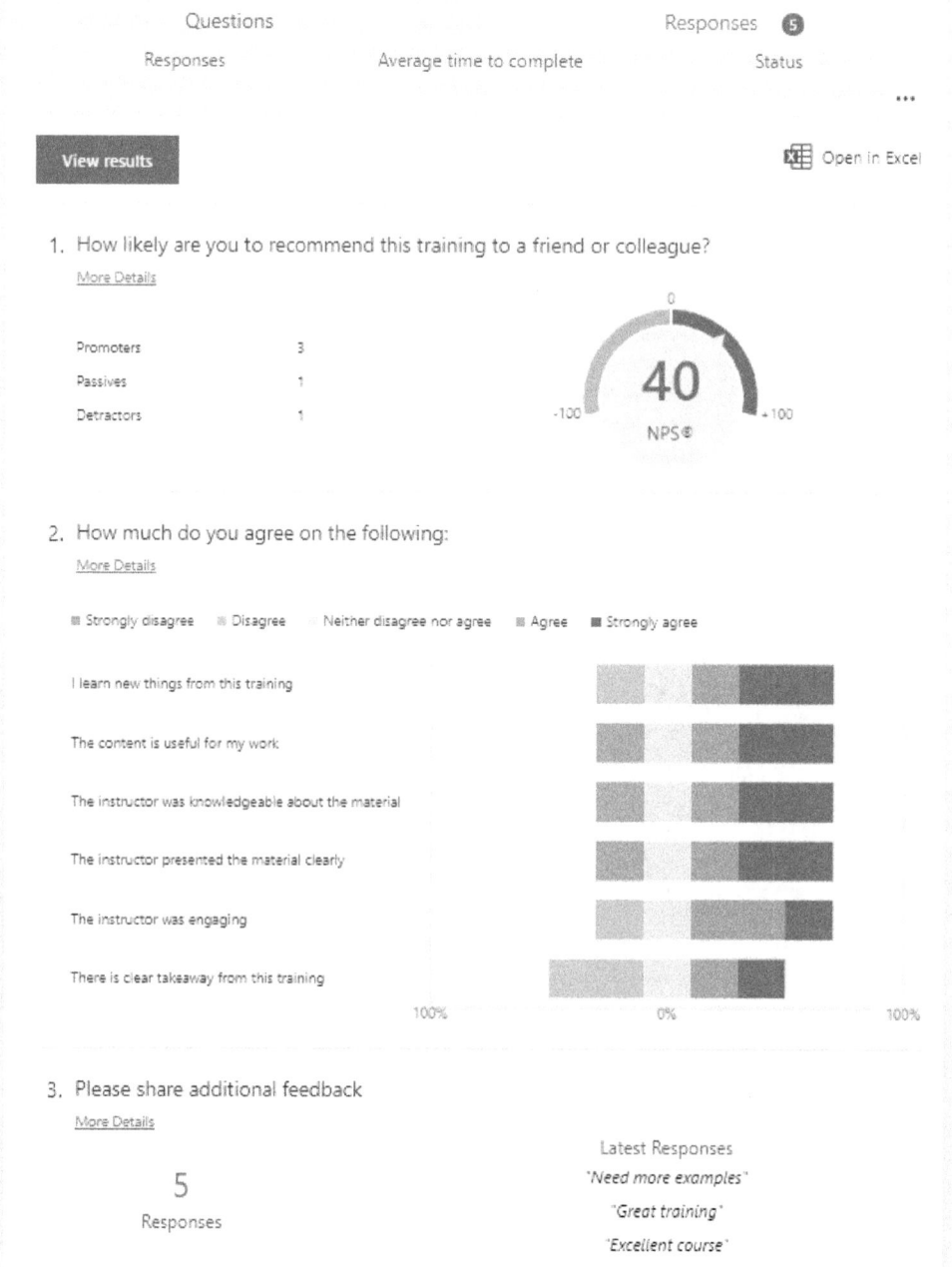

Figure 5.25 – Training feedback results

As discussed in *Chapter 3, Creating a Survey with Microsoft Forms*, you can view individual responses by clicking **View results**, and you can download all responses by clicking **Open in Excel**.

While Microsoft Forms enables you to easily create a feedback form for your training, its use case is limited to a single class-training event. If you have multiple training courses that you would like to use the same feedback form for, with the ability to filter the results for different courses, then you can use Dynamics 365 Customer Voice.

Using Customer Voice to collect multi-course training feedback

Dynamics 365 Customer Voice is built on top of the Microsoft Forms simple survey creation experience and adds advanced functionalities to support enterprise feedback management scenarios. One of the advanced capabilities is the functionality to define survey variables to personalize a survey and to filter a report based on survey variables. We will discuss how you can use survey variables to support collecting feedback for multi-course training sessions.

As an example, suppose that you are conducting three training courses, as follows:

- **TRG101**: Create surveys with Dynamics 365 Customer Voice
- **TRG102**: Introduction to Office client customization
- **TRG103**: Introduction to Azure fundamentals

With Microsoft Forms, you can create a separate feedback form for each training course and view the result separately. Using Customer Voice, you can create a single survey and use survey variables to identify the training ID and training title as part of the survey. With this approach, you can get a combined survey result across all training courses, with the ability to filter results for a specific training course.

Creating a survey

To create multi-course training feedback using Customer Voice, follow these steps:

1. Go to `https://customervoice.microsoft.com` to get started.

> **Important note**
>
> Customer Voice requires a separate license than Office 365. If your organization does not have a Customer Voice license, you can sign up for a 30-day trial at `https://aka.ms/customervoice`.

2. Select a blank template and click **Next** to continue. Note that Customer Voice provides several out-of-the-box templates for common feedback scenarios; however, it does not yet include an event or training feedback template, so we will create a new survey from a blank template for our example, as illustrated in *Figure 5.26*:

Figure 5.26 – Template selection screen in Customer Voice

3. Select a default location and click **Create** to continue, as illustrated in *Figure 5.27*:

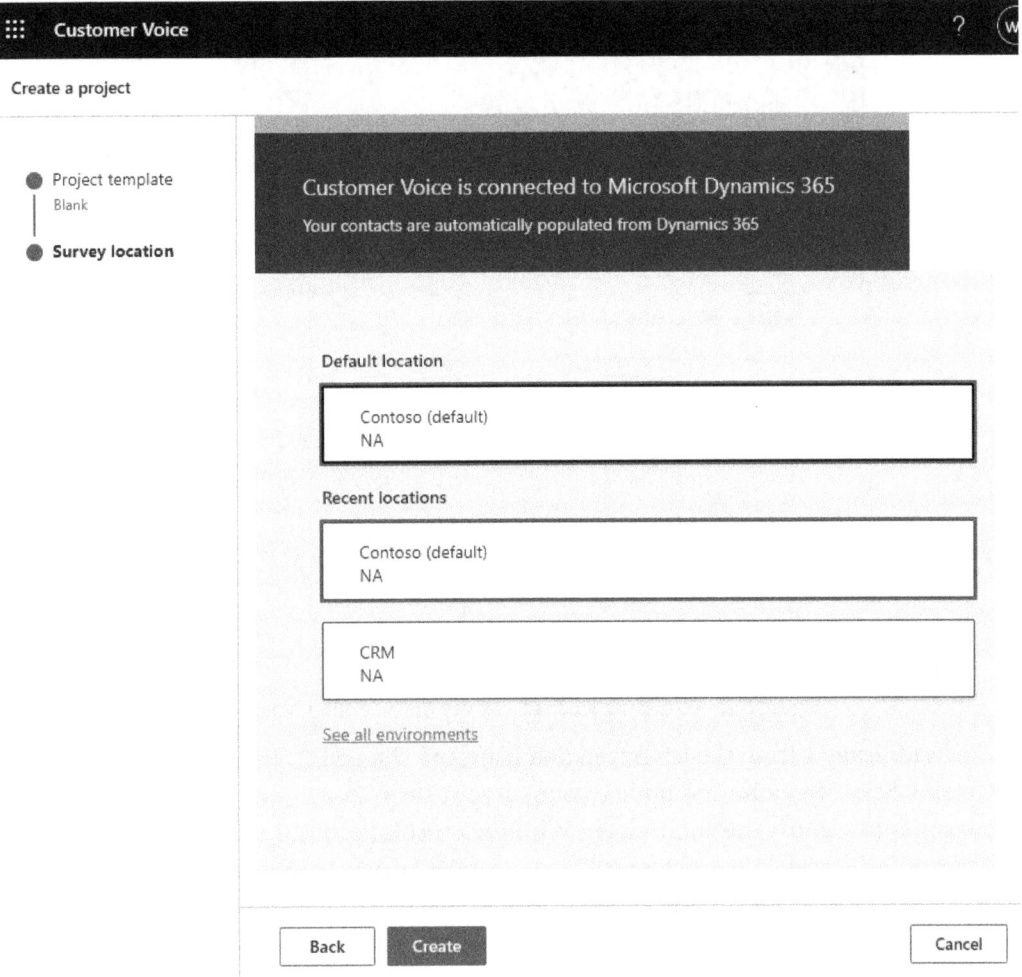

Figure 5.27 – Survey location selection in Customer Voice

> **Important note**
>
> **Survey location** specifies where you store the survey response data. If you
> are using Microsoft business applications such as **Dynamics 365** or **Power
> Apps**, you can use the same **Dataverse** location and automatically connect
> your survey with application data. If you are not using a Microsoft business
> application, then you can use the default location.

4. Create a survey by adding a survey title and survey questions, as shown *Figure 5.28*:

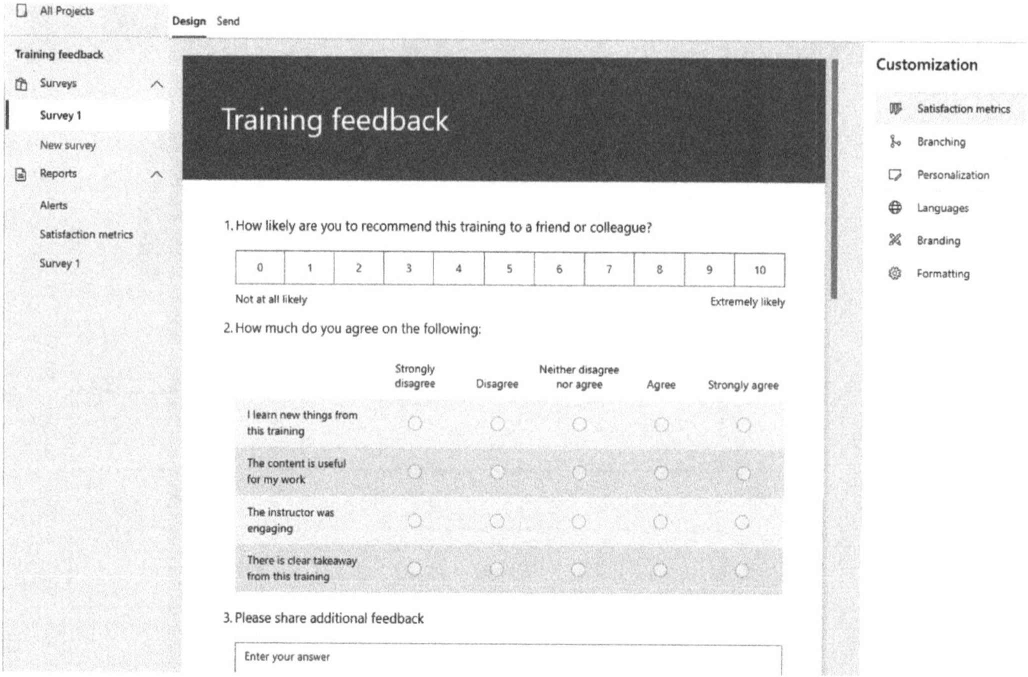

Figure 5.28 – Training feedback survey on Customer Voice

5. Select **Survey 1** from the left navigation pane and click on **...** to open a command menu. Select **Rename** and update your survey title to 2021 training to make it easier to identify the survey later. While Microsoft Forms use the survey header text as the survey title, Customer Voice separates survey titles and survey headers. This allows you to use a more generic header text (such as We want your feedback) to encourage more participation, and a more specific survey title to identify the survey for reporting purposes. The process is illustrated in the following screenshot:

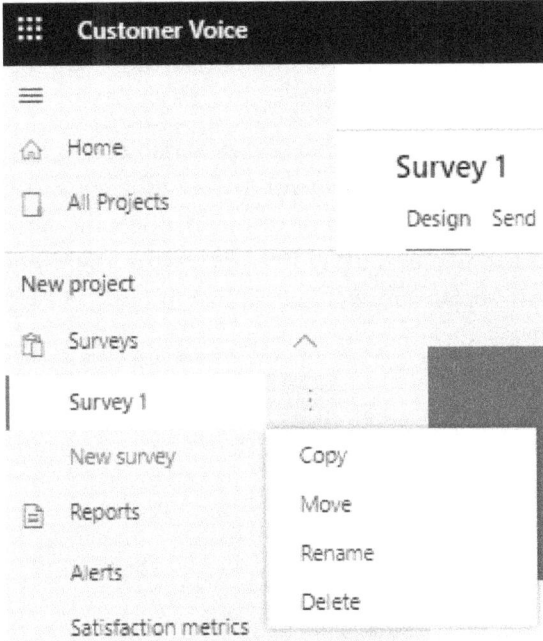

Figure 5.29 – Renaming a survey command

6. Open the **Personalization** setting from the **Customization** pane on the right (see *Figure 5.28*) to create survey variables. Add two survey variables, TrainingID and TrainingTitle, then click **Save**, as shown in the following screenshot:

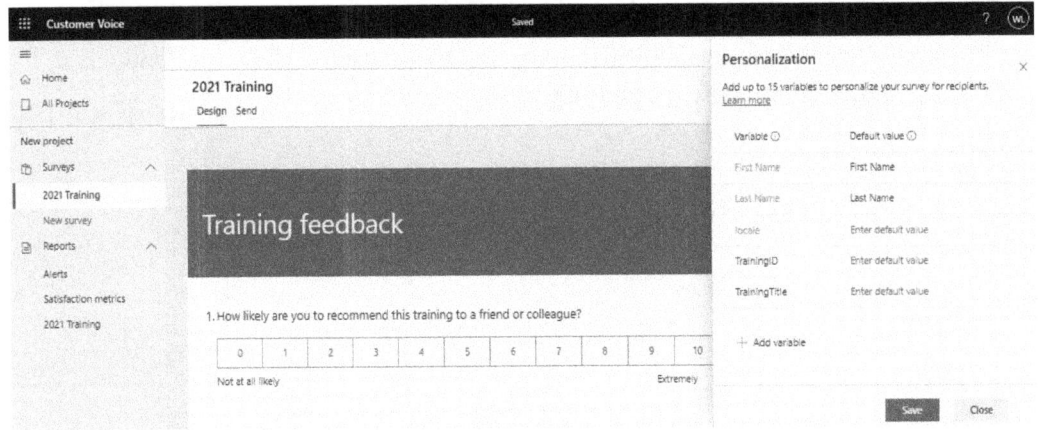

Figure 5.30 – Adding survey variables to Customer Voice survey

You can use the survey variables to personalize your survey questions. The `TrainingTitle` survey variable will be automatically replaced with the actual training name, as shown later in the steps.

7. To personalize a survey question with a survey variable, select a question to insert the survey variable, place the cursor to a location (or a word) to insert the survey variable, and then, from the toolbar menu, select the variable. For example, highlight the word `this` from the **Net Promoter Score** (**NPS**) question, then select `TrainingTitle` to replace the word, as shown in *Figure 5.31*:

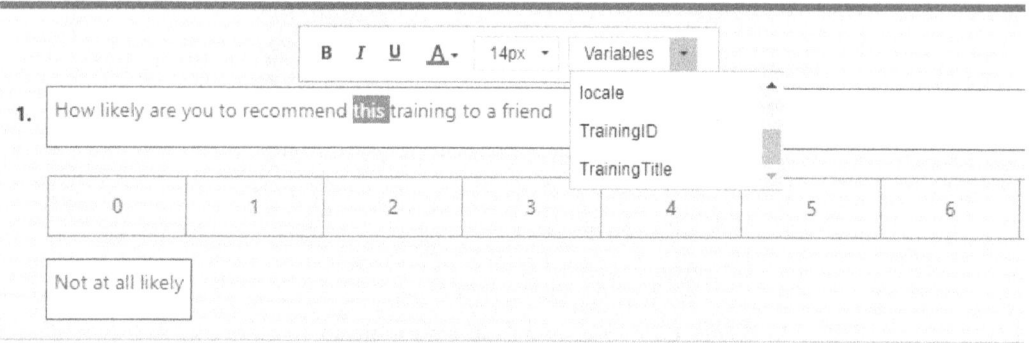

Figure 5.31 – Inserting a survey variable into a survey question

By using the survey variable in the text question, you can specify the title of the training course when sending the survey, and the question text will be automatically updated based on the value of the survey variable.

8. To personalize the survey link with survey-variable values, click on the **Send** tab at the top of the survey and click on **Link**, as shown in *Figure 5.32*:

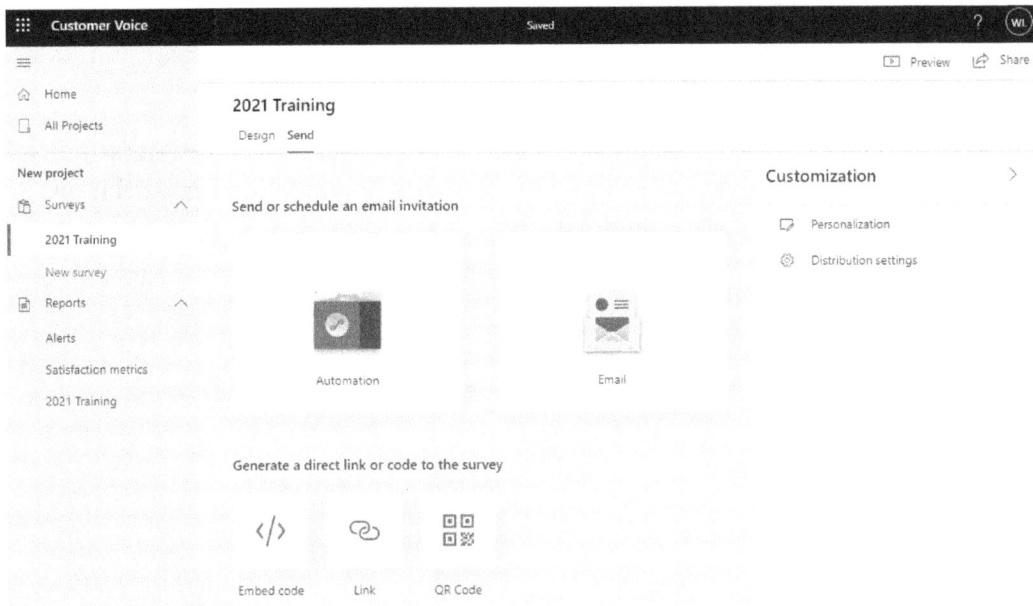

Figure 5.32 – Options for sending survey

9. On the **Survey links** panel, click **Create link** under the **Custom links** section, as shown in *Figure 5.33*:

Survey links   ✕

Copy link

https://ncv.microsoft.com/pOA2RB9oID

This is a generic link that won't track personal information.   ▦ QR code

Custom links

Group responses by region, language, or other categories with a custom URL.

╋ Create link   ↦ Export

Figure 5.33 – Creating a custom survey link

The **Custom links** feature in Customer Voice enables you to create a unique link for a specific combination of your survey-variable values. In our example, we can create a separate survey link for each of the three training courses.

10. On the **Create link** panel, select the variables (for example, `TrainingID` and `TrainingTitle`) to generate a custom link, then add values for each variable by clicking **Add more values**, as shown in *Figure 5.34*:

← **Create link**

Select your variables

☐ First Name   ☐ Last Name   ☐ locale

☑ TrainingID   ☑ TrainingTitle

Add values for each variable

TrainingID	TrainingTitle
TRG01	Create surveys wit...
TRG02	Introduction to Of...
TRG03	Introduction to Azur

╋ Add more values

⌄ Advanced options

[Create]   [Cancel]

Figure 5.34 – Creating a link for each survey-variable value

Note that if you have many courses, you can download a `.csv` template from Advanced options section populate the file with the training course information, then upload the file using the **Upload** button.

11. Click the **Create** button to generate the links.

12. In the **Survey links** panel you can find a link for each training course, as shown in *Figure 5.35*:

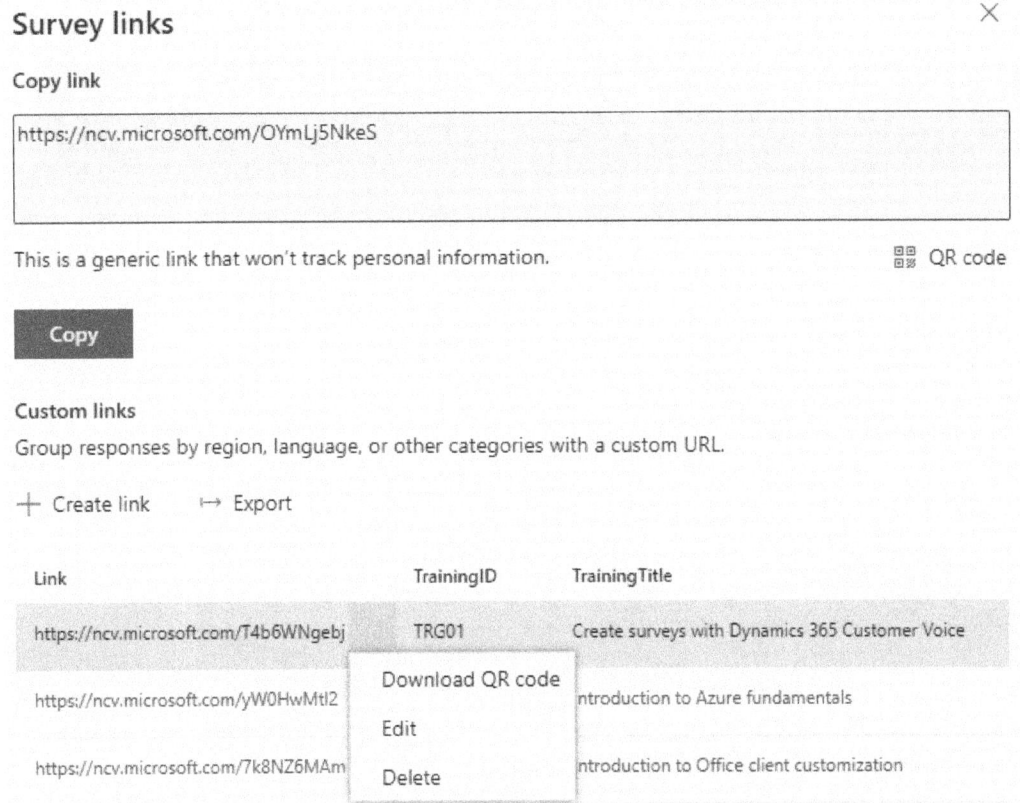

Figure 5.35 – Unique survey link for each survey-variable value

You can also get a QR code for each link by selecting the link and selecting **QR code** from the pop-up menu.

Collecting feedback

After you have generated survey links for all your training courses, you can share a link to each course instructor for them to include this in their training. Each course will use one corresponding survey link for the course, and the instructors can include this link as part of their course material.

When a trainee provides feedback, the link opens a personalized survey for the training they attended. For example, clicking the link for `TRG101` (for example, `https://ncv.microsoft.com/V4TxJPT72R`) would open a survey similar to the one shown in the following screenshot, with the first question personalized with the name of the **Create surveys with Dynamics 365 Customer Voice** training included in the *NPS* question:

Training feedback

1. How likely are you to recommend **Create surveys with Dynamics 365 Customer Voice** training to a friend or colleague?

0	1	2	3	4	5	6	7	8	9	10

Not at all likely   Extremely likely

2. How much do you agree on the following:

	Strongly disagree	Disagree	Neither disagree nor agree	Agree	Strongly agree
I learn new things from this training	○	○	○	○	○

Figure 5.36 – Personalized survey for the custom link

The survey variable would not only be used for personalizing the survey, but the variable can also be used as a filter for the feedback results.

Viewing feedback results

Once all feedback across all three courses has been received, you can view the results, as shown in the following screenshot:

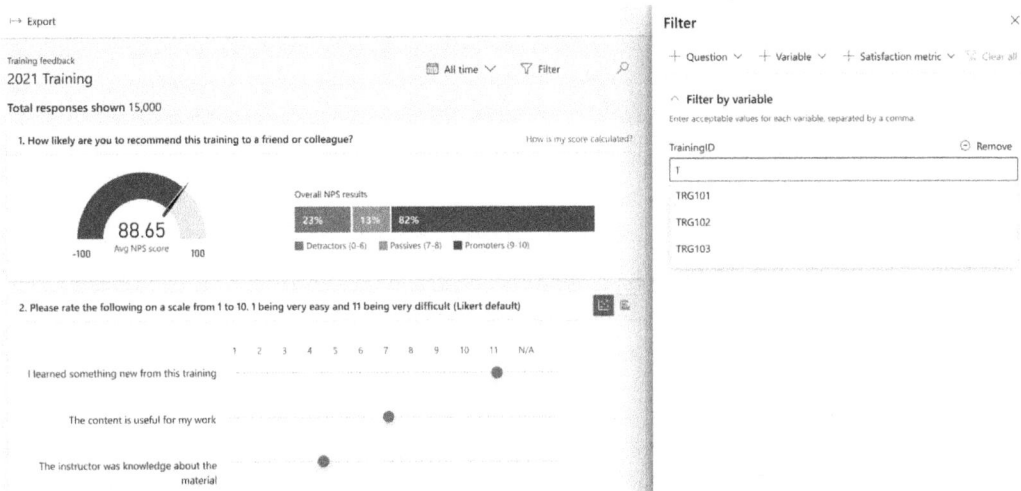

Figure 5.37 – Unfiltered survey results

You can filter the results to a specific course by clicking the **Filter** button at the top of the survey report.

On the **Filter** panel, locate the **Variables** section, then select `TrainingID` as the variable for filtering. From the list of possible variable values, select the specific training for which you would like to see feedback. For example, selecting `TRG101` would filter the feedback results so that they only come from the `TRG1010` course, as shown in the following screenshot:

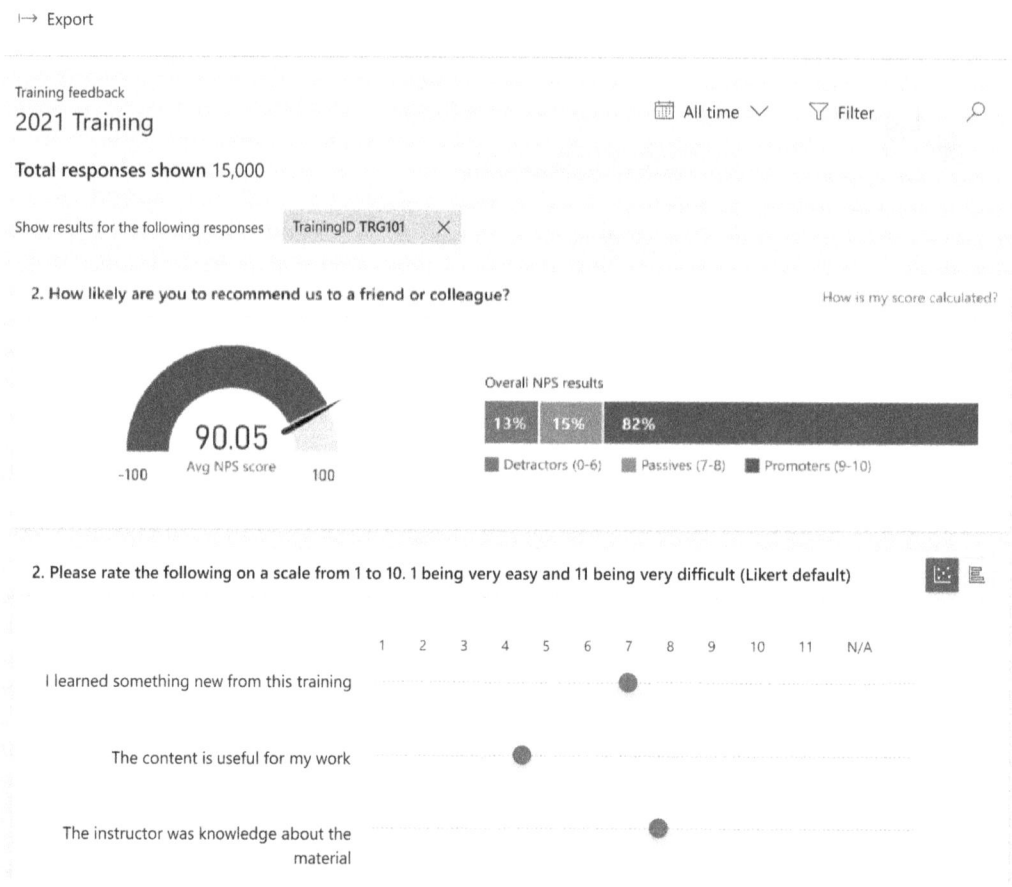

Figure 5.38 – Filtered survey results

The filtering capabilities of Customer Voice enable you to get better insights, especially in cases where you need to aggregate feedback across multiple training sessions. The filtered result is not only reflected in the report page, but the filter is also applied when you export the data through the **Export** button shown at the top of the page in *Figure 5.38*.

Summary

Microsoft Forms provides the ability for you to create a quiz to test students' or training attendees' knowledge. In addition to a quiz, you can also create a form to collect feedback following a training course. If you are delivering training across multiple courses, you can use Customer Voice and leverage the survey-variable functionality to use the same survey across different courses but allow each survey to be personalized with course-specific information, such as training title, as part of the survey question. Using the same survey across multiple training courses enables you to view aggregate feedback reports across all training courses and use survey variables to filter for a specific training course.

In this chapter, we introduced Customer Voice and its survey-variable functionality to enable additional capabilities beyond what is available through Microsoft Forms. In the next few chapters, we will go over more advanced functionalities of Customer Voice across common employee and customer feedback scenarios. We will start with an employee feedback scenario in the next chapter.

6
Conducting an Employee Survey with Dynamics 365 Customer Voice

Successful businesses recognize that employees are a company's biggest asset. In an article, *Forbes* describes employees as the *face of your company*, becoming your best brand ambassadors. (See `https://www.forbes.com/sites/forbesbusinessdevelopmentcouncil/2019/12/12/five-reasons-employees-are-your-companys-no-1-asset`.) You need to make sure that you are bringing in high-quality talent and that employees are in the best environment to fully realize their talent and potential.

Surveys have long been used as a tool to measure employee experiences, from the time they are hired and continuing throughout their employment. To conduct an effective employee feedback survey, you will need additional capabilities.

Dynamics 365 Customer Voice is built on Office Forms and adds advanced capabilities to support organizational surveys. Despite the *Customer* in its name, Customer Voice is not limited to only being used for external customer feedback.

In this chapter, we will review Customer Voice capabilities in the context of common employee-feedback scenarios. By the end of this chapter, you will understand how to use Customer Voice to collect feedback from your employees.

This chapter covers the following topics:

- Automating new employee hire feedback
- Conducting an anonymous employee engagement survey

Note that this chapter includes a more advanced topic to create a workflow using **Microsoft Power Automate**. Power Automate is a low-code and no-code tool to enable citizen developers to create workflow to automate business process. If you are new to Power Automate, you can follow the steps to learn. With that said, let's start with how you can automate the collection of feedback as part of employee onboarding.

Automating new employee hire feedback

As we discussed in *Chapter 1, Introducing Microsoft Forms and Customer Voice*, Dynamics 365 Customer Voice is built on top of Office Forms and adds further capabilities to support organizational surveys. One such capability in Customer Voice is the ability to automatically send a survey based on your business process event (such as a new employee hire). In this section, I will walk through creating a new employee survey that is automatically sent 2 weeks after an employee starts in their post. These are the high-level steps involved in this process:

- Creating a new employee survey in Customer Voice
- Creating an email template
- Creating a workflow to automate the sending of a new employee survey

We will start by creating a new employee survey in Customer Voice.

Creating a new employee survey in Customer Voice

Customer Voice requires a separate license. If you do not have a Customer Voice license, you can sign up for a free 30-day trial from `https://aka.ms/customervoice`. Once the trial signup process is complete, you will be taken to the **Project template** selection screen in Customer Voice. If you have an existing Customer Voice license, you can return to Customer Voice by going to `https://customervoice.microsoft.com` and then create a new project. Either way, you will land on the **Project template** selection screen. Customer Voice includes several out-of-the-box templates for common feedback scenarios. These are shown in *Figure 6.1*:

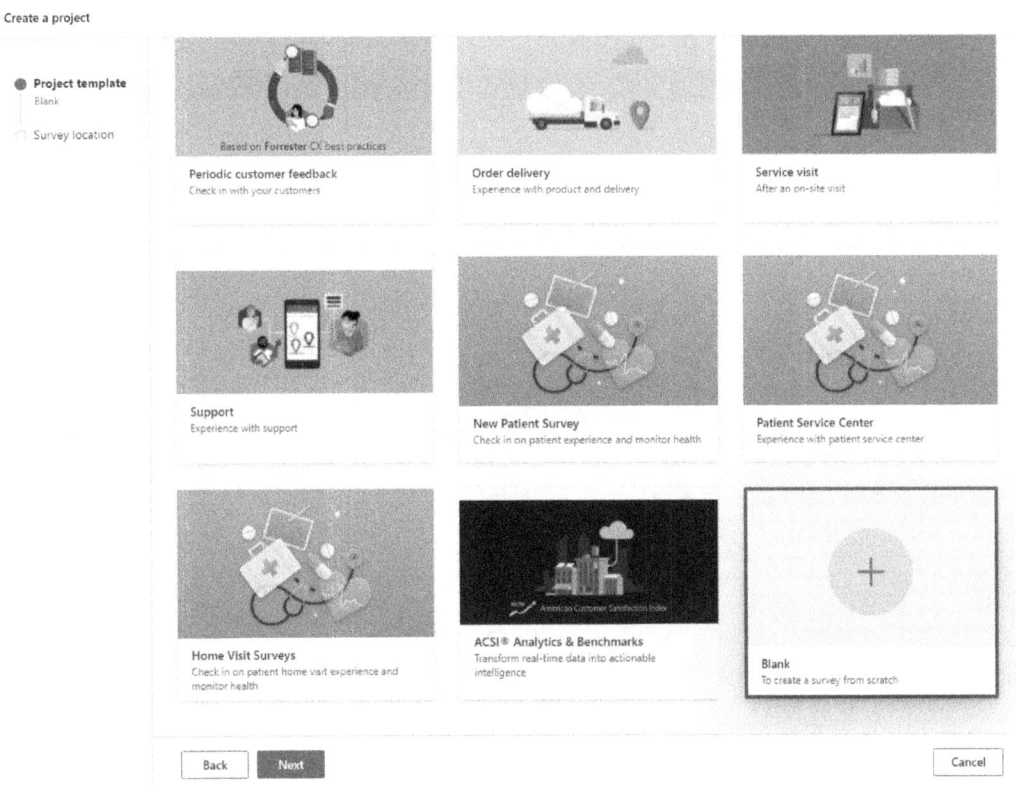

Figure 6.1 – Project template selection screen in Customer Voice

The templates include customizable survey questions and workflows to automate the sending of a survey. If you do not find a template for your scenario, you can create a new survey project using a blank template. Since Customer Voice does not include (as of the writing of this book) an employee feedback template, we will use the **Blank** project template in this chapter.

Follow these steps to create a new employee survey:

1. Select the **Blank** project template and click **Next**.

2. Select a project location to store your data and click **Create**, as illustrated in *Figure 6.2*:

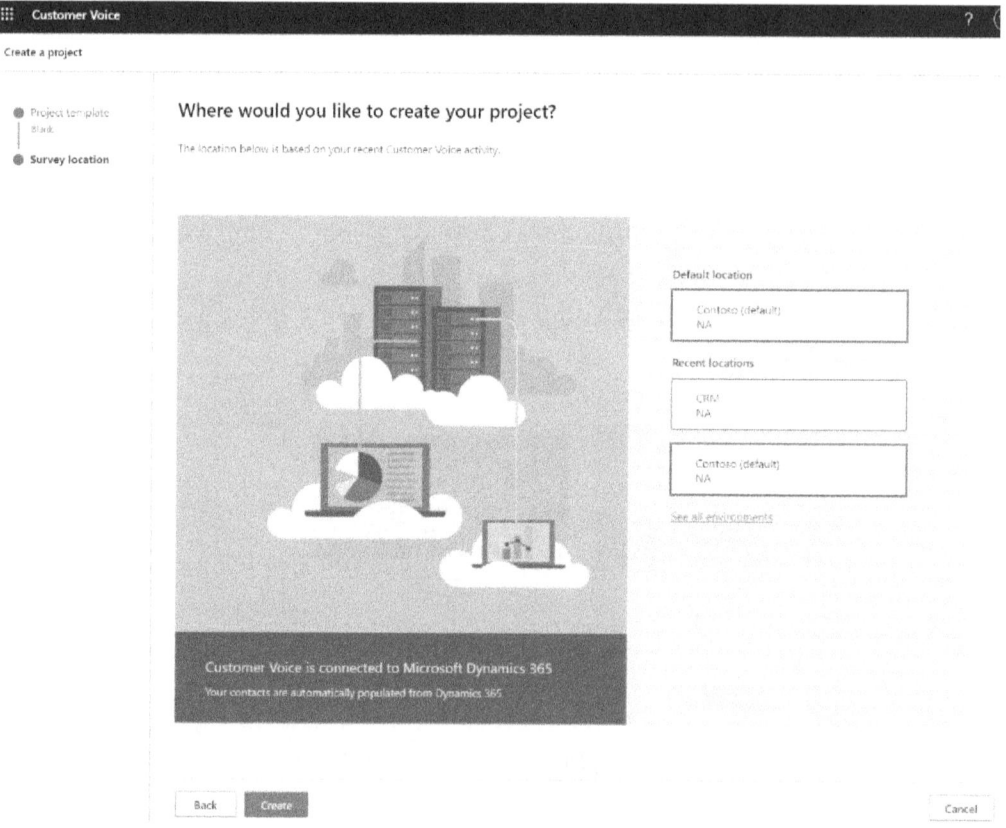

Figure 6.2 – Survey project location selection in Customer Voice

> **Important note**
> **Survey project location** specifies where you store the survey response data. If you are using Microsoft business applications such as Dynamics 365 or Power Apps, you can use the same Dataverse environment for the location and Customer Voice automatically connects your survey with all applications using the same environment. If you are not using Microsoft business applications, then you can use the default location.

3. Create a survey by adding a survey title and survey questions. See *Figure 6.3* for an example:

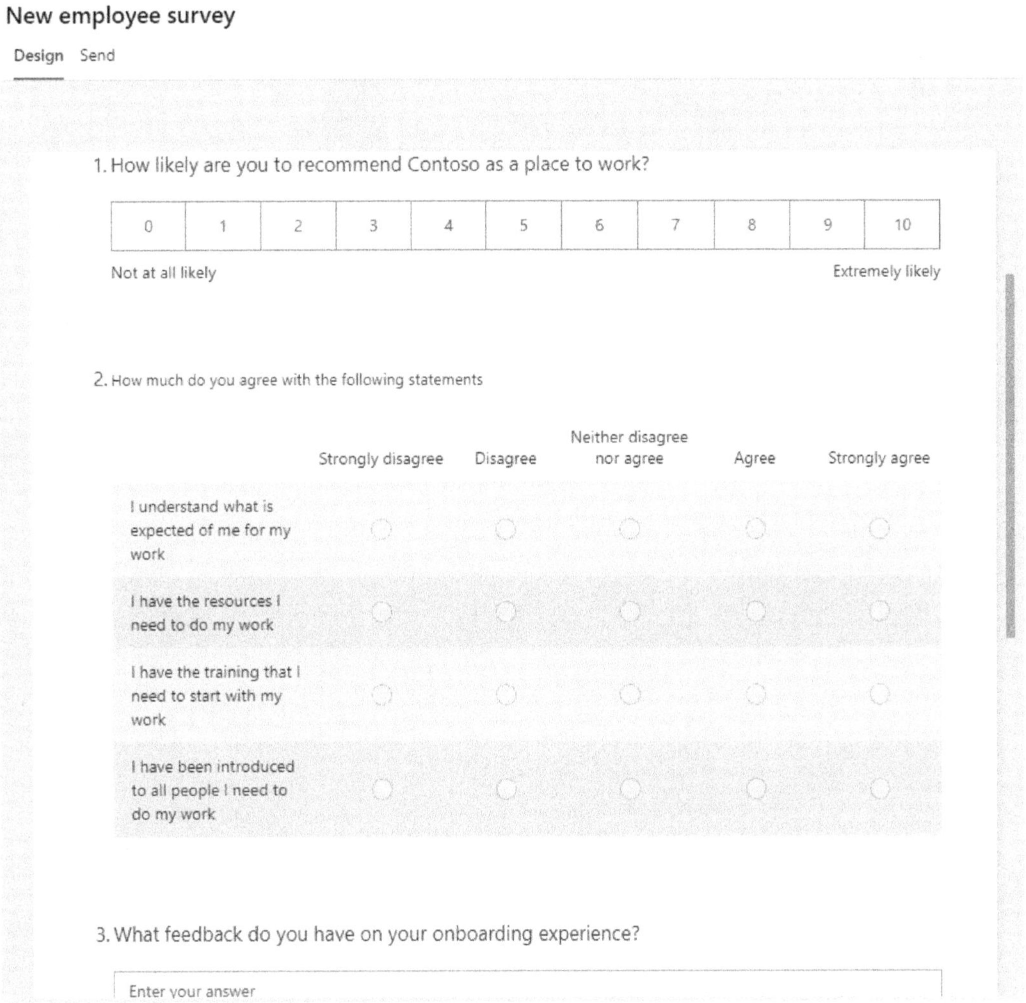

Figure 6.3 – An example of a new employee survey

4. Rename the survey to make it easier to identify by clicking the **...** drop-down menu on the left navigation page (see *Figure 6.4*):

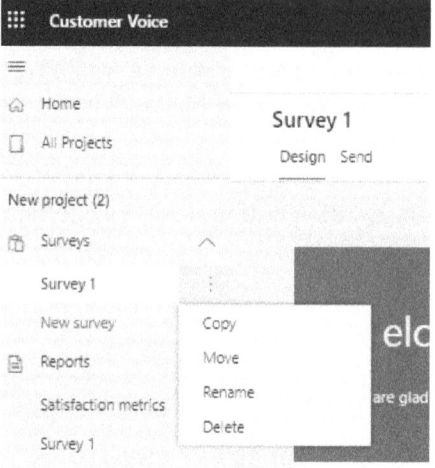

Figure 6.4 – Rename survey command

5. Expand the **Customization** panel on the right and click on **Satisfaction metrics** to specify **Key Performance Indicator (KPI)** metrics in your survey, as illustrated in *Figure 6.5* (refer to *Chapter 2, Best Practices for Collecting Feedback through Surveys* for a discussion on KPI metrics):

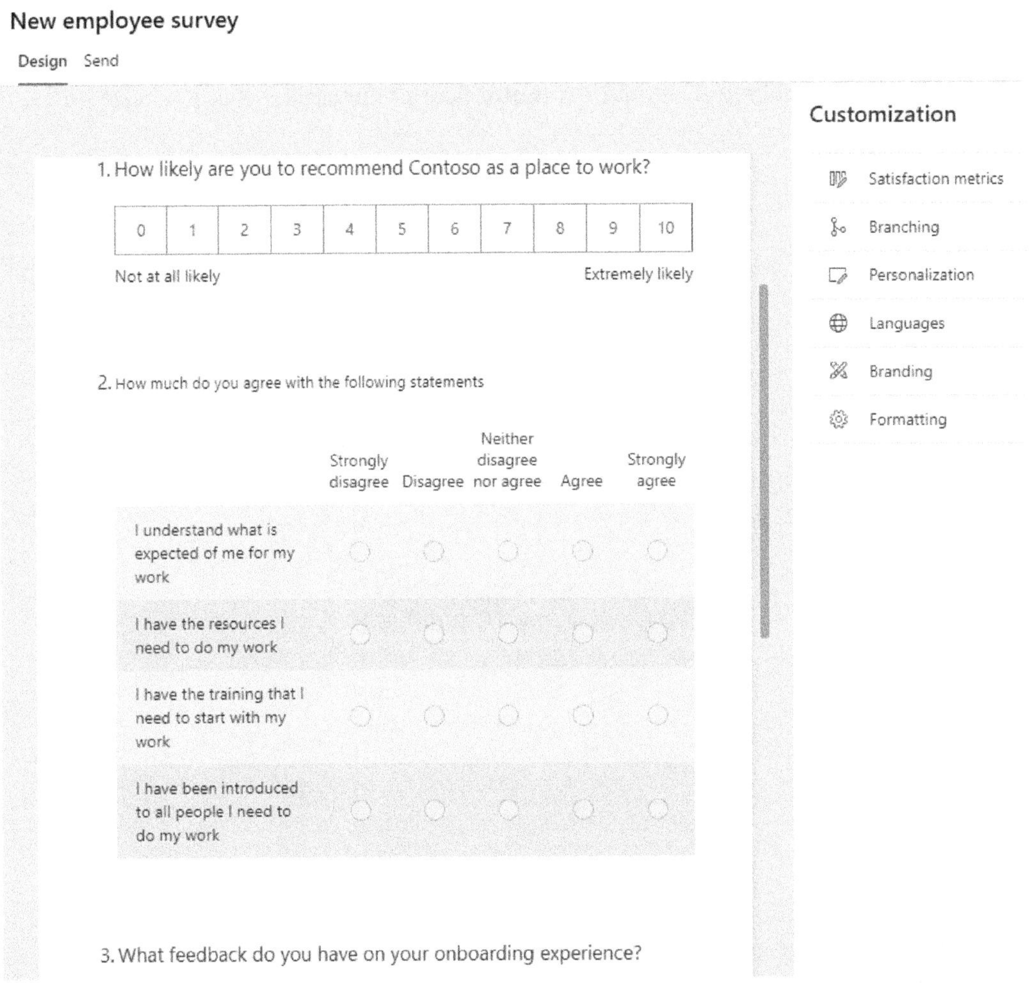

New employee survey

Design   Send

1. How likely are you to recommend Contoso as a place to work?

0	1	2	3	4	5	6	7	8	9	10

Not at all likely   Extremely likely

2. How much do you agree with the following statements

	Strongly disagree	Disagree	Neither disagree nor agree	Agree	Strongly agree
I understand what is expected of me for my work	○	○	○	○	○
I have the resources I need to do my work	○	○	○	○	○
I have the training that I need to start with my work	○	○	○	○	○
I have been introduced to all people I need to do my work	○	○	○	○	○

3. What feedback do you have on your onboarding experience?

Customization

- Satisfaction metrics
- Branching
- Personalization
- Languages
- Branding
- Formatting

Figure 6.5 – Customization panel for Customer Voice survey design

6. Add a new metric by clicking the **Add metrics** button and select the metric type. For our example, since the survey is using **Net Promoter Score** ® to measure overall satisfaction, we will select the **Net Promoter Score** ® metrics type, as illustrated in *Figure 6.6*:

You don't have any satisfaction metrics added

Add satisfaction metrics for a project to track trends across surveys

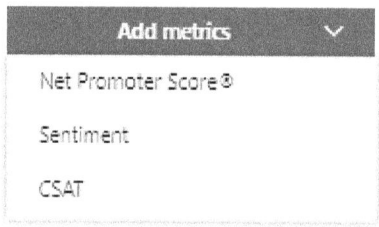

Figure 6.6 – Add metrics menu

7. Name the metric (for example, New employee satisfaction), then map the metric to the **Net Promoter Score** ® question on your survey and click **Save** to finish (See *Figure 6.7*):

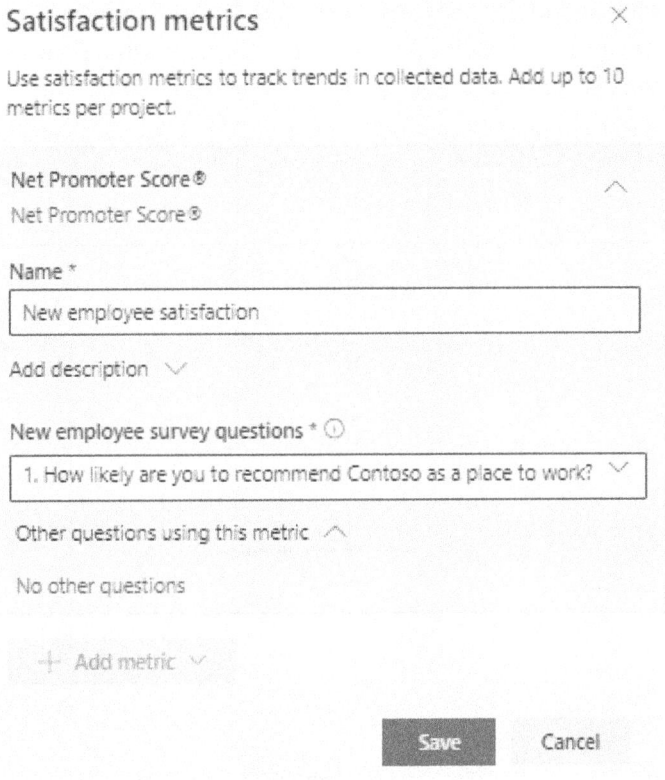

Figure 6.7 – Satisfaction metrics creation pane

8.   Close the **Satisfaction metrics** pane to go back to the **Customization** pane.

9.   Select **Personalization** from the **Customization** pane (see *Figure 6.5*).

10. The **Personalization** pane enables you to create **survey variables** to be added to your survey that can be used to personalize your survey (such as dynamically inserting a survey recipient name into your survey question). The survey variable values can be included as part of the survey responses to provide more context. In our example, we will add an *employee number* to the survey so that we can associate the response with the corresponding employee record in the **Human Resources (HR)** system.

11. Click **Add variable** and click **Save** to finish, as illustrated in *Figure 6.8* (note that you can optionally set a default variable value—in our example, the default value for **EmployeeNumber** is not necessary, so we can leave it empty):

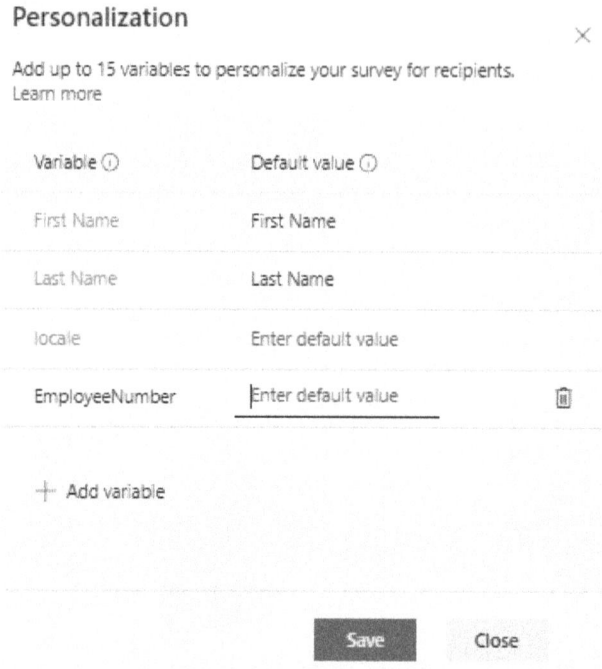

Figure 6.8 – Add variable panel

12. Rename your survey project by clicking on **All Projects** from the top-left navigation panel (see *Figure 6.9*) to go to the **My projects** view, then select your project and select **Rename** from the **triple-dot** drop-down menu, as illustrated in the following screenshot (as an example, you can rename the project as Employee onboarding to make it easier to identify the project and get back to it later):

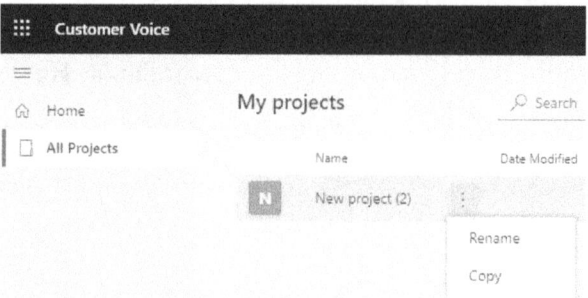

Figure 6.9 – Renaming a project

After this step, you are ready to start sending the survey. However, before sending it, you need an email template that you can use to send an email to the new employee, inviting them to fill out the survey.

Creating an email template

Customer Voice supports the sending of a survey invitation email and enables you to customize this. Here are the steps to create a customized email template:

1. Open the `Employee onboarding` project from the **All projects** view in Customer Voice.

2. Click on the **Send** tab on **New employee survey** to view different options for distributing your survey, as illustrated in *Figure 6.10*:

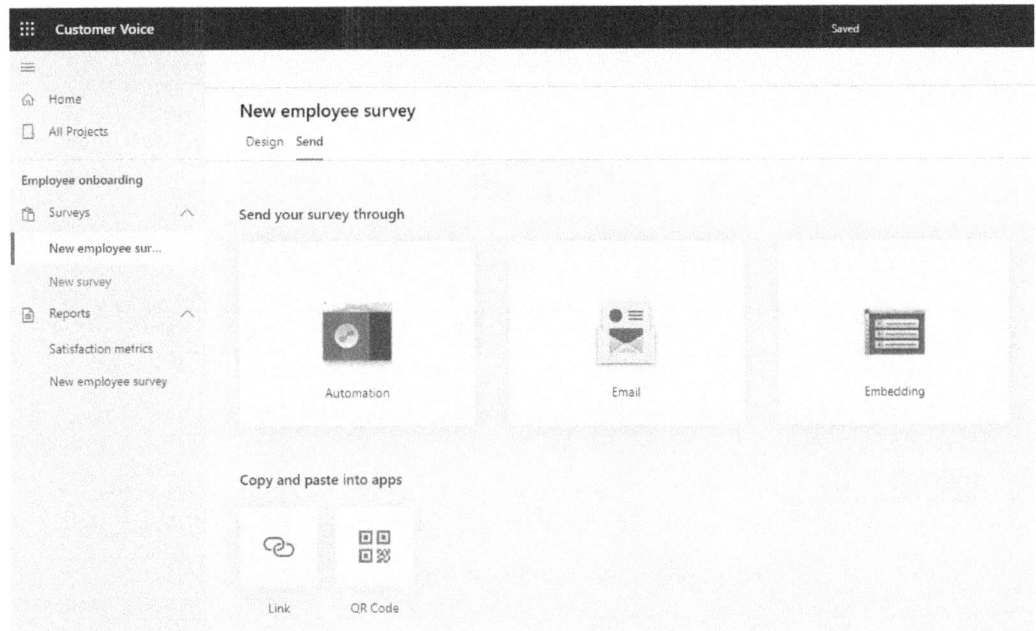

Figure 6.10 – Options to distribute survey

3. Click on the **Email** option to open the survey invitation email editor page, as shown in *Figure 6.11*:

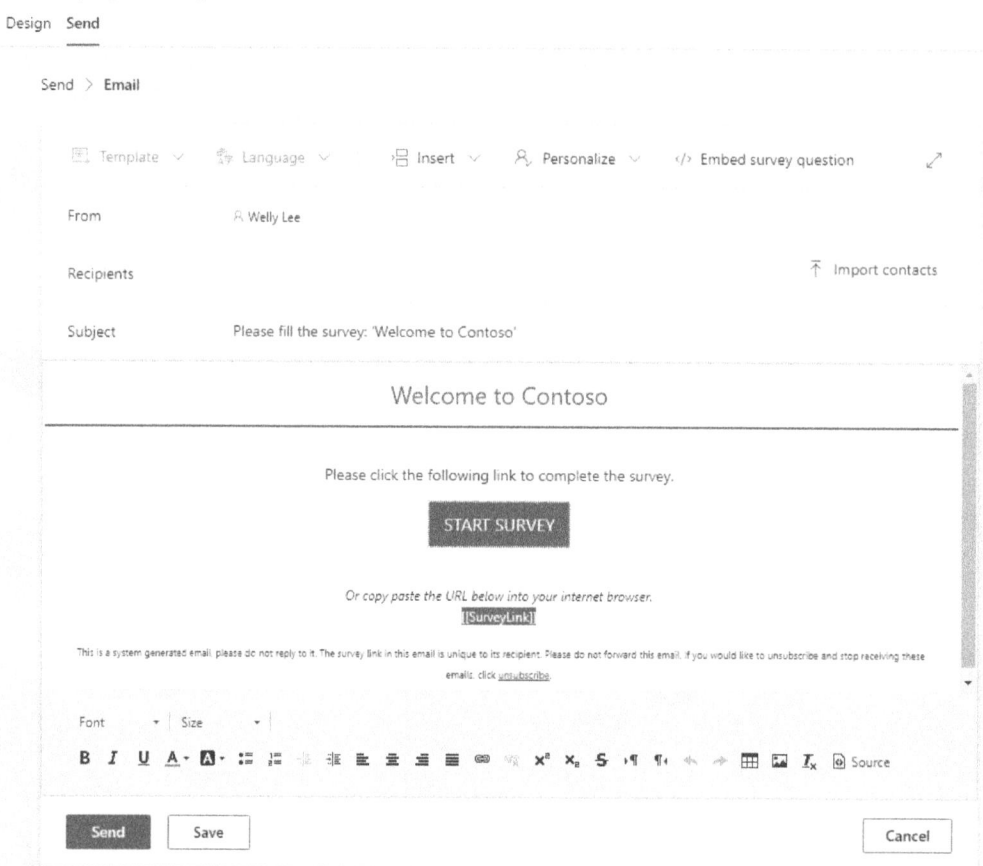

Figure 6.11 – Survey invitation email editor

> **Important note**
> Even though we are going to automate the sending of the survey, you still need to use an email to send the survey invitation. Hence, you still need to first create an email invitation before selecting the **Automation** option.

4. To customize an email template, remove the existing email content by clicking anywhere on the email body, use *Ctrl + A* to select all existing content, and press *Delete* to remove. You should have an empty email template, like the one shown in *Figure 6.12*:

New employee survey

Design Send

Subject   Please fill the survey: 'Welcome to Contoso'

Segoe UI ▾ | 14px ▾ |

B *I* U̲ A̲ ▾ ◼ ▾ ⋮☰ ☰ ⫤ ⫣ ☰ ☰ ☰ ☰ ⊕ x² x₂ S̶ ·¶ ¶· ↩ ↪ ⊞ 🖼 I꜀ ⧉ Source

[Send]   [Save]   [Cancel]

Figure 6.12 – Empty email template

5. You can create the email template directly on the email editor pane using the toolbar
    highlighted in green in *Figure 6.12*. One of the options includes **Source** editing,
    which allows you to author the email template using **HyperText Markup Language
    (HTML)**. Alternatively, you can create HTML email content elsewhere and copy
    and paste the email content on the email editor (see *Figure 6.13* for an example):

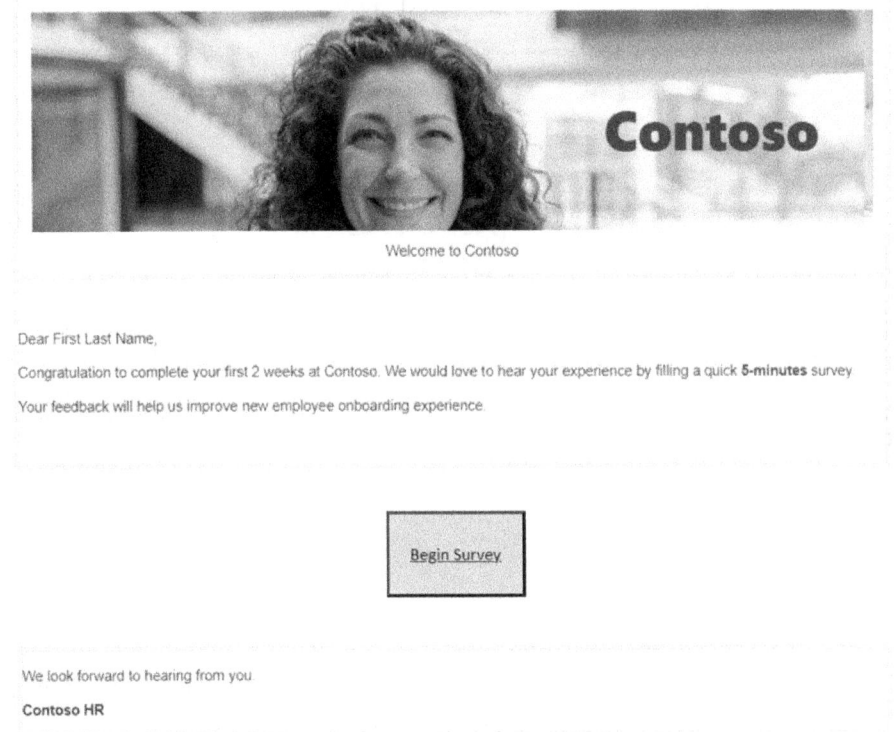

Figure 6.13 – Example of survey invitation template

> **Important note**
>
> When using an image as part of an email template, the image must be first uploaded to an online location and linked from the email template. The email template has size limitations, and if you try to embed an image directly on it, you will get the following error: **The email message has exceeded the maximum limit of 255000 characters. Try a shorter email message.**

6.   The email template must include a survey link. To insert a survey link on a custom email template, using the mouse highlight the text/image to insert the link (for example, the **Begin Survey** text on the email template in *Figure 6.14*), then under the **Insert** menu, select **Survey link**, as illustrated in the following screenshot:

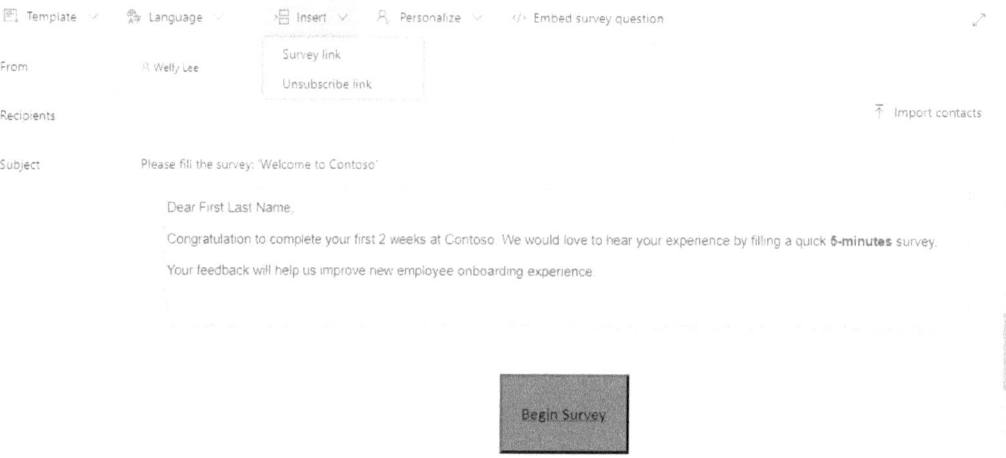

Figure 6.14 – Insert survey link to the email template

7.   You can also personalize the email by inserting a survey variable that will be replaced by the actual value for each survey recipient when the email is sent. For example, highlight the **First** text using your mouse, then open the **Personalize** menu to insert the **First Name** variable to replace the text, as illustrated in the following screenshot:

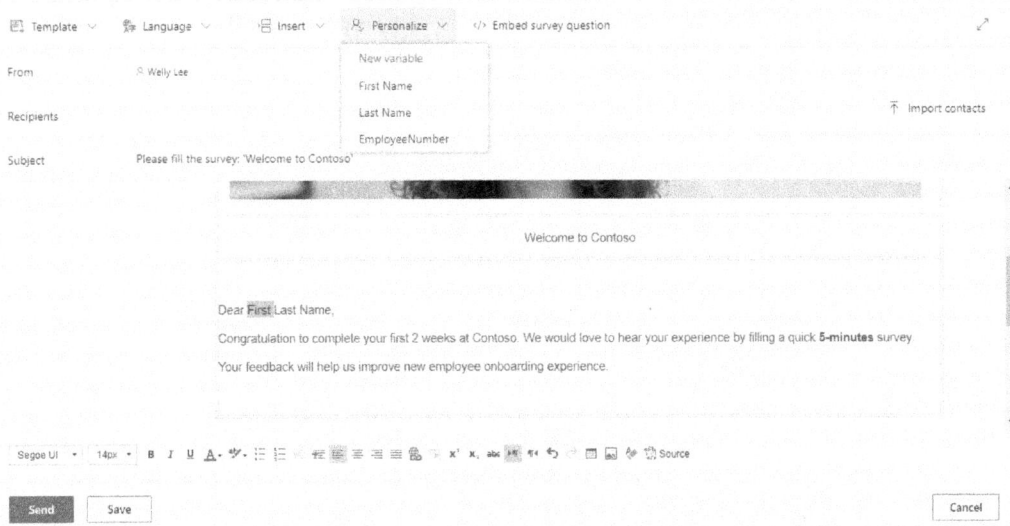

Figure 6.15 – Personalize email template by inserting a survey variable

8. Repeat the step for **Last Name**. After you complete this step, the email template should look like what's shown in *Figure 6.16*:

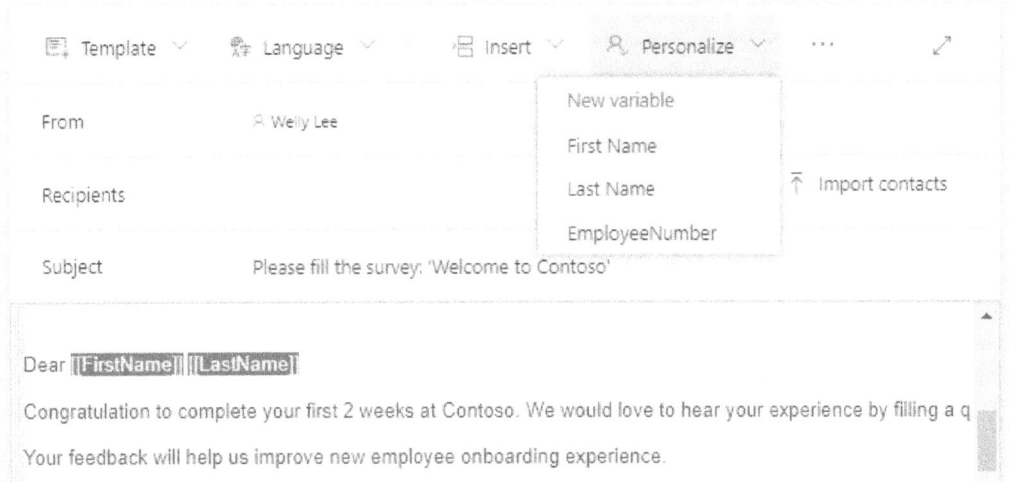

Figure 6.16 – FirstName and LastName variables added to the email template

9. Replace the subject text (for example, **Welcome to Contoso**) and save the template by clicking the **Save** button at the bottom of the screen, as illustrated in *Figure 6.17*:

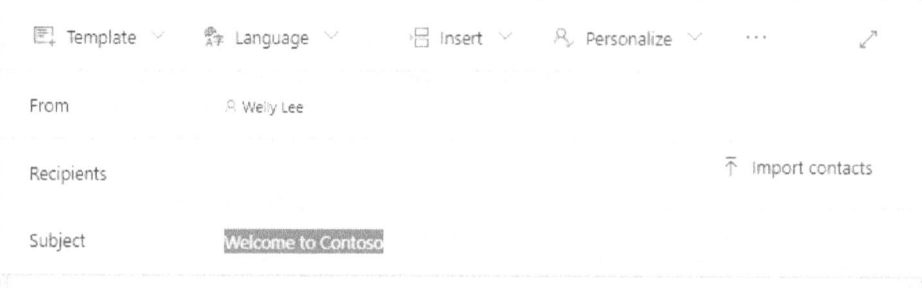

Figure 6.17 – Saved email template

The email template will be saved by using the **Default Template** option. You can rename the template by clicking the **Template** menu and clicking **triple-dot** menu and then selecting **Rename**, as shown in *Figure 6.18*:

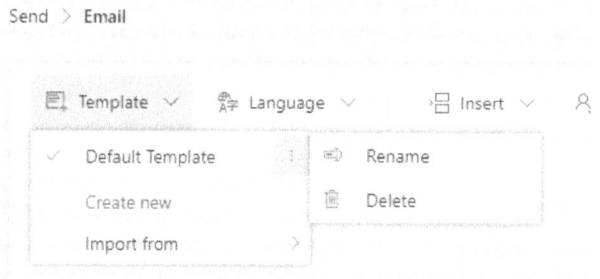

Figure 6.18 – Rename email template

Now that you have the email template ready, you can create a workflow to automatically send the survey.

Creating a workflow to automate the sending of a new employee survey

Customer Voice supports the automatic sending of a survey based on an event in your existing business application—for example, when a new employee record is added to your HR system. You can create an automation workflow through Microsoft Power Automate, the workflow automation product from Microsoft. Integration with Power Automate enables you to use 300+ connectors to connect Customer Voice with your existing business application. If there is no connector to the business application you are using (such as when you are using a homegrown application), then you can create a custom connector in Power Automate.

I will use an example where Customer Voice is integrated with a Dynamics 365 Human Resources application to trigger the sending of a survey when a new employee record is added to the HR system. You can use this example as a reference and replace the steps to connect to Dynamics 365 with the HR application you are using.

We will set up a workflow to send the survey 2 weeks after the new employee starts, based on the employment start date.

To create the automation workflow, follow these steps:

1. Go to `https://flow.microsoft.com` to create a workflow.

> **Important note**
> If you are connecting to Dynamics 365 or Power Apps, make sure to select the same **Dataverse** environment as in your instance of Dynamics 365 or Power Apps.

2. Select **Create** from the left navigation pane and select the **Scheduled cloud flow** option, as illustrated in *Figure 6.19*:

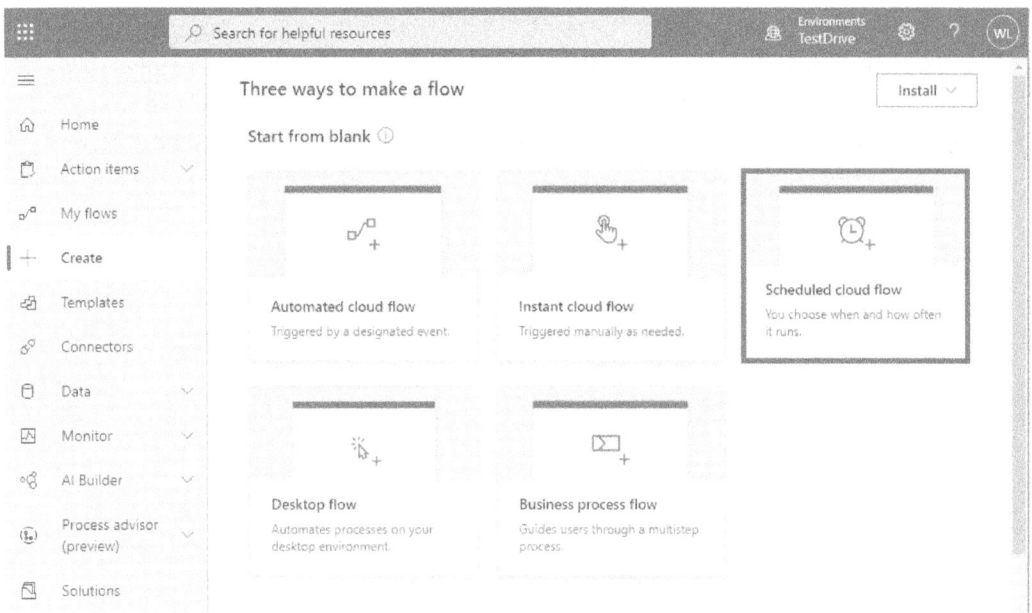

Figure 6.19 – Create a new workflow option

3.   Name the workflow and set the run frequency to daily, as illustrated in *Figure 6.20*:

Build a scheduled cloud flow   ✕

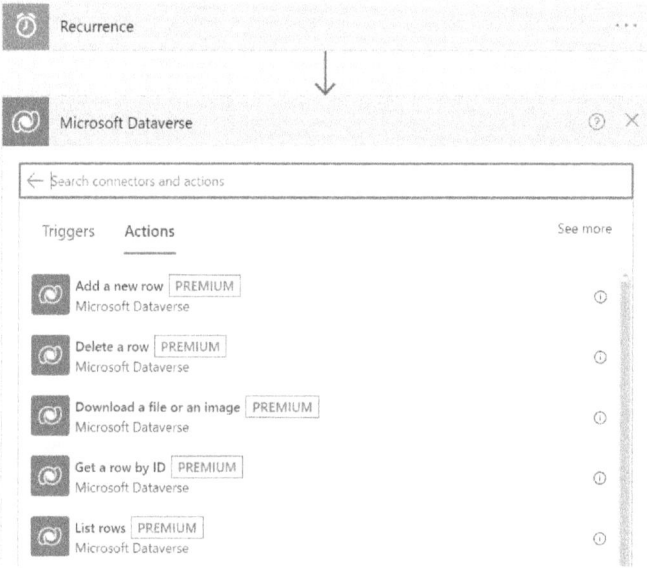

Stay on top of what's important without the effort—you choose
when and how often the flow runs.

Examples:
*   Automate team reminders to submit expense reports
*   Auto-backup data to designated storage on a regular basis

Flow name

New employee survey

Run this flow *

Starting   5/3/21   📅 * at   10:00 AM   ⌄

Repeat every   1   * Day   ⌄ *

This flow will run:

Every day

Skip   **Create**   Cancel

Figure 6.20 – Create new flow screen

4.   Add a **New step** and select your HR application connection. In our example,
we will connect to the **Dynamics 365 Human Resources** system. Select the
Dataverse connector and select a **List rows** action, as illustrated in *Figure 6.21*:

Figure 6.21 – Dataverse connector and action

5. Select the **Employments** table and specify **Filter Query** to get all records where **Employment Start Date** (cdm_employmentstartdate) is greater than today's date (15 days) and less than today's date (14 days), as follows:

```
cdm_employmentstartdate gt @{addDays(utcNow(),-15)} and
cdm_employmentstartdate le @{addDays(utcNow(),-14)}
```

Refer to *Figure 6.22* for how you add the filter condition on the workflow:

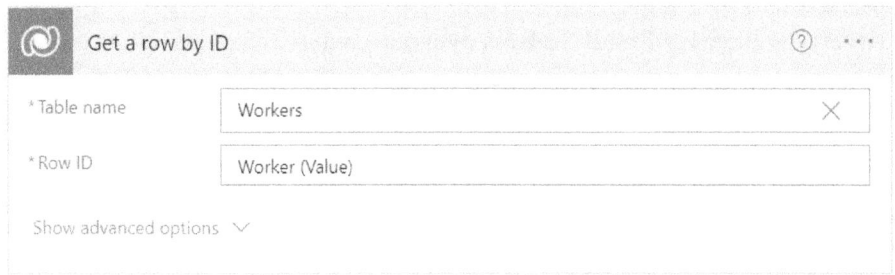

Figure 6.22 – List rows configuration

The **Employments** entity in Dynamics 365 Human Resources stores employment information such as an employee's start date. However, information such as an employee's name and email address are stored in a separate entity called **Workers**. To get these employee details, you will need a separate step.

6. Add a new step, search for **Dataverse**, and select the **Get a row by ID** action (see *Figure 6.21*).

7. Select the **Workers** table and select **Worker (Value)** as **Row ID**, as illustrated in *Figure 6.23*:

Figure 6.23 – Get a row by ID configuration

8. Add a new step, search for **Customer Voice**, and select the **Send a survey** action, as illustrated in *Figure 6.24*:

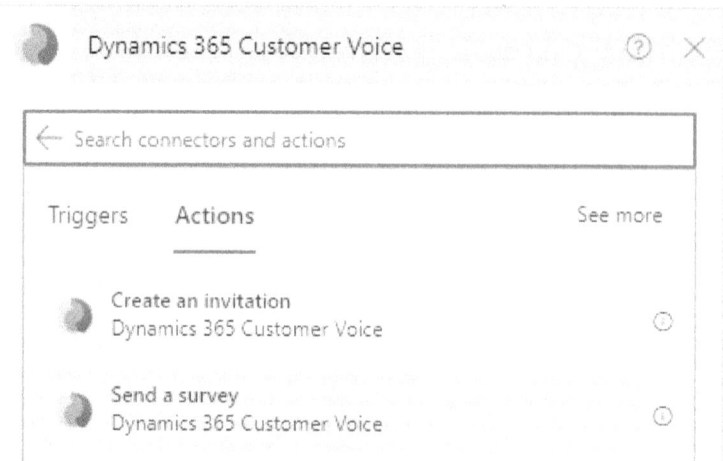

Figure 6.24 – Customer Voice workflow actions

> **Important note**
>
> Using the **Send a survey** action, Customer Voice will send an email invitation. The **Create an invitation** action only generates the survey link, and you will need to send the link on your own. The latter option should be used when you need to use another email service in your application or when you need to distribute the survey to other channel such as via **short message service (SMS)** or social media.

9. Configure the **Send a survey** action as follows:

    To: Insert the **Primary Email Address** dynamic content from the **Get a row by ID** step.

    Project: Select **Employee onboarding** (name of the project created in the prior steps) from the dropdown.

    Survey: Select **New employee survey** (name of the survey created in the prior steps) from the dropdown.

    First Name: Insert the **First Name** dynamic content from the **Get a row by ID** step.

    Last Name: Insert the **Last Name** dynamic content from the **Get a row by ID** step.

    EmployeeNumber: Insert **Worker Number** from the **Get a row by ID** step.

    The preceding fields are illustrated in *Figure 6.25*:

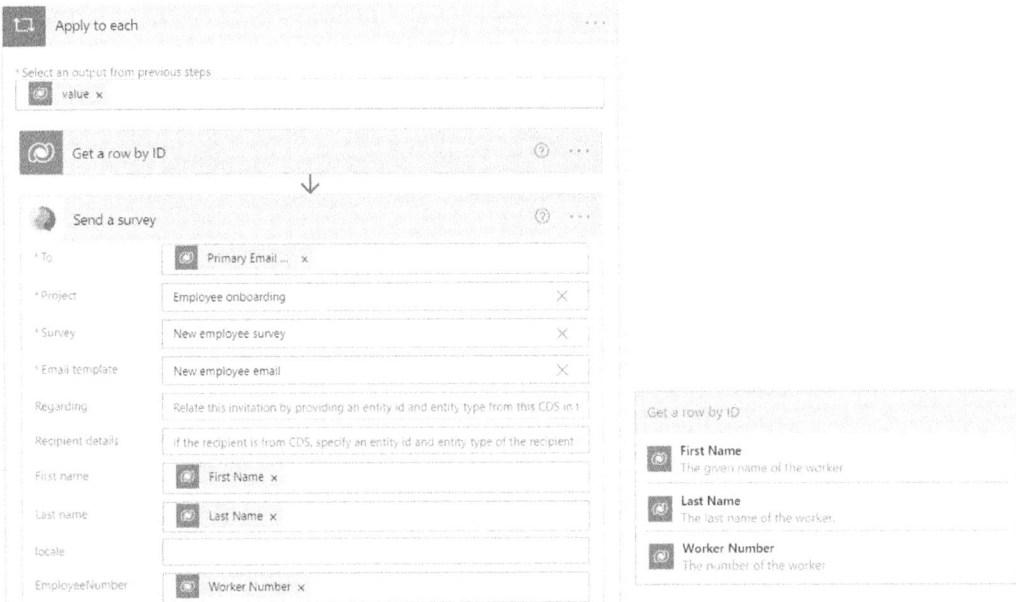

Figure 6.25 – Send a survey configuration

10. Save the workflow.

When a new employee is hired, after 2 weeks the new employee will get an email like the one shown in *Figure 6.26*:

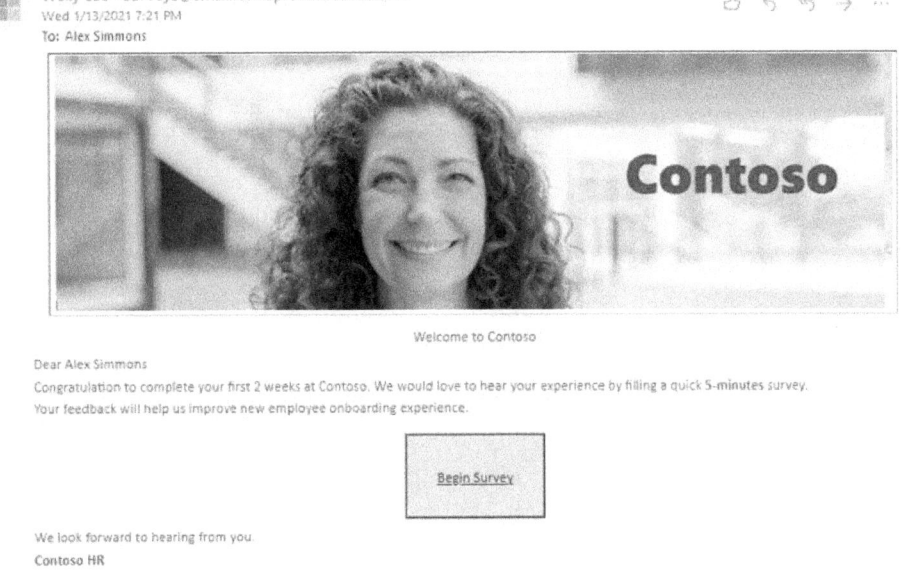

Figure 6.26 – Survey invitation email

Clicking the survey invitation link opens an online survey, as shown in *Figure 6.27*:

Welcome to Contoso

We are glad to have you join and would like to hear how you are doing in your first few weeks

1. How likely are you to recommend Contoso as a place to work?

0	1	2	3	4	5	6	7	8	9	10

Not at all likely   Extremely likely

2. How much do you agree with the following statements

	Strongly disagree	Disagree	Neither disagree nor agree	Agree	Strongly agree
I understand what is expected of me for my work	○	○	○	○	◉
I have the resources I need to do my work	○	○	○	○	◉
I have the training that I need to start with my work	○	○	○	○	◉
I have been introduced to all people I need to do my work	○	○	○	○	◉

3. What feedback do you have on your onboarding experience?

It would be great if you can send the employment paperwork ahead of time.

Submit

Figure 6.27 – New employee survey

After you receive the employee responses, you can view the results through Customer Voice reports. The first report is a **Satisfaction metrics** dashboard report that provides you with a score and a trend for each satisfaction metric you define in your project. The following screenshot shows the **New employee satisfaction** metric dashboard that we defined in *Figure 6.28*:

Figure 6.28 – Satisfaction metrics dashboard

HR can view a survey summary report from Customer Voice, as illustrated in *Figure 6.29*:

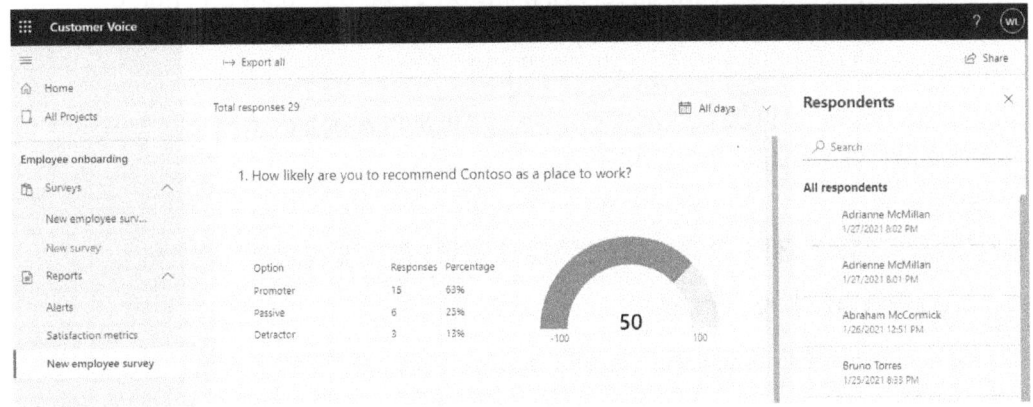

Figure 6.29 – Survey report

The **Respondents** panel on the right shows the details of employees who have filled out the survey. Double-clicking the employee name will show the survey response detail, as well as personalized data including the **EmployeeNumber**, as shown in *Figure 6.30*:

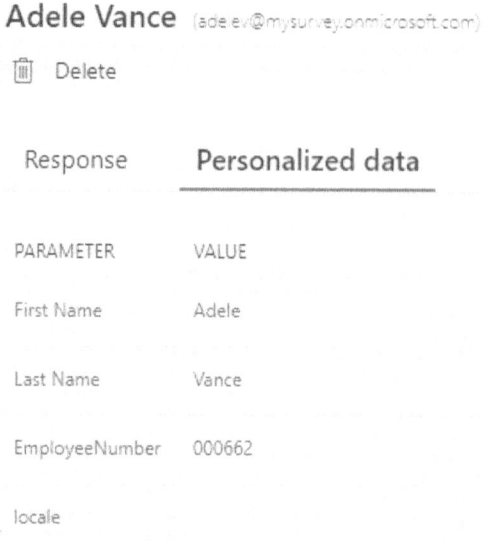

Figure 6.30 – Personalized survey data report

In addition to sending an onboarding survey, many organizations conduct periodic employee pulse surveys to measure employee engagement. For example, Microsoft conducts an annual employee survey called **MS poll**.

In the next section, we will discuss how you can conduct an anonymous employee engagement survey with Customer Voice.

Conducting an anonymous employee engagement survey

Employee engagement surveys are often collected anonymously to allow employees to express themselves more freely. In *Chapter 3, Creating a Survey with Microsoft Forms*, we discussed how you can use Microsoft Forms to collect anonymous employee feedback. Customer Voice supports the collection of feedback that excludes personal identifiable information while capturing some general information about the employee. It is often necessary to group the feedback so that you can create a report that compares feedback across different groups, such as by department or location.

Let's see how you can set up an anonymous survey while capturing generic employee information using Customer Voice.

Creating a survey

To start, go to `https://customervoice.microsoft.com` to create your survey and select the **Blank** template. Then, create your **Employee engagement survey** questionnaire, an example of which is given in *Figure 6.31*:

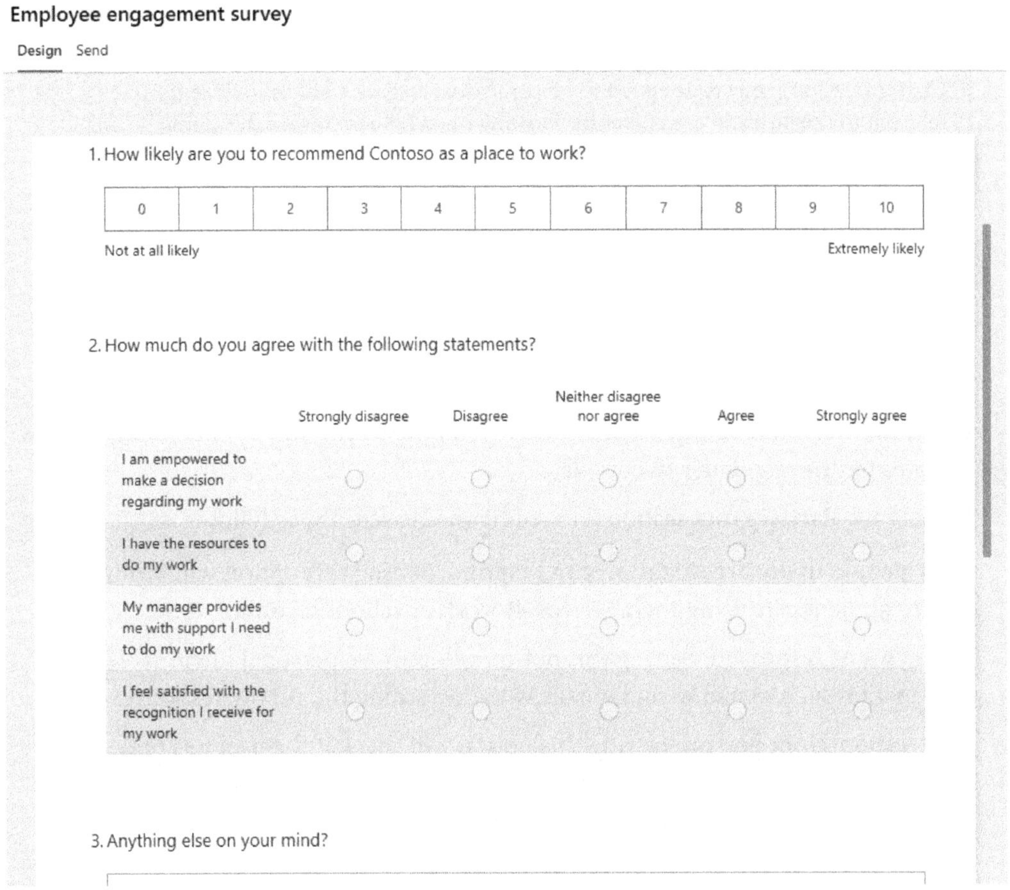

Figure 6.31 – An example of an employee engagement survey questionnaire

After you finish with your survey, click on the **Send** tab to configure the distribution settings.

Sending your survey

Use the following steps to configure anonymous sending of the survey:

1. Select the send survey through **Email** option.

2. Expand the **Customization** panel on the right to view the **Distribution Setting** options.

    > **Important note**
    >
    > The **Customization** panel is available on both the **Design** and **Send** tabs. However, the options are different depending which tab you are on. The **Customization** panel is designed to be contextual so that it only shows options relevant to the task you are currently working on, whether you are designing the survey or distributing the survey.

3. Click on the **Distribution settings** option.

4. Expand the **Participant** setting and enable **Save survey progress**. This setting enables the survey responders to fill out the survey incrementally—for example, the survey responder can start filling out the survey on a mobile device and close the survey before hitting **Submit**, and can then open the same link on a PC to pick up where they off. This setting is useful when you have a long survey that requires a few minutes for the responder to complete it.

5. Expand the **Participants** section and configure the settings as follows:

    Only people in my organization can respond: Setting this option will prompt the user to authenticate using their Microsoft work or school account.

    Anonymous responses: Setting this option will remove personal identifiable information such as names and emails when recording the survey response.

    One response per person: Setting this option will check if the user has previously submitted a response. A user who previously submitted a response will be shown a message and blocked from opening the survey again.

Save invited participants as Contacts: This option is mostly used for tracking results over time for non-anonymous surveys.

Save survey progress: This option allows the survey respondent to answer survey in multiple sessions and Customer Voice will save the progress to enable the respondent to pick up where they left off.

The preceding fields are shown in *Figure 6.32*:

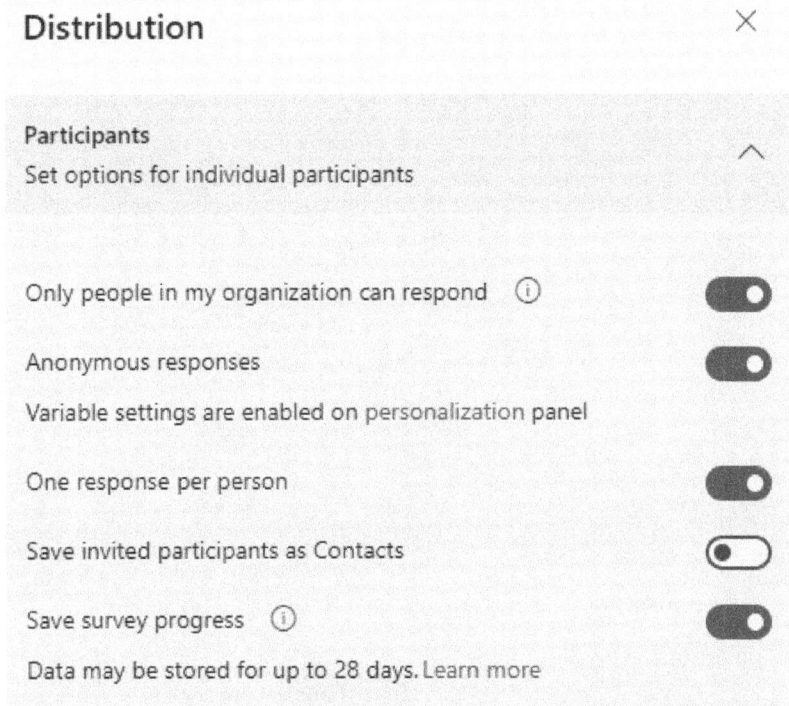

Figure 6.32 – Participant setting options for an anonymous employee survey

6. Under the **Anonymous responses** setting, click on the **personalization** link inside **Variable settings are enabled on personalization panel** to open the **Personalization** panel.

7.   On the **Personalization** panel, click **Add variable** to add new variables for general employee information you would like to include in your reporting—such as `Title`, `Department`, and `Location`—and click the **Save** button when finished, as illustrated in *Figure 6.33*:

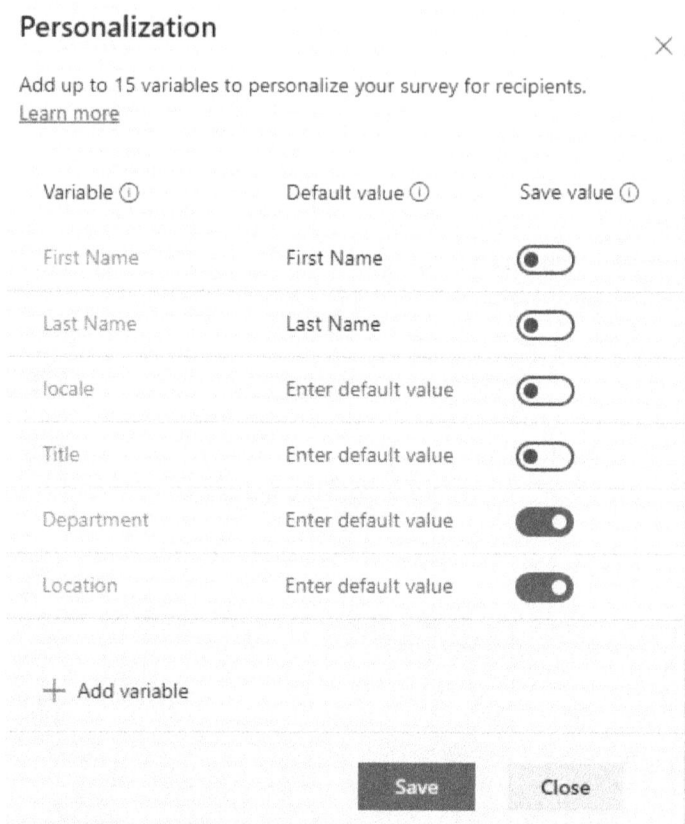

Figure 6.33 – An example of variables to include in an employee survey

Important note

Make sure that **Save value** is turned off for **First Name** and **Last Name** to exclude this information from being recorded as part of anonymous survey responses.

You also need to make sure that the employee attribute is not so specific that it reveals employee identity. For example, **Title** may be too specific (such as, if there is only one salesperson per location), so you may want to exclude collecting the title as part of your reporting to avoid revealing employee identity.

8. Back on the email editor, click **Import contacts** for the survey recipients, as illustrated in *Figure 6.34*:

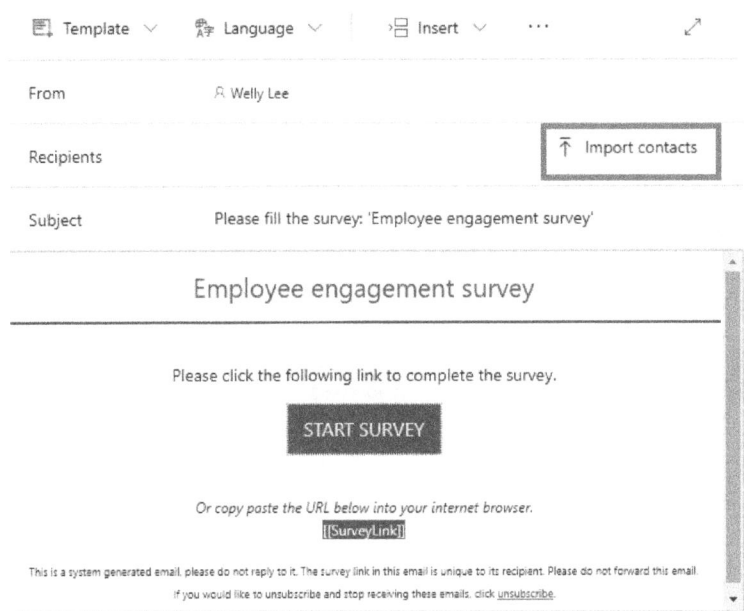

Figure 6.34 – Import contacts for survey recipients

9. On the **Import contacts** panel, click **Download template** to get a template you can use to fill out your employee information. See *Figure 6.35* for an example of the employee information you might use for your reporting:

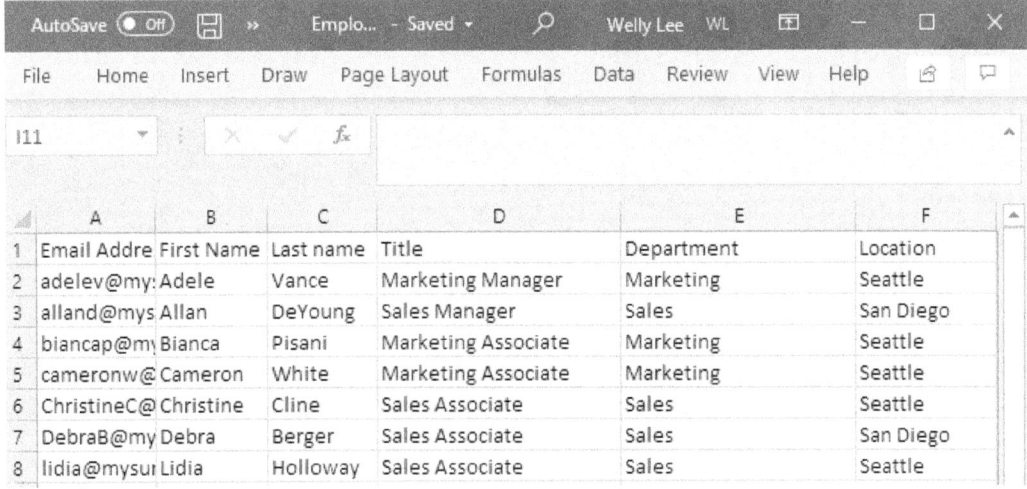

	A	B	C	D	E	F
1	Email Addre	First Name	Last name	Title	Department	Location
2	adelev@my:	Adele	Vance	Marketing Manager	Marketing	Seattle
3	alland@mys	Allan	DeYoung	Sales Manager	Sales	San Diego
4	biancap@m	Bianca	Pisani	Marketing Associate	Marketing	Seattle
5	cameronw@	Cameron	White	Marketing Associate	Marketing	Seattle
6	ChristineC@	Christine	Cline	Sales Associate	Sales	Seattle
7	DebraB@my	Debra	Berger	Sales Associate	Sales	San Diego
8	lidia@mysu	Lidia	Holloway	Sales Associate	Sales	Seattle

Figure 6.35 – An example of employee information

10. Upload the completed employee list file from the **Import Contacts** panel.

11. Click **Send** at the bottom of the email editor (see *Figure 6.34*) to distribute the survey.

After you receive the responses, you can view and analyze the results.

Analyzing the survey results

You can view the survey response summary from the Customer Voice summary report page, where the **Respondents** panel shows individual survey responses. Note in *Figure 6.36* that the respondent names are all listed as **Anonymous** since the survey was configured as anonymous in the previous steps:

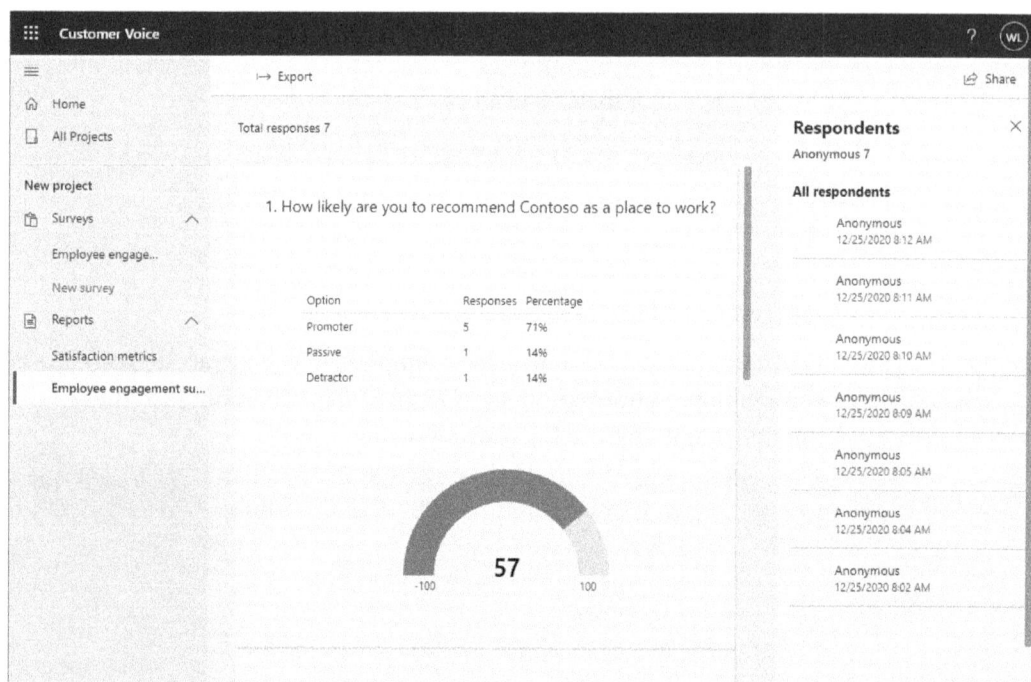

Figure 6.36 – Survey response summary report

Double-click on a respondent to view their individual response as well as the survey variable value. Since we set the survey to be anonymous, names and emails of the survey recipients were removed from the survey responses. However, specified survey variables such as **Department** and **Location** are collected and shown through the **Personalized data** tab when you double-click on the survey response record, as illustrated in *Figure 6.37*:

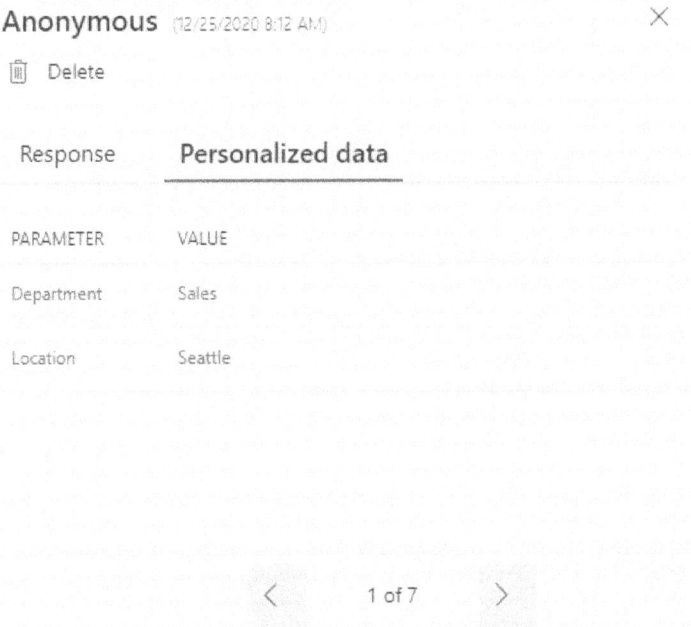

Figure 6.37 – Survey variable value

The survey variables are also included when you download the results to Excel. To download to Excel, click **Export** on the command bar on the top of the survey. *Figure 6.38* shows the exported survey results in Excel:

	A	B	C	D	E	F	G	H	I	J	K	L
1	ID	Start time	Completion time	Email	Name	How likel	I am empowered	I have the resourc	My manager pro	I feel satisfied	Anything els	Personalized data
2	1	5/25/21 8:02:38	5/25/21 8:02:47	anonymous		10	Strongly agree	Strongly agree	Agree	Strongly agree		Department:Marketing;Location:Seattle;
3	2	5/25/21 8:03:47	5/25/21 8:04:06	anonymous		8	Agree	Agree	Neither disagree r	Neither disagree	Compensation	Department:Sales;Location:San Diego;
4	3	5/25/21 8:04:39	5/25/21 8:05:13	anonymous		10	Strongly agree	Agree	Strongly agree	Strongly agree	More flexible w	Department:Marketing;Location:Seattle;
5	4	5/25/21 8:09:21	5/25/21 8:09:47	anonymous		9	Disagree	Disagree	Neither disagree r	Disagree	Need better tra	Department:Marketing;Location:Seattle;
6	5	5/25/21 8:10:12	5/25/21 8:10:36	anonymous		10	Strongly agree	Strongly agree	Agree	Strongly agree		Department:Sales;Location:Seattle;
7	6	5/25/21 8:11:01	5/25/21 8:11:07	anonymous		10	Strongly agree	Strongly agree	Strongly agree	Strongly agree		Department:Sales;Location:San Diego;
8	7	5/25/21 8:12:04	5/25/21 8:12:18	anonymous		3	Strongly disagree	Strongly disagree	Strongly disagree	Disagree		Department:Sales;Location:Seattle;

Figure 6.38 – Exported survey results

Notice that since the survey is set as **anonymous**, all rows in the **Email** column are marked as **anonymous** and the rows under the **Name** column are all empty.

All survey variables are stored under a single column called **Personalized data** (see *Figure 6.38*). To make it easier for you to filter based on those values, you may want to create separate columns for each of the survey variables (such as **Department** and **Location**).

Excel has a **Flash Fill** feature (see https://support.microsoft.com/en-us/office/using-flash-fill-in-excel-3f9bcf1e-db93-4890-94a0-1578341f73f7) that you can use to create separate columns for survey variables.

To use **Flash Fill**, simply create a new column next to the **Personalized data** column and start typing the value of the first few rows. Excel will automatically detect the pattern and pre-fill the rest of the row, as illustrated in *Figure 6.39*:

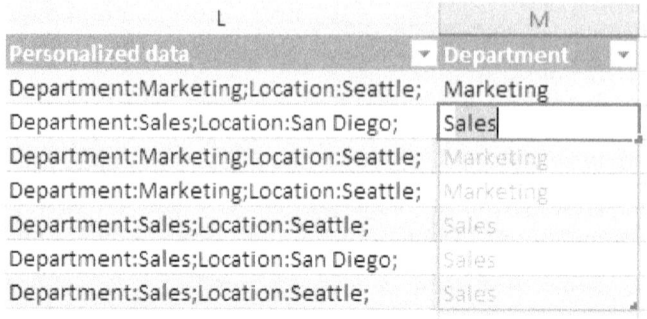

Figure 6.39 – Flash Fill feature in Excel automatically populates the values after a few examples

In *Figure 6.39*, you start typing the department value for the first two rows (for example, Marketing, Sales), then Excel will show suggested values. Press *Enter* to accept the suggestion.

Repeat the steps for the **Location** variable and you should get an updated Excel sheet, like the one shown here:

ID	Start time	Completion ti	Email	Ho	I am empowere	I have the resou	My manager	I feel satisfie	Anything	Personalized data	Departme	Location
1	5/25/21 8:02:38	5/25/21 8:02:47	anonymous	10	Strongly agree	Strongly agree	Agree	Strongly agree		Department:Marketing;Location:Seattle;	Marketing	Seattle
2	5/25/21 8:03:47	5/25/21 8:04:06	anonymous	8	Agree	Agree	Neither disagree	Neither disagree	Compensati	Department:Sales;Location:San Diego;	Sales	San Diego
3	5/25/21 8:04:39	5/25/21 8:05:13	anonymous	10	Strongly agree	Agree	Strongly agree	Strongly agree	More flexibl	Department:Marketing;Location:Seattle;	Marketing	Seattle
4	5/25/21 8:09:21	5/25/21 8:09:47	anonymous	9	Disagree	Disagree	Neither disagree	Disagree	Need better	Department:Marketing;Location:Seattle;	Marketing	Seattle
5	5/25/21 8:10:12	5/25/21 8:10:36	anonymous	10	Strongly agree	Strongly agree	Agree	Strongly agree		Department:Sales;Location:Seattle;	Sales	Seattle
6	5/25/21 8:11:01	5/25/21 8:11:07	anonymous	10	Strongly agree	Strongly agree	Strongly agree	Strongly agree		Department:Sales;Location:San Diego;	Sales	San Diego
7	5/25/21 8:12:04	5/25/21 8:12:18	anonymous	3	Strongly disagree	Strongly disagree	Strongly disagree	Disagree		Department:Sales;Location:Seattle;	Sales	Seattle

Figure 6.40 – Excel file with separate columns for survey variables

With each survey variable in a separate column, you can now filter and analyze the survey results based on the survey variable value—for example, viewing all results from the **Seattle** location.

Summary

Collecting feedback from employees is an important part of an organization in terms of understanding employees' concerns and improving the culture of a company. Customer Voice includes features to enable you to automate the internal employee feedback process as well as enable anonymous feedback collection, to allow your employees to express their opinions more freely.

In the next chapter, we will discuss how you can use Customer Voice to collect feedback from external customers.

7
Collecting Periodic Customer Feedback with Customer Voice

Collecting customer feedback periodically such as quarterly or annually is a common way to understand the mood of your customers. Customer feedback must be integrated with your **Customer Relationship Management (CRM)** system and survey responses must be linked to the customer records in the system. This is important so that you can get a complete insight into your customers, and the feedback can be available to anyone who needs to interact with the customer. When a customer complain to you, it expects everyone in your organization to know about the complaint.

Customer Voice enables you to integrate survey data with your customer records in your business application. If you are using Microsoft business applications such as Dynamics 365, then you can use the built-in integration functionalities in Customer Voice. If you are not using Dynamics 365, you can connect to your business application through Power Automate workflow. In this chapter, we will discuss an example using Dynamics 365 and will add notes on how you can do similar integration if you are not using Dynamics 365.

We will cover viewing survey results using the out-of-the-box reports in Customer Voice as well as using custom dashboards in Power BI.

Customer Voice writes survey responses to a dedicated online database for your organization called **Dataverse**. Dataverse is the application and data platform for Microsoft and is used by Microsoft business applications such as Power App, Power BI, and Dynamics 365. If you are using Dynamics 365 Customer Engagement (sales, customer service, or marketing), then you can select the same Dataverse instance to automatically connect survey responses to your customer record. If you are not using Dynamics 365, then the survey response is written to the default Dataverse instance that comes as part of your Microsoft 365 subscription. You can then use Power BI to connect directly to Dataverse to create a custom dashboard for your specific reporting needs.

In this chapter we will use an example of a customer experience manager at a bank who sends monthly customer feedback surveys to a customer list provided by the operations team. We will start by creating a personalized survey based on your customer type, and then brand the survey, send the survey, and link the results to the customer records. To conclude, we will discuss how you can use Power BI to create a custom report that combines survey responses with information in Dynamics 365 Customer Engagement. At the end of this chapter, you will understand how to implement an integrated customer feedback management solution.

The chapter is organized as follows:

- Creating a personalized survey
- Branding the survey
- Sending the survey
- Viewing survey results

We will start by creating a survey.

Creating a personalized survey

For this example, you would like to send a feedback survey from a list you receive from your operation team. The list includes customer types such as online customers who conduct business through a mobile app and branch customers who visit a branch location. You would like to send personalized surveys that ask different questions based on the customer type.

To create a personalized survey, do the following:

1. Create a new project at `https://customervoice.microsoft.com`.

2. Select a blank template.

3. On the location selection screen, select the same location that your company uses for Dynamics 365.

> **Tip**
>
> If you are using Dynamics 365 and would like to connect survey responses to your customer records, you must change the default location to the same Dataverse environment as your Dynamics 365 instance. You also need to be granted the Project Owner role in Dynamics 365 to connect. Please see *Chapter 10, Administering Microsoft Forms and Dynamics 365 Customer Voice*, for details on assigning Customer Voice roles in Dynamics 365.

4. On the **Design** tab, create a survey with all the questions for both branch and mobile app customers (see an example survey in *Figure 7.1*):

1. How likely are you to recommend us to a friend or colleague?

0	1	2	3	4	5	6	7	8	9	10

Not at all likely   Extremely likely

2. Thinking about your branch visit experience, how much do you agree with the following:

	Strongly disagree	Disagree	Neither disagree nor agree	Agree	Strongly Agree
I can talk to a teller quickly	○	○	○		○
I am satisfied with the courtesy and helpfulness of the teller	○	○	○	○	○
I am satisfied with the speed my financial transaction was completed	○	○	○	○	○

3. When using our mobile app, how much do you agree with the following:

	Strongly disagree	Disagree	Neither disagree nor agree	Agree	Strongly Agree
I can easily find information	○	○	○	○	○
I am satisfied with the time for information being updated	○	○	○	○	○
I am satisfied with the reliability of the app	○	○	○	○	○

4. Anything else on your mind?

Enter your answer

Figure 7.1 – An example of a bank survey

5. In the **Customization** panel, open the **Personalization** setting.

    Personalization enables you to create survey variables that you can use to personalize your survey. For our example, let's add the following survey variables:

    `MobileCustomer`: This variable will be used to indicate if the customer is an online customer who uses the mobile app. Set the default value to No.

    `BranchCustomer`: This variable will be used to indicate if the customer is a branch customer. Set the default value to Yes.

`PrimaryBranch`: This variable will be used to store the name of the primary branch for the customer. Leave the default value to empty.

> **Tip**
> If you are using a CRM system other than Dynamics 365, you can use a survey variable to store the record ID from your CRM system. The survey variable value will be included as part of the survey response and you can use a Power Automate workflow to push the survey response to your CRM system and use the survey variable value to link the survey response to the relevant record in your CRM system.

The updated personalization setting looks like *Figure 7.2*:

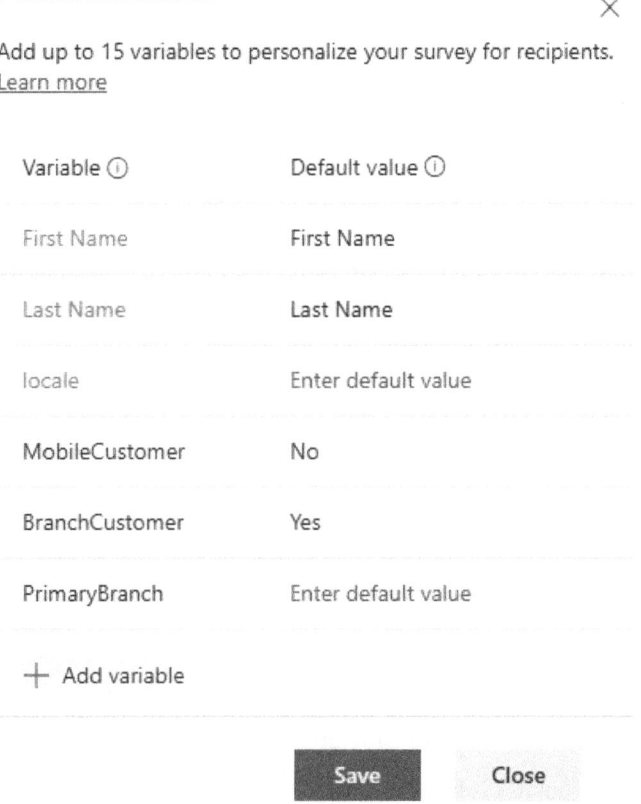

Figure 7.2 – Updated personalization settings

Click **Save** to create the variables. You can now use the survey variable to personalize your survey questions and to set up a branching rule to conditionally show question(s) based on the value of the survey variable.

6. In the **Customization** panel, open **Branching**.

7. Create a new rule by clicking the **Customize** button.

8. Give your rule a name that describes the branching logic purpose (for example: Show mobile feedback questions).

    The branching rule enables you to specify one or more conditions based on how the user responds to the survey questions or based on the value of a survey variable. In our example, we will use the survey variable as the condition for the rule.

9. Add a condition and select **Survey variable** from the first dropdown, then select the **MobileCustomer** variable from the second dropdown. In the last text box, type Yes as the survey variable value to trigger the condition (see *Figure 7.3*):

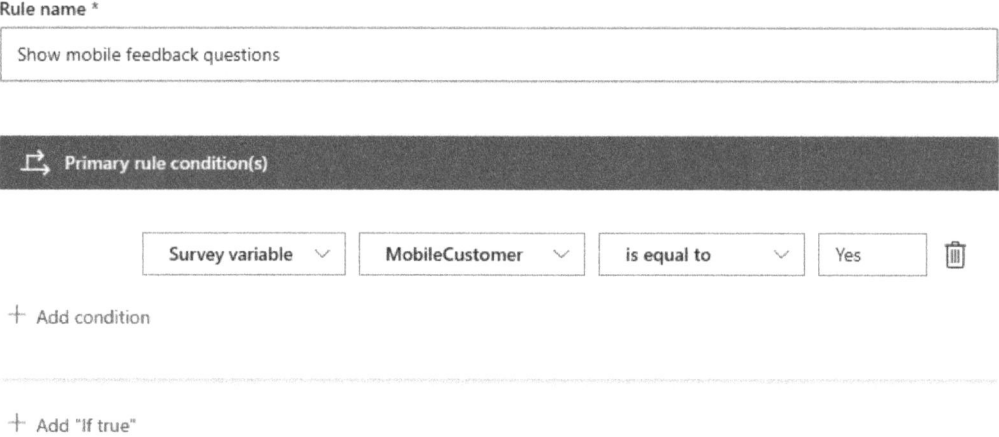

Figure 7.3 – Branching rule condition for mobile customer type

10. Click **Add "If true"** and click **Add action** to specify the action when the condition occurs.

    You can set the action to show or hide question(s) or to navigate the user to another question, the end of the survey, another survey (a chained survey), or to a URL.

11. Select **Show** > **Question**, and the questions to appear for mobile customers.

12. Click **Add "If false"** and click **Add action** to hide the questions for non-mobile customers.

The completed rule is shown in *Figure 7.4*. Click **Save** to finish:

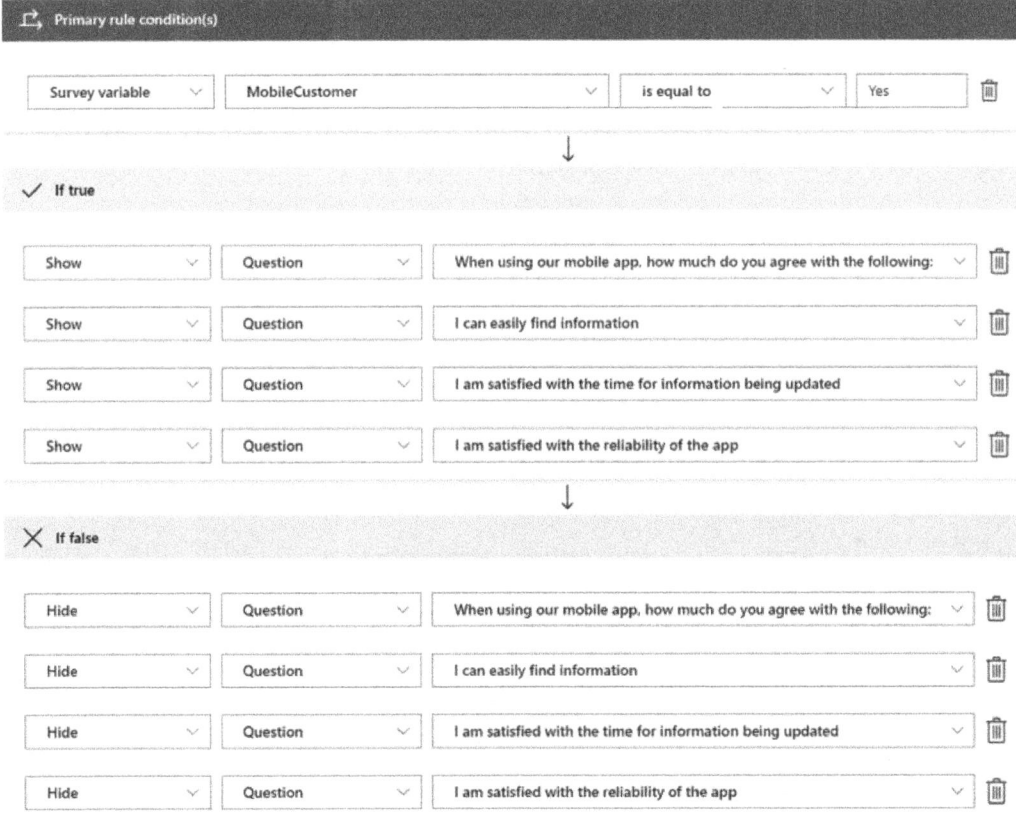

Figure 7.4 – Branching rule for mobile customers

13. Repeat the step for branch customer condition. See *Figure 7.5* for the completed branching rule for branch customers:

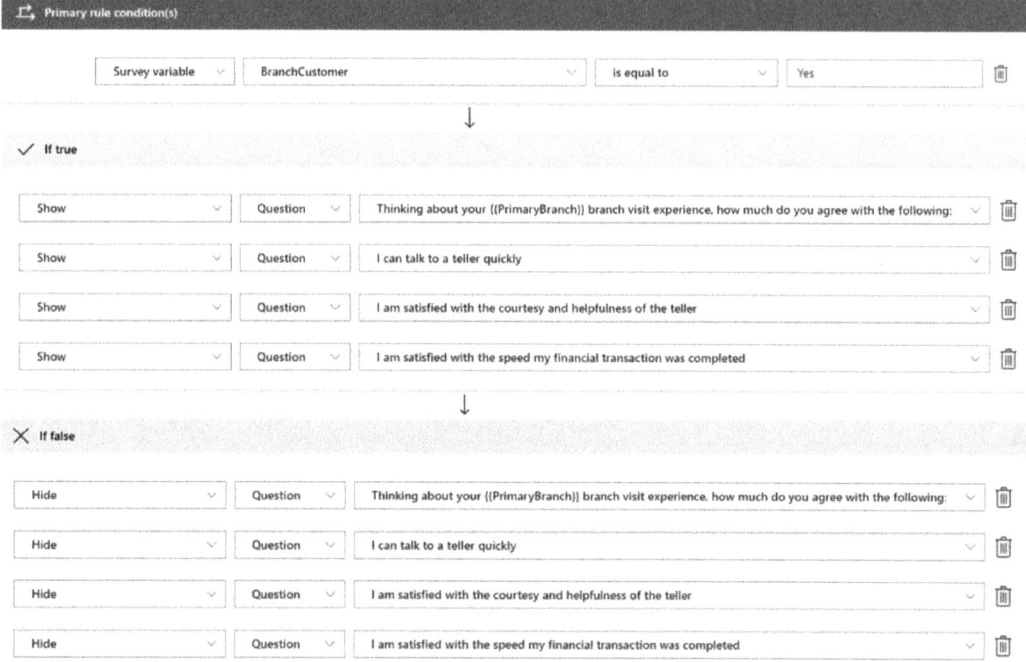

Figure 7.5 – Branching rule for branch customers

14. Close the branching panel.

15. Select the **Likert** question for the mobile app customers and set the **Visible** setting to *off*. This setting will hide the question by default and only show based on the branching rule (see *Figure 7.6*):

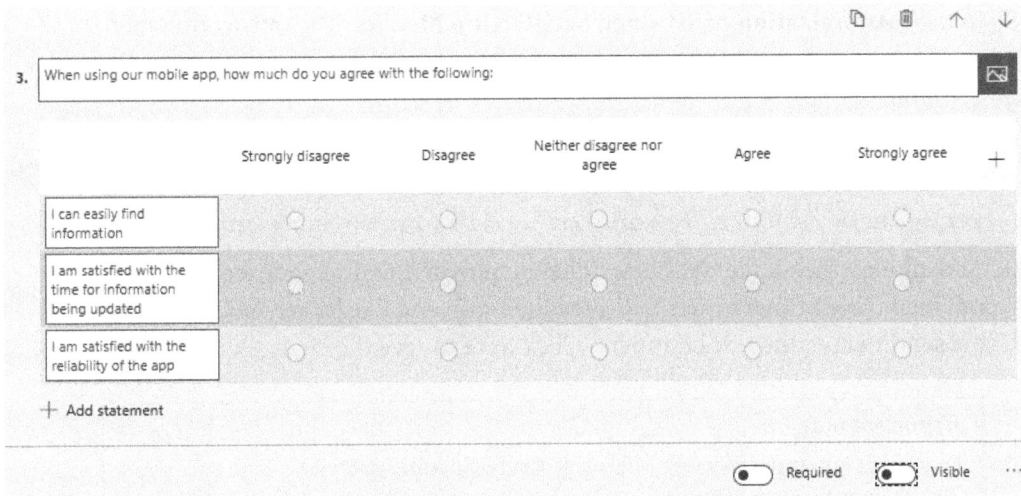

Figure 7.6 – Turn the Visible setting off for the mobile app feedback question

16. Make the same visible setting change to the branch customer feedback question.

   In addition to using a survey variable for branching, you can also use the variable as part of the survey question to make your survey more personalized.

17. Place your cursor to where you would like to add and select variable to insert from the dropdown (see *Figure 7.7*):

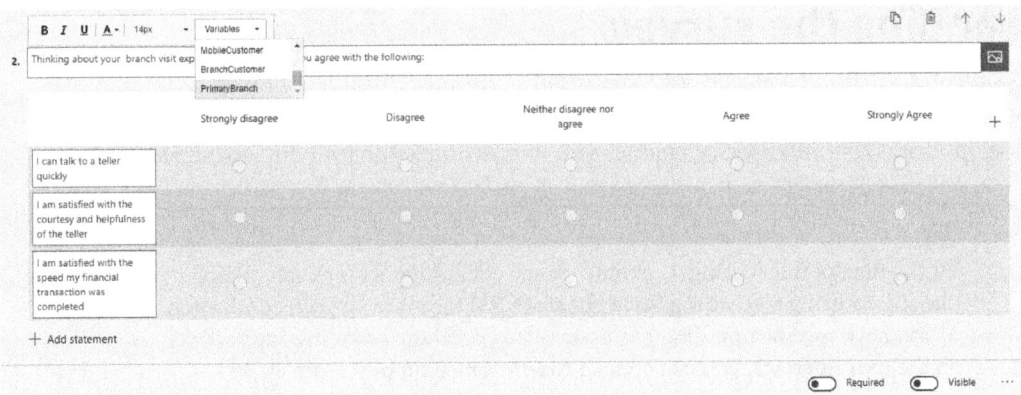

Figure 7.7 – Insert survey variable into the text question

18. In the **Customization** panel, open **Satisfaction Metrics**. The satisfaction metric enables you to define key metrics for your survey and map them to your survey question.

19. Create a new metric by selecting **Net Promoter Score®** from the **Add metrics** dropdown. Then map the metric to the question `How likely are you to recommend us to a friend or colleague?` in our example.

20. Add another metrics by selecting **Sentiment** from the **Add metrics** dropdown. You can map the sentiment metric to a text question and Customer Voice will calculate the sentiment of the text comment. Click **Save** to save the changes.

> **Important note**
>
> Sentiment is computed using Microsoft Azure Cognitive Service's Text Analytics model (see `https://docs.microsoft.com/en-us/azure/cognitive-services/text-analytics/text-analytics-user-scenarios`). At the time of the writing of this book, Customer Voice only supports English text for sentiment analysis. The plan is to support more languages in 2021.

After you have added all the questions and the logic, you can modify the look and feel by customizing the survey branding.

Branding the survey

In *Chapter 3, Creating a Survey with Microsoft Forms*, we discussed how you can add a background image, upload a logo, and customize the color. In addition to support for those options, Customize Voice enables you to customize the font and survey header.

> **Tip**
>
> At the time of this writing, Customer Voice offers support for customizing the survey using **Cascading Style Sheets** (**CSS**) for more style customization. If you have specific branding requirements beyond the branding support in the user interface, you can contact the customer support team at `customervoice@microsoft.com` to request enabling CSS in your organization.

Customizing fonts

Customer Voice supports customizing the font used for your survey. To customize the font, go to your survey's **Design** tab and open the **Customization** panel. Open **Branding** and expand the **Font** section. You can use a different font for your header, which includes the survey header and the section header, as well as for your survey body (see *Figure 7.8*):

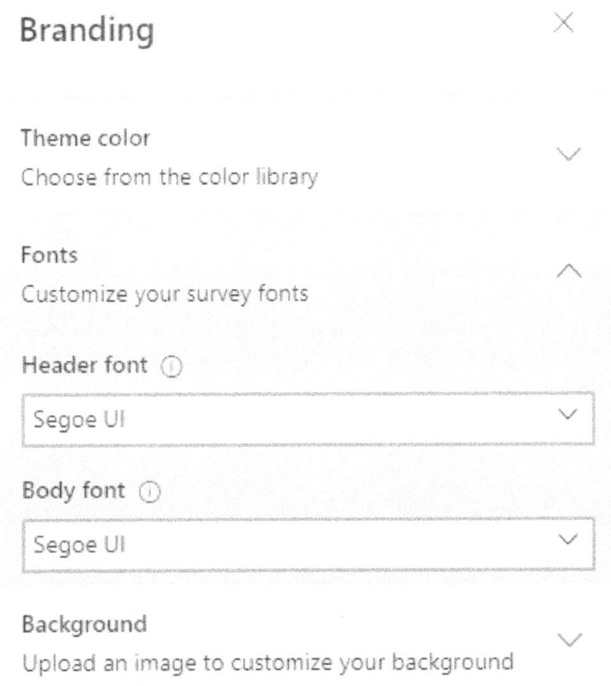

Branding   ×

Theme color   ⌄
Choose from the color library

Fonts   ⌃
Customize your survey fonts

Header font ⓘ

Segoe UI   ⌄

Body font ⓘ

Segoe UI   ⌄

Background   ⌄
Upload an image to customize your background

Figure 7.8 – Font customization

In addition to customizing the font for the survey header, you can also upload an image and a logo for the header section.

Customizing the survey header

The survey header is perhaps the most visual part of your survey, and you need to make the survey look familiar to your customers. As we discussed in *Chapter 2, Best Practices for Collecting Feedback through Surveys*, aligning the look of your survey with your websites makes it easier for your survey respondents to recognize your brand and increase the user's trust that the survey is legitimate.

Customer Voice makes it easy for you to change the look and feel of the survey header. To customize the survey header, select the survey header area by clicking or navigating to the survey header title. A customization toolbar appears with the following options (see *Figure 7.9*):

- **Style**: Select a header from a set of image and header styles.
- **Theme color**: Select a theme color for the header and the survey (including accent and button color).
- **Image**: Select from out-of-the-box images or upload your own image.
- **Logo**: Upload your logo.

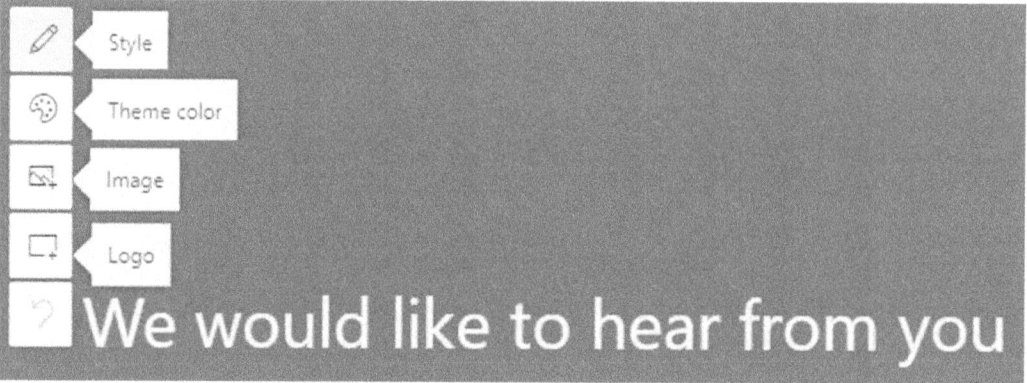

Figure 7.9 – Header customization toolbar

For our example, we will import a custom image for our header image.

Image

To import an image into the header, click on the image button in the toolbar and select the **Upload image** option:

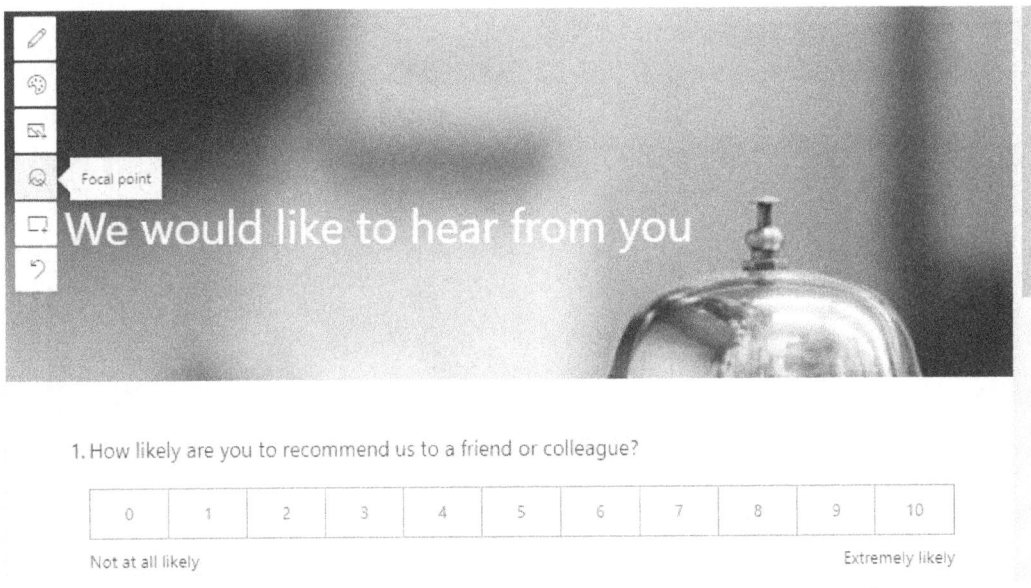

Figure 7.10 – Custom survey header

After you upload the image, you can use the **Focal point** option (see *Figure 7.10*) to pan the image and set the image's focal point to make sure the focal point is always visible when the image is resized to account for the width of the browser on different desktop and mobile devices.

If the image you are using for the survey header does not already include your organization's logo, you can upload your logo image separately.

Logo

Upload the logo from the toolbar menu, as shown in *Figure 7.9*. After you upload the logo, specify the size (small, medium, large) and placement (left, center, or right and top, middle, or bottom) using the toolbar, as shown in *Figure 7.11*:

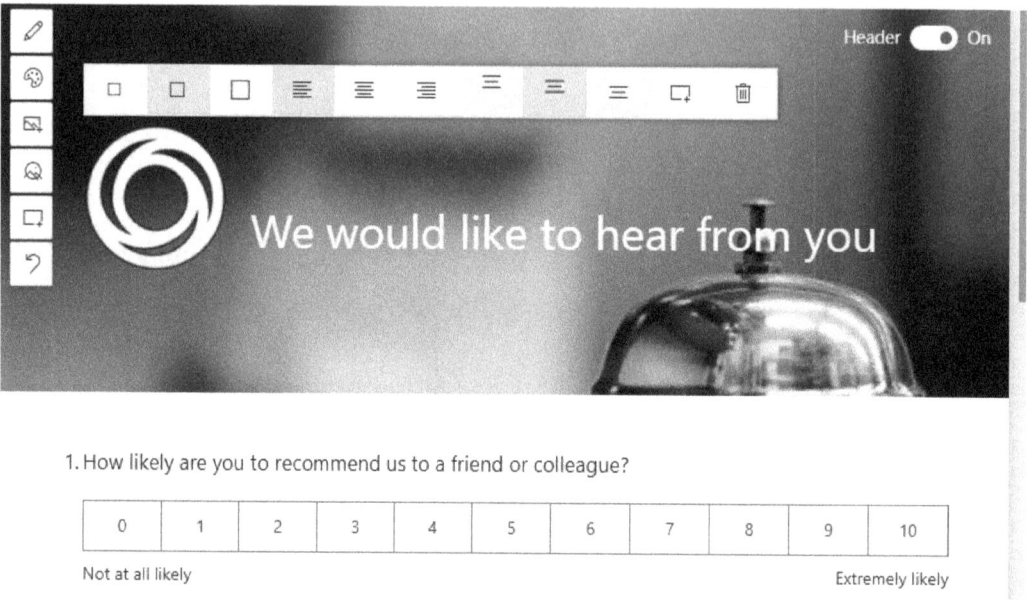

Figure 7.11 – Survey header with logo

A similar toolbar to set the placement of the logo is also available to set the position for the survey title.

We are now done with the survey design, and we are ready to distribute the survey.

Sending the survey

Follow these steps to send the survey:

1. Customize the email template (refer to *Chapter 6, Conducting an Employee Survey with Dynamics 365 Customer Voice*, for steps to customize the email template). One option for the email template, which was discussed in *Chapter 2, Best Practices for Collecting Feedback through Surveys*, is to embed the first question in the email template. To insert the first question, place your cursor on the location where you would like the question to be inserted, then click on **Embed survey question** in the toolbar (see *Figure 7.12*):

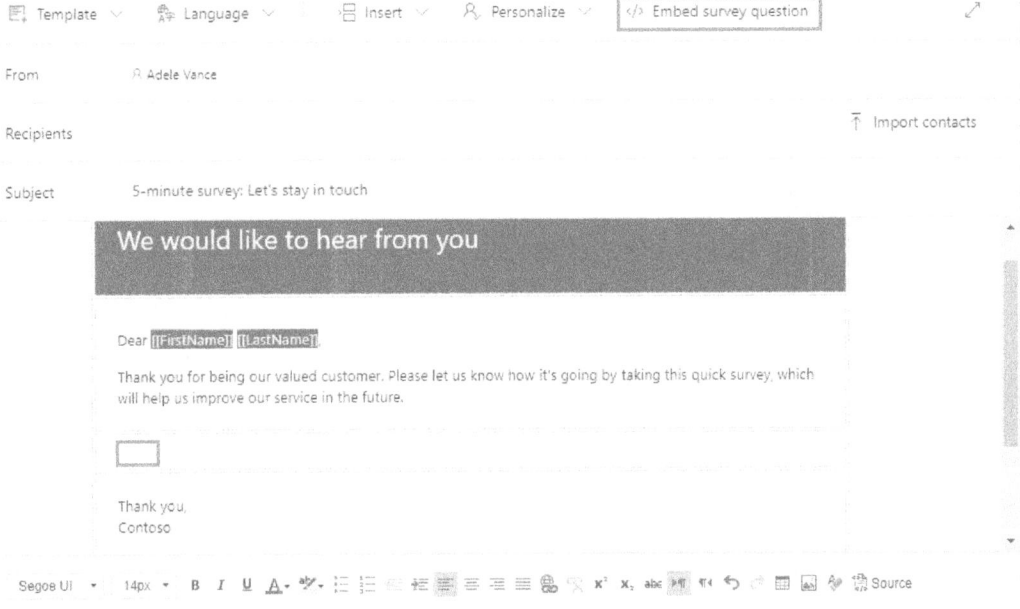

Figure 7.12 – Inserting a survey question in the email invitation

2. After you have the email template ready, you can proceed with uploading the survey recipient list.

3. Click on the **Import contact** link in the email recipient field in the email editor to download the import contact templates (see *Figure 7.13*):

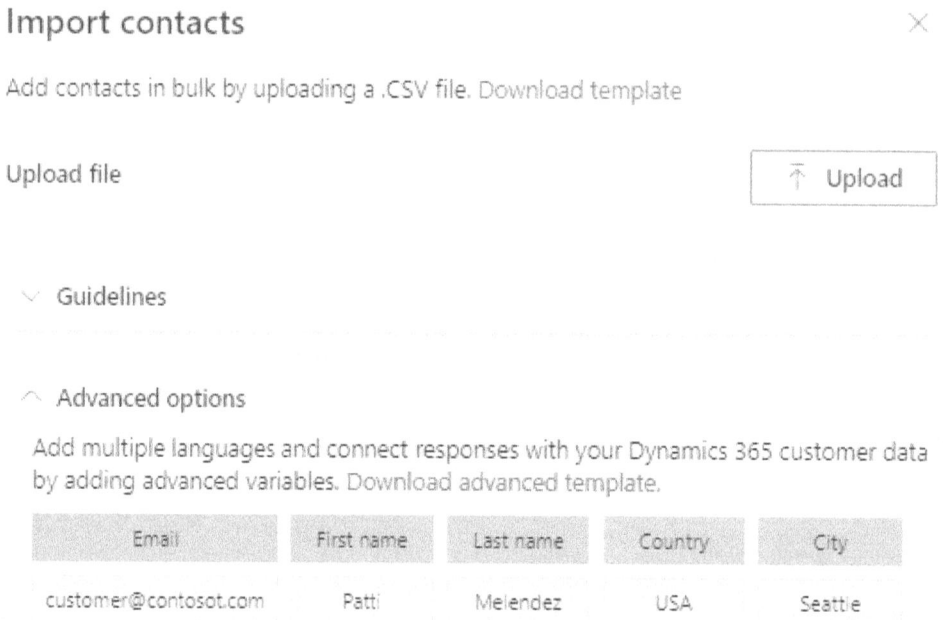

Figure 7.13 – Import contact panel

There are two types of templates for uploading the list of recipients:

Basic template – Use this template if you do not use Dynamics 365 as your CRM system and do not need to automatically connect survey responses with customer records in Dynamics 365.

Advanced template –This includes fields to map recipients to record IDs in Dynamics 365.

4. For this example, you need to connect the survey response to Dynamics 365, so click **Download advanced template** and populate the file with the survey recipient information, making sure the variables are populated accurately with values that are relevant to each contact (see *Figure 7.14* for an example of a completed file).

> **Important note**
>
> To obtain a contact entity's ID, you can export contact records from the Dynamics 365 contact view. The exported Excel file by default hides the contact record IDs. You can unhide the columns and the record IDs should be in column **A**.

	A	B	C	D	E	F	G	H	I
1	Email Address	First Name	Last name	MobileCustomer	BranchCustomer	PrimaryBranch	locale	RegardingID	RegardingEntityName
2	susanb@M365	Susan	Burk	Yes	Yes	Seattle	en-us	c6d00c79-d947-e	contact
3	renev@M365B	Rene	Valdes	Yes	Yes	San Diego	en-us	c0d00c79-d947-e	contact
4	yvonnem@M3(	Yvonne	McKay	Yes	Yes	San Diego	en-us	b0d00c79-d947-e	contact
5	sydneyh@M36	Sydney	Higa	Yes	Yes	Seattle	en-us	b8d00c79-d947-e	contact
6	susannas@M36	Susanna	Stubberod	Yes	Yes	Seattle	en-us	b2d00c79-d947-e	contact
7	scotts@M365B	Scott	Konersmann	Yes	Yes	San Diego	en-us	bad00c79-d947-e	contact
8	robertl@M365E	Robert	Lyon	No	Yes	San Diego	en-us	bcd00c79-d947-e	contact
9	patricks@M365	Patrick	Sands	No	Yes	Seattle	en-us	c4d00c79-d947-e	contact
10	paulc@M365B7	Paul	Cannon	No	Yes	Seattle	en-us	bed00c79-d947-e	contact
11	nancya@M365E	Nancy	Anderson	No	Yes	San Diego	en-us	b4d00c79-d947-e	contact
12	mariac@M365E	Maria	Campbell	Yes	No		en-us	b6d00c79-d947-e	contact
13	thomasa@M36	Thomas	Andersen	Yes	No		en-us	c8d00c79-d947-e	contact
14	jimg@M365B7	Jim	Glynn	Yes	No		en-us	c2d00c79-d947-e	contact

Figure 7.14 – An example of the completed recipient list

5. Upload the completed list by clicking the **Upload** button in the import contact panel (see *Figure 7.13*).

6. Click **Send** on the email editor page to start distributing the survey.

> **Important note**
>
> For each recipient on the list, Customer Voice generates a personalized email invitation with a unique survey link. Through this unique link, Customer Voice identifies who responded to the survey without requiring the recipient to log in. When the survey response is received, Customer Voice looks up the contact identity and, if there is a **Regarding Identifier** associated with the survey invite, Customer Voice automatically links the survey response to the Dynamics 365 record. The survey invitation and response are added as activities to the contact and automatically appear on the activity timeline.

Now that you have sent the survey invite, you can monitor the status of the survey invitation in Customer Voice.

Monitoring survey invite status

When sending survey invites through Customer Voice, you can monitor progress by opening the **Send** tab for your survey. For example, when **Susan Burk** receives the email invitation and reads the email, the number of invitations with the **Read** status is updated (see *Figure 7.15*). Opening the **Details** pane will list the invitees and their status:

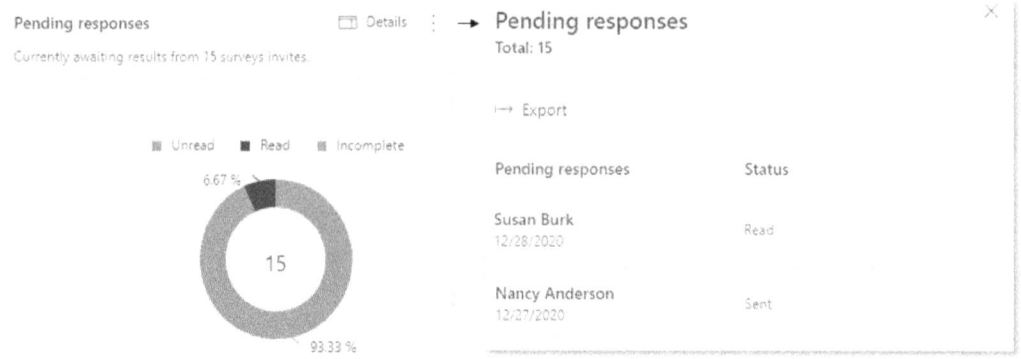

Figure 7.15 – Read status report

When Susan opened the survey link, a survey page is opened, as shown in *Figure 7.16*. Notice that the survey is personalized with the primary branch information (such as **Seattle**). Since the survey variable values for **MobileCustomer** and **BranchCustomer** are set to Yes for Susan (refer to the recipient list in *Figure 7.14*), she sees questions for both branch experience and mobile app experience:

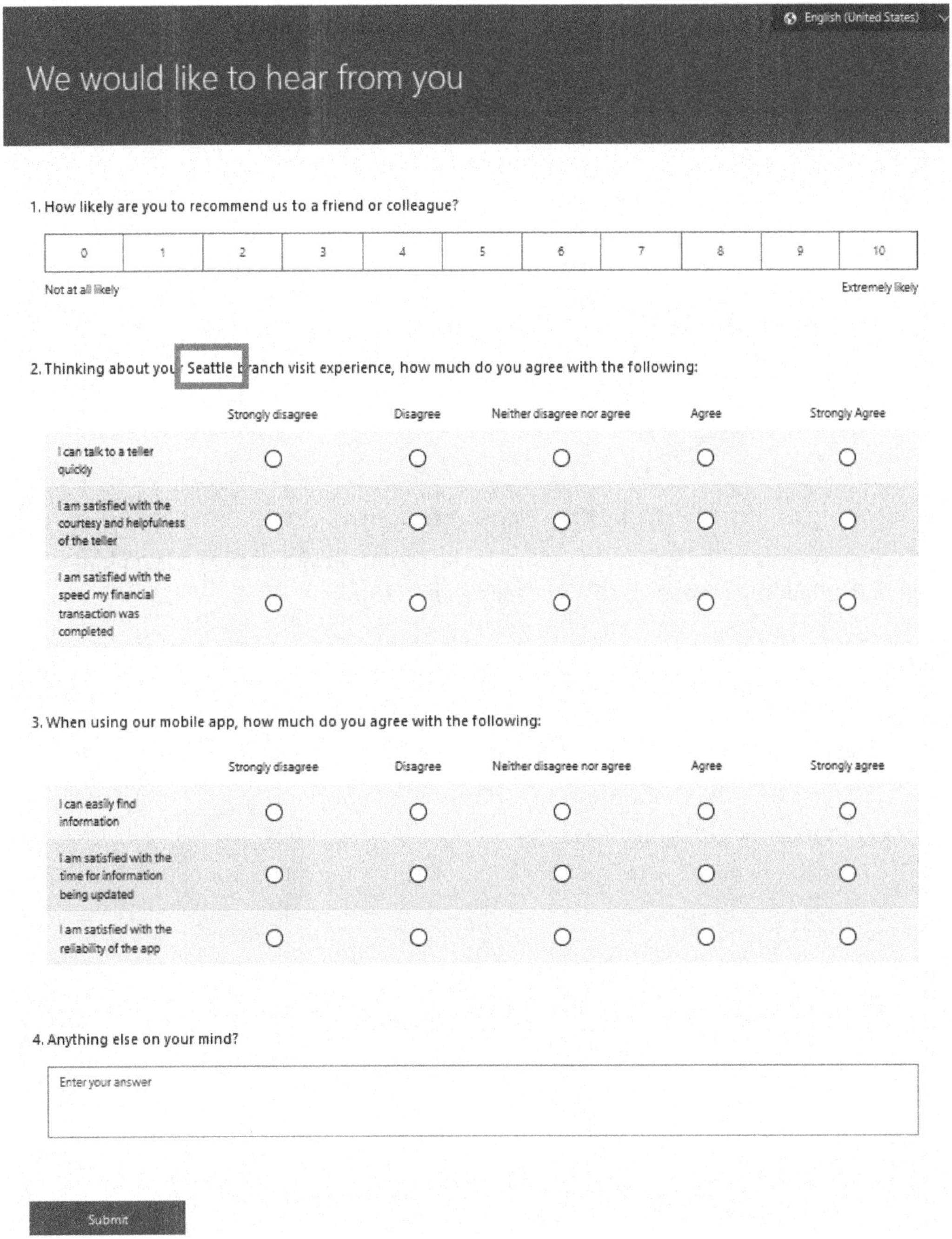

Figure 7.16 – Personalized survey page shown to the recipient

When Susan opens the link, the status on the Customer Voice **Pending response** report is updated to **Opened** (see *Figure 7.17*):

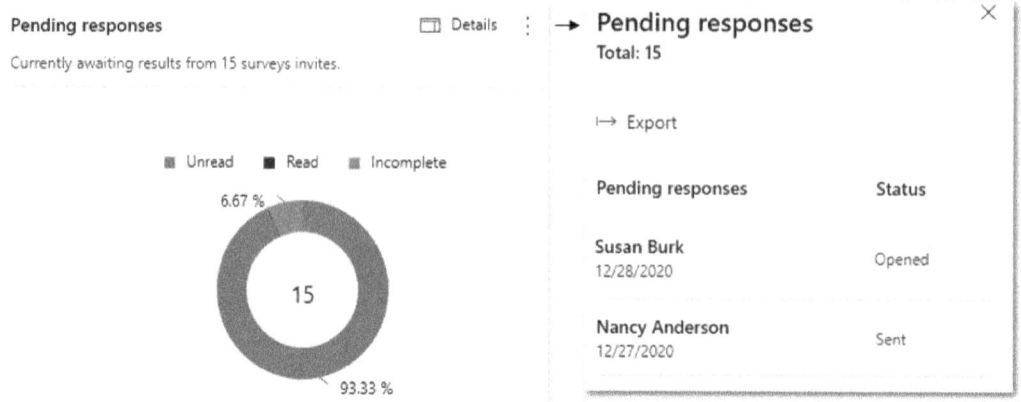

Figure 7.17 – Opened status report

After Susan responds to the survey, her status is changed to **Responded** and is no longer tracked in the **Pending responses** section (see *Figure 7.18*):

Figure 7.18 – Updated report after a survey is complete

After a while, if you still do not get the responses you need, you can send a survey reminder through Customer Voice with the following steps:

1. Click **Send a reminder** in the **Pending responses** section to open the reminder settings.

2. Configure the reminder settings (see *Figure 7.19*):

    When: You can send the reminder immediately or send the reminder at a time when your recipients are likely to check their email. You can also send reminders automatically when you do not hear from the respondent after a few days.

    Send to recipients with: Specify the number of days to send a reminder. If the respondents do not respond after that day, then a reminder email is automatically sent:

Send a reminder ✕

When

○ Send now

○ Schedule for later

◉ Automatically

Send to recipients with

Pending responses **10** days after the original invite

10	days

Summary

A reminder will be sent **automatically** to recipients with pending responses **10** days after the original invite is sent

[Next]   Cancel

Figure 7.19 – Send a reminder setting

3.   Create a survey reminder email template.

4.   Click **Create new** in the template dropdown (see *Figure 7.20*). By default, the email template uses the same email template as the original invite. You must create a new template if you want to have a different email template for the reminder:

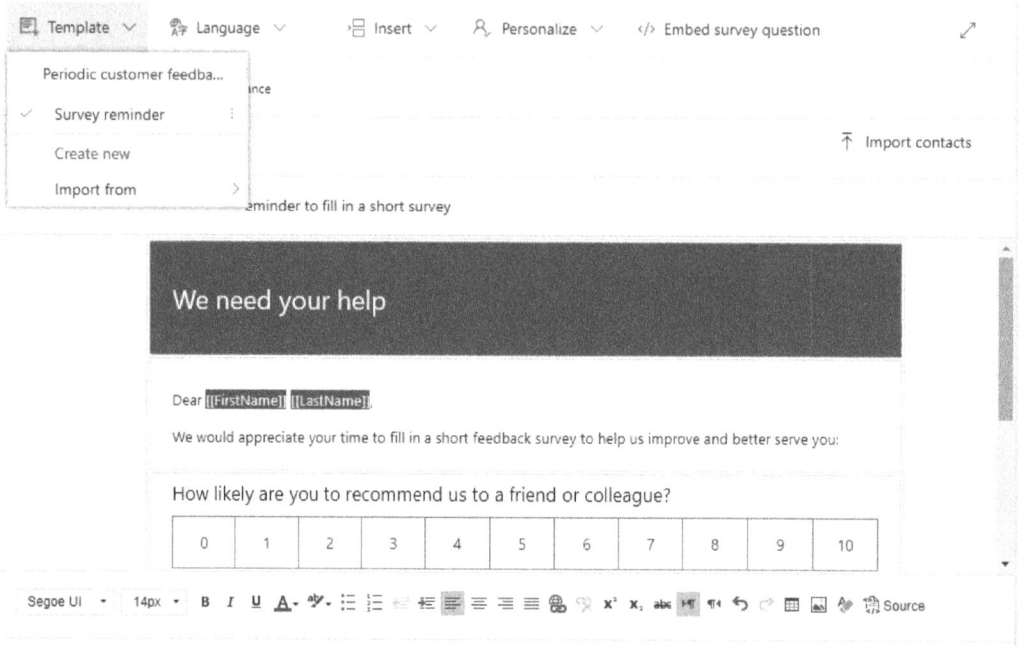

Figure 7.20 – Survey reminder email template

5.   After you send the reminder, the **Pending responses** section is updated with the reminder activity and its status (see *Figure 7.21*):

Active: The reminder is scheduled or in progress. You can modify active reminders by clicking **See all reminders** and selecting the **Edit** or **Delete** menu.

Completed: The reminder is sent to your recipients who have not responded. You can no longer edit completed reminders:

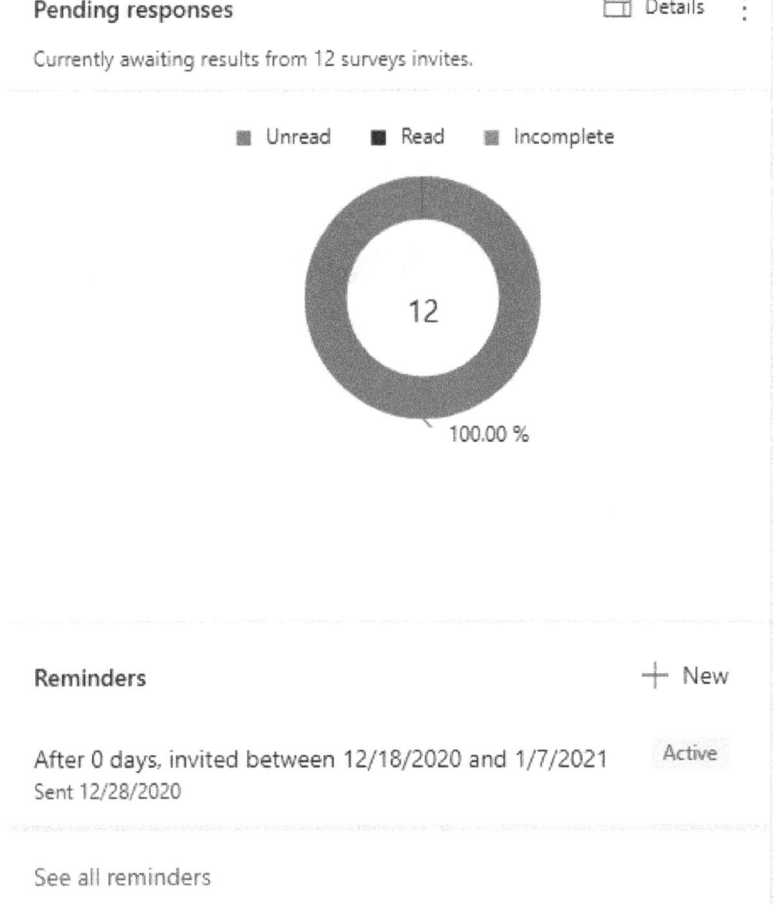

Figure 7.21 – Reminder activity history

When you have received the survey responses, you can start viewing the results.

Viewing survey results

Customer Voice provides different ways to view the survey results:

- View survey results in Customer Voice reports.
- View survey results in Dynamics 365.
- Create a custom dashboard using Power BI.

Let's look at each of these in turn.

View survey results in Customer Voice reports

There are two reports available in Customer Voice. The first is the satisfaction metrics dashboard report. For each satisfaction metric you defined in your project, Customer Voice reports the latest score and trend so you can measure your progress over time. In our example, we use two metrics: **NPS** and **sentiment**. *Figure 7.22* shows an example of a satisfaction metrics dashboard report:

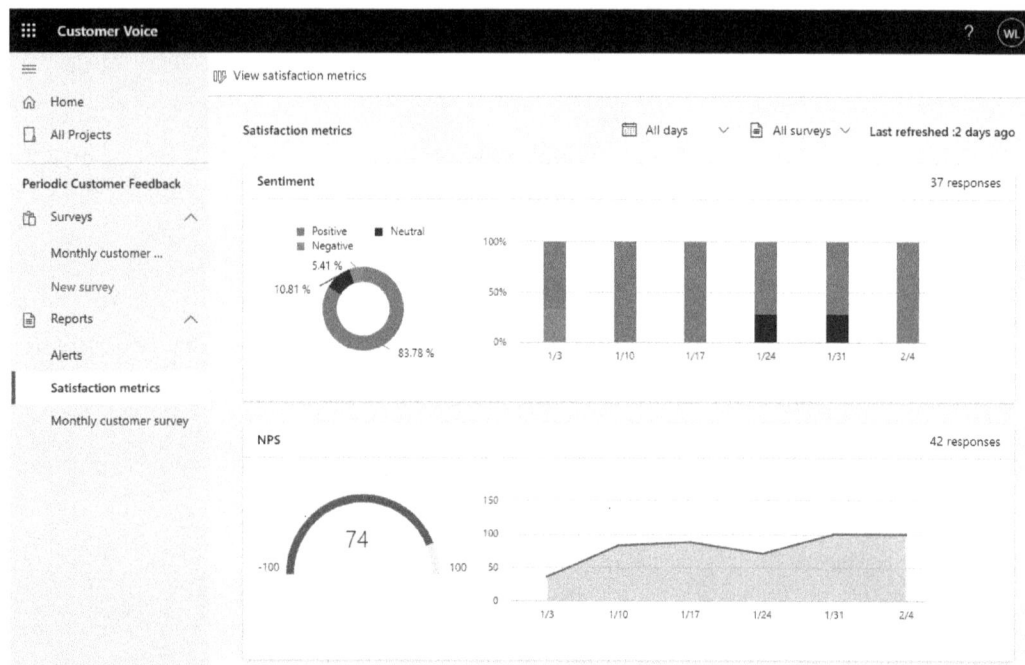

Figure 7.22 – An example of a satisfaction metrics dashboard

You can view individual survey reports in the **Reports** section in the left menu. The survey report summarizes the results from each question, and you can also view the individual survey responses by clicking the **Respondents** pane on the right and double-clicking the name of the recipient to view the detailed response (see *Figure 7.23*):

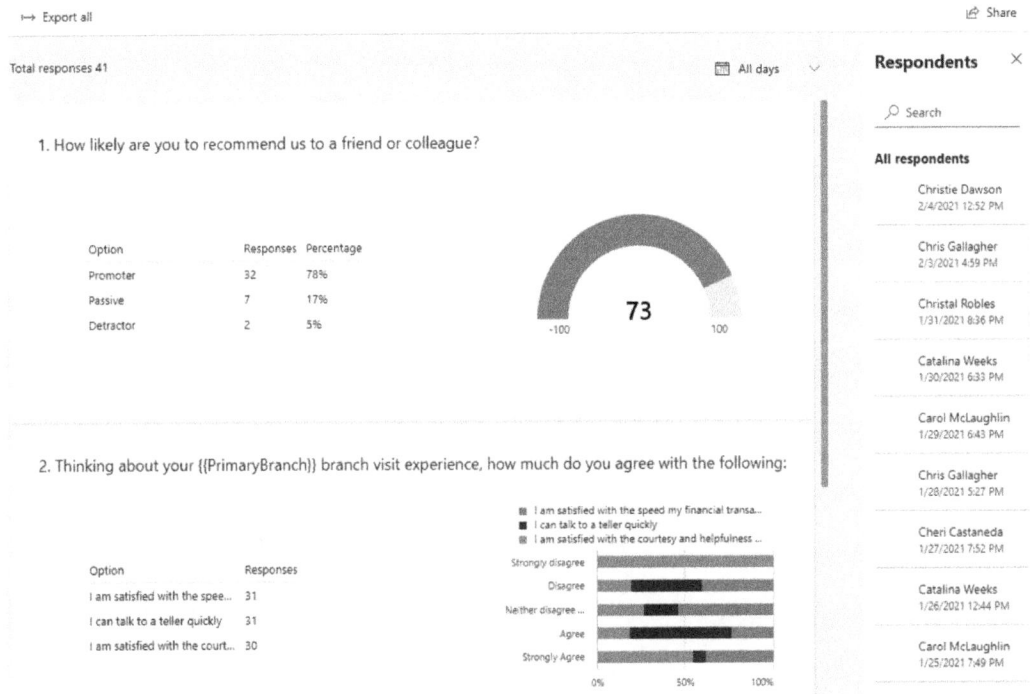

Figure 7.23 – Survey report summary

In addition to viewing the results in Customer Voice, you can view the survey results directly in Dynamics 365.

View survey results in Dynamics 365

When you associate the survey with Dynamics 365 entity records, the survey invites and survey responses automatically appear in the activity timeline for the record (see *Figure 7.24*):

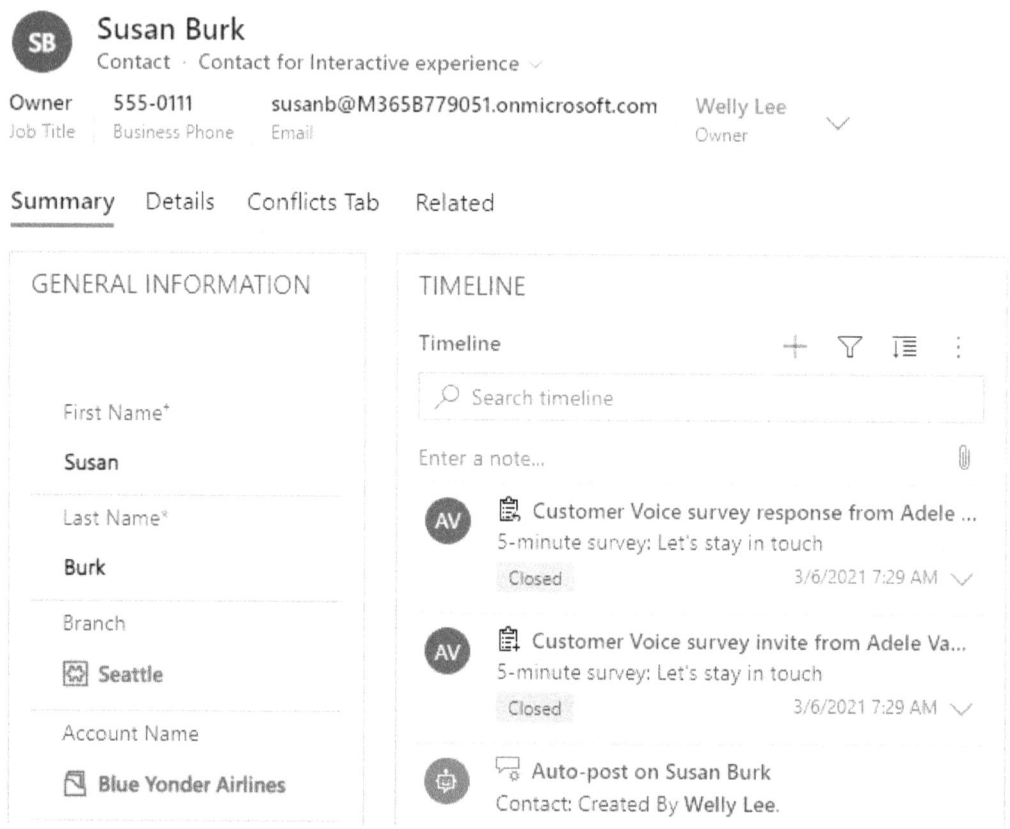

Figure 7.24 – Survey invites and survey response activities on Dynamics 365

Opening the Customer Voice survey response activity will show the detailed response, as shown in *Figure 7.25*:

5-minute survey: Let's stay in touch						Normal	12/28/2020 10:09 AM	Open	Adele Vance	∨
Customer Voice survey response						Priority	Due Date	Activity Status	Owner	

General   Related

🔒 Name	1	🔒 Subject	5-minute survey: Let's s...	🔒 Submit date	12/28/2020 📅
🔒 From	🏴 Susan Burk	🔒 Respondent	Susan Burk	🔒 Respondent email address	susanb@M365B779051.on...
🔒 Survey	● Monthly customer su...	🔒 Survey Invite	📋 5-minute survey: Let'...	🔒 Survey response URL	https://customervoice.... ⊕
🔒 Regarding	🏴 Susan Burk	🔒 Start Date	12/28/2020 📅 10:09 AM	🔒 Language	{"localeId":"en-us","localeN...
🔒 Locale	---	🔒 NPS Score	10	🔒 Sentiment	Positive
🔒 Other properties	---	🔒 Context Data	{"EmbedContextPara meters":null,"PipeData ▼	🔒 Created By	○ 👤 Adele Vance
				🔒 Source survey identifier	OSH9Ht8nM0ePrpnFfa9ny...

Response Details

Responses   Satisfaction metrics   Personalization

Question	Response
How likely are you to recommend us to a friend or colleague?	10
Thinking about your {{PrimaryBranch}} branch visit experience, how much do you agree with the following:	

Figure 7.25 – Survey response detail

Anyone who can access the contact's activities will be able to view the survey responses. This is important so that anyone who needs to work with the customer can get the feedback. In addition to the survey responses, you can also view survey variables and satisfaction metrics values by opening the different tabs in the **Response Details** section.

As survey responses are linked to the customer records, you can create a custom dashboard that combines survey response data and customer records in your Dynamics 365 system.

Create a custom dashboard using Power BI

Customer Voice integrates with Power BI to enable you to create a custom report. Power BI is a flexible reporting tool that enables you to create a report that's specific to your needs. Since Customer Voice survey responses are saved to your organization's Dataverse, you can use the built-in connector in Power BI to connect to Dataverse for your dashboard without requiring you to export survey data and import it again to your reporting platform. For our example, as shown in *Figure 7.26*, I created a custom dashboard to link the survey response to the customer information in Dynamics 365:

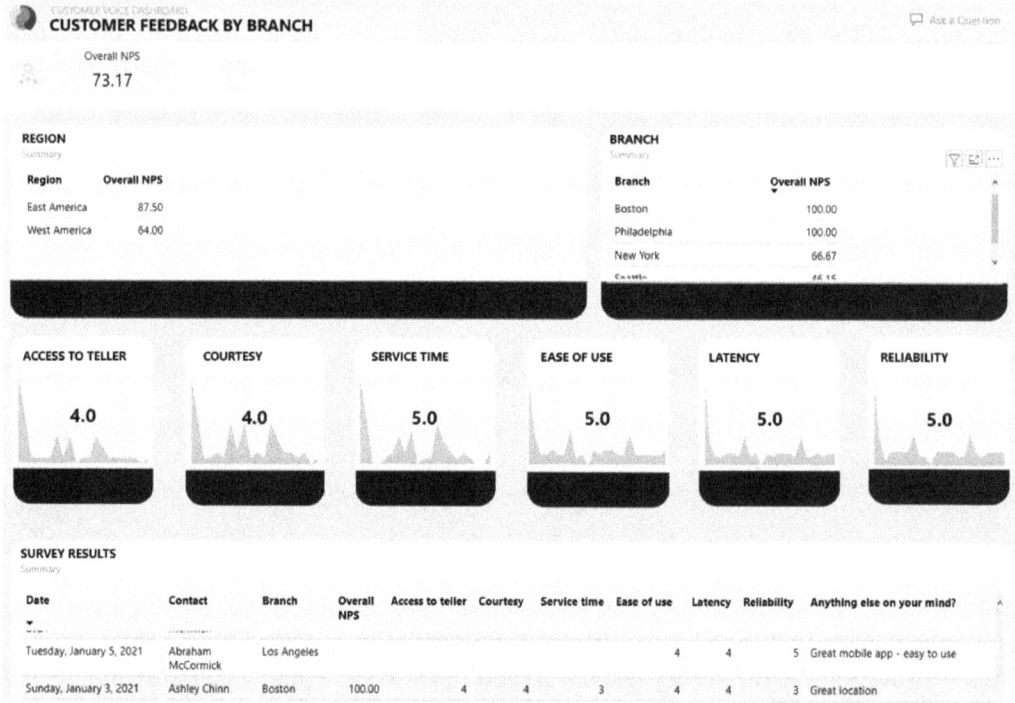

Figure 7.26 – An example of a dashboard that shows survey results by region and branch

I recorded a step-by-step video walkthrough to create the preceding dashboard, which you can find at the following links:

https://bit.ly/3upDWku

https://bit.ly/3vqYtGE

Summary

In this chapter, we went over an example of a customer experience manager at a bank who collects feedback from her customers each month using a list of customers provided by her operations team. This example is based on real-life scenarios from two bank customers I have worked with.

We discussed how you could send surveys, which are linked to her Dynamics 365 system. The survey responses are automatically captured in Dynamics 365 so that anyone in the company working with the customer can get the latest customer feedback. You can also create a custom Power BI dashboard to view the survey results and combine the customer feedback with other customer information. Since the Power BI dashboard is connected directly to the backend system, you do not need to export data from the survey system and import it into the reporting system. The Power BI dashboard can be refreshed periodically so that everyone will always get the latest information.

In the next chapter, we will discuss how to automate sending surveys based on business transactions such as when a support case is resolved in your CRM system.

8
Automating Customer Support Surveys with Dynamics 365 Customer Voice

Collecting feedback after a customer service call is standard practice for a customer service process. After a customer support issue is resolved, the customer often gets given a survey to ask for their feedback. Customer Voice includes a template to help you implement feedback in your customer service process. The template not only includes common survey questionnaires for customer service feedback but also includes a workflow to automate sending the feedback request when a support case is resolved. In addition, Customer Voice provides a Power BI report template to show the feedback results in the context of support cases.

In this chapter, we will look at how you can use and customize those templates. Note that we will go over a workflow as part of the template and require some working knowledge of Power Automate. If you are new to Power Automate, please check out Microsoft learn resource at `https://docs.microsoft.com/en-us/learn/modules/ get-started-flows`. In addition to review the support template, we will also discuss additional ways you can collect feedback as part of your customer support process, such as collecting feedback through text messages and chat.

The chapter covers the following:

- Customizing Customer Voice support templates
- Customizing Customer Voice report templates
- Additional ways to collect customer support feedback

We will start with using and customizing Customer Voice support templates.

Customizing Customer Voice support templates

Customer Voice includes several out-of-the-box templates for common customer feedback scenarios. At the time of writing, it includes eight templates with more currently being developed. You can use a template to create a Customer Voice project using the following steps:

1. Go to `https://customervoice.microsoft.com` and click **New project**.
2. From the template selection screen, select **Support** and click **Next**.
3. On the location selection screen, select the Dynamics 365 environment you are using for Customer Service. Click **Create** to create the project.

> **Tip**
> If you are not using Dynamics 365 for your CRM system, you can use the default location provided by Customer Voice.

Customer Voice will then create a project that includes survey questions, satisfaction metrics, email templates, and the Power Automate workflow. After it is finished, you will see the project as shown in *Figure 8.1*:

Hi {{First Name}},

We appreciate your business, and we hope you had a great experience with our customer service. Please share your feedback so we can make the experience even better.

1. How would you rate the overall quality of our customer service?

Dissatisfied ☆ ☆ ☆ ☆ ☆ Satisfied

2. How long did it take us to address your questions and concerns?

○ Longer than expected

○ As expected

○ Shorter than expected

3. How would you rate your satisfaction with our customer service representative in terms of:

	Very dissatisfied	Dissatisfied	Neutral	Satisfied	Very satisfied
Timeliness of resolution	○	○	○	○	○
Courtesy and professionalism	○	○	○	○	○
Product knowledge and competence	○	○	○	○	○
Ability to resolve issue during the first call	○	○	○	○	○

4. Please share any other feedback on how we can improve our service:

Enter your answer

Figure 8.1 – Project created from a support template

The project template creates a survey with common questions for a customer service scenario. The questions are just a starting point for you and can be modified.

Customizing survey questions

Customize the survey questions by removing the questions that you do not need and adding questions based on your business requirements.

> **Important note**
>
> The first question, **How would you rate the overall quality of our customer service?**, is a rating metric question that is used by Dynamics 365 for Customer Service to auto-populate CSAT scores in the app. If you remove the CSAT metrics or any related questions, the CSAT score for a case is no longer populated.

In addition to adding and removing questions, you can personalize and brand your survey as we have discussed in the previous two chapters. One thing to note is that you can also translate your survey questions into different languages. This is important when you have customers that speak different languages.

To translate survey questions, use the following steps:

1. From the **Customization** panel, open the **Language** setting. The language setting allows you to translate the survey questions into other languages.

2. Click **Add language** to create a translated survey. For example, select **Español** to add the Spanish translation.

3. Add the translation by editing the language via clicking the *edit* (pencil) icon next to the language name, or click **download an Excel template here** to get a translation file. We will use a translation file in this example:

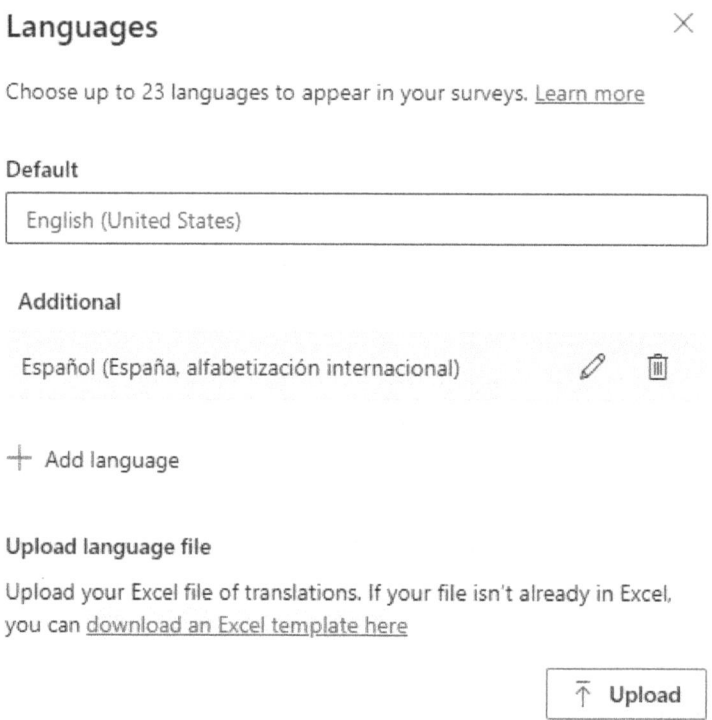

Figure 8.2 – Editing survey translation

4. Open the downloaded file and add the translated text under the provided language column (see the completed file in *Figure 8.3*):

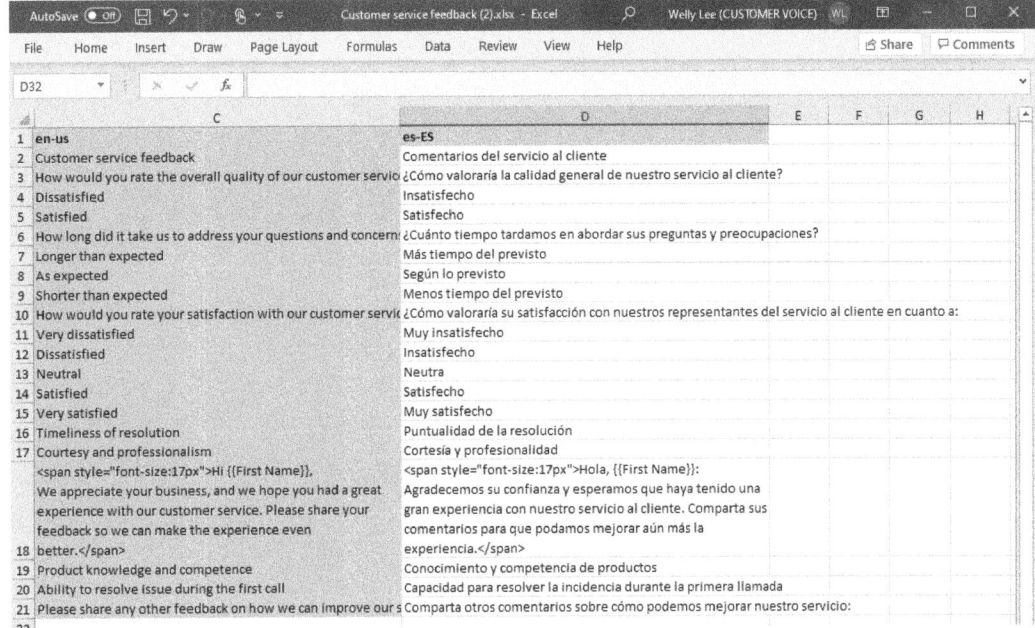

Figure 8.3 – Completed survey translation file

> **Important note**
>
> When you add multiple languages, each language appears as a separate column in the same file.
>
> If you are using a survey variable in the text question, make sure to start with {{ and end with }}.
>
> By default, Customer Voice supports all languages supported by Dynamics 365. If you would like to translate your survey beyond the supported language, you can add a column directly on the translation file and include the language code as the first row. See `https://docs.microsoft.com/en-us/dynamics365/customer-voice/create-multilingual-survey` for the list of language codes to use.

5. Return to the language setting and upload the completed translation file.

6. Review the translated language by previewing the survey and select the language from the dropdown in the upper right. See *Figure 8.4* for the survey preview:

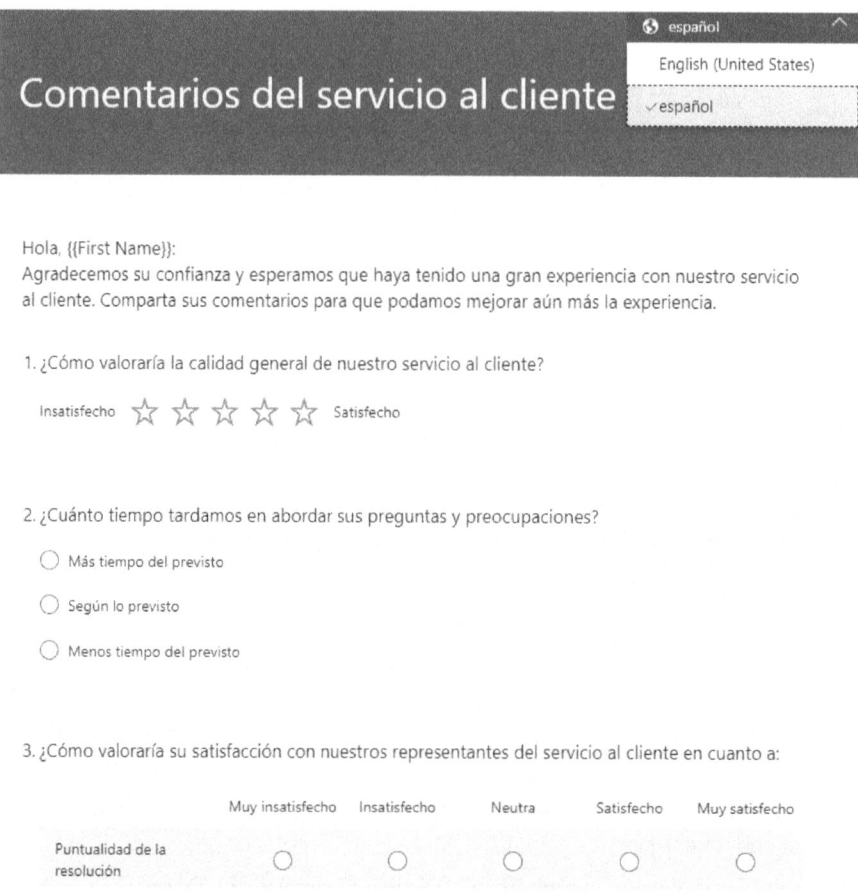

Figure 8.4 – Previewing the survey in another language

Important note

Customer Voice automatically shows the translated survey based on the user's browser language. A dropdown appears at the top of the survey to allow the user to switch to another language.

If there is no matching language, Customer Voice will use the closest language available (for example, if the user's browser language is fr-be and there is no French Belgian translation, it will use the French (fr-fr) translation). If there is no close language translation available, Customer Voice will use the primary language defined in the survey.

Now that you have the survey questions ready, you can proceed to customizing the automation workflow.

Customizing email templates

The Customer Voice support template includes an automation workflow; here, the workflow sends a survey invitation link via email when a support case is resolved in Dynamics 365. You can use the steps we discussed in *Chapter 6, Conducting an Employee Survey with Dynamics 365 Customer Voice*, to customize the email template. In addition, if you are translating your survey questions into a different language, you should also translate your email template according to the survey language.

The following are the steps for translating the survey invitation email:

1. Create an email template (refer to the steps for creating an email in *Chapter 6, Conducting an Employee Survey with Dynamics 365 Customer Voice*).

    Since the survey is created in both English and Spanish, you need to create a separate email template for Spanish.

2. Add a language to the email template through **Language>Choose language** (see *Figure 7.10*):

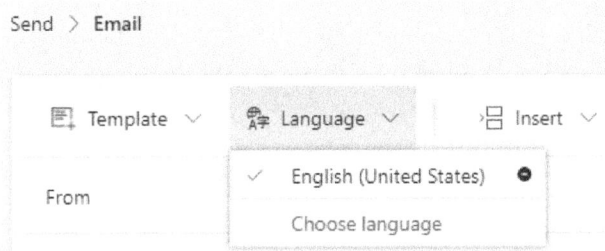

Figure 8.5 – Add the language for the survey email template

3. Select the language to create the email template. Note that you can only select from the languages defined in your survey. For example, if your survey is translated into Spanish, then the list will include **español**. Click **Add** to add the language for your email template.

4. Select the added language (**español**) to translate the email template (see *Figure 8.6*):

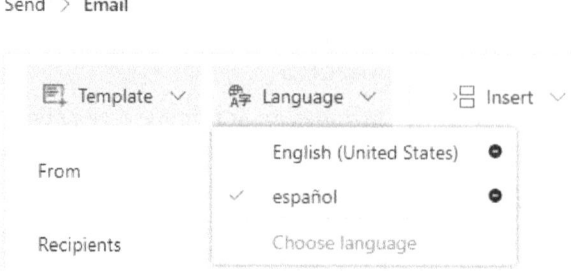

Figure 8.6 – Email template language selector

5. Translate the email template (see *Figure 8.7* for an example translation):

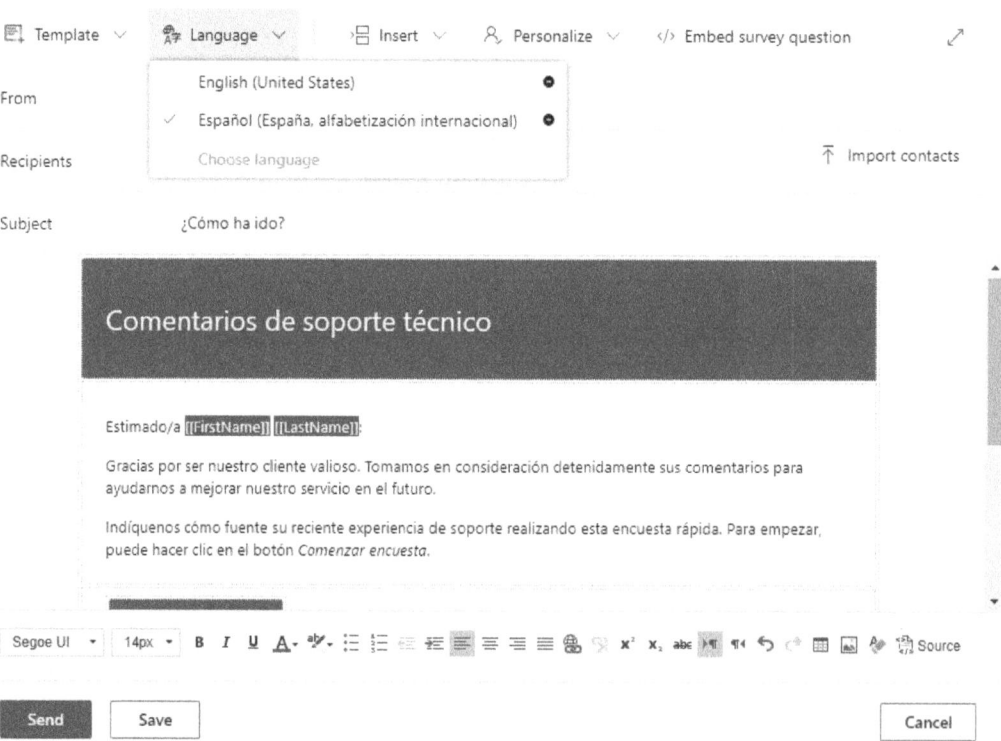

Figure 8.7 – An example of a translated email template

> **Important note**
>
> To align with your organization's policy and any regulatory requirements, such as the **CAN-SPAM** Act in the United States, you may need to include an unsubscribe link in the email to allow your recipient to opt out from receiving emails in the future.
>
> Customer Voice supports unsubscribe functionality that you can add to the survey invitation email. If your recipient clicks on the link, the email is stored in the **Customer Voice unsubscribed recipients** table in your Dataverse instance.
>
> When you use Customer Voice to send a survey invitation email (either from the Customer Voice web interface or through Power Automate), Customer Voice first checks whether the email address exists in the **Customer Voice unsubscribed recipients** table. If the email address exists in that table, Customer Voice will not send emails to it and will show status of **Unsubscribed** in the survey invitation report.
>
> If you have an existing email unsubscribe system, you can use a Power Automate workflow to synch the **Customer Voice unsubscribed recipients** table with your email unsubscribe system.

After you are done with the email template, you can proceed with setting up the workflow.

Customizing the automation workflow

Customer Voice includes built-in integration with Power Automate. The out-of-the-box support template includes a workflow to automate sending the feedback survey when a support case is resolved in Dynamics 365.

> **Important note**
>
> The support template automates sending a survey link based on activity in Dynamics 365. If you are using Salesforce to manage your customer support, you can remove the default workflow and replace it with a **Send a survey when a case is closed in Salesforce** workflow template for Customer Voice. If you are using another customer support app, you need to customize the template by replacing the workflow trigger with that of your application.

You can find the workflow using your browser by going to `https://flow.microsoft.com`. Make sure to select the right environment according to your Customer Voice project (see *Figure 8.8*):

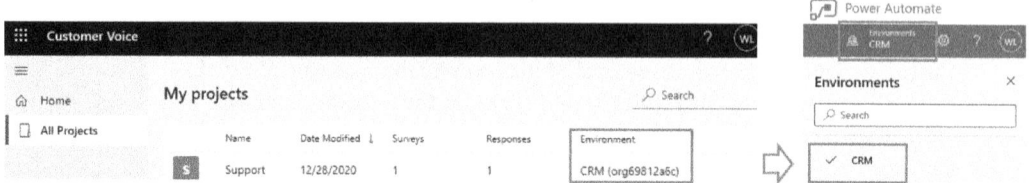

Figure 8.8 – Environment selector in Power Automate

Click on **My flows** from the left navigation pane and look for **Send a survey when a case is resolved in Dynamics 365**. This flow is created when you create a project using the **Support** template in Customer Voice (see *Figure 8.9*):

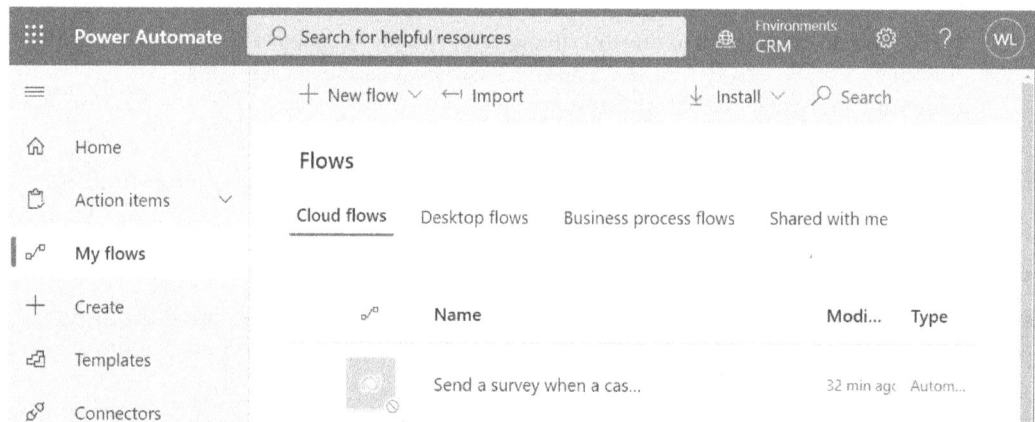

Figure 8.9 – A flow created by the Customer Voice support template

Select the flow and click on **Edit** to open the flow.

The flow uses a **Microsoft Dataverse** trigger when a case is resolved (in Dynamics 365). You can view the triggering condition by expanding the box and clicking **….** In the pane that opens, click **Settings** (see *Figure 8.10*):

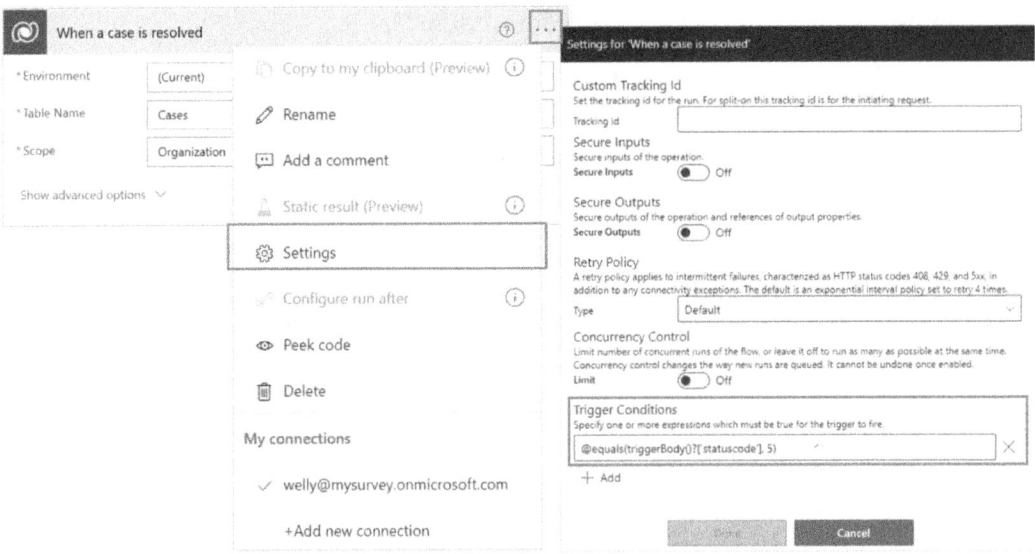

Figure 8.10 – Accessing Settings on the workflow trigger

The **Settings** pane shows a trigger condition, `@equals(triggerBody()?` `['statuscode'], 5)`, which means the flow will start when the **statuscode** field in the **Cases** table is changed to 5.

> **Important note**
> Make sure to check whether your system is using the same resolve status code in Dynamics. I have been in several troubleshooting sessions where a flow failed to start because of a different status code being used in Dynamics.

Back in the flow, we take the following steps:

1. When a case is resolved, we check the type of customer record associated with the case. In Dynamics 365, you can link a support case to a customer contact (individual) or an account (company). Depending on the type of customer, you will need to get different information to complete the flow.

2. Get the contact detail information based on the primary contact ID from *Step 1*.

3. Send the survey to the contact email address from *Step 2*.

    See *Figure 8.11* for the flow based on this sequence:

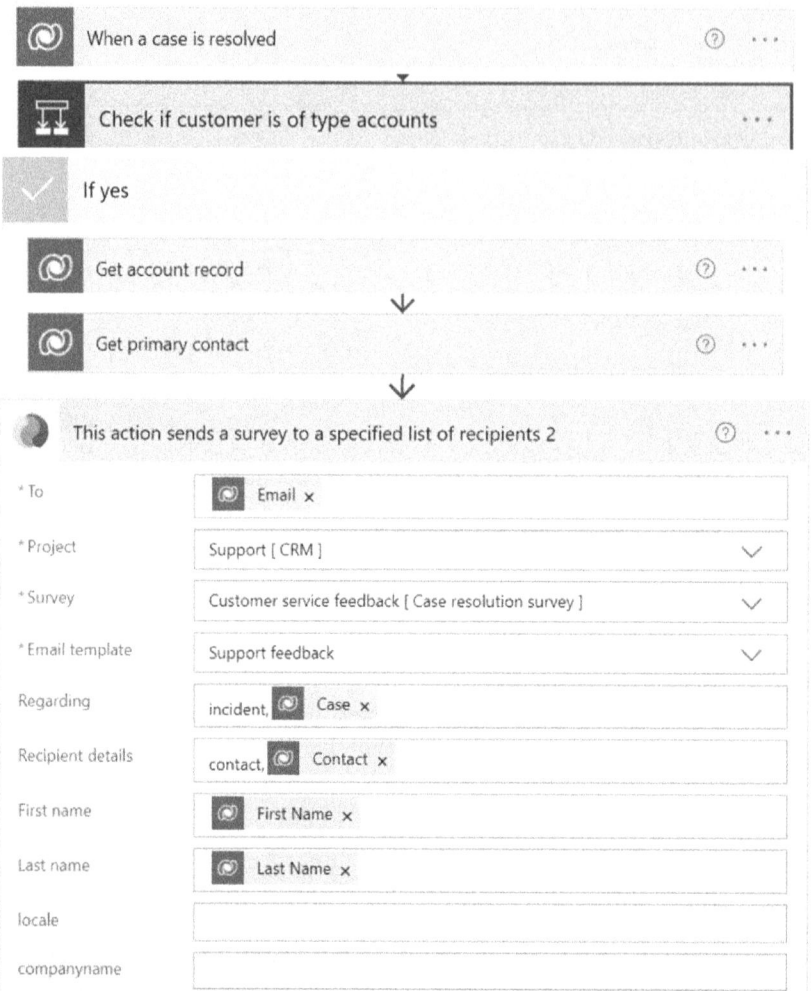

Figure 8.11 – Flow to automate sending a survey when a case is resolved in Dynamics 365

The flow uses the Customer Voice **Send a survey** action, which has the following parameters:

- **To**: Email address to receive the survey.

- **Project**: Customer Voice project name.

- **Survey**: Survey name (filtered based on the selected project).

- **Email template**: Email template name to be used when sending the survey. If the email template has multiple languages, you can specify the language code in the **Locale** field.

- **Regarding**: Record ID to associate the survey invitation and response with (from the case details).

- **Recipient details**: Contact record ID to associate the survey invitation and response with (from the contact information). Note that Customer Voice only supports linking survey records to the contact table. If you would like to link the survey response to another table, use the corresponding field.

- **First name**: First name of the recipient (from the contact record).

- **Last name**: Last name of the recipient (from the contact record).

- **Locale**: Language code for the survey email template and survey. If you leave this blank, Customer Voice will use the primary language for the email template and will use the user's language browser setting to display the survey language.

- **companyname**: A survey variable from the Support template. The companyname variable is used to replace the signature at the end of the email template. You can either type your company name or, if you modify the email template and are not using the survey variable value to sign your email, you can ignore this field and leave it empty.

If you use additional survey variables in the survey, the survey variables are automatically listed after you pick the survey name from the dropdown. You can then populate the value by using **Dynamic content** in Power Automate.

In addition to selecting **Project** and **Survey** names from the dropdown, you can use **Dynamic content** (see *Figure 8.12*):

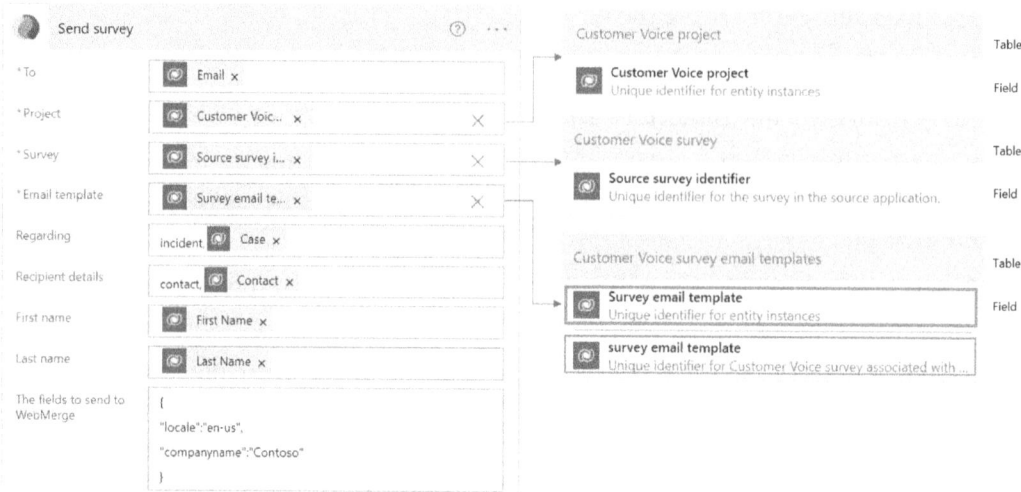

Figure 8.12 – Using Dynamic content to specify a Customer Voice project, survey, and email template

However, if you use **Dynamic content**, then the survey variables are not automatically listed and you need to specify the survey variables using JSON format as follows: `{"locale":"<LOCALE>","companyname":"<NAME>"}`, where `locale` and `companyname` are the survey variables.

The **Send a survey** action in Power Automate uses the Customer Voice email service to send the survey invitation. Customer Voice uses the same scalable email service that Dynamics 365 Marketing uses to send large volumes of emails. The email service platform includes email tracking capability (to report if the recipient opens the email) and **reputation management** support to minimize the likelihood that your recipients' email service providers (for example, **Outlook**, **Gmail**, and **Yahoo**) flag the email as spam. The Dynamics 365 Marketing team actively monitors email traffic and engages with major email service providers to resolve any issues. Note that you do not need a Dynamics 365 Marketing license to send survey invitations with Customer Voice.

To increase the response rate, you can send an email to remind your customers of the survey if you haven't heard from them.

Customizing survey reminders

Customer Voice supports automatically sending a reminder if the recipient has not responded after a few days. Follow these steps to configure this:

1. Go to `https://customervoice.microsoft.com` and open your project.

2. Click on the **Send** tab to open the survey distribution report (see *Figure 8.13*):

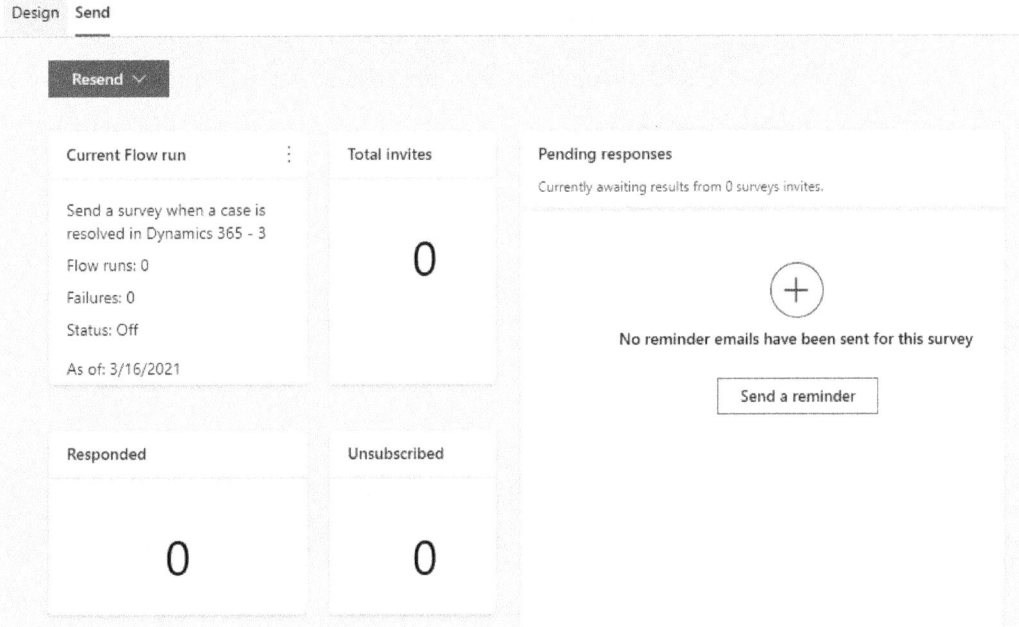

Figure 8.13 – Survey distribution report

3. Click **Send a reminder** to create a survey reminder schedule.

4. Select the **Send automatically** option and specify the number of days from the invite sent date to send a reminder. For example, if you specify 3 days, then if after 3 days from the survey invitation date the recipient has not responded, a reminder email with the same survey link will be sent to the recipient.

5. Edit the survey reminder email template. Make sure to edit the template for all languages you are using in your survey (see an example in *Figure 8.14*):

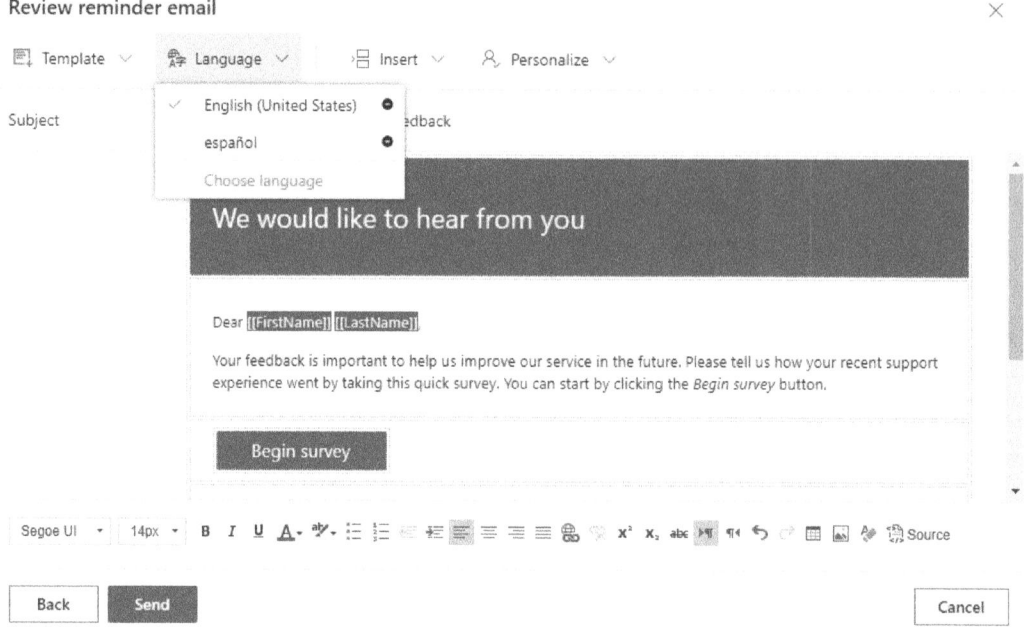

Figure 8.14 – Survey reminder email template

Another setting you may want to consider is to set the limit on how frequently your customers receive a survey.

Setting a survey limit

To minimize contacting customers for feedback, many organizations have a contact policy for how frequently a customer can receive feedback requests. Customer Voice supports setting a number of days before your customer can receive another survey.

To set this up, follow these steps:

1. From the **Send** tab, open the **Customization** panel on the right.

2. Open the **Distribution** setting.

3. Expand the **Email** section.

4. Turn on **Contact frequency limits** and specify a number of days before the next survey invite can be sent (see *Figure 8.15*):

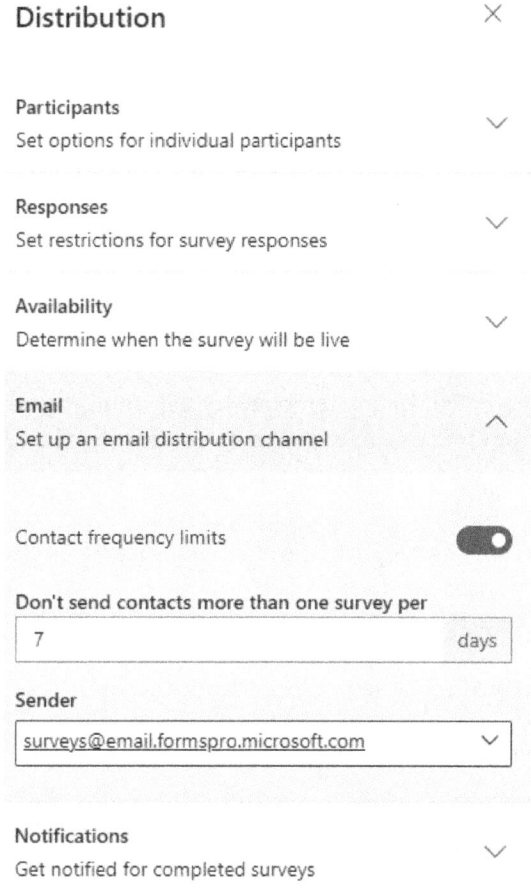

Figure 8.15 – Contact limit setting

When the automated workflow triggers sending a survey, Customer Voice first checks the last time the recepient (using the email address as the identifier) received a survey. If the number of days is less than what is specified, the invite will not be created.

After you receive a survey response, you can use a Customer Voice report to analyze the results.

Customizing the Customer Voice report template

When using the support template, the Customer Voice survey invitations and survey responses are automatically added to the contact and support case's activity timeline in Dynamics 365. Opening the survey response activity will show the Dynamics 365 user the survey results, as we discussed in *Chapter 7, Collecting Periodic Customer Feedback with Customer Voice*.

Since the survey response is linked to the case, you can create a custom Power BI report that can combine case information with survey results.

Customer Voice provides a Power BI app template to help you get started. You can download the template from `https://aka.ms/customervoice/pbi/support`.

The dashboard has three pages:

- **Overview**: CSAT scores by support case attribute, such as location, case priority, case origin, case type, and product

- **Agent Performance**: CSAT scores by support agent handling the case

- **Customer Satisfaction**: CSAT scores by customer account

Figure 8.16 shows the average CSAT score from the survey for each customer support agent handling the case:

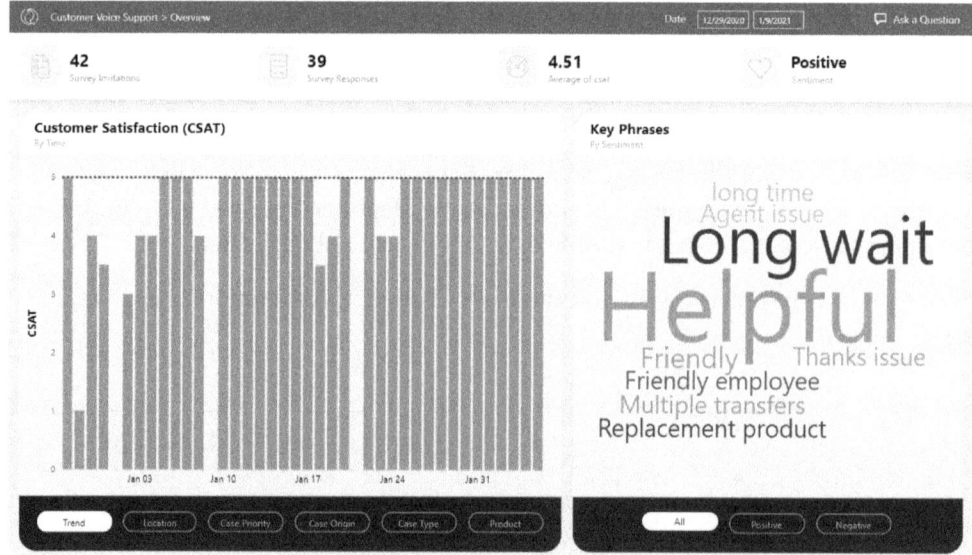

Figure 8.16 – Customer satisfaction by Agent Performance

The report also shows a **word cloud** of key phrases from the text comments from the surveys to summarize what the customers have been saying. Clicking the name of the agent filters the word cloud to show only the text comments related to that specific agent.

So far, we have discussed how you can use and customize the support template in Customer Voice. The template includes a Power Automate workflow to automatically send an email with a personalized survey link to the customer.

In the next section, we will discuss other options available for you to collect feedback as part of your customer service process.

Additional ways to collect customer support feedback

Customer Voice provides flexibility as to when you can send a survey, how to deliver survey invitations, and how to collect feedback. Let's start with sending the survey invitation.

Sending surveys on demand from Dynamics 365

In addition to sending a survey automatically when a case is resolved in Dynamics 365, Customer Voice also provides an add-on solution that you can install on your Dynamics 365 instance to enable users to send surveys on demand when working on a support case record in Dynamics.

Customer Voice publishes the **Send Survey** solution in **App source** (see `https://aka.ms/SendSurveyApp`). The **Send Survey** solution is designed to allow Dynamics 365 users to send a survey without needing to be given access to Customer Voice. The Customer Voice survey owner can share the survey broadly with their team using the standard share function in Dynamics 365. All shared-with users will then be able to send the survey to their customers without needing to go to Customer Voice. The shared users also do not have edit access to the survey, to secure the survey from unauthorized modification.

After you install the app, go to your Dynamics 365 security administration area and assign the **Survey Sender** security role to the users in your Dynamics 365 instance who you would like to share surveys with.

The app also uses a Power Automate workflow to send surveys. Complete the flow configuration using the following steps:

1. Go to `https://flow.microsoft.com` and select **Solutions** from the left pane.

2. Find and open the **Send Customer Voice survey from Dynamics 365** solution.

3. Find and open the **Send survey on create of custom entity record** cloud flow solution.

4. Edit the flow, complete the authentication steps when prompted, and then save the changes.

5. Complete any pending connection setup steps (any steps with warning symbols on the action header).

6. Turn on the workflow.

Once you have the solution installed, you can open an entity such as **Contact**, **Account**, **Lead**, **Opportunity**, or **Case** and see that the **Send Survey** command has been added at the top of the record form. Note that **Send Survey** is only supported for a single record, so it only appears when you open the record form (it does not appear in the list view).

Use the following steps to send the survey:

1. Click **Send Survey** to open a dialog box (see *Figure 8.17*):

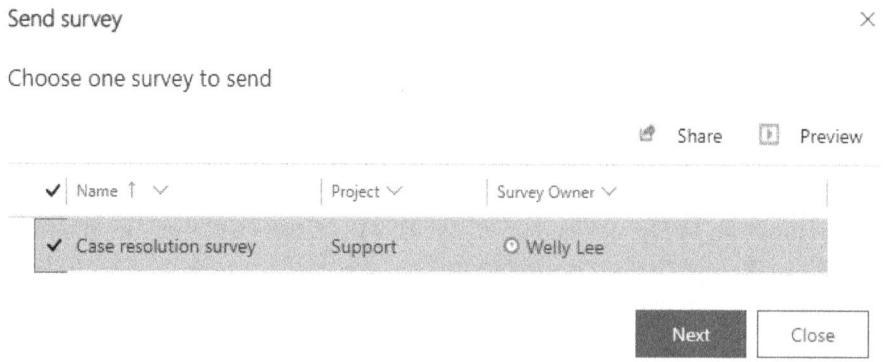

Figure 8.17 – The Select survey dialog box

2. Review and update the survey parameters, including the **Recipient** and **Email Template** parameters (see *Figure 8.18*), and click **Send** to complete:

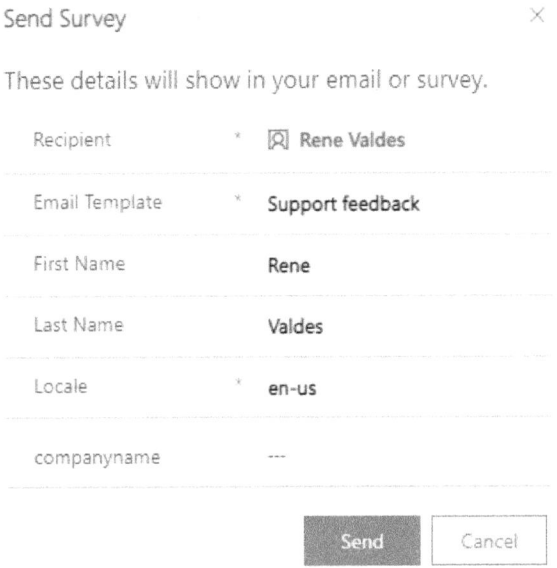

Figure 8.18 – Send survey parameters

Tip

After you send the survey, a new request is created in the **Customer Voice Send survey history** table. A Power Automate workflow is then triggered when there is a new record in this table and the survey is sent through the workflow. The **Status Reason** field shows three possible values: **Sending** (initial status), **Sent** (when the survey invite has been successfully sent), and **Failed**. *Figure 8.19* shows examples of survey invitations with **Sending** and **Sent** statuses:

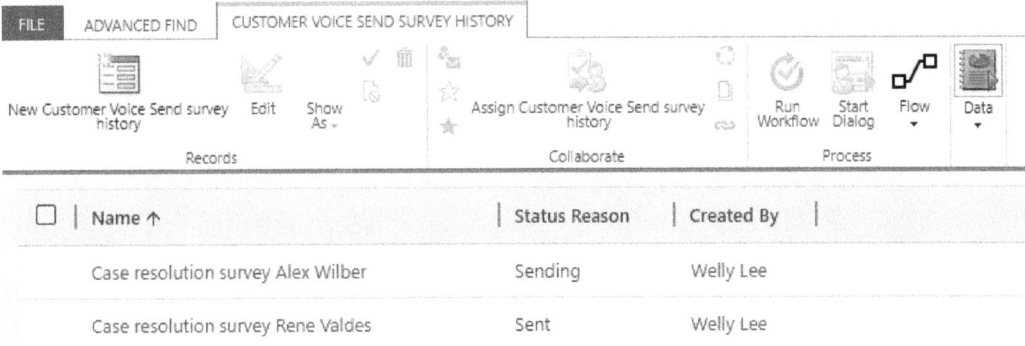

Figure 8.19 – Status reasons

After the survey is sent, you will see that the Customer Voice survey invite activity has appeared on the activity timeline (see *Figure 8.20*):

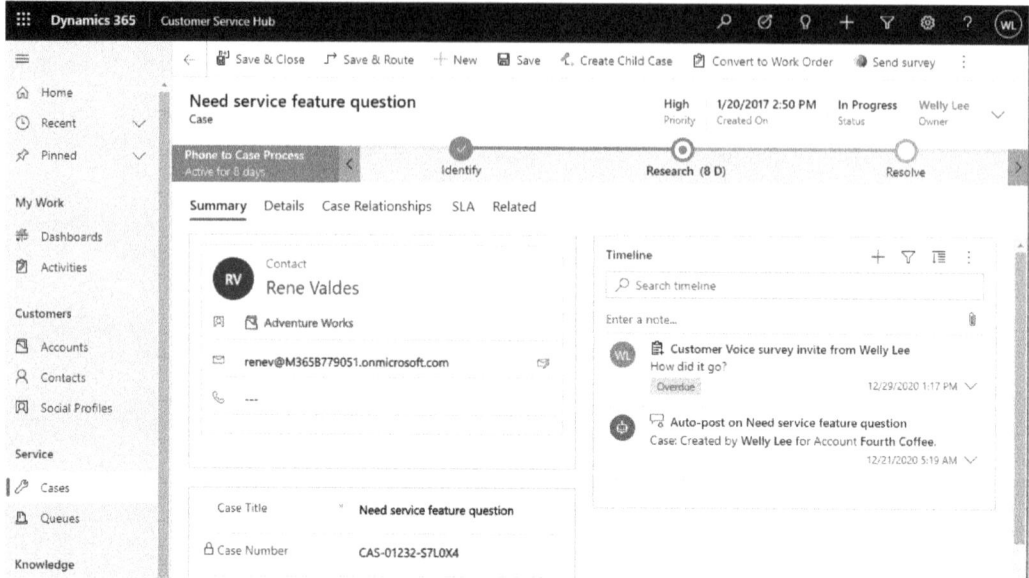

Figure 8.20 – The Customer Voice survey invite on the activity timeline

After the survey recipient has responded to the survey, the survey response is automatically added to the activity timeline (see *Figure 8.21*):

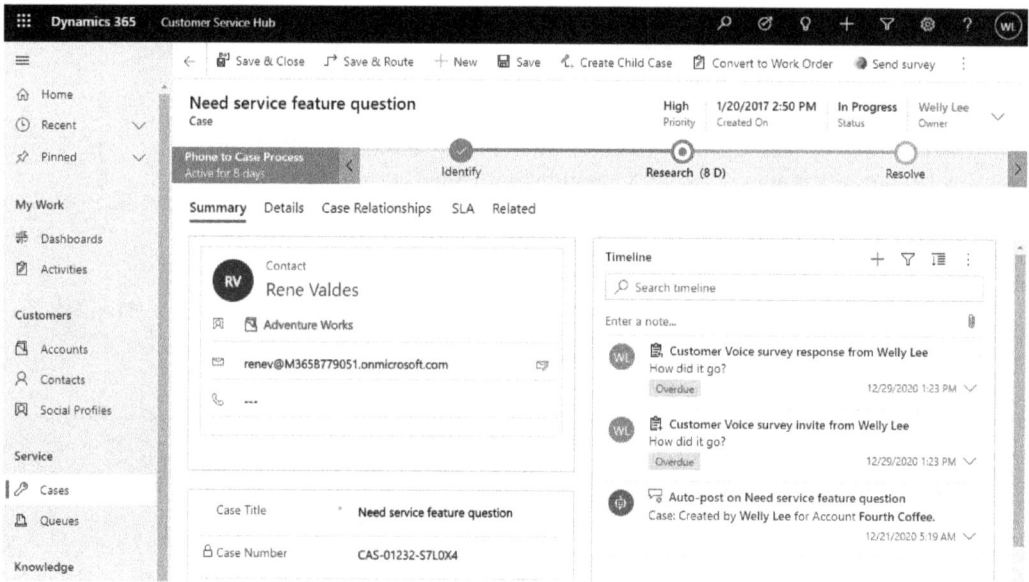

Figure 8.21 – Customer Voice survey response on the activity timeline

Anyone who can access the case record in Dynamics 365 will be able to view the survey response (see *Figure 8.22*):

| How has it been?
Customer Voice survey response | Normal
Priority | 1/10/2021 4:33 PM
Due Date | Open
Activity Status | Welly Lee
Owner | ⌄ |

General   Related

Question	Response
How would you rate the overall quality of our customer service?	★★★★★
How long did it take us to address your questions and concerns?	Shorter than expected
How would you rate your satisfaction with our customer service representative in terms of:	
Timeliness of resolution	Very satisfied
Courtesy and professionalism	Very satisfied
Product knowledge and competence	Very satisfied
Ability to resolve issue during the first call	Very satisfied

Figure 8.22 – Customer Voice survey response details

The survey invites and survey responses are added not only to the entity record that the survey is sent with regard to (that is, a case record) but also to the contact whom the survey is sent to. Anyone who works with the customer can access the survey response from the customer to make sure everyone has the latest information. If the customer submits a complaint, everyone will know and be able to engage appropriately with the customer. It would be frustrating for the customer if they submitted a complaint but the next employee who called them did not know anything about the complaint.

Customer Voice, by default, sends survey invitations using email. You can modify the Power Automate workflow to send surveys through an alternate communication channel such as SMS.

Sending survey invitation links through SMS

In addition to the **Send a survey** action, you can use the **Create an invitation** action in the Power Automate flow. Customer Voice generates a unique link for each recipient to identify people outside your organization who respond to the survey. Based on this link, the survey response is automatically linked to the recipient information, and if you are using Dynamics 365, the survey response is added as part of the activity for the contact and case record. *Figure 8.23* shows how to find and use the **Create an invitation** action:

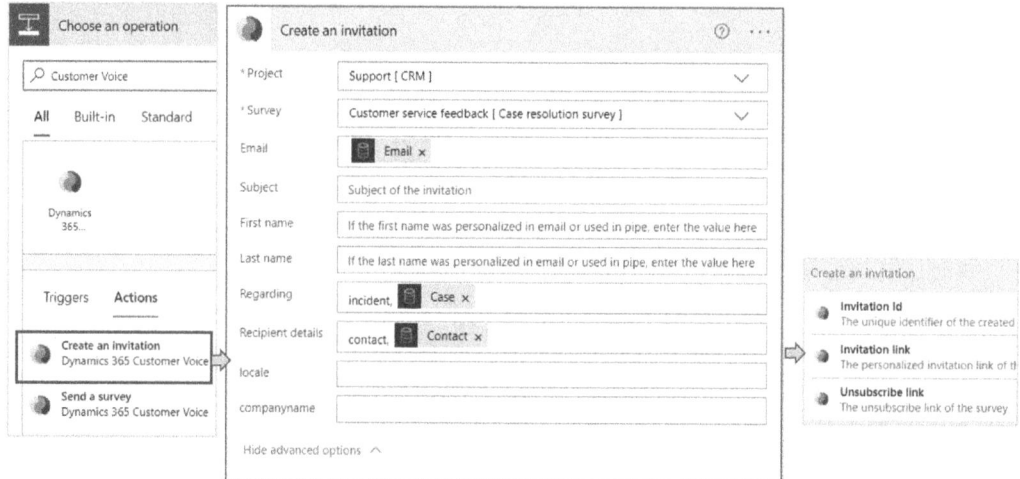

Figure 8.23 – The Create an invitation action

The **Create an invitation** action uses recipient details to link the contact record and generates the following output:

- **Invitation Id**: Record ID for the Customer Voice survey invites table

- **Invitation link**: Unique survey URL for the contact record

- **Unsubscribe link**: A link you can include in the email to enable your recipient to unsubscribe

After you get the link, you can use an SMS provider such as Twilio to send the survey link. For our example, we will use Twilio's **Send Text Message (SMS)** action in Power Automate. When using Twilio for the first time in Power Automate, you will need to set up a connection to an existing account in Twilio by providing your account ID and access token as shown in *Figure 8.24*:

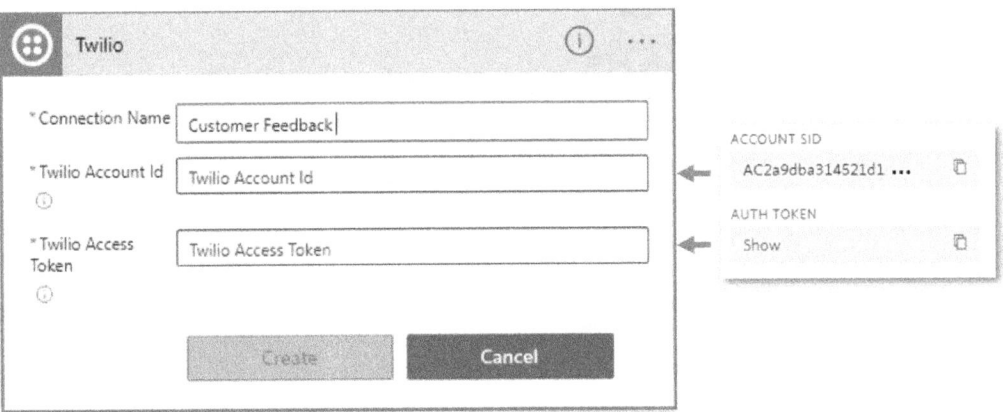

Figure 8.24 – Setting up a connection in Power Automate

Modify the Power Automate workflow and replace the **Send a survey** action with the **Create an invitation** action, then add Twillio's **Send Text Message (SMS)** action. The modified workflow should look as shown in *Figure 8.25*:

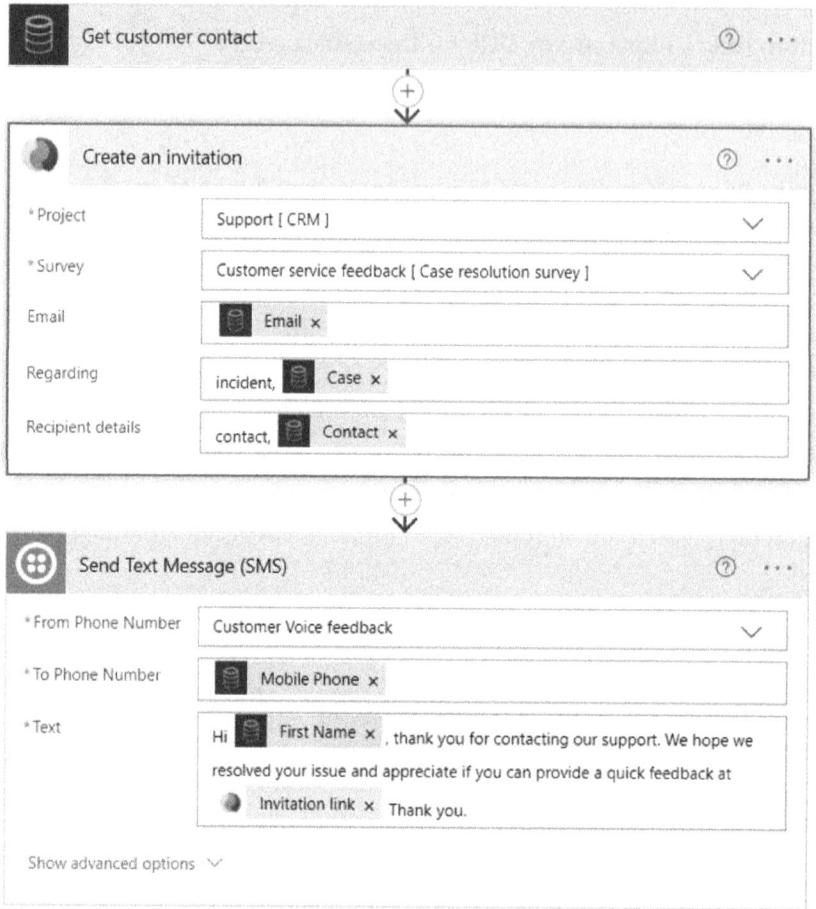

Figure 8.25 – Modified workflow to send a survey link using SMS

The resulting SMS message is shown in *Figure 8.26*:

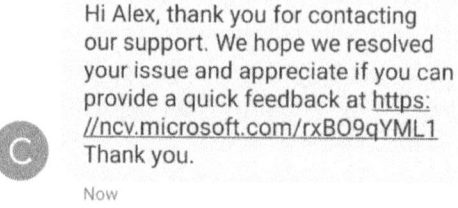

Figure 8.26 – An example survey invitation text message

The resulting link is a personalized link, so that when Alex responds to the survey, the survey response will be automatically associated with Alex's record in Dynamics 365.

In addition to presenting a link to the survey, you can also embed the survey as part of your web application

Embedding Customer Voice survey in a web application

To embed survey in your web application, you need to obtain embed script to show the survey. To generate the embed script, select the **Embed** option in your survey's **Send** tab. You can choose from **inline**, **pop-up window**, or **button** embed style and copy the **Embedded code** which you can send to the web application developer to integrate.

The embedded code includes survey variables so the application can pass context. For example, I created a new variable called `sessionID`, which can be used to link the survey response with the user session on the application (see *Figure 8.27*):

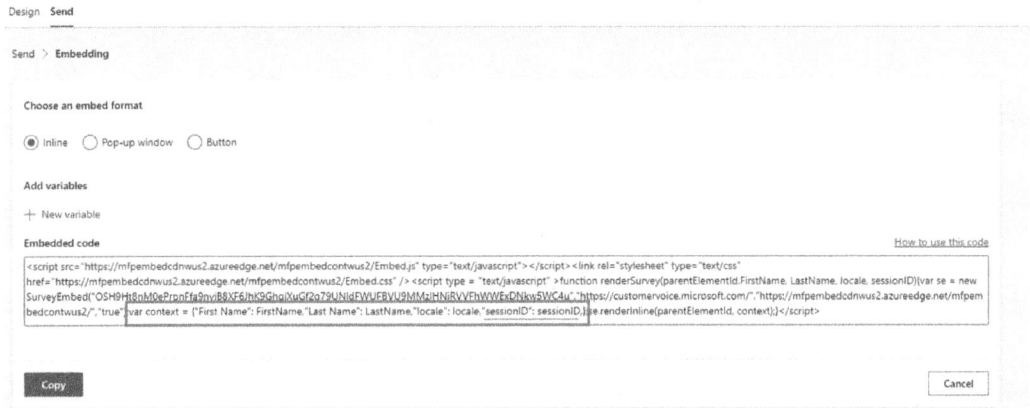

Figure 8.27 – Embedded code with the sessionID variable

If you are using a Dynamics 365 Customer Service omnichannel application for chat as part of your customer support process, then you can use the built-in Customer Voice survey embedding functionality.

Integrating Customer Voice with a support chat app

The Customer Voice survey can be configured so that it appears automatically at the end of a chat session using the Dynamics 365 Customer Service omnichannel feature.

You can use the same survey as your other support channel survey, or alternatively, you can create a separate survey on the same project.

Creating a chat feedback survey

Follow these steps to create a chat feedback survey on an existing project:

1. Open your project.

2. From the left pane, click the **New survey** link in the **Surveys** section.

3. Create a simple survey as appropriate for your chat experience (see an example in *Figure 8.28*):

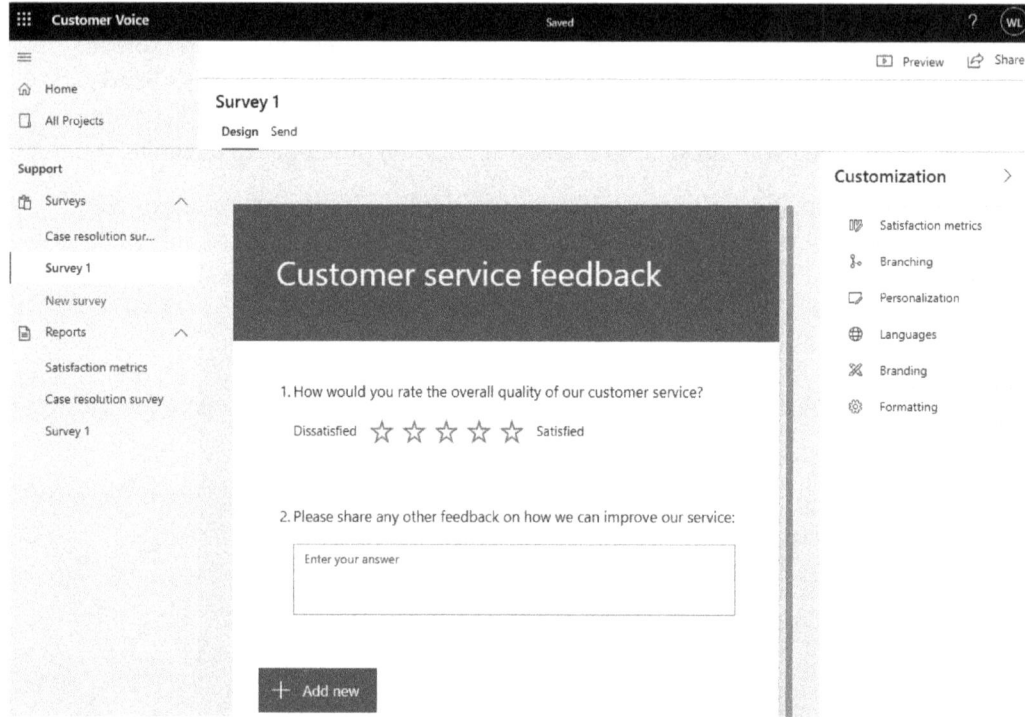

Figure 8.28 – An example of a chat feedback survey

4. From the **Customization** pane, click **Satisfaction metrics** and open the **CSAT** metrics.

5. Map the **CSAT** metrics to the rating question on your new survey (see *Figure 8.29*). Mapping the question to the same metrics enables Customer Voice to aggregate feedback data from multiple surveys. So, regardless of whether a customer provides feedback from an email survey or a chat survey, the results will be reported through the same metrics on the built-in **Satisfaction metrics** dashboard:

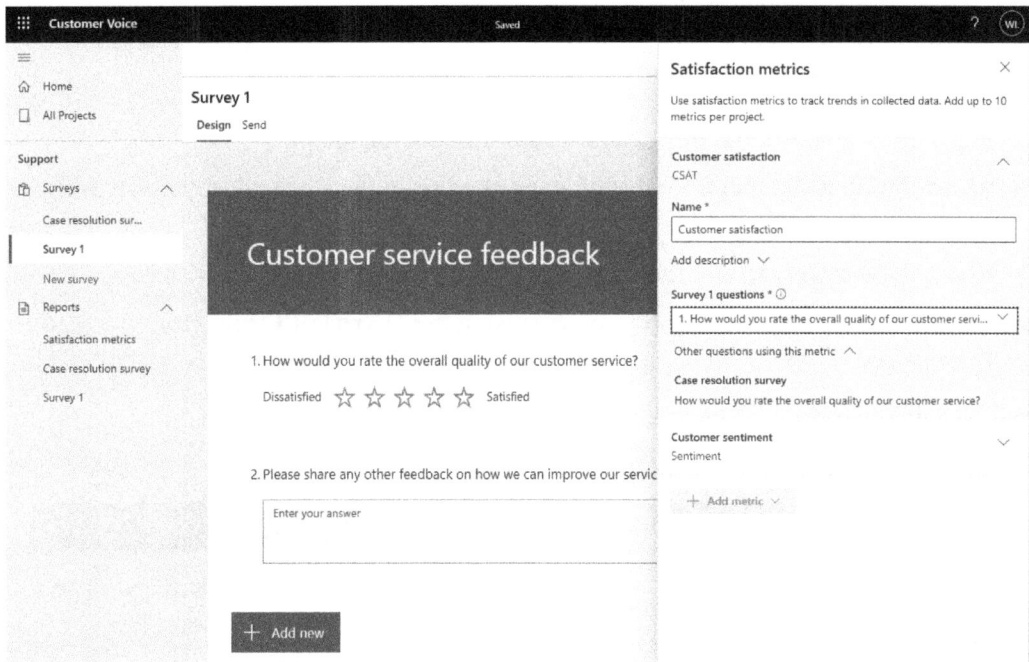

Figure 8.29 – Mapping customer satisfaction metrics to the survey question

6. Map the **Customer sentiment** metric to the text comment question #2. This enables Customer Voice to calculate sentiment based on the text feedback. Save the changes to continue.

7. Rename the survey by clicking **...** on **Survey 1** on the left pane and select **Rename**. For example, you can rename it Chat feedback.

After you have created the survey, you can add the survey to the chat widget in the **Omnichannel for Customer Service** app.

Important note

The following section provide instruction on enabling Customer Voice survey to the chat widget. To configure chat widget in Dynamics 365 Omnichannel for Customer Service app, refer to https://docs.microsoft.com/en-us/dynamics365/customer-service/configure-live-chat.

Adding a Customer Voice survey to the chat widget

Use the following steps to add a survey to the chat widget:

1. Open the Dynamics 365 **omnichannel administration app**.

2. Open the **Chat** channel from the left pane, then open the chat widget you are using for your chat experience.

3. Go to the **Surveys** tab and then turn on the **post-conversation** survey.

4. Look for the name of the survey you created in the **Microsoft Forms Pro survey** field.

5. Save the changes.

The completed configuration looks like *Figure 8.30*:

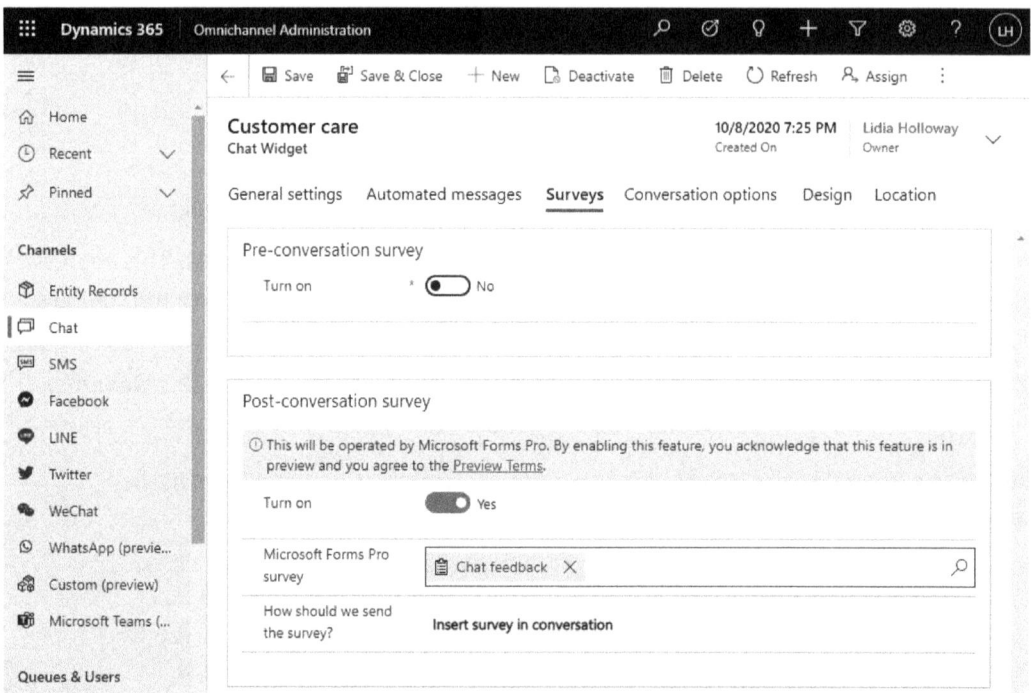

Figure 8.30 – Enable the post-conversation survey on your chat widget

6. After you have added the survey to the chat widget, the survey will be automatically shown at the end of a chat experience (see *Figure 8.31*):

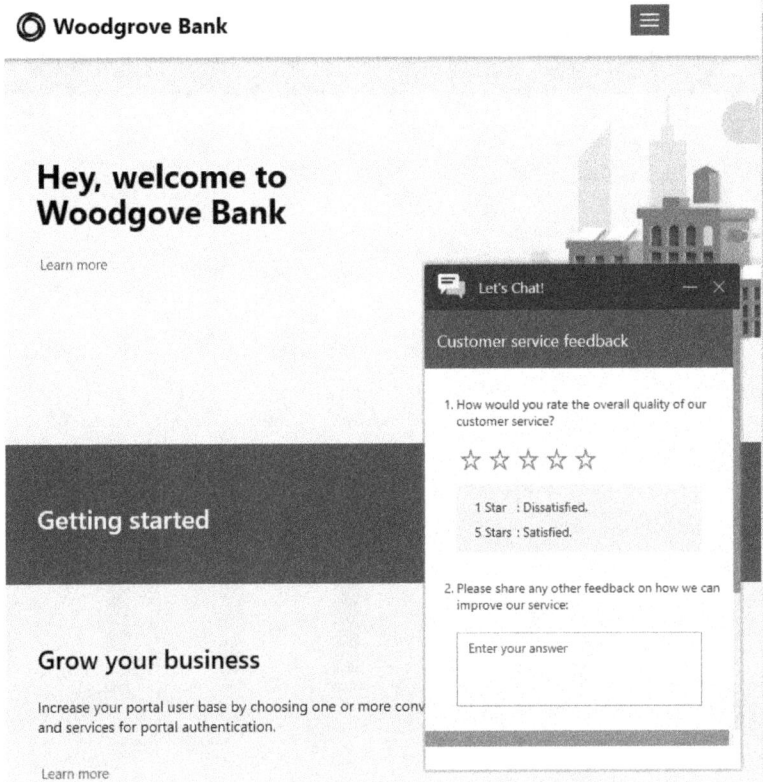

Figure 8.31 – Feedback survey at the end of a support chat session

Collecting feedback right at the end of the customer support chat experience provides a more engaging experience and an increased response rate, and it helps you to identify potential issues right away.

When you have created two surveys in the same project that share the same satisfaction metrics, the survey results, whether they are collected via email surveys or chat surveys, are aggregated; you can view the results using the **Satisfaction metrics** dashboard as shown in *Figure 8.32*:

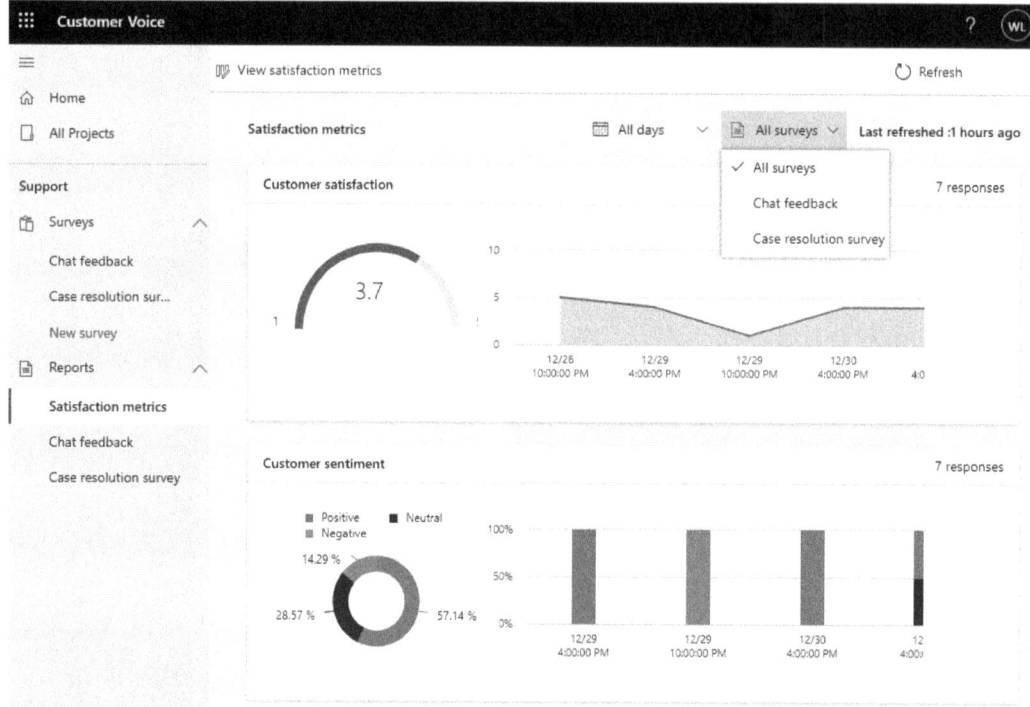

Figure 8.32 – The Satisfaction metrics dashboard for customer support surveys

Summary

Customer service is often the cornerstone of customer experience. Customer Voice provides functionalities to make it easy for you to implement customer feedback that is integrated with your customer service system. If you are using Dynamics 365 for Customer Service as your CRM system, Customer Voice provides out-of-the-box integration templates to automate sending surveys when a case is resolved in Dynamics or to collect feedback at the end of a chat session. There is no code and only minimal setup is required to enable you to get the system running quickly. In this chapter, we discussed how you use the support template in Customer Voice, including coverage of using the Power Automate workflow and the Power BI report template to integrate survey response data with your support case. We also discussed additional options to extend collecting feedback beyond the email survey.

In the next chapter, we will discuss how you can use Customer Voice to close the feedback loop and have timely follow-up actions with your customers.

9
Closing a Feedback Loop with Customer Voice

Closing a feedback loop is an important step in customer feedback management. If you have an unhappy customer, you must get back to the customer promptly, otherwise you risk losing your customer.

One of our auto manufacturer customers sends a survey after their customer picks up a new car. If the customer gives a poor NPS score, an alert is automatically generated to the dealer manager where the car was purchased so that the manager can follow up with the customer to resolve the issue. Another organization I worked with operates restaurants in Europe. They include a QR code on the dining table where customers can provide feedback. If a customer is not happy with their experience, they are provided with the restaurant's contact information so that they can speak with the manager in real time.

In this chapter, we are going to show how to implement follow-up actions as in the preceding examples with Customer Voice. We will start with an out-of-the-box follow-up action in Customer Voice, and then discuss how you customize the follow-up workflow. We will use Power Automate for the follow up workflow. As mentioned in the earlier chapter, Power Automate is a low-code and no-code tool to enable citizen developers to create workflow to automate business process. If you are new to Power Automate, some content in this chapter may be a bit more technical, but I encourage you to follow along as this may be a good way for you to learn Power Automate which you can use to automate various business process.

Finally, we will conclude the chapter by showing you how you can also use Power Automate to create workflows not only for Customer Voice survey but also to automate responses from Microsoft forms survey.

By the end of this chapter, you will understand how to implement a closed-loop feedback system, what you can do out of the box with Customer Voice, and how you can use a Power Automate workflow to create custom follow-up workflows for both Customer Voice and Microsoft Forms surveys.

The chapter is organized as follows:

- Real-time action with post-survey messages
- Alert notifications for satisfaction metrics
- Custom follow-up workflow with Power Automate
- Microsoft Forms response workflow with Power Automate

Let's look at how you can configure a conditional thank you for a real-time feedback loop.

Real-time action with post-survey messages

In the earlier example, I talked about a restaurant chain that collects feedback from its customers. The restaurant would like to allow a customer who is unhappy about the food or their experience to talk directly with the restaurant manager (refer to the example in *Figure 9.1*):

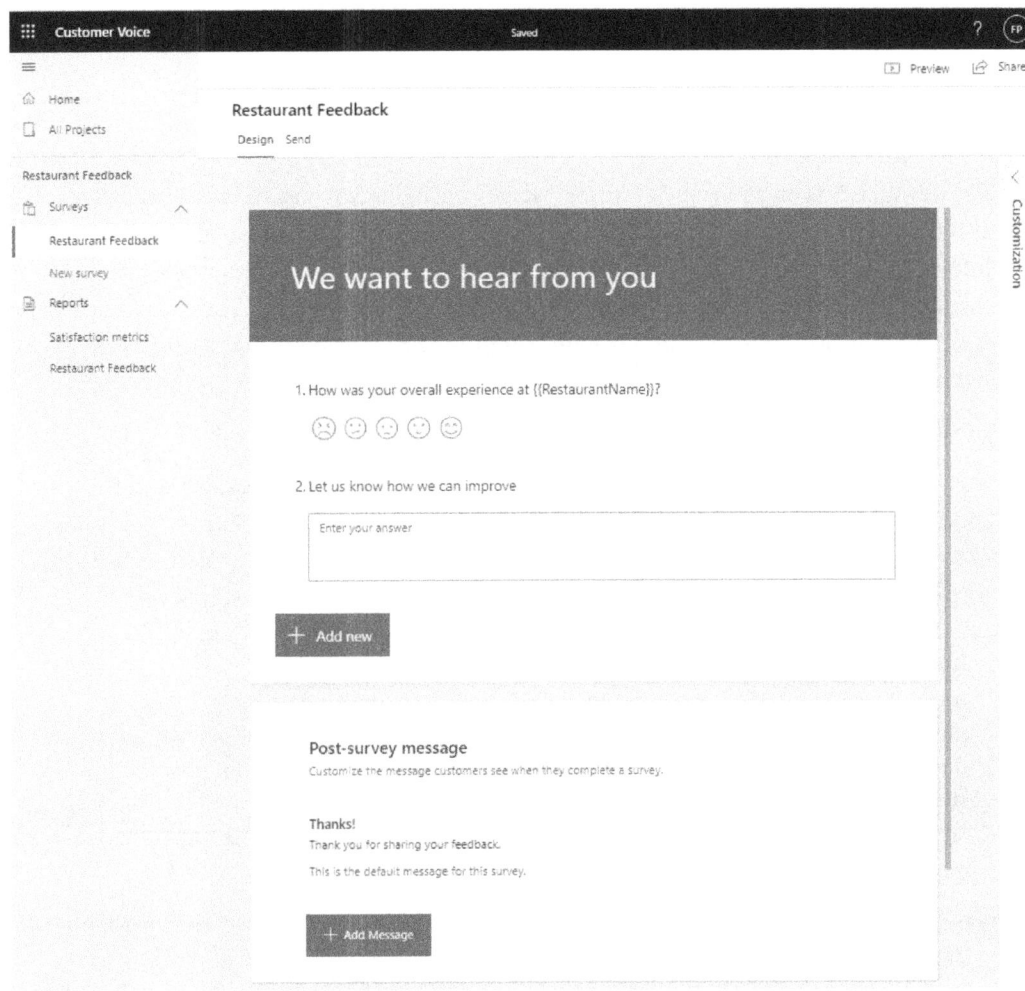

Figure 9.1 – An example of restaurant feedback

Customer Voice provides support for conditional post-survey messages to enable you to specify relevant messages.

To customize, perform the following steps:

1. Click **Add Message** in the **Post-survey message** section (see *Figure 9.1*).

2. Specify the post-survey message heading and main message.

   For the survey message, you can insert survey variables such as `ManagerName` and `ContactInfo`, which would be replaced with the actual name and contact information for the specific restaurant location. You can create the survey variable through the **Personalization** setting on the **Customization** panel. Refer to *Chapter 6, Conducting an Employee Survey with Dynamics 365 Customer Voice*, for the steps to create survey variables.

3. Click **Add condition** to show the custom post-survey message.

   Customer Voice supports the addition of multiple post-survey messages and the specification of conditions to show the post-survey message. In our case, we would like to show the custom message when the response to `How was your overall experience at this restaurant` is less than a 4 smiley rating level.

   > **Important note**
   > If you do not specify a condition or when there are multiple post-survey messages where the condition is met, then Customer Voice will use the first message that meets the condition. If no condition is met, then the default post-survey message will be used.

4. The completed message is shown in *Figure 9.2*:

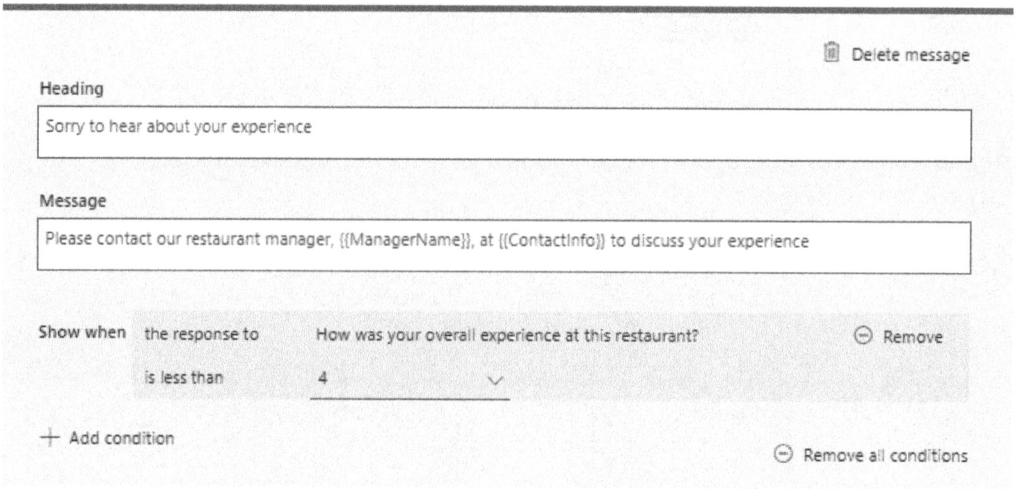

Figure 9.2 – Post survey message and condition

After you have created the survey, you will need to generate a link and QR code for each restaurant location so that you can specify the name of the restaurant manager and their contact information. To generate a unique survey link and corresponding survey variable values, follow these steps:

1. Go to the **Send** tab on your survey.
2. Click the **Link** option for sending the survey.
3. On the expanded **Survey links** panel, click **Create links** (See *Figure 9.3*):

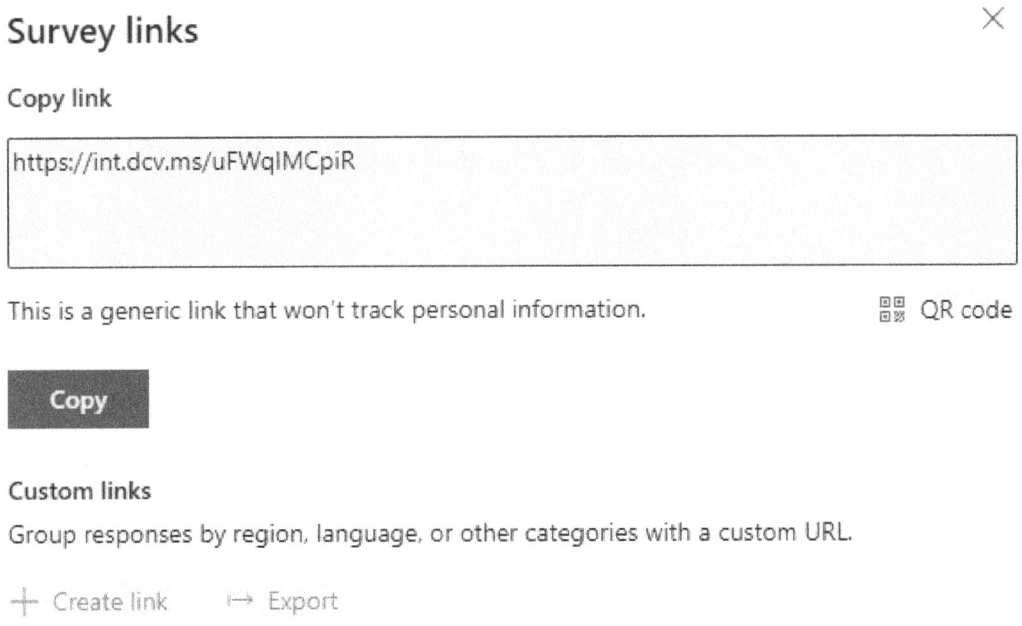
Survey links
Copy link
https://int.dcv.ms/uFWqIMCpiR
This is a generic link that won't track personal information.
QR code
Copy
Custom links
Group responses by region, language, or other categories with a custom URL.
Create link
Export

Figure 9.3 – Creating custom links for each restaurant location

4. On the **Create links** panel, select the `restaurant name`, `manager name`, and `contact info` variables and then click **Create** to generate a unique link for each restaurant site. Repeat this step for each restaurant location.

> **Important note**
>
> After you select the variables to generate a unique link, you can download a template to populate survey variable values. This option is available if you need to generate a large number of links.

5. Download the QR code for each restaurant location.

> **Important note**
>
> The QR code functionality generates a QR code image corresponding to the survey URL. You are not limited to using a QR code generator in Customer Voice. Once you have the link, you can use any tools to generate the QR code image. For example, BING.com offers a free QR code generator, which you can access by searching for *QR code* as a search term.

Once you get the QR code, you can test the experience by submitting the response. When you submit a survey response with a smiley rating of less than level 4, you will see the post-survey message as in *Figure 9.4* after you submit the survey:

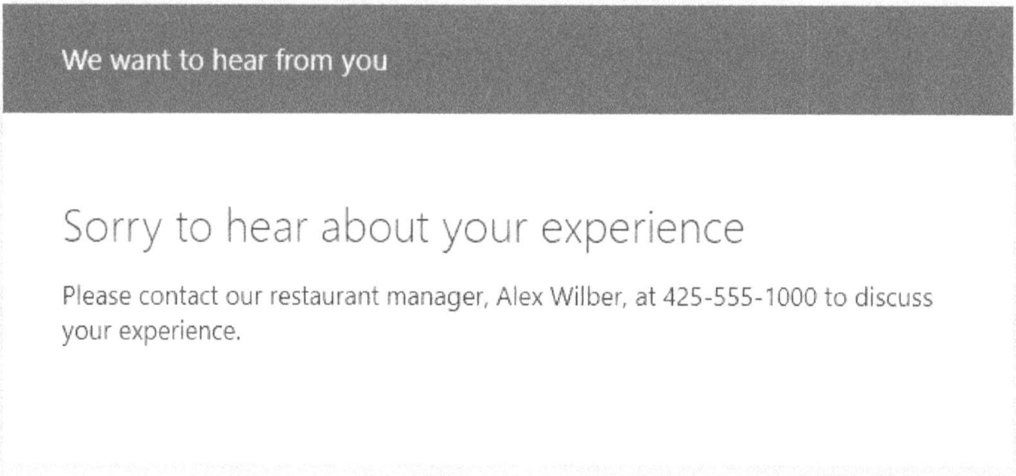

We want to hear from you

Sorry to hear about your experience

Please contact our restaurant manager, Alex Wilber, at 425-555-1000 to discuss your experience.

Figure 9.4 – Conditional post-survey message

In addition to using a post-survey message to follow up, you can also use alert functionality in Customer Voice.

Alert notifications for satisfaction metrics

At the beginning of the chapter, I shared a use case of an automotive manufacturer that sends a customer feedback survey to a new car owner. If the customer is not happy with the car, an alert is generated.

To implement this scenario, you can use the alert notification feature in Customer Voice. An alert is generated based on a satisfaction metric value. Customer Voice supports the definition of satisfaction metrics on your project and maps the metric to survey questions in the same project. In addition to the standard metrics, such as **Net Promoter Score®** **(NPS)** and **Customer Satisfaction (CSAT)**, you can also create custom metrics based on your specific scenario.

Figure 9.5 shows an example of a new car survey that measures different aspects of customer experience (question 2):

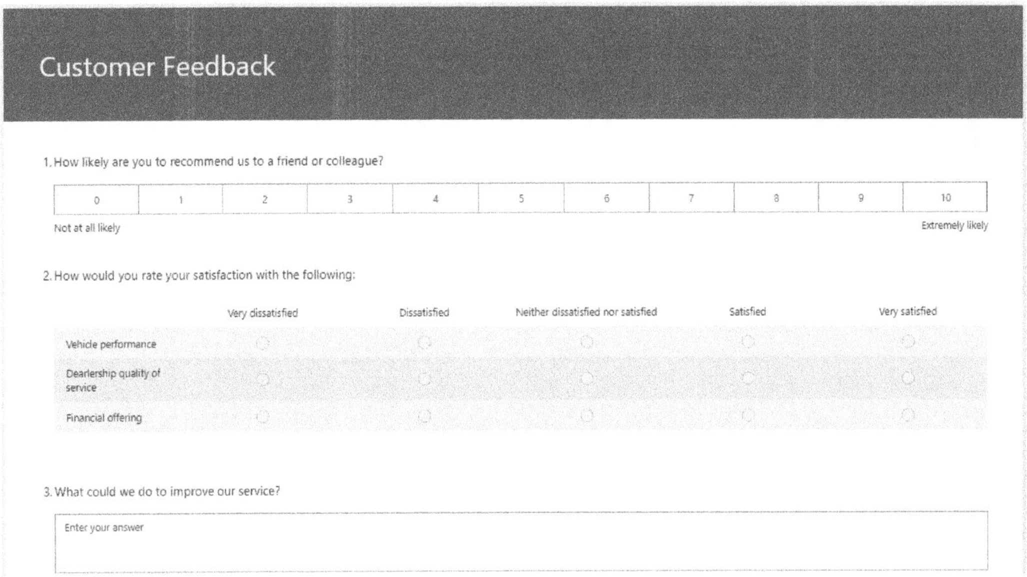

Figure 9.5 – An example survey question for an automotive dealer

You can create a custom satisfaction metric that calculates the combined score from different statements in your Likert question type. Perform the following steps to create the satisfaction metric:

1. Open the **Satisfaction metrics** setting from the **Customization** panel.

2. Create a new metric and select the **Net Promoter Score®** option.

3. Select the following question: **1. How likely are you to recommend us to a friend or colleague?.**

4. Save the metric.

5. Create a second new metric and select the **Custom score** option.

6. Name the custom score (such as Customer Satisfaction).

7. From the multi-select dropdown, select all questions you would like to include in the score. Note: the custom score metric supports *rating*, *choice*, and the *Likert* question type.

8. Click **Edit score** and adjust the scoring for each scale and the weight for each statement. In our example, adjust the weight for vehicle performance to 3 to afford more weight (see *Figure 9.6*):

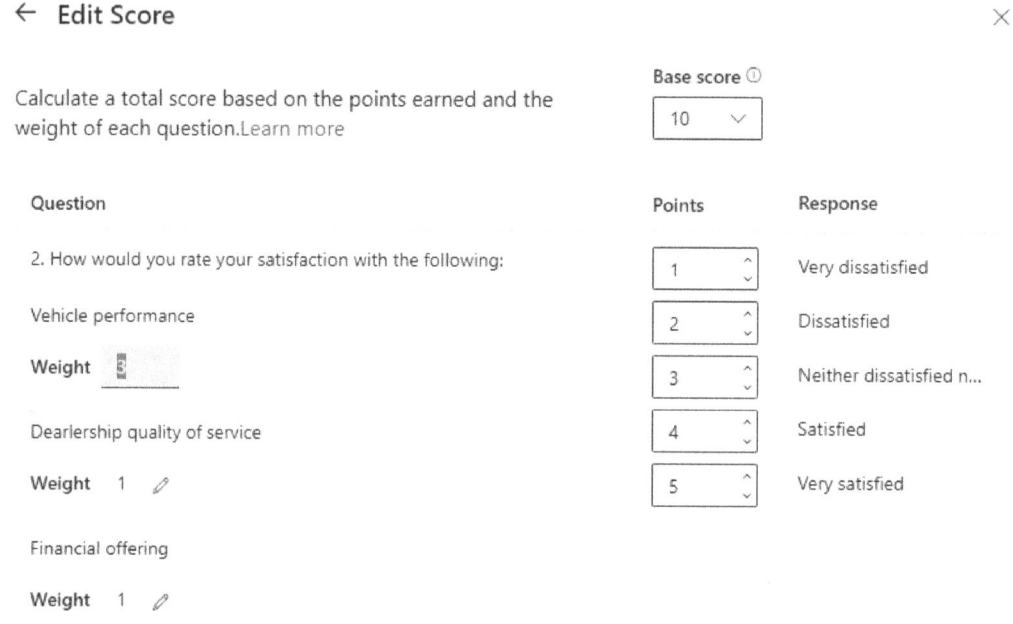

Figure 9.6 – Custom score options

The following settings can be customized for the custom scoring calculation:

- **Base Score (B)**: The range of the custom score. For example, for a base score of 100, then the points from the question included in the calculation will be converted to a maximum score of 100. If a user gives 5 (out of 5 stars), then the user will get 100 points. If the user gives 1 star, then the user will get 0 points. If the user answers in between, then they will get a prorated score of between 0 and 100.

- **Points (P)**: The points to assign for each rating scale or choice question. You can assign any positive number, including 0. By default, each scale is assigned a number starting from 1. If you have a rating or choice question that starts with a positive to negative outcome, such as question 3 (where the first choice, **Lower rate than competitor**, is more desirable than the last option, **Higher than competitor**), then you will need to reverse the points allocated.

- **Weight (W)**: The weight to assign for each question. In the example from *Figure 9.6*, the first question has a weight of 3, so the score is multiplied by a factor of 3 divided by 5, which is the total weight across all questions in this metrics (3+1+1).

Custom scoring is calculated based on the formula in *Figure 9.6*. For example, if a user responds to the survey with the following (on a scale from 1 to 5):

- **Vehicle performance**: 5
- **Dealership quality of service**: 1
- **Financial offering**: 2

The weighted score for base 100 will be 65 (see *Figure 9.7*):

Question	Survey Response (P)	Min Score (P_{min})	Max Score (P_{max})	Weight (W)	Score ($(P-P_{min})$ / $(P_{max}-P_{min})$ x W)
Vehicle performance	5	1	5	3	(5-1) / (5-1) x 3 = 3
Dealership quality of service	1	1	5	1	(1-1) / (5-1) x 1 = 0
Financial offering	2	1	5	1	(2-1) / (5-1) x 1 = 0.25
Total				5	3.25

$$\left(\frac{\Sigma\, W \left(\frac{P - P_{min}}{P_{max} - P_{min}} \right)}{\Sigma\, W} \right) \times B \ = \ \left(\frac{3.25}{5} \right) \times 100 \ = \ 65$$

Figure 9.7 – Formula for custom scoring

Note that the three questions we are using in our example have the same scale (1-5). If you are calculating the score from a different question with a different scale, then P_{min} and P_{max} will be different for each row in *Figure 9.7*.

> **Important note**
>
> When you are using a choice question with the **Other** option and allow a user to input their own text, the custom score will calculate the score only when the user enter an additional text. If the user selects the **Other** option, but does not leave any additional text, then the custom score will skip the empty response from the calculation.

The satisfaction metric is defined at the project level, so if you have multiple surveys in your project, questions from the survey can be mapped to the same metrics. For example, if you would like to collect a survey from customers visiting your website, you can create a separate survey for your website visit on the same project using the same metrics as NPS and map the NPS question on your second survey to the same NPS metric. That way, no matter which survey the customer uses to provide your feedback, you will get the NPS score aggregated across all your surveys.

The satisfaction score is displayed on the **Satisfaction metrics** dashboard under the **Reports** section on the left pane, as seen in *Figure 9.8*. The satisfaction metrics display the latest score and trend over time. You can filter the time, such as **Last 7 days**, **Last 28 days**, **Last 90 days**, or specify specific date ranges. Similarly, you can view the metrics across all surveys or filter on a specific survey:

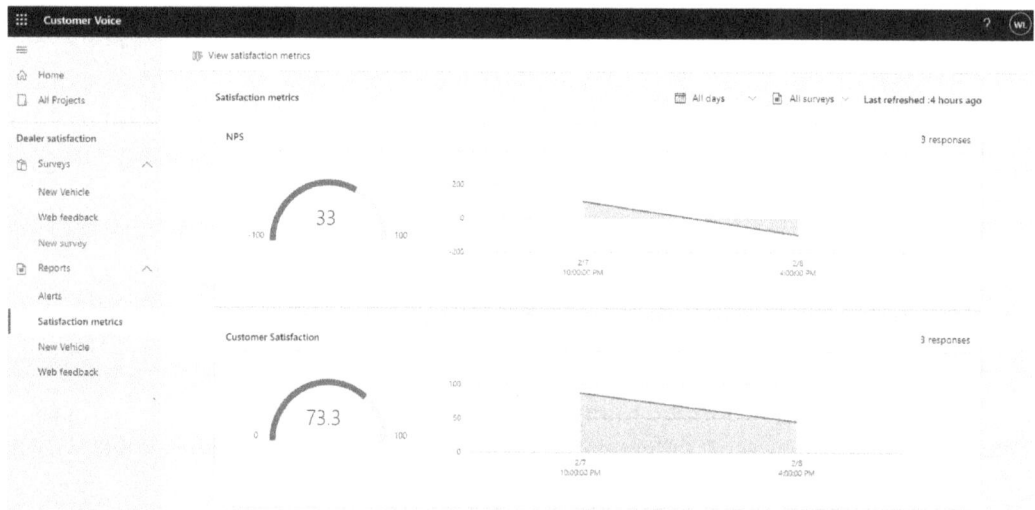

Figure 9.8 – Satisfaction metric dashboard

After you create the satisfaction metrics, you can create an alert to be notified when you receive a survey from the customer below a certain threshold.

Perform the following steps to create an alert:

1. From the left pane, click **Alerts**.
2. Click **Create alert rule**.
3. Name the alert.
4. Select the satisfaction metrics to monitor, such as **Net promoter score**.
5. Select the condition to generate the alert, such as **Less than Promoters**.

The completed alert setting is shown in *Figure 9.9*:

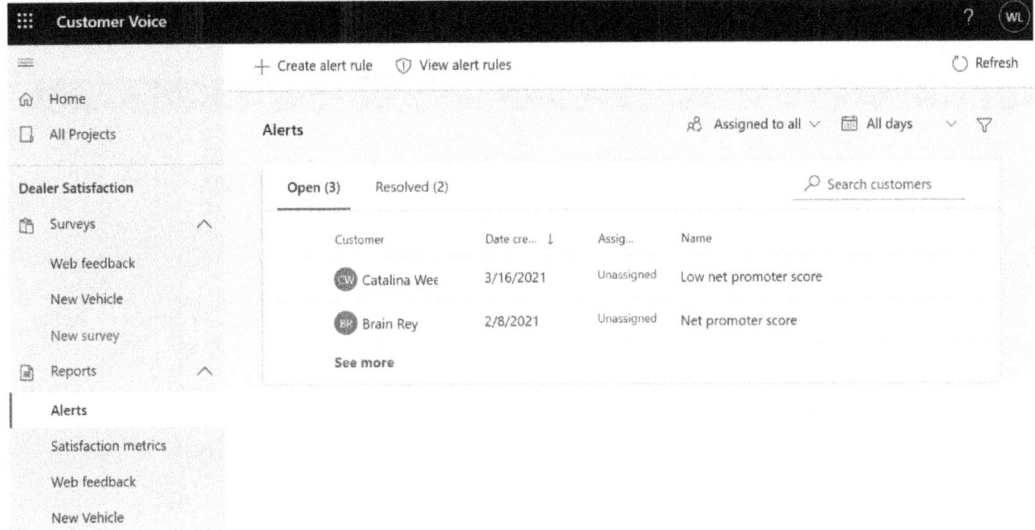

Figure 9.9 – An example of an alert rule

When you receive new feedback from your customer that resulted in less than promoter score, an alert is generated. You can find all the alerts from the **Alerts** dashboard under the **Reports** section, as shown in *Figure 9.10*:

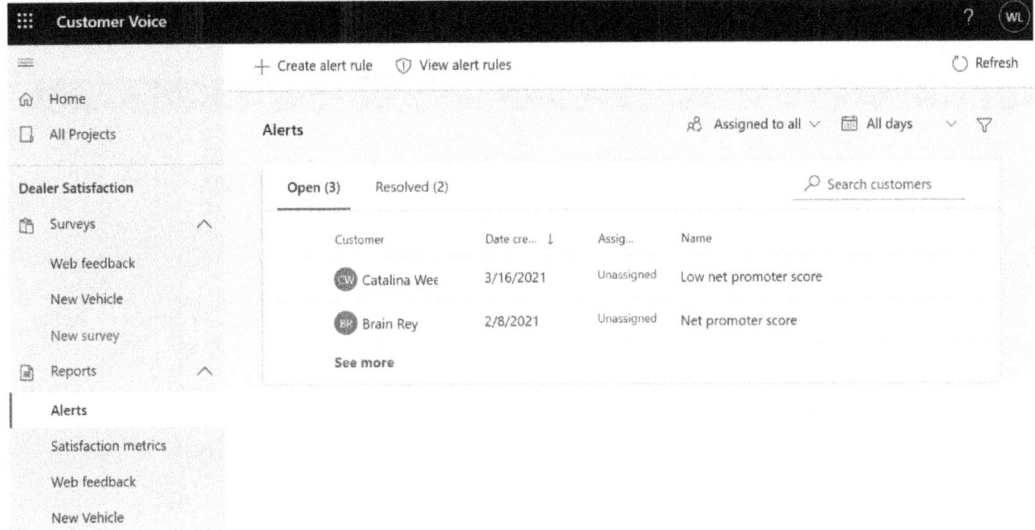

Figure 9.10 – Alerts dashboard

Opening the alert opens a panel that provides the details, such as **survey responses** and **survey respondent**. You can assign the alert to your colleague and update notes. You can also resolve the alert and add comments (see *Figure 9.11*):

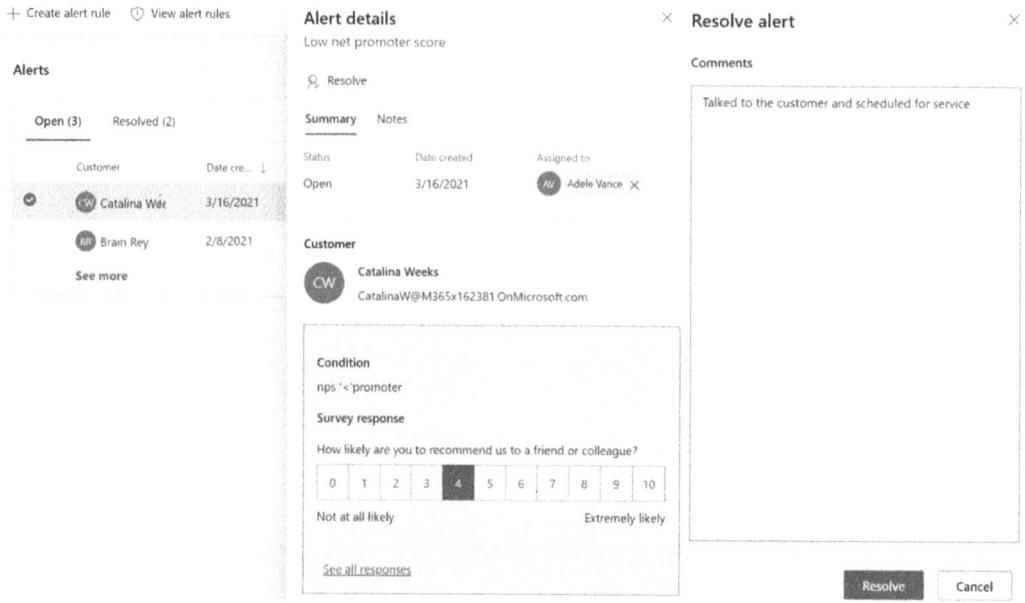

Figure 9.11 – Alert details panel

After you resolve the alert, the alert is moved out of the **Open** alert tab and is added to the **Resolved** alert tab (see *Figure 9.12*):

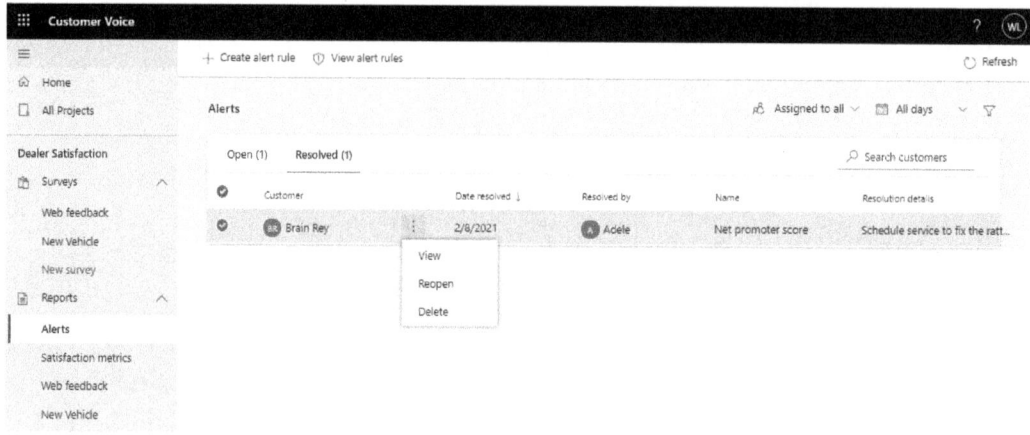

Figure 9.12 – Resolved Alerts view

From the **Resolved** alerts view, you can select a record, click **…** to open the option to view the details, reopen the alert (and move the alert back to the **Open** alert tab), or **Delete** the record.

Custom follow-up workflow with Power Automate

In addition to the out-of-the-box follow-up action through an alert, Customer Voice supports the creation of a custom follow-up action through a Power Automate workflow. For our example, the automotive manufacturer would like to send an email to the relevant dealer manager regarding customer feedback with a low NPS score.

> **Important note**
> You can find the video recording for creating custom follow-up workflow at the following links:
> https://bit.ly/2Swx3Az
> https://bit.ly/3vmldI4.

To implement the custom workflow, go to https://flow.microsoft.com to create a Power Automate workflow.

Switch the environment to match the environment for your Customer Voice project. You can find the environment information from the **All Projects** view in Customer Voice (see *Figure 9.13*):

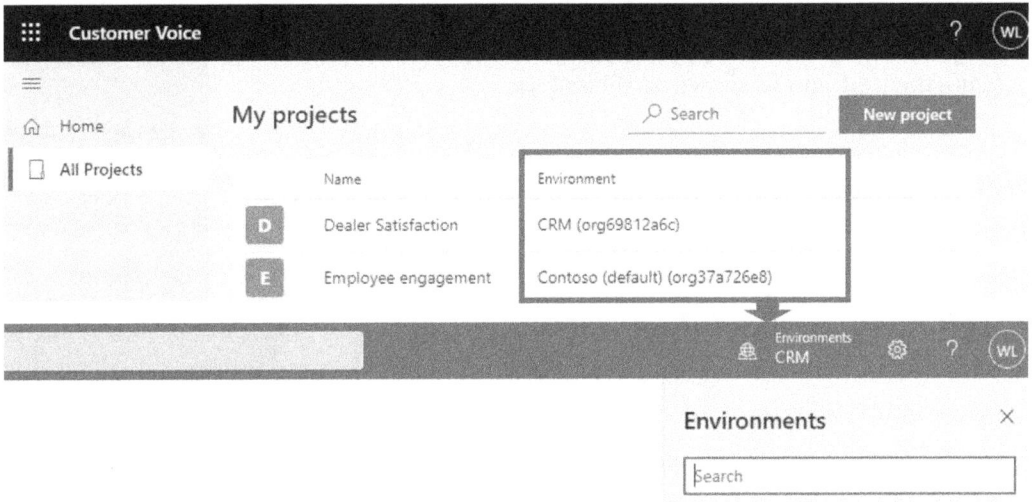

Figure 9.13 – Selecting the Power Automate environment

Create a workflow by clicking **Create** on the left pane and then select the **Automated cloud flow** option from the main screen, as shown in *Figure 9.13*.

Name your workflow, search for the Dataverse trigger, and then select **When a record is created** (see *Figure 9.14*):

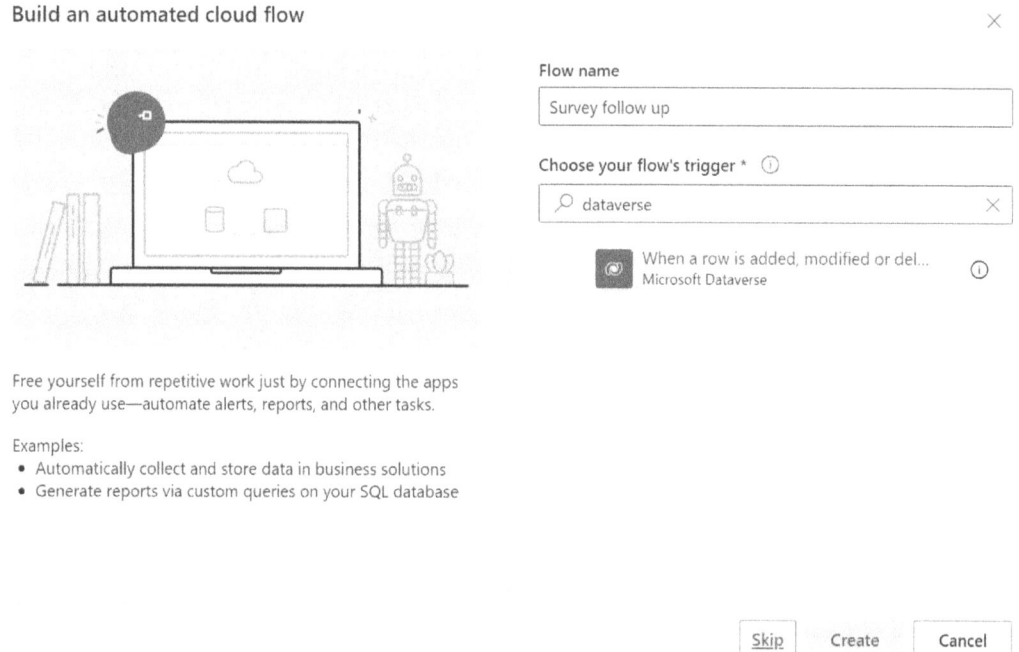

Figure 9.14 – Creating an automated workflow

Configure the workflow as shown in *Figure 9.15*:

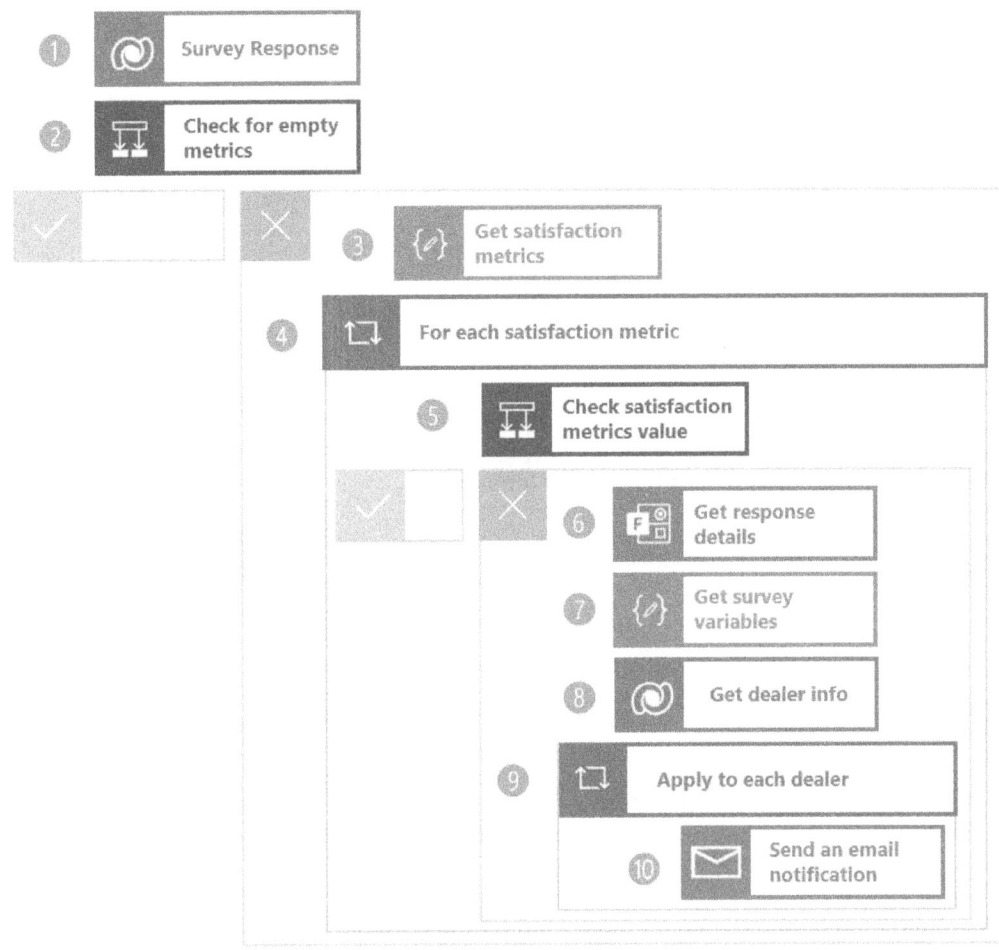

Figure 9.15 – Workflow to send an email when receiving a low NPS survey response

We will review each step in the workflow in the following section.

Survey Response (1)

The workflow will need to start when you receive a new survey response and a new record is created in the **Customer Voice survey response** table in **Dataverse**. To set up the workflow, use the **When a record is created** trigger and configure it as follows:

- **Change type**: Select **Create** to trigger the workflow when a new response is created.
- **Table Name**: Select **Customer Voice survey responses**.
- **Scope**: Select **User** to include records that the user has access to.

Then, click the **...** menu on the trigger header as shown in *Figure 9.16* to open an additional menu option and click **Settings**:

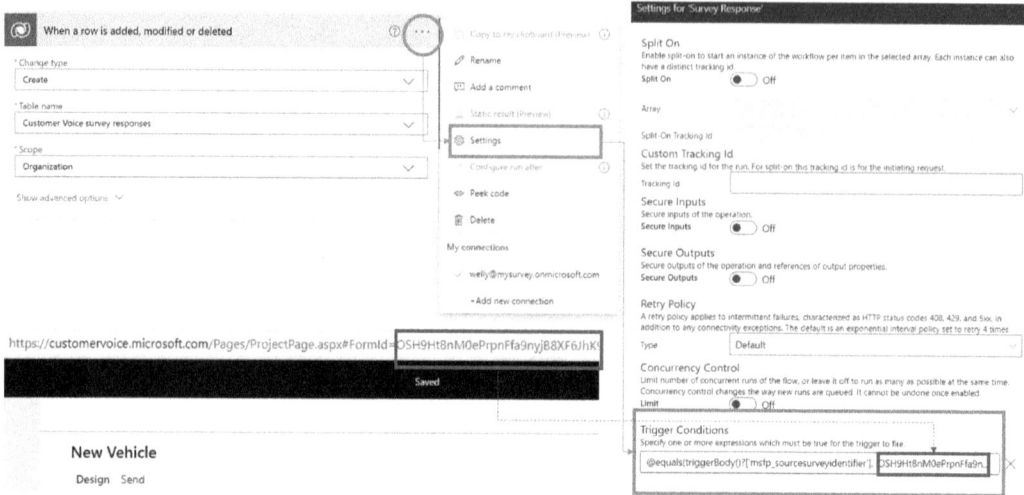

Figure 9.16 – Configuring a survey response trigger

To limit things so that the workflow only starts for a specific survey, you can add a trigger condition. From the setting dialog window, add a new trigger condition and enter the following:

`@equals(triggerBody()?['msfp_sourcesurveyidentifier'], '<Form ID>')`. Replace `<Form ID>` with the value from the URL on your survey (See *Figure 9.16*).

In our example, the trigger condition value is `@equals(triggerBody()? ['msfp_sourcesurveyidentifier'], 'OSH9Ht8nM0ePrpnFfa9nyj B8XF6JhK9GhgjXuGf2q79URUFMVERDV0JNRFc4MFBJMVhCREVRTEQ2MC4u')`.

Click **Done** to save the trigger condition setting. Rename the trigger to better identify the step, for example, `Survey Response`.

Check for empty metrics (2)

There could be a case where satisfaction metrics may be removed from the survey definition, so to accommodate such a situation, you can optionally add a condition to check whether the satisfaction metric is present. Add a new step to your workflow and select the **Condition** control. On the left side of **Condition**, select **Satisfaction metric value** under **Survey Response** from the **Dynamic content** dialog window. On the right side of the condition, open the **Expression** tab on the dialog window, type `null`, and then click **OK**, as shown in *Figure 9.17*:

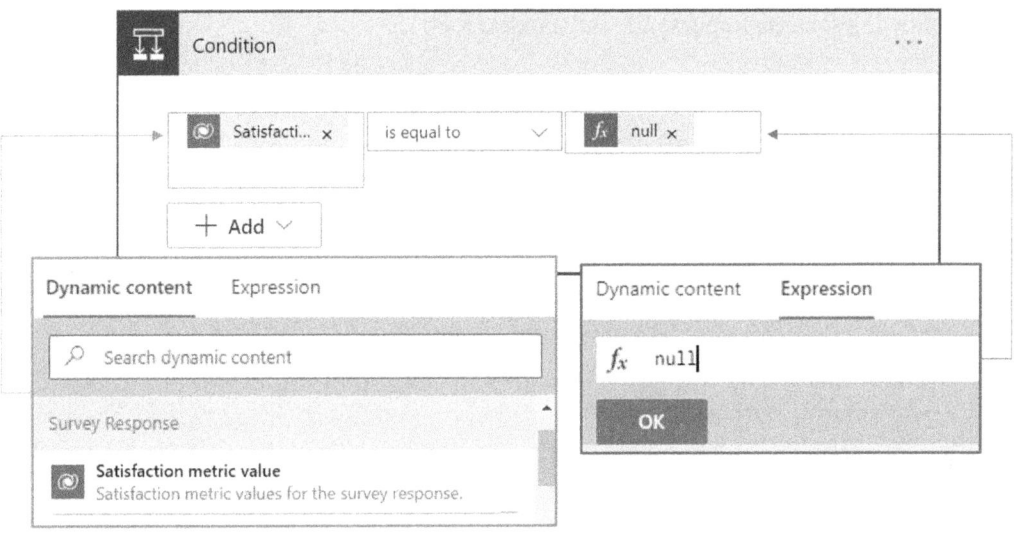

Figure 9.17 – Checking for an empty satisfaction metrics value

Get satisfaction metrics (3)

The satisfaction metrics value is calculated for each survey response and the result is stored in **Satisfaction metrics value** (`msfp_satisfactionmetricvalue`) in the **Customer Survey Response** table. Since there can be multiple metrics associated with the survey response, the values are stored in JSON format, so you need to parse the values in order to use it.

To read the satisfaction metrics value in Power Automate, add a new step under the **If No** section following the condition action and select the **Parse JSON** action. Then, select **Satisfaction metric value** from **Dynamic content**, as shown in *Figure 9.18*:

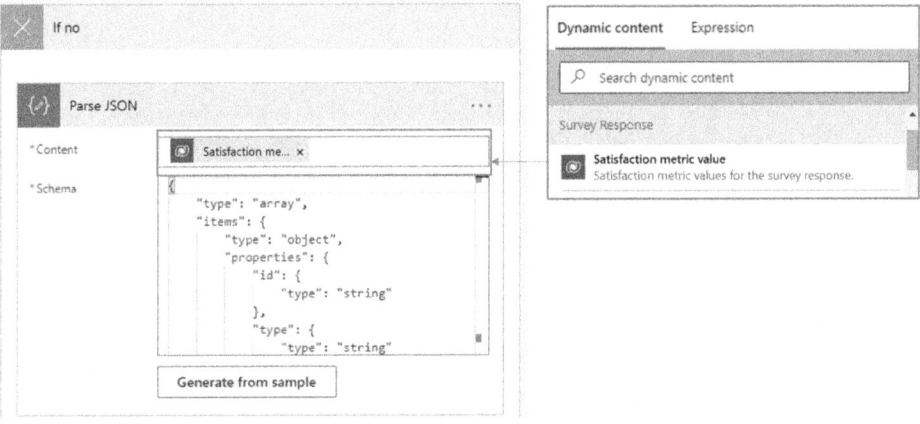

Figure 9.18 – Getting a satisfaction metrics value

Use the following schema to parse the satisfaction metrics:

> **Important note**
>
> You can find the complete code for this chapter on GitHub: `https://github.com/PacktPublishing/Working-with-Microsoft-Forms-and-Customer-Voice/tree/main/Chapter09`.

```
{
    "type": "array",
    "items": {
        "type": "object",
        "properties": {
            "id": {
                "type": "string"
            },
            "type": {
                "type": "string"
            },
            "value": {
                "type": "string"
            }
        },
        "required": [
            "id",
            "type",
            "value"
        ]
    }
}
```

Name your parse step `GetSatisfaction metrics` to reference it later.

For each satisfaction metric (4)

Since there could be more than one satisfaction metric, you need to evaluate each of the metric's values. To do so, add an action and select the **Apply to each** control. For the input, select **Body** from the previous step (**Satisfaction metrics**). Rename the control `Foreach satisfaction metric`.

Check satisfaction metrics value (5)

For each of the satisfaction metrics, evaluate the satisfaction metrics value. Add an action and select the **Condition** control. Add id and value from the **Get satisfaction metrics** action to the **And** condition as shown in *Figure 9.19*. Rename the control Check satisfaction metric value:

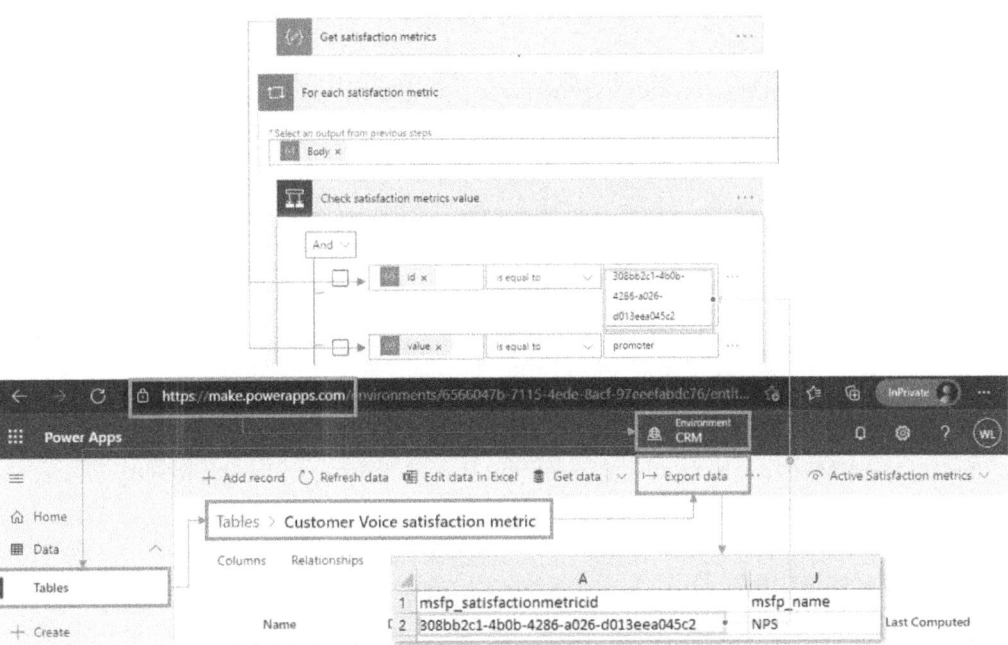

Figure 9.19 – Checking for a satisfaction metrics value

To configure the condition control, you need the satisfaction metrics identifier. To get the identifier for the metrics, perform the following steps:

1. Go to https://make.powerapps.com.

2. Select your **Dataverse** environment.

3. Navigate to the **Tables** section under **Data** from the left navigation.

4. Look for the **Customer Voice satisfaction metric** table. If you do not see the table, click on **Don't see the items you're looking for? Reset the filter above to see more** at the bottom of the page.

5. Export the data to Excel.

6. Open the Excel file and locate the ID of the satisfaction metrics record.

Once you get the satisfaction metric ID, enter the value to the condition control for id, as shown in *Figure 9.19*. The satisfaction metrics value for NPS is one of the following: promoter, passive, and detractor. For this workflow, we would send a notification when you receive anything less than promoter, hence, we can check whether the value is equal to promoter and set up the follow-up action when the condition is false.

Get response details (6)

To get the survey responses, you can use the Microsoft Forms **Get response detail** action and use Source response identifier from the **Survey Response** step, as shown in *Figure 9.20*:

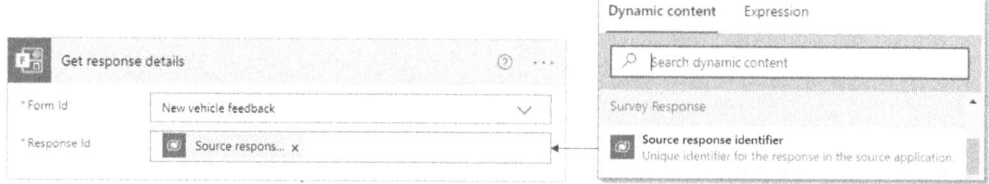

Figure 9.20 – Obtaining a survey question response

The question responses are then available for you to use in the workflow, and we will use them shortly.

Get survey variables (7)

Your survey may contain survey variables to provide additional information about the survey. The survey variable values are stored in **Context Data** (msfp_ embedcontextparameter) in the Customer Voice survey response. As there are multiple variables in the survey, the variable values are stored in JSON format. To parse the survey variable values, use the **Parse JSON** action and select **Context Data** for **Content**, as shown in *Figure 9.21*:

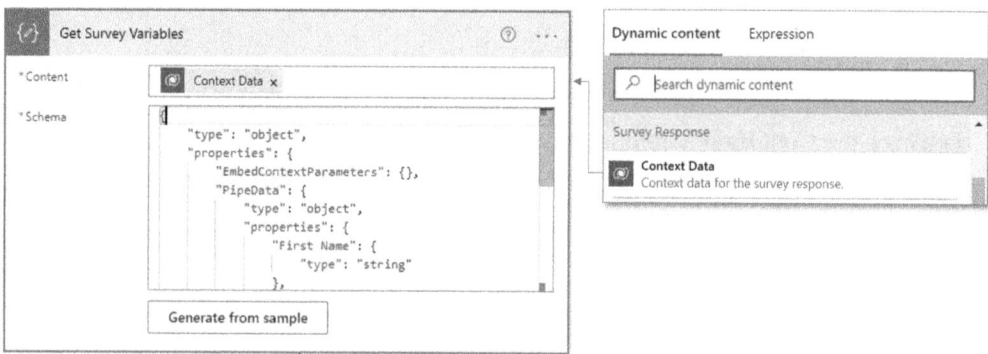

Figure 9.21 – Parsing survey variables

You can use the following schema and repeat the `<Survey Variable>` name for each variable you defined in your survey:

```
{
    "type": "object",
    "properties": {
        "EmbedContextParameters": {
            "type": "object",
            "properties": {
                "<Survey Variable>": {
                    "type": "string"
                },
            }
        }
    }
}
```

For example, if you have `First Name`, `Last Name`, `Dealer`, and `locale` as your survey variables, the schema looks as follows:

```
{
    "type": "object",
    "properties": {
        "EmbedContextParameters": {
            "type": "object",
            "properties": {
                "Dealer": {
                    "type": "string"
                },
                "First Name": {
                    "type": "string"
                },
                "Last Name": {
                    "type": "string"
                },
                "locale": {
                    "type": "string"
                }
```

```
                    }
                }
            }
        }
```

Rename the parse step to `Get Survey Variable`.

Get dealer info (8)

The survey variable includes dealer information. We can then use the information to look up the contact information for the dealer. In this example, I am storing the dealer contact information in the `Dealers` table in **Dataverse** and using the **List Rows** action for **Common Data Service** to retrieve the contact information filtered using the `Dealer` survey variable value, as shown in *Figure 9.22*:

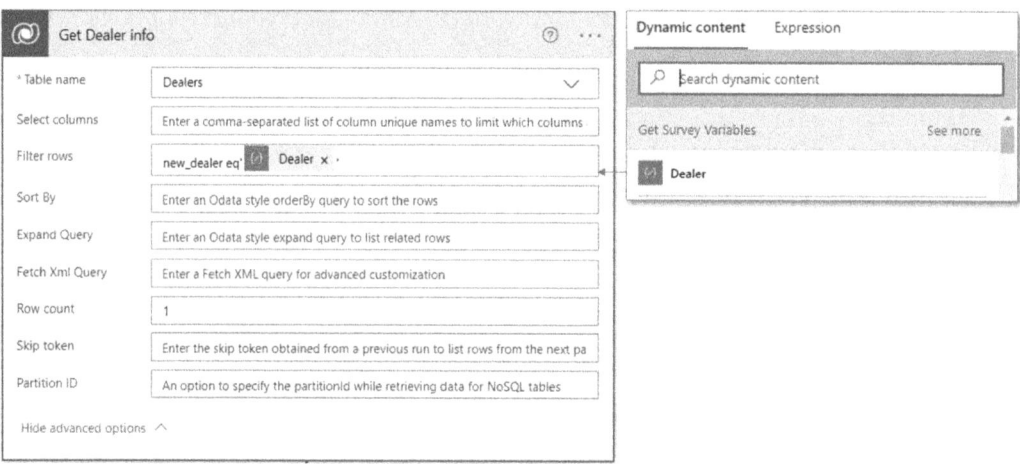

Figure 9.22 – Getting dealer contact information

Important note

A survey variable is an important capability when it comes to enabling you to integrate Customer Voice with business application systems. For example, if you are using Salesforce for your **Customer Relationship Management (CRM)** system, you can trigger surveys based on business activity in Salesforce and store a Salesforce record ID in the survey variable. When you receive a response, you can use the value in the survey variable to look up the record in Salesforce and connect the survey response to the relevant record.

Apply to each dealer (9)

As discussed previously, you need to add the **Apply to each** action for **List** rows and use the values from the previous step as input.

Send an email notification (10)

After we get the dealer's contact information, we can use the **Send an email notification** action to send an email. In the email body, you can insert the survey response from *Step 6* as shown in *Figure 9.23*. In addition to the survey responses, you can include additional information from the survey, including the following

- **Regarding** (regardingobjectid): A Dynamics 365 record ID related to the survey (if specified)

- **Respondent** (msfp_respondent): The respondent's full name

- **Respondent email address** (msfp_respondentemailaddress): The email address of the survey respondent

- **Submit date** (msfp_submitdate): The date and time when the survey response was submitted:

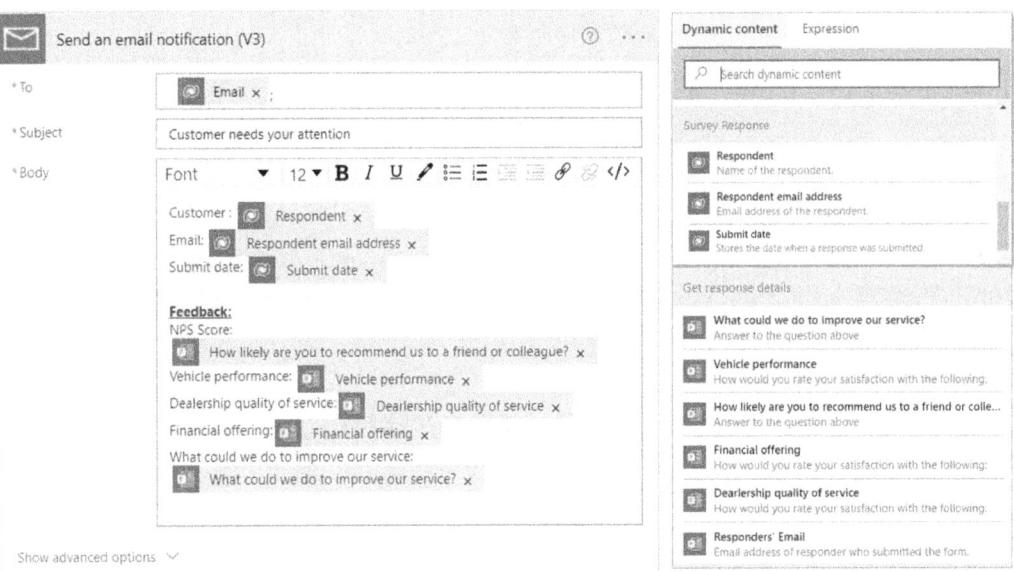

Figure 9.23 – Sending an email to a dealer

When a customer submits a survey response with a low NPS score, the workflow automatically sends an email to the relevant dealer manager. *Figure 9.24* shows an example of the email notification to the dealer manager:

Microsoft Power Apps and Power Automate
<microsoft@powerapps.com>
Tue 3/16/2021 10:20 AM
To: Adrienne McMillan

Customer: Catalina Weeks
Email: CatalinaW@M365x162381.OnMicrosoft.com
Submit date: 2021-03-16

Feedback:
NPS Score: 4
Vehicle performance: Dissatisfied
Dealership quality of service: Satisfied
Financial offering: Satisfied
What could we do to improve our service:
Rattling sound from the back seat

If you want to unsubscribe from these emails, please use this form.

Reply | Forward

Figure 9.24 – Email notification to the dealer

The Power Automate workflow is also available for surveys sent through Microsoft Forms. In the next section, we will go through an example of creating a workflow for a Forms survey response.

Microsoft Forms response workflow with Power Automate

When receiving responses from Microsoft Forms, you can create a workflow to automate follow up actions. One of the common use case for this automation workflow is to copy the survey response to another location such as to a SharePoint list.

Copying an Microsoft Forms response to a SharePoint list

Figure 9.25 shows the Microsoft Forms training feedback survey we used in *Chapter 5, Post-Training Assessment and Feedback*:

1. How likely are you to recommend this training to a friend or colleague?

0	1	2	3	4	5	6	7	8	9	10

Not at all likely   Extremely likely

2. How much do you agree on the following:

	Strongly disagree	Disagree	Neither disagree nor agree	Agree	Strongly agree
I learn new things from this training	○	○	○	○	○
The content is useful for my work	○	○	○	○	○
The instructor was knowledgeable about the material	○	○	○	○	○
The instructor presented the material clearly	○	○	○	○	○
The instructor was engaging	○	○	○	○	○
There is clear takeaway from this training	○	○	○	○	○

3. Please share additional feedback

Enter your answer

Figure 9.25 – Training feedback form

For our example, we will create a workflow that copies the survey response from this training feedback to a SharePoint list.

To start, create a SharePoint list to store the survey responses. Create a separate column for every question you would like to capture. For example, in our survey, we have eight questions (including each statement in the Likert), so you can add eight new columns to the SharePoint list as shown in *Figure 9.26*. Note that each of the SharePoint columns must be created as a **single line of text** or a **multiple lines of text** column type. The column does not have to have the same text as the question in your survey, as we will map the workflow later:

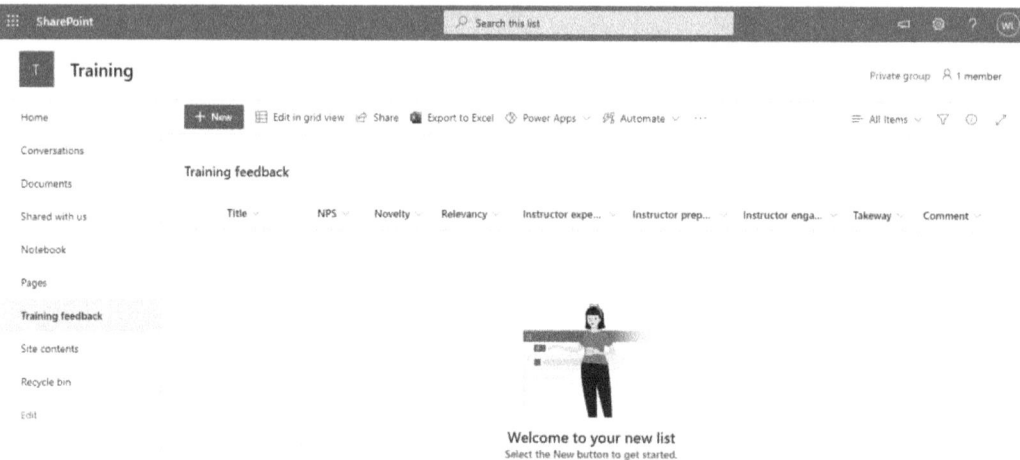

Figure 9.26 – SharePoint list to store survey feedback

After you create the SharePoint list, go to Power Automate, create a new automated workflow, and select **When a new response is submitted** for the flow's trigger (see *Figure 9.27*):

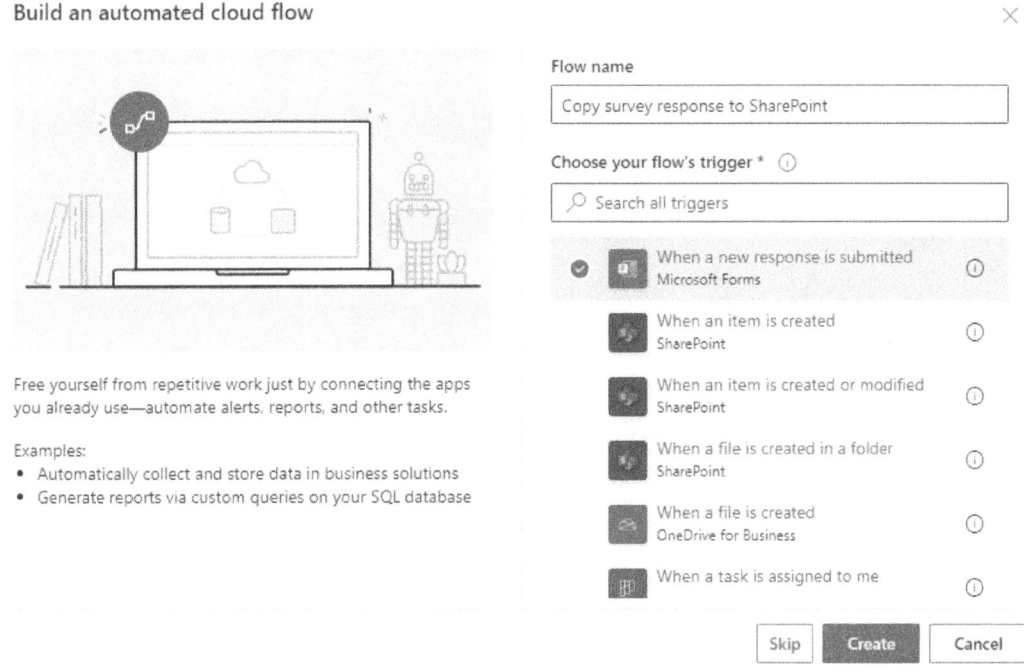

Figure 9.27 – Workflow trigger for the Microsoft Form survey response

Select the form's name (for example, **Training feedback**) and add a new action to **Get response details**. Select the form name and add **Response ID** from the previous step, as shown in *Figure 9.28*:

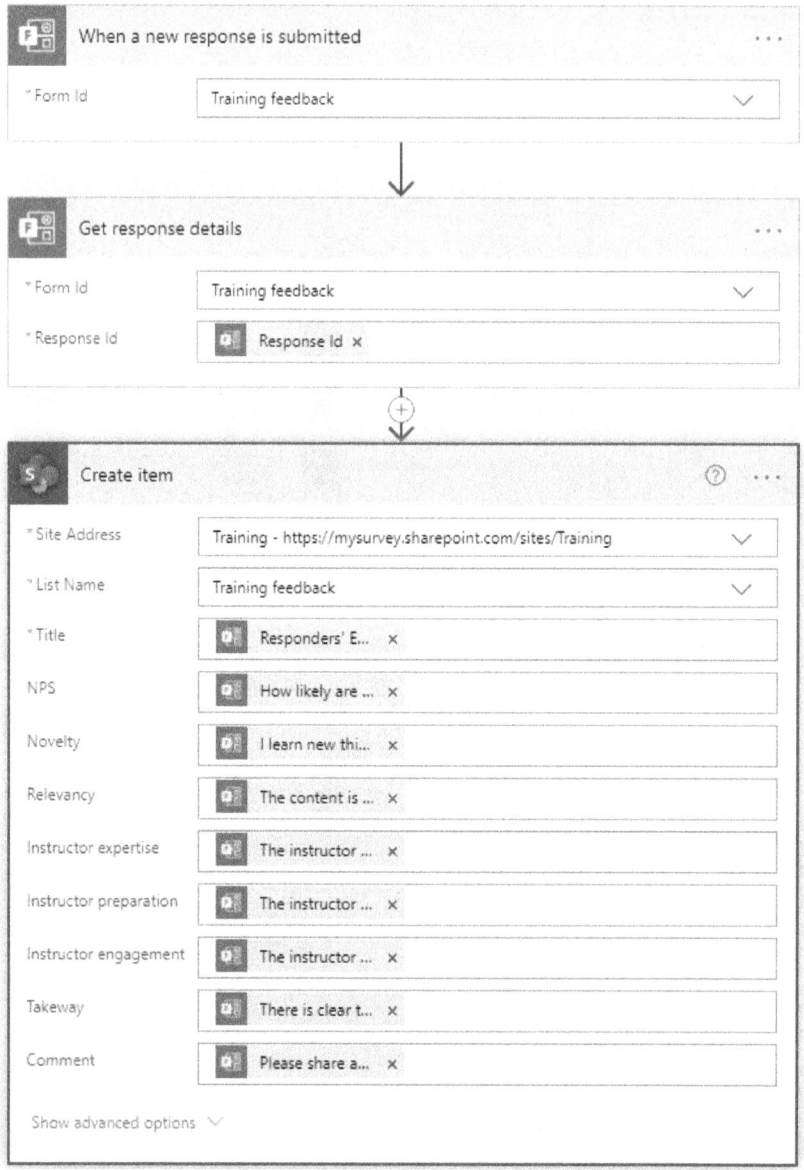

Figure 9.28 – Workflow for copying a survey response to SharePoint

Then, add a new action to create an item in SharePoint, specify the SharePoint site's URL and list name, and then map the survey question response to the SharePoint column as shown in *Figure 9.28*.

When you submit a new survey response, the workflow will automatically create a new item in the SharePoint list with the information from the survey response, as shown in *Figure 9.29*:

Title	NPS	Novelty	Relevancy	Instructor expe...	Instructor prep...	Instructor enga...	Takeway	Comment
welly@mysurvey.onmicrosoft.com	10	Agree	Strongly agree	Strongly agree	Strongly agree	Agree	Agree	Great training

Figure 9.29 – Survey response in a SharePoint list

The workflow makes a copy of the Microsoft Forms response to a SharePoint list. When you have a file attachment in your survey, you can copy the response and its file attachment to a SharePoint document library, which we will discuss next.

Copying Microsoft Forms file attachments to the SharePoint document library

For example, if you are using a survey form similar to *Figure 9.30* where you include a file upload question in your survey:

1. How likely are you to recommend this training to a friend or colleague?

0	1	2	3	4	5	6	7	8	9	10

Not at all likely   Extremely likely

2. How much do you agree on the following:

	Strongly disagree	Disagree	Neither disagree nor agree	Agree	Strongly agree
I learn new things from this training	○	○	○	○	○
The content is useful for my work	○	○	○	○	○
The instructor was knowledgeable about the material	○	○	○	○	○
The instructor presented the material clearly	○	○	○	○	○
The instructor was engaging	○	○	○	○	○
There is clear takeaway from this training	○	○	○	○	○

3. Please share additional feedback

> Enter your answer

4. Please share a picture from the training

⬆ Upload file

Figure 9.30 – Survey with file attachment

By default, the file is created on OneDrive for Business of the survey owner. In some cases, you may want to copy the file to a SharePoint document library to make it easier to share. To do this, you can create a Power Automate workflow to copy the file to your team's SharePoint list.

Perform the following steps to modify the workflow we created to include steps to copy the file:

1. Create a SharePoint document library and add a hyperlink column to store the link to the survey feedback, as shown in *Figure 9.31*:

Figure 9.31 – SharePoint document library to store the Forms attachment

2. Since the survey may not always include an attachment, we need to check in the workflow whether a file attachment is empty. Modify the workflow by adding a new **Condition** control at the end of the last step, as shown in *Figure 9.32*. In the left side of the condition, type empty() in the pop-up dialog window's **Expression** tab and then place your cursor in between the parentheses before switching to the Dynamics content to pick the file upload question type and then click **OK**. On the right-hand side, type true on the **Expression** tab and then click **Update**:

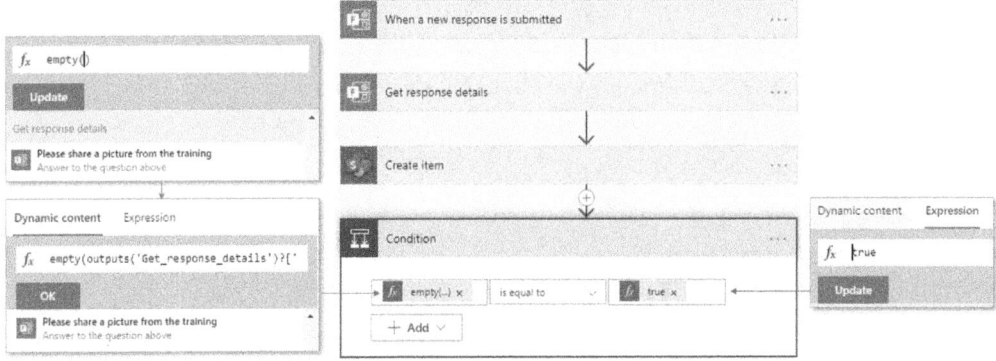

Figure 9.32 – Condition to check whether there is an attachment in the response

In our example, the full expression would be
`empty(outputs('Get_response_details')?['body/`
`r36b4af2360494caaab5ab80832f5996d']).`

3. The file attachment information is using JSON format, so to extract the information, you need to add a new **Parse JSON** action, as shown in *Figure 9.33*:

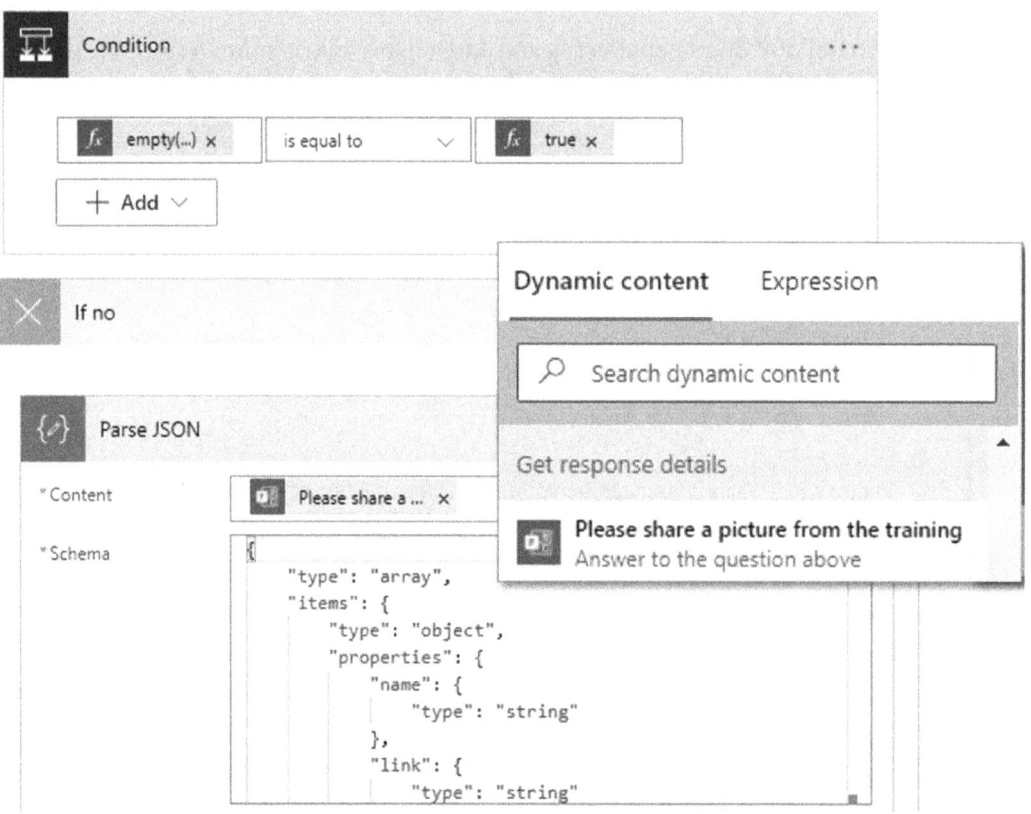

Figure 9.33 – Getting Microsoft Forms attachment information

Use the following as a schema for the **Parse JSON** action:

```
{
    "type": "array",
    "items": {
        "type": "object",
        "properties": {
            "name": {
                "type": "string"
```

```
        },
        "link": {
            "type": "string"
        },
        "id": {
            "type": "string"
        },
        "type": {},
        "size": {
            "type": "integer"
        },
        "referenceId": {
            "type": "string"
        },
        "driveId": {
            "type": "string"
        },
        "status": {
            "type": "integer"
        },
        "uploadSessionUrl": {}
    },
    "required": [
        "name",
        "link",
        "id",
        "type",
        "size",
        "referenceId",
        "driveId",
        "status",
        "uploadSessionUrl"
    ]
    }
}
```

4. Add an **Apply to each** control for each file attached to the Forms response and use `Body` from the previous step as the input (see *Figure 9.34*).

5. Add **Get file content** from the **One Drive for Business** action and use `id` from the **Parse JSON** action as the input (see *Figure 9.34*).

6. Add **Create file** from SharePoint, select the SharePoint site and document library from the dropdown, and then the map name from **Parse JSON** and `File content` from **Get file content** from the One Drive for Business step (see *Figure 9.34*).

7. As the last step, add **Update the file property** from **SharePoint** with the link to the **Forms** record we created in the SharePoint list (see *Figure 9.34*):

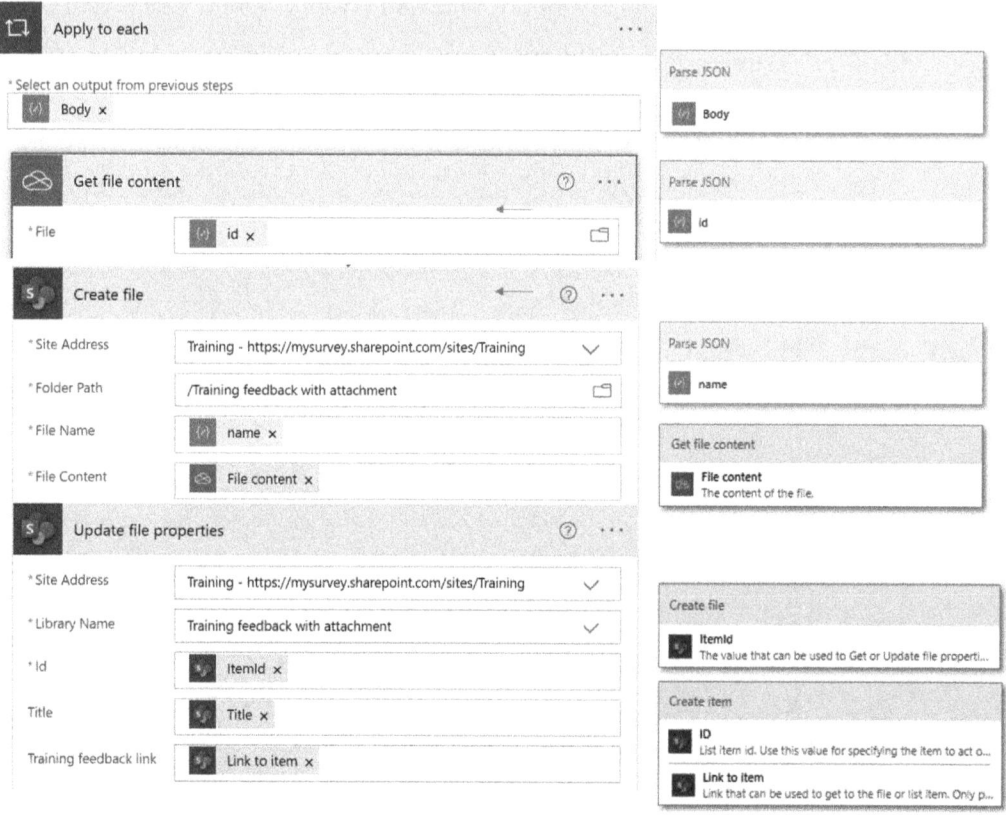

Figure 9.34 – Workflow steps for copying a file attachment to the SharePoint library

When a form is submitted with a file attachment, the file is automatically uploaded to the document library with a link to the training feedback (see *Figure 9.35*):

Training feedback with attachment

	Name ⌄	Modified ⌄	Modified By ⌄	Training feedba... ⌄
	IMG_20200206_192855_Welly Lee.jpg	A few seconds ago	Welly Lee	https://mysurvey.share...

Figure 9.35 – Uploaded file attachment in SharePoint

Summary

In this chapter, we discussed the built-in follow-up action capabilities in Customer Voice to notify you when receiving poor feedback and to enable you to close the loop with the respondent promptly. Follow-up action is one of the key areas of investments in Customer Voice and you can expect more capabilities to make it easier for you to close the loop for common feedback scenarios. When you have specific follow-up action workflow requirements, Customer Voice and Microsoft Forms include built-in integration with Power Automate so you can create custom workflow actions based on survey responses.

The follow-up workflow is not limited to performing an action within Microsoft applications such as Dynamics or Office, but the workflow can include actions to any system that you can connect through Power Automate. At the time of this writing, Power Automate has 453 connectors (you can find the latest list of available connectors at `https://docs.microsoft.com/en-us/connectors/connector-reference/connector-reference-powerautomate-connectors`). Power Automate also supports custom connectors, meaning you can build your own connector if you are using a system where there is no available out-of-the-box connector.

In the last few chapters, we discussed end user capabilities for Microsoft Forms and Customer Voice. In the remaining chapters, we will talk about administering the applications.

Section 3: Administering Microsoft Forms and Dynamics 365 Customer Voice

This section will go over the administration settings for Microsoft Forms and Dynamics 365 Customer Voice and when to use them.

This section contains the following chapters:

10
Administering Microsoft Forms and Dynamics 365 Customer Voice

Microsoft Forms and Dynamics 365 Customer Voice provide some administrative settings to enable administrators to set policies for creating surveys in their organization. In addition, Customer Voice saves survey data to Dataverse, and there is some setup that a Dataverse administrator has to complete before connecting Customer Voice with Dataverse.

In this chapter, we will review the administration settings for Forms and Customer Voice, walk through process of setting up users in Dataverse for Customer Voice, and review functionalities to help you to move Customer Voice projects from development to test and product environments.

The chapter is organized as follows:

- Administration settings for Microsoft Forms
- Administration settings for Customer Voice

- Managing permissions for Customer Voice
- Managing project deployment for Customer Voice

By the end of the chapter, you will understand what settings are available for you to manage policies for Microsoft Forms and Dynamics 365 Customer Voice.

Administration setting for Microsoft Forms

Microsoft Forms administration settings are available through the **Microsoft 365 admin center** (admin.microsoft.com). To access the Microsoft Forms settings, navigate to **Settings>Org Settings** and select **Microsoft Forms** from the list of the applications to open a settings panel, as shown in *Figure 10.1*:

Microsoft Forms

External sharing

Control how people in your org can collaborate on forms with people outside your org.

☑ Send a link to the form and collect responses

☑ Share to collaborate on the form layout and structure

☑ Share the form as a template that can be duplicated

☑ Share form result summary

Record names of people in your org

By default, your forms will capture the names of people in your org who fill them out. This setting can be changed on individual forms.

☑ Record names by default

Allow YouTube and Bing

☑ Include Bing search, YouTube videos
   Allow users in your organization to add images from Bing and YouTube videos to Forms. Note: If unchecked, previously added images from Bing will remain, but any previously added YouTube videos will be converted into a YouTube link that will launch outside of Forms.

Phishing protection

Help protect against personal data loss of a compromised account.

☑ Add internal phishing protection
   Proactively scan forms that only allow in-org responses, and automatically block them from being shared or distributed if common phishing questions are detected, such as requests for personal or sensitive information. Admins will be notified via the Message Center when a form is blocked due to

Figure 10.1 – Microsoft Forms settings

We'll describe the settings in the following section.

External sharing

External sharing settings restrict how you can collaborate or send surveys to people outside your organizations.

Send a link to the form and collect responses

Enabling this setting allows users in your organization to send surveys to people outside the organization. When the setting is unchecked, the **Anyone can respond** option is disabled, as shown in *Figure 10.2*:

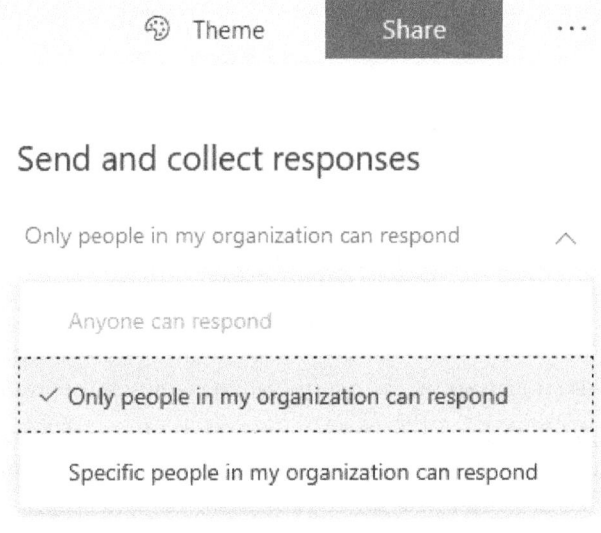

Figure 10.2 – Disabled external sharing option

When the link is shared to people outside the organization, the recipient will be asked to log in to their Microsoft work or school account, and if the user is not part of the same organization, an error message like in *Figure 10.3* is shown:

Sorry, something went wrong

IT policy prevents external user from responding this form.

∨ Technical details

Create my own form

Powered by Microsoft Forms | Privacy and cookies | Terms of use

Figure 10.3 – Error message shown to survey recipients outside the organization

In addition to sharing the link for the recipient to respond, Microsoft Forms also supports setting a limit on who you can share the link with to collaborate on the survey.

Share to collaborate on the form layout and structure

To restrict the people with whom survey owners in your organization can collaborate on a survey, you can disable the setting for **Share to collaborate on the form layout and structure** in the **External sharing** section. When this setting is disabled, survey owners can no longer select the option to share with people outside the organization, as shown in *Figure 10.4*:

Share to collaborate

People in my organization can view and edit   ∧

Users with an Office 365 work or school account
can view and edit

✓ People in my organization can view and edit

Specific people in my organization can view and
edit

Figure 10.4 – Disabled external collaboration option

When the link is shared anyway, recipient of the links will be prompted to log in, and users outside the organization will be shown the error message like the one in *Figure 10.5*:

Sorry, something went wrong

IT policy has disabled the collaboration feature.

∨ Technical details

Figure 10.5 – Error message shown to collaborators outside the organization

Another way survey owners can share a survey design is to share the survey as a template.

Share the form as a template that can be duplicated

Microsoft Forms supports sharing a survey template link to enable the recipient of the link to create a new survey with the same questions and styling. By default, the survey template link is available to users who are internal and external to the organization to make a copy of the survey. By disabling the **Share the form as a template that can be duplicated** checkbox, the link is only available to users from the same organization. *Figure 10.6* shows a comparison of the **Share as a template** panel where the setting is disabled and enabled:

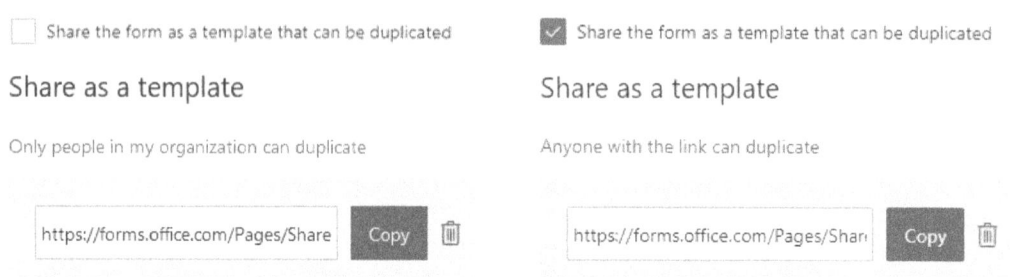

Figure 10.6 – Difference in share as a template based on the admin setting values

When the link is opened by users outside the organization, the user will be shown an error message saying **IT policy prevents external user from copying this form**.

Share form result summary

As discussed in *Chapter 3, Creating a Survey with Microsoft Forms*, Microsoft Forms supports sharing the summary report with people who are both internal and external to your organization. Anyone with the summary link can view the report. As an administrator, you can restrict sharing the summary report link to only people within your organization. When the survey owner generates a summary link, a message is displayed stating that only people in the organization can view the summary, as shown in *Figure 10.7*:

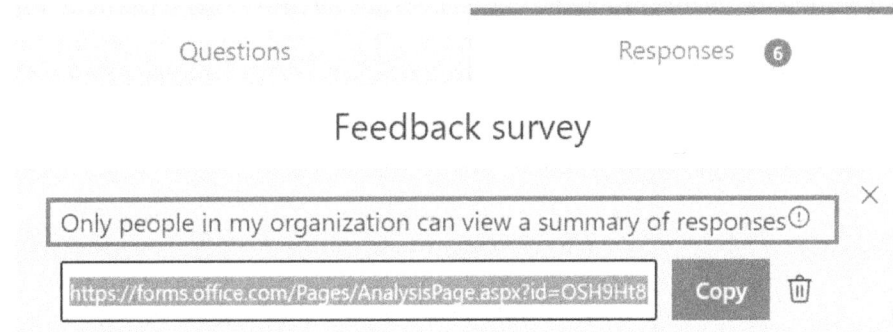

Figure 10.7 – Sharing the summary link when external sharing is disabled

When the link is accessed by users outside the organization, the following message is displayed: **IT policy prevents external user from viewing responses summary of this form**.

Record names of people in your organization

Microsoft Forms gives survey owners the chance to record the names of the survey responders when selecting **Only people in my organization can respond**, as shown in *Figure 10.8*:

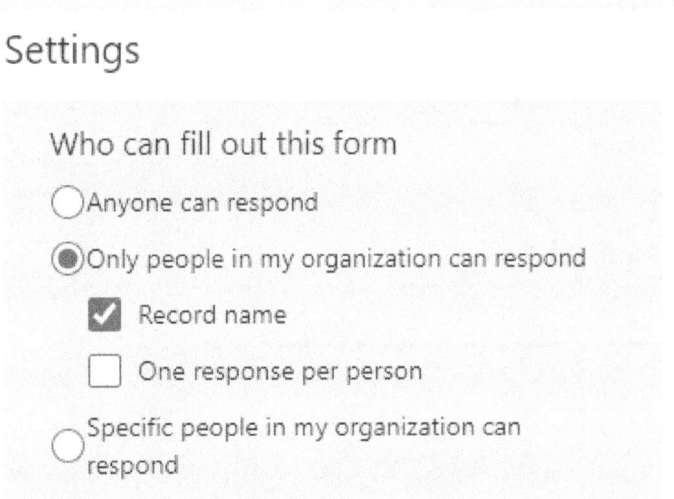

Figure 10.8 – Settings to share survey to only people in the organization

The **default setting** for the **Record name** option depends on the setting selected by your organization administrator. If the administrator disabled **Record names by default**, then the survey owner would need to explicitly change the setting for the specific survey to record the name. Otherwise, the survey response would be recorded as **Anonymous** in the survey report (see *Figure 10.9*):

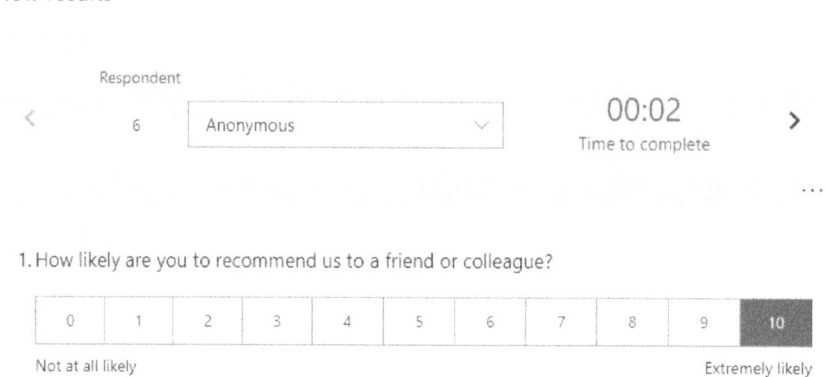

Figure 10.9 – Survey response when the Record name setting is not selected

You can also set the policy that prevents using publicly available images or videos as part of survey questions to minimize the risk of content rights violations.

Allow YouTube and Bing

When creating a survey question, you can insert a **YouTube** video or an image from **Microsoft Bing**, as shown in *Figure 10.10*:

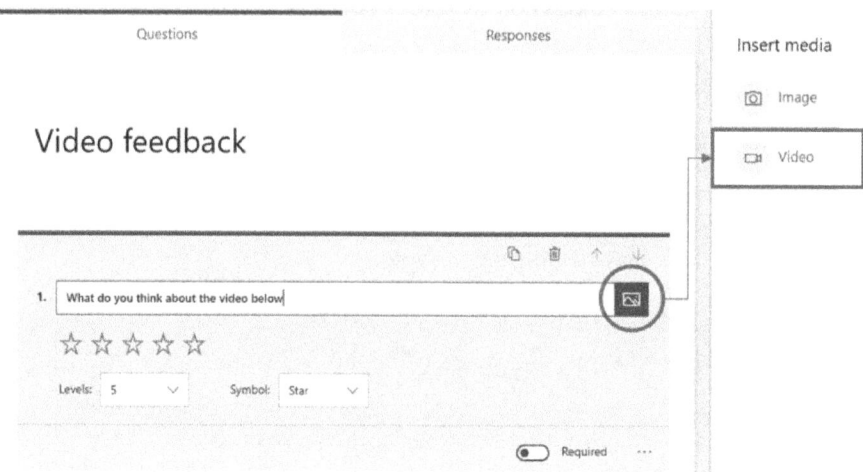

Figure 10.10 – Inserting a video on a survey question

After inserting a YouTube video link, the video is embedded into the survey question, as shown in *Figure 10.11*:

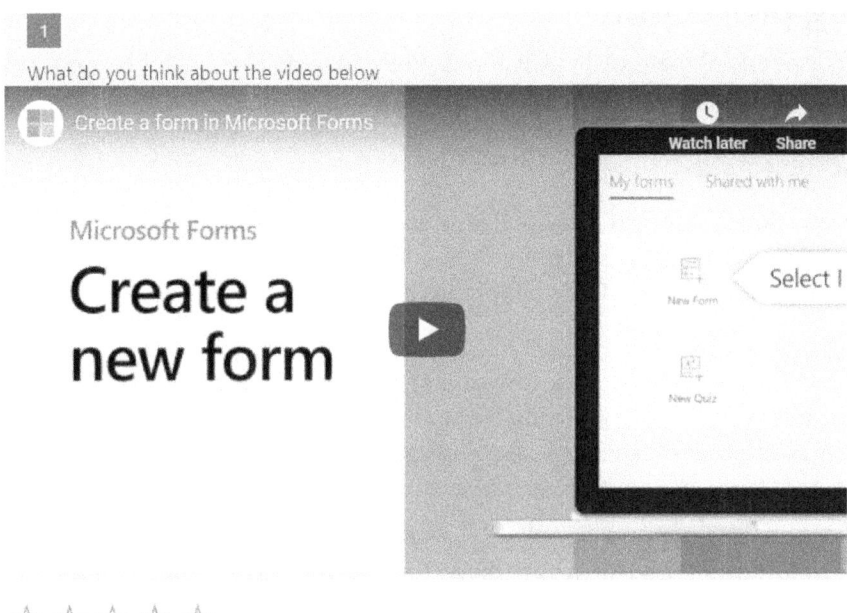

Figure 10.11 – Embedding a YouTube video into a survey question

The use of the images and videos depends on the content rights of the content owner. To minimize the risk of content rights violations, you can disable the **Include Bing search, YouTube videos** setting. When this setting is disabled, survey owners will get an error message, as shown in *Figure 10.12*:

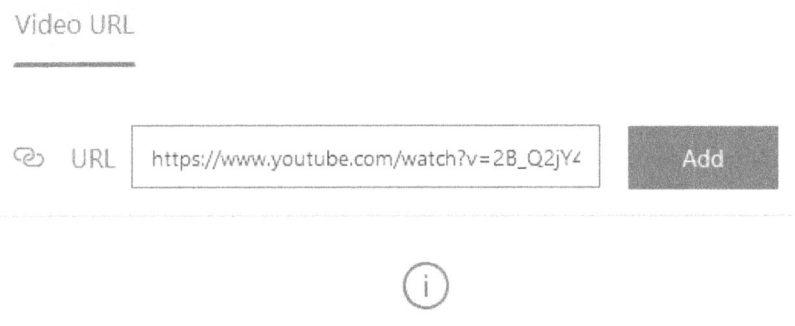

Figure 10.12 – Message while inserting a video when an admin disables the setting

The last administrator setting for Microsoft Forms is for phishing protection.

Phishing protection

Microsoft Forms and Dynamics 365 Customer Voice include anti-phishing protection, which means that if your survey is suspected to be a cover for a phishing attack to obtain personal information, your survey would be disabled by default and you would be unable to collect any responses.

Phishing protection is automatically applied to surveys that collect responses from people outside the organization, and you cannot disable it. Phishing protection is enabled, by default, for surveys with the **Only people in my organization can respond** setting enabled.

If you may need to collect personal information through surveys and would like to prevent your internal survey from being blocked as potential phishing, then an admin can disable the **Add internal phishing protection** setting. Disabling this setting skips anti-phishing protection checks for internal surveys.

Now that you have learned about the administration settings for Microsoft Forms, let's take a look at the settings for Customer Voice.

Administration settings for Customer Voice

Dynamics 365 Customer Voice is often used for collecting feedback from customers outside your organization, and the settings are simplified to reflect the scenario. You can access the settings for Customer Voice from the same **Org Settings** page in **Microsoft 365 admin center** as for Microsoft Forms. The settings for Customer Voice are shown in *Figure 10.13*:

Dynamics 365 Customer Voice

Capture, analyze, and act on customer and employee feedback with a simple-yet-powerful enterprise survey solution.Learn how to create a survey

Record names of people in your org

By default, your surveys will capture the names of people in your org who fill them out. This setting can be changed on individual surveys.

☑ Record names by default

Phishing protection

Help protect against personal data loss of a compromised account.

☑ Add internal phishing protection

Proactively scan surveys that only allow in-org responses, and automatically block them from being shared or distributed if common phishing questions are detected, such as requests for personal or sensitive information. Admins will be notified via the Message Center when a survey is blocked due to phishing.

Send surveys from a custom email address

+ Add domain

Domain	Status	
customervoicedemo.com	Pending Verification	... ∨

Figure 10.13 – Admin settings for Customer Voice

The first two settings, **Record names of people in your org** and **Phishing protection**, are the same as in Microsoft Forms.

The additional setting that is unique for Customer Voice is the setting to customize the email address surveys are sent from.

Send survey from a custom email address

Customer Voice supports sending a personalized survey invitation email to your survey recipients. The email is tracked so you can get a report when the survey recipient opens the email. When sending the survey invitation, Customer Voice by default uses the following email address: `surveys@email.formspro.microsoft.com`. You can customize the email sender address with your organization's email address by adding a domain in the administration settings. Complete the following steps:

1. Click **Add domain** from the setting page (See *Figure 10.13*).

2. Specify your organization's email domain address, as shown in *Figure 10.14*, and click **Next**:

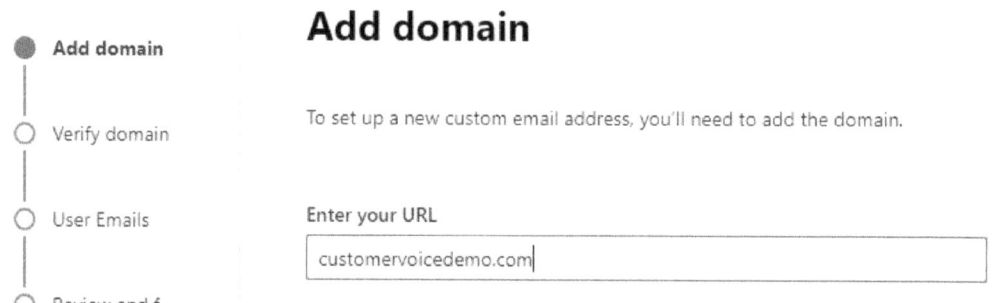

Figure 10.14 – Specifying the domain

3. Get the information that you need to add to your DNS record to verify that you own the domain specified in the previous step:

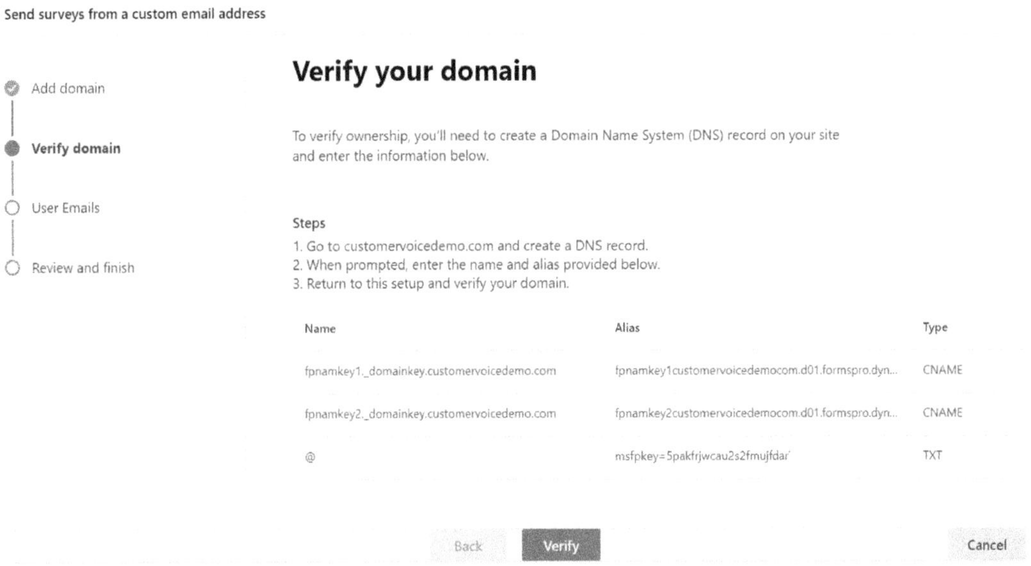

Send surveys from a custom email address

Verify your domain

- ● Add domain

- ● **Verify domain**

- ○ User Emails

- ○ Review and finish

To verify ownership, you'll need to create a Domain Name System (DNS) record on your site and enter the information below.

Steps

1. Go to customervoicedemo.com and create a DNS record.
2. When prompted, enter the name and alias provided below.
3. Return to this setup and verify your domain.

Name	Alias	Type
fpnamkey1._domainkey.customervoicedemo.com	fpnamkey1customervoicedemocom.d01.formspro.dyn...	CNAME
fpnamkey2._domainkey.customervoicedemo.com	fpnamkey2customervoicedemocom.d01.formspro.dyn...	CNAME
@	msfpkey=5pakfrjwcau2s2fmujfdar'	TXT

Back   Verify   Cancel

Figure 10.15 – Domain information for Customer Voice custom email verification

> **Important note**
>
> The DNS verification steps need to be done by your network administrator. Depending on who manages your DNS, the steps may vary. The following steps are an example where the DNS is managed directly from `admin.microsoft.com`.

4. On a new tab, open `https://admin.microsoft.com` and navigate to **Settings**>**Domains**, click on **DNS records**, and then click **Add record** (see *Figure 10.16*):

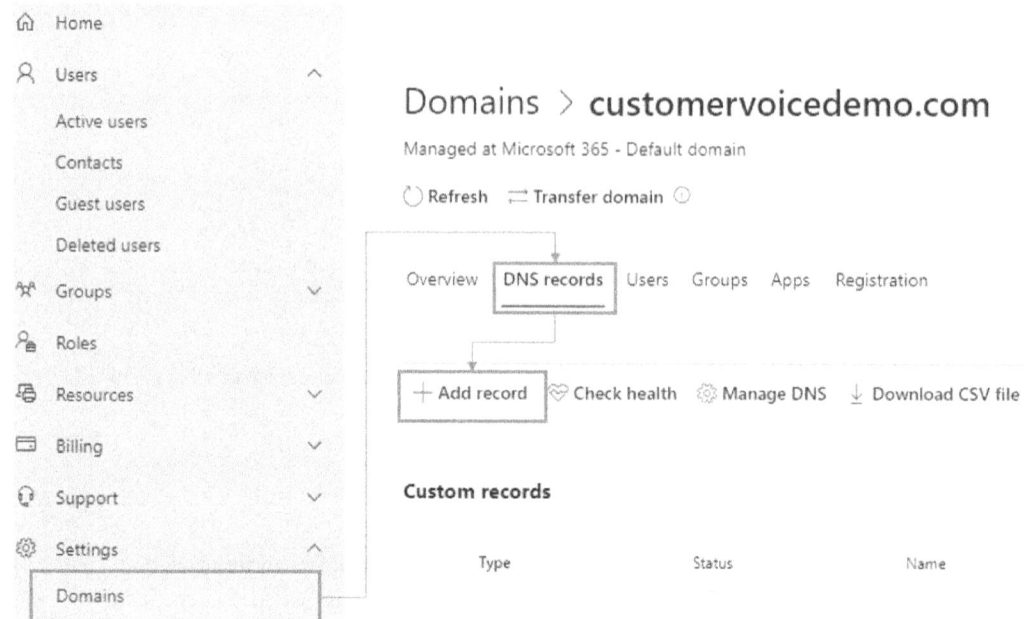

Figure 10.16 – Adding a new record to your domain

5. Create a new record for each of the three entries from the preceding *step 2*. See *Figure 10.17* as an example for the three entries:

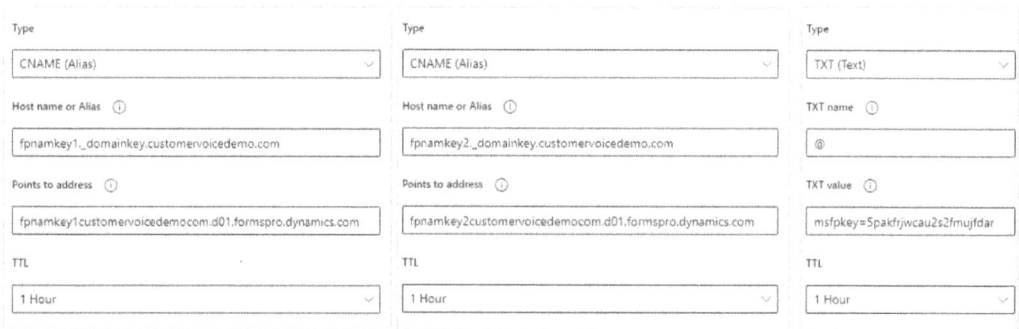

Figure 10.17 – Example of DNS record entries

> **Important note**
> The alias values from *step 3* may not display fully. Make sure the alias entry
> ends with `.dynamics.com`.

6. After adding the entry, your DNS records should look like what is shown in *Figure 10.18*:

Domains > **customervoicedemo.com**

Managed at Microsoft 365 - Default domain

↻ Refresh   ⇌ Transfer domain ⓘ

Overview   DNS records   Users   Groups   Apps   Registration

+ Add record   ♡ Check health   ⊚ Manage DNS   ↓ Download CSV file   ↓ Download zone file   🖨 Print

Custom records

Type	Status	Name	Value	TTL
TXT	⋮	@	msfpkey=5pakfrjwcau2s2fmujfdar	1 Hour
CNAME	⋮	fpnamkey1._domainkey	fpnamkey1customervoicedemocom.d01.formspro.dynamics.com	1 Hour
CNAME	⋮	fpnamkey2._domainkey	fpnamkey2customervoicedemocom.d01.formspro.dynamics.com	1 Hour

Figure 10.18 – Completed DNS record entries

7. Return to the Customer Voice admin setup page (*step 2*) and click **Verify**.

8. Specify the **Email address**, **Display name**, and users who can use the email domain, as shown in *Figure 10.19*:

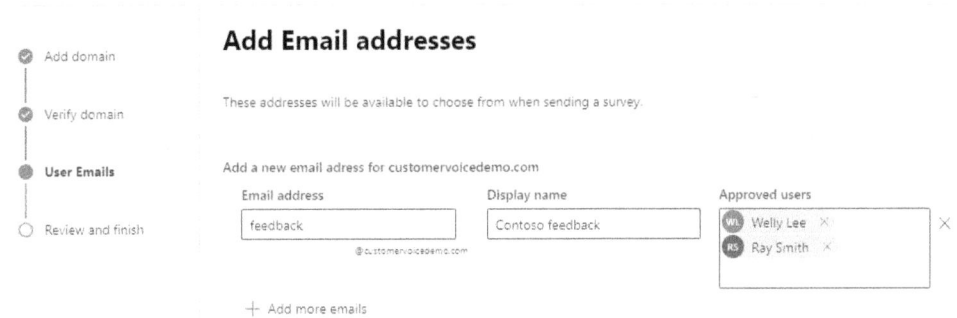

Figure 10.19 – Email address and approved users setup

9. Verify the information and complete the setup.

After you have completed the domain setup, the users listed in *step 7* can change the sender email address through the **Distribution** pane, as shown in *Figure 10.20*:

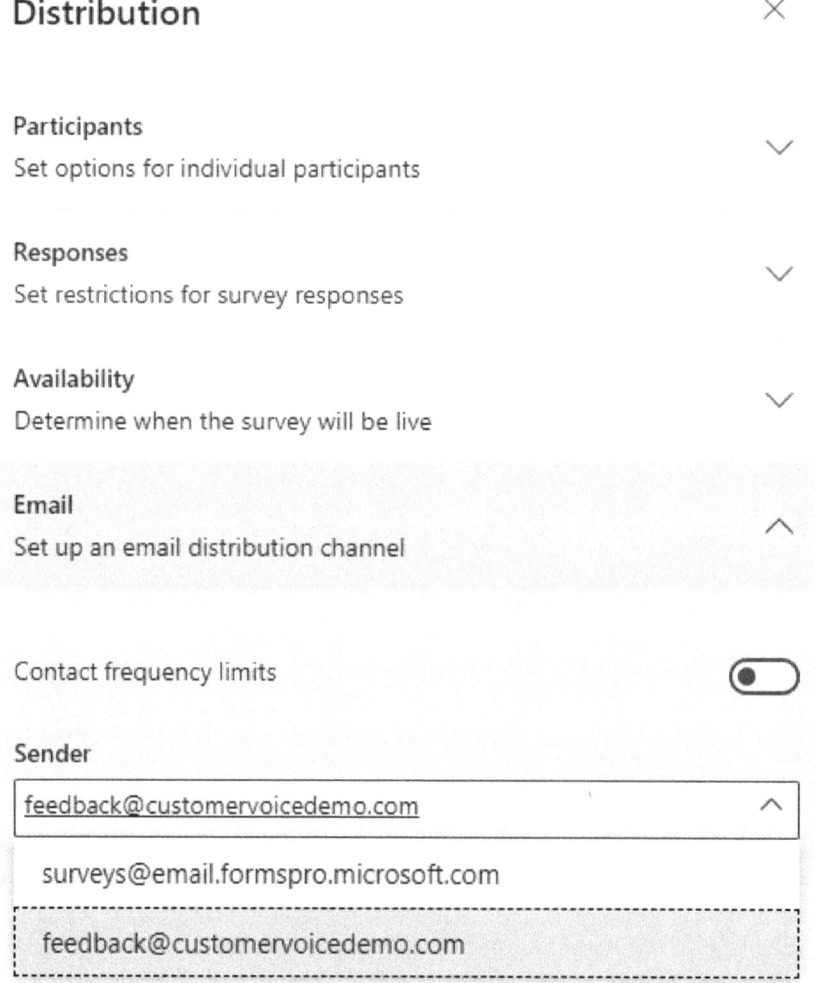

Figure 10.20 – Email sender setting

In addition to configuring settings, as an admin, you will also need to manage permissions for Customer Voice.

Managing permissions for Customer Voice

Customer Voice stores survey definitions, survey invites, and response data in its own cloud service and the data is then copied to your organization's Dataverse (for more information about Dataverse, go to `https://docs.microsoft.com/en-us/powerapps/maker/data-platform/data-platform-intro`). If you are using Dynamics 365 or Power Apps, then you can use the Dataverse associated with the application to store the Customer Voice survey data. If you are not using Dynamics 365 or Power Apps, then Customer Voice uses the default Dataverse instance for your organization. In the next section, I will cover how you can manage permissions when using default Dataverse and what additional steps you must follow to manage permissions for Customer Voice in Dynamics 365 or Power Apps.

Using the default Dataverse for Customer Voice

The first time you use Customer Voice, a user account is created in the default Dataverse instance (for more information about default Dataverse, go to `https://docs.microsoft.com/en-us/power-platform/admin/environments-overview#the-default-environment`). The default Dataverse is a shared database that is used by other applications, such as Power Apps. If there is no default Dataverse instance, Customer Voice will automatically create the default Dataverse and associated tables to store the survey data (see `https://docs.microsoft.com/en-us/dynamics365/customer-voice/developer/entity-reference` for Customer Voice schemas in Dataverse).

The user created by Customer Voice will be automatically assigned the **Project Owner** role in the default Dataverse to enable the user to write and read their own data. In Dataverse, a record must have an owner. Survey definition, survey invite, and survey response records are owned by the user who creates the project in Customer Voice.

Customer Voice uses **Microsoft 365 Group** to share a project with others. When a user shares a project, the user must select a group or create a new group.

You can share a project from the **All Project** view in Customer Voice or click the **Share** button when you are in a project.

The following are the steps to share a project in Customer Voice:

1. Select an existing group or create a new **Microsoft 365 Group**. Note that if the administrator disables this setting, then the option to create groups is removed (see *Figure 10.21*).

2. When creating a new group, provide the **Group Name** and **Email address** information, and add at least one member to share the survey with.

3. Click **Share** to finish:

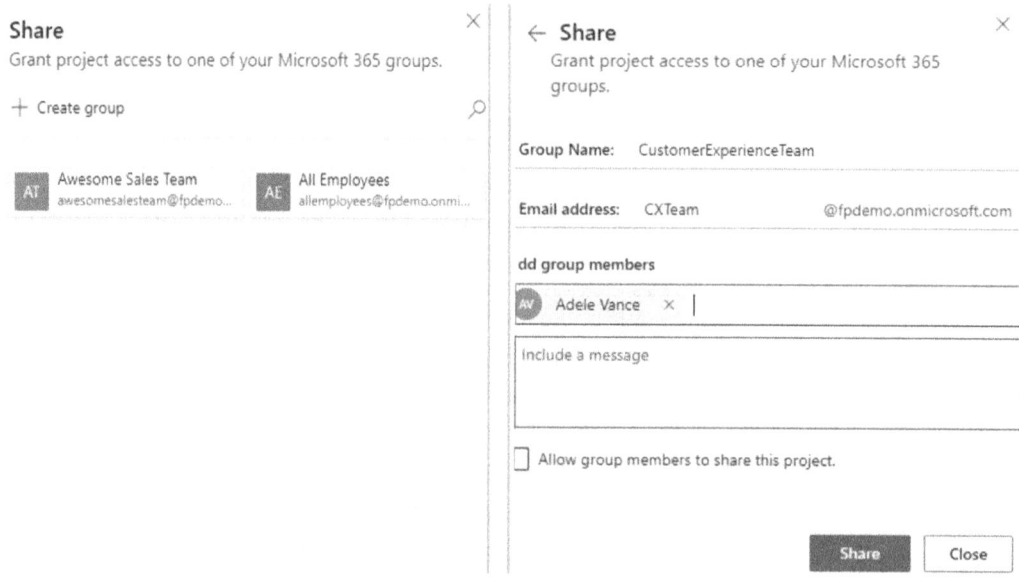

Figure 10.21 – Share a Customer Voice project

When you share a project, Customer Voice automatically creates a **Team** in Dataverse and assigns the **Project Owner** role to the team. Any subsequent survey records are created using the Dataverse team as the record owner. Any member you add to the group gets access to the record in Dataverse.

User account creation and role assignment are done automatically when you use the default Dataverse option. If you connect to an existing Dataverse instance for Dynamics 365 or Power Apps, then you need to manage permissions manually.

Managing Customer Voice permissions in Dataverse

Any user who needs to create a project and send a survey needs to have permissions in an existing Dataverse instance for Dynamics 365 and Power Apps. By default, Customer Voice is installed automatically as part of the Dynamics 365 customer engagement application (such as Sales, Customer Service, and Marketing). If you are using an existing Dataverse instance for Power Apps, then you need to install Customer Voice from `https://aka.ms/CustomerVoiceApp` on your existing Dataverse instance. The app installs tables, roles, and the application user account used by Customer Voice to write data to Dataverse.

To enable users to select the Dataverse instance, the user must be assigned the **Project Owner** role, as shown in *Figure 10.22*:

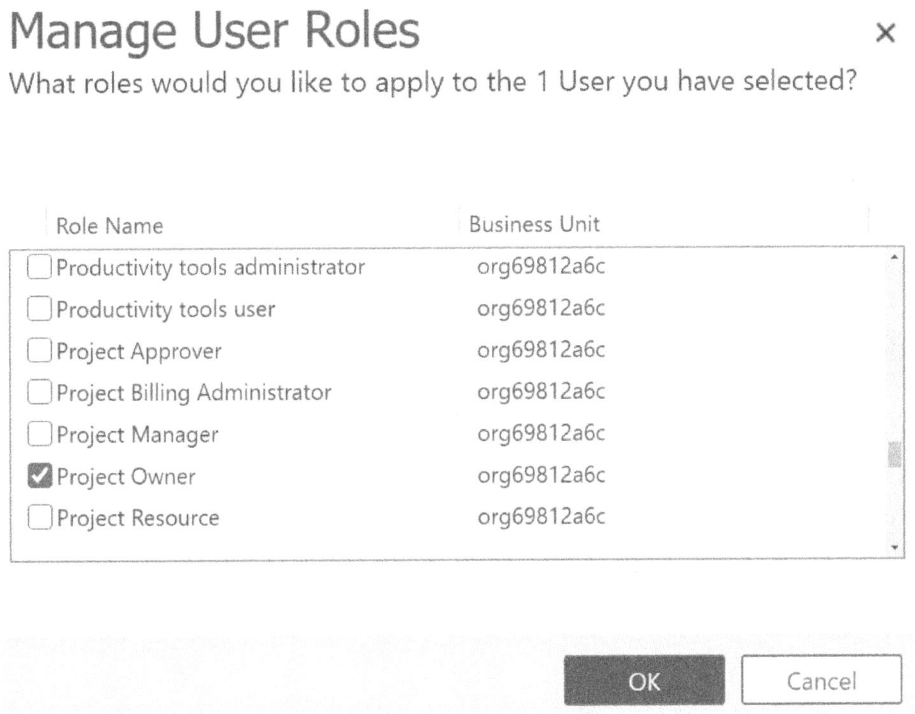

Manage User Roles   ✕

What roles would you like to apply to the 1 User you have selected?

Role Name	Business Unit
☐ Productivity tools administrator	org69812a6c
☐ Productivity tools user	org69812a6c
☐ Project Approver	org69812a6c
☐ Project Billing Administrator	org69812a6c
☐ Project Manager	org69812a6c
☑ Project Owner	org69812a6c
☐ Project Resource	org69812a6c

OK   Cancel

Figure 10.22 – Project owner role for a Customer Voice user

The Project Owner role assigns the necessary privileges to enable users to create survey records in Dataverse. The user will need to have a separate role to access other Dataverse records to send a survey and associate the survey with that record. For example, to send a survey to an existing contact in Dynamics 365, you must have additional permission to access the contact. Without it, the user will not be able to select the contact to send the survey.

> **Important note**
>
> When you are using a Power Automate workflow using a service account, you must share the Customer Voice project to the service account so the workflow can send the survey invites.

The **Project Owner** role includes privileges for related records, such as the privilege to create a contact. When you send a survey invitation email, by default, Customer Voice creates a contact record. You can turn this option off (see *Figure 10.23*):

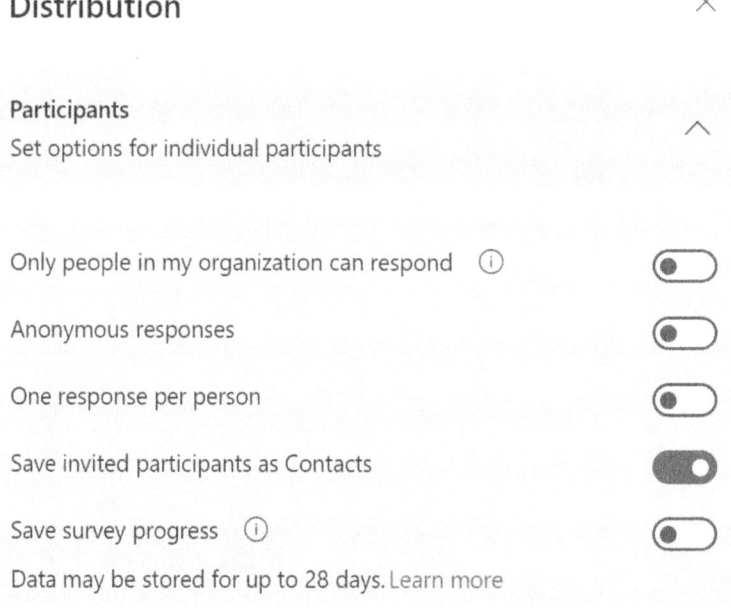

Figure 10.23 – Survey distribution settings

When working on a business solution, organizations often use different environments for development, testing, and production. Each environment has a different owner, and changes to the solution are first made in the development environment before they are moved to the testing environment. After the testing is complete, the changes are deployed to production.

Customer Voice supports multi-environment deployment, which we will discuss next.

Managing project deployment for Customer Voice

You can copy a project between environments within the same organization or across organizations. We will start with copying within the same organization.

Copying a project within the same organization

You can start by creating a Customer Voice project in your development environment. When you are ready to copy the project to a production environment, go to **All Projects**, select your project, click on the **…**, and select **Copy** from the pop-up menu, as shown in *Figure 10.24*:

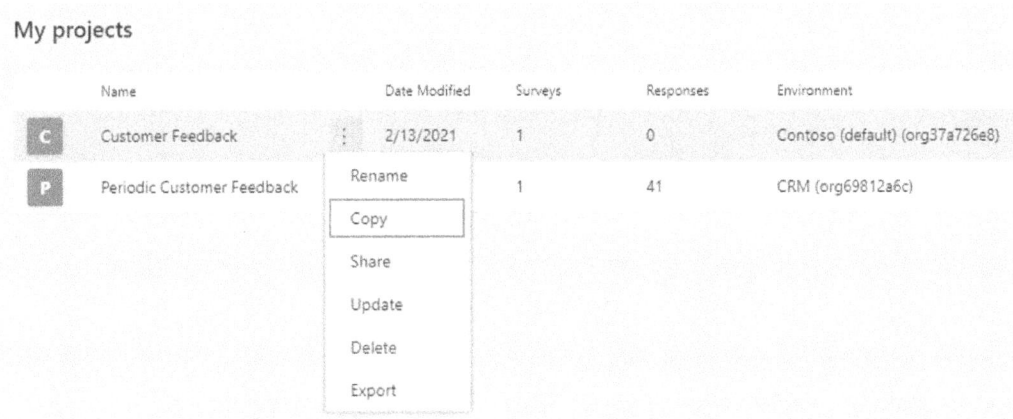

Figure 10.24 – Copying a project

Select the environment to copy to, as shown in *Figure 10.25*:

Copy to   ✕

Select where you'd like to copy your project

Current location

◯ Contoso (default) (org37a726e8)

Recent locations

◉ CRM (org69812a6c)

All locations ⌄

Copy   Cancel

Figure 10.25 – Selecting the destination environment to copy the project to

The copied project will have - **copy** appended to the project name, and you can use the **Rename** option to change the name, as shown in *Figure 10.26*:

Figure 10.26 – Renaming a project

If you are making changes to the project, you can do this in your development environment. When you are ready to deploy the changes to production, on the related production project, select **Update**, as shown in *Figure 10.27*:

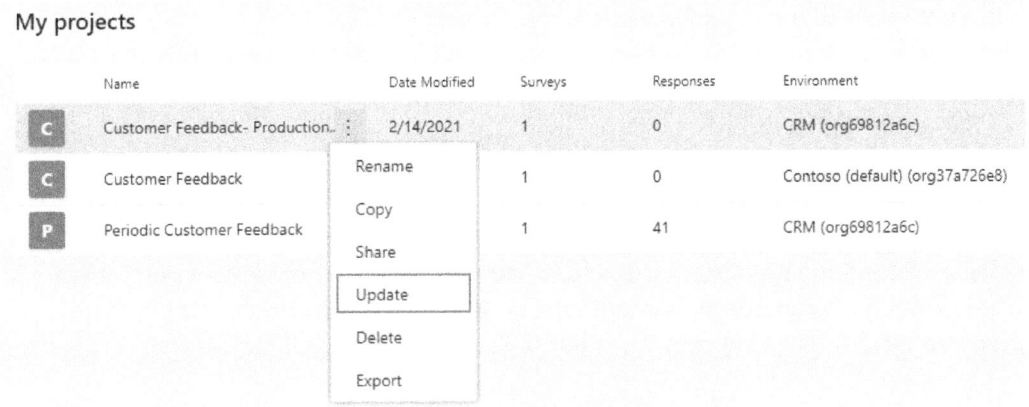

Figure 10.27 – Updating a project

In the dialog window, select the project to copy from (see *Figure 10.28*):

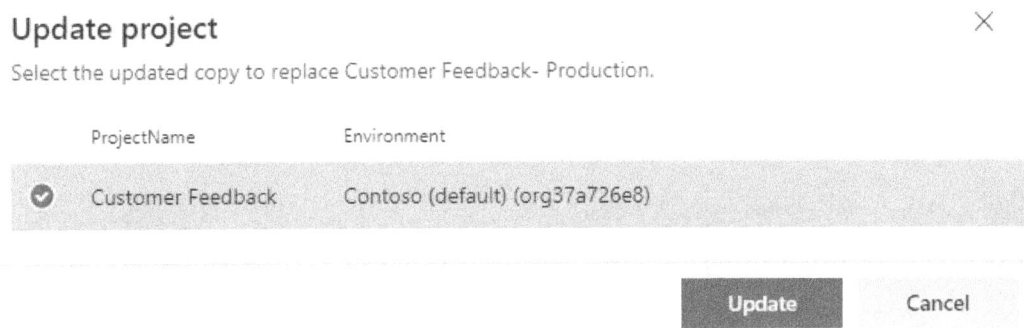

Figure 10.28 – Update project dialog window

The project will be updated based on the changes in the source project. Changes that are included in the copy include the following:

- Changes in the survey question, including branding, branching logic, personalization, and satisfaction metrics
- Survey translations
- Survey invitation email templates

What is not included in the project update is as follows:

- Permission/sharing
- Survey invitation records
- Survey response records

Sometimes you need to copy a project across different organizations; for example, you may have different organizations for sandbox and production. Another use case is when you are working with an external system integrator that creates a project within their organization and you need to copy it to your organization when it is ready.

Copy a project across organizations

To copy a project across organizations, follow these steps:

1. Select the project you would like to copy and, from the **...** menu, select **Export** (see *Figure 10.29*):

My projects

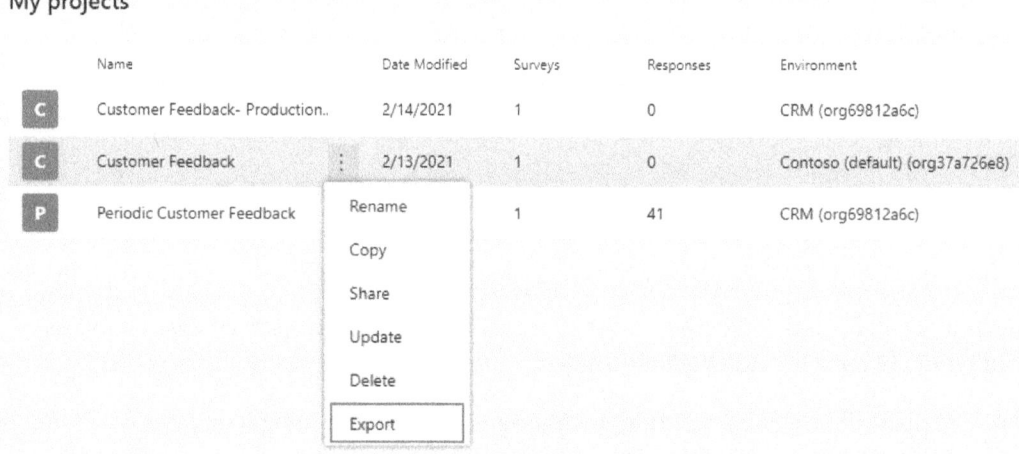

Figure 10.29 – Export project option

2. In the dialog box, copy the **Link to exported project** URL (as shown in *Figure 10.30*):

Link to exported project   ✕

https://customervoice.microsoft.com/nam/cvtemplateorch/api/CopyTemplate/e0b80473-9d55-490b-a3ca-a719f9aa458a/6be19d18-2f76-41eb-9790-71bc66a632d9

Copy   Cancel

Figure 10.30 – Link to the exported project

3. Log in to the destination organization by going to `https://customervoice.microsoft.com`.

4. Paste the URL in your browser.

The project will be created in the destination organization.

Summary

In this chapter, we reviewed the administrative settings for Microsoft Forms and Dynamics 365 Customer Voice to enable you to set the policy for surveys created in your organization. Customer Voice includes built-in integration with Dataverse. You can use the default Dataverse instance or a Dynamics 365-based Dataverse instance. When you connect Customer Voice to Dynamics 365 instances, you need to assign additional roles in the Dynamics 365 to ensure that only authorized users can send surveys to your contacts in Dynamics. Finally, we reviewed how to copy Customer Voice projects from one environment to another for multi-environment deployments.

In the next and last chapter of this book, we will review Customer Voice licensing and how you can manage license allocation.

11
Managing Usage with Dynamics 365 Customer Voice

Dynamics 365 Customer Voice requires a separate license and is based on the number of survey responses received. As an administrator, you would need to monitor usage and plan for the licenses to make sure your organization has adequate capacity for how you plan to use Customer Voice surveys in your business.

In this last chapter of the book, we will review the Customer Voice license model and how you can get usage reports and discuss the departmental capacity management that is being previewed in Customer Voice.

The chapter is organized as follows:

- The Customer Voice license model
- Survey response usage report
- Departmental capacity management

By the end of the chapter, you will understand how to plan and manage your Customer Voice licenses for your organization.

The Customer Voice license model

The Customer Voice license model is based on the number of survey responses received. You can send as many survey invitations as you need; what is measured is the actual responses to the survey. When you purchase a Customer Voice license, you start with the base license of 2,000 responses per month and you can purchase add-on licenses in the increment of 1,000 responses per month. For example, if you plan to receive 5,500 survey responses every month, then you need to buy the base license of 2,000 responses and four add-ons to get 6,000 responses per month (since the add-on is available in increments of 1,000, you need to round it up to the next 1,000).

If you have a Dynamics 365 for Enterprise license, which includes Dynamics 365 Sales Enterprise, Customer Service Enterprise, Field Service, Marketing, Human Resources, and Project Service Automation (see the complete and up-to-date list at `https://aka.ms/CustomerVoice`), then your first 2,000 responses per month are included and you purchase add-ons if you need more.

Note that the Customer Voice response capacity is set at the organization level and not at the user level, which means that regardless of whether your organization has 1 or 1,000 seats of a qualifying Dynamics 365 license, your organization would be entitled to the same 2,000 responses per month.

Customer Voice also does not limit the number of users who can create and send a survey. You could give access to everyone in your organization without needing to purchase a user license. Note that everyone in the organization consumes from the same response capacity pool and so the more users who can create and send a survey, the faster you will consume the capacity.

To limit the number of survey makers, Customer Voice provides a $0 Customer Voice **user license** (**USL**). This license is intended to give control to the administrator over who can create a survey in the organization. A user who has a Dynamics 365 license is automatically allowed to create a Customer Voice survey and the administrator can remove access by following the steps at `https://docs.microsoft.com/en-us/dynamics365/customer-voice/purchase#disable-dynamics-365-customer-voice-for-a-user`.

Customer Voice survey response monitoring

Customer Voice measures your survey response usage based on 12-month consumption, which enables you to use the Customer Voice monthly capacity to conduct a quarterly or annual survey. For example, if you purchase the base license of 2,000 responses per month, Customer Voice sets your capacity at 12 x 2,000 = 24,000. Your usage is calculated against the 24,000 capacity. As long as you do not accumulate more than 24,000 responses within the 12-month period, you are fine.

When your 12-month cumulative responses add up to 80% of your capacity, Customer Voice sends a warning. If you do not do anything, your surveys stop receiving responses at the capacity. If you need more time to purchase, you can request an extension by contacting Microsoft support.

Estimating survey response

Given that Customer Voice uses survey responses, how do you estimate what license you should purchase? You should start with estimating what type of feedback you would like to collect and how you'll collect the feedback, such as collecting feedback from your website visitors, through email surveys, or through SMS or social channels.

Next, you need to estimate the annual volume of the number of times you are asking customers or employees to fill out the survey. For example, if you are sending a quarterly survey to your 1,000 employees, then the annual volume would be 4 quarters/year x 1,000 employees = 4,000. If you are collecting feedback from your website visitors, then find out your annual website visits. If you are sending a survey after a support case is resolved, then determine the number of cases in the last 12 months.

For each survey, estimate the number of users responding to the survey. In general, internal employee surveys typically have a higher response rate than external customer feedback. For internal employee surveys, I have come across response rates from 40% for periodic and voluntary employee pulse checks to 80-90% for annual employee surveys where participation is highly encouraged. For external email surveys, many organizations use 10% as an average response rate estimate. Web feedback is typically less than 5% but depends on how you prompt your website visitors for feedback.

Then, multiply each response rate by the annual volume to get the total responses annually, as shown in *Figure 11*:

Channel	Annual volume	Estimated response rate	Estimated annual response
Customer feedback – email survey	10,000 cases	10%	1,000 responses
Employee feedback – email survey	4,000 surveys	40%	1,600 responses
Website visit	100,000 web visits	1%	1,000 responses
		Total	3,600 responses

Figure 11.1 – An example of annual response estimation

Finally, you can calculate what Customer Voice license you need to purchase.

After you purchase Customer Voice, you can use the Customer Voice usage report in the Microsoft 365 admin center.

Survey response usage report

To check the usage of Customer Voice, go to https://admin.microsoft.com, then click on **Usage** under the **Reports** section in the left navigation. Click on the **View More** button under **Dynamics 365 Customer Voice Activity** to open the report, as in *Figure 11.2*:

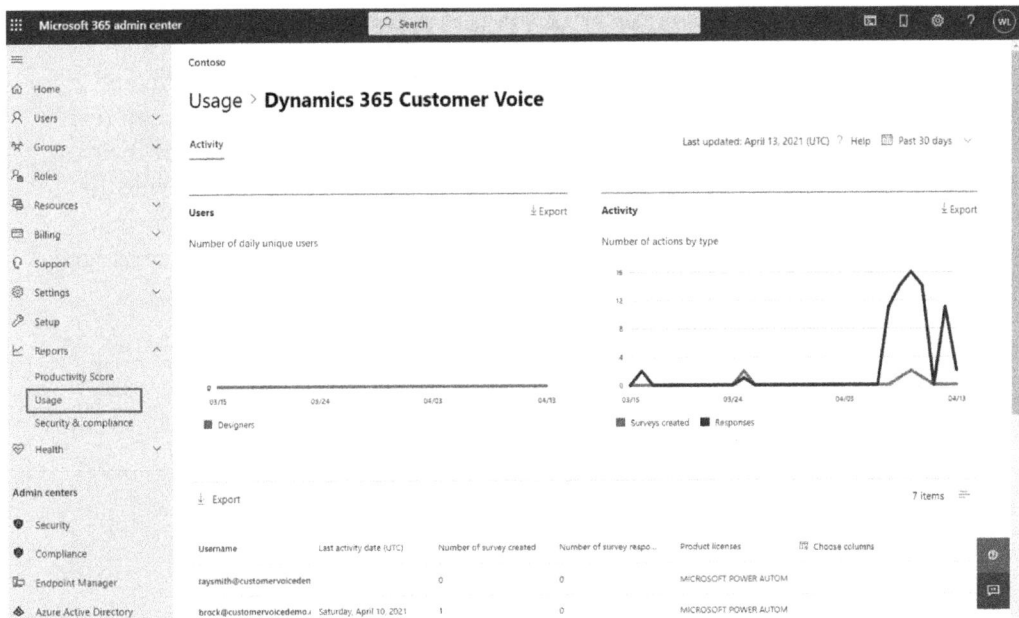

Figure 11.2 – Customer Voice usage report

The activity usage report in *Figure 11.2* shows the number of survey responses, the survey owner, and the number of responses received for each survey.

> **Important note**
>
> The usage report only goes back to the last 180 days. To get the complete response activities, you need to create a Power BI report. Refer to `https://aka.ms/CustomerVoiceUsageReport` for a video tutorial on how to create a report that aggregates results from Dataverse.

While the usage report provides information about who uses Customer Voice, it provides the information after the Customer Voice survey has been completed and it does not limit Customer Voice by department or prevent departments from using Customer Voice beyond the allocated capacity. For departmental capacity management, you need to use the allocation management feature in Customer Voice.

Departmental capacity management

For large enterprises, you may want to allocate a Customer Voice license to different departments. For example, the marketing department may have a need to send surveys for market research purposes and would like to purchase additional licenses for their project. Customer Voice is working on a feature to enable administrators to divide the license into multiple allotments and allocate an allotment to a different department. A tenant administrator must first create allotment(s); then the survey owner can assign the allotment to their project.

> **Important note**
>
> The tenant allotment feature is still being tested at the time of writing. The feature is planned to be available as a preview feature in summer 2021.

Creating and assigning allotments

Use the following steps to create and assign license allotments:

1. Go to `https://admin.microsoft.com` and navigate to **Licenses** under the **Billing** section, as shown in *Figure 11.3*. Click **Create allotment** to start:

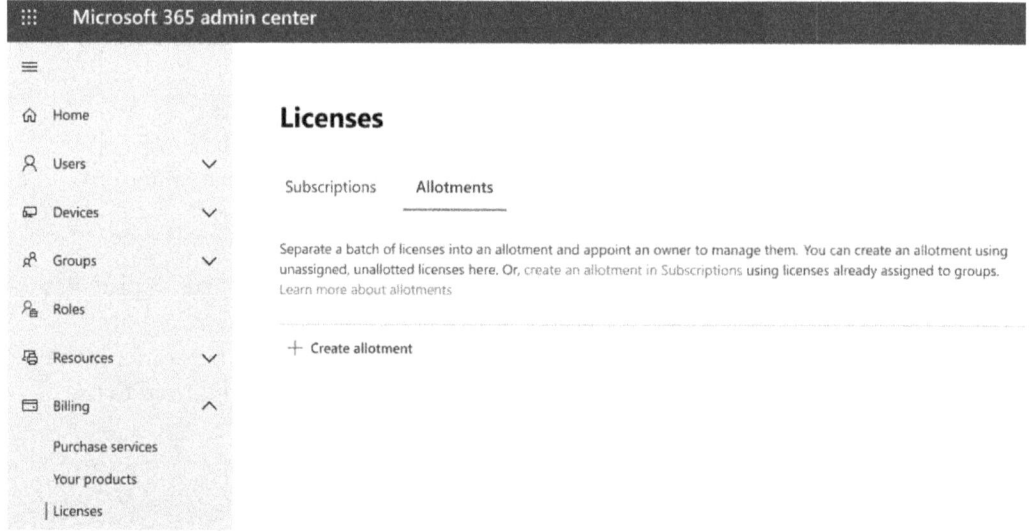

Figure 11.3 – License management in the admin center

2. Name your allotment and select the security group whose members can access the allotment (see *Figure 11.4*):

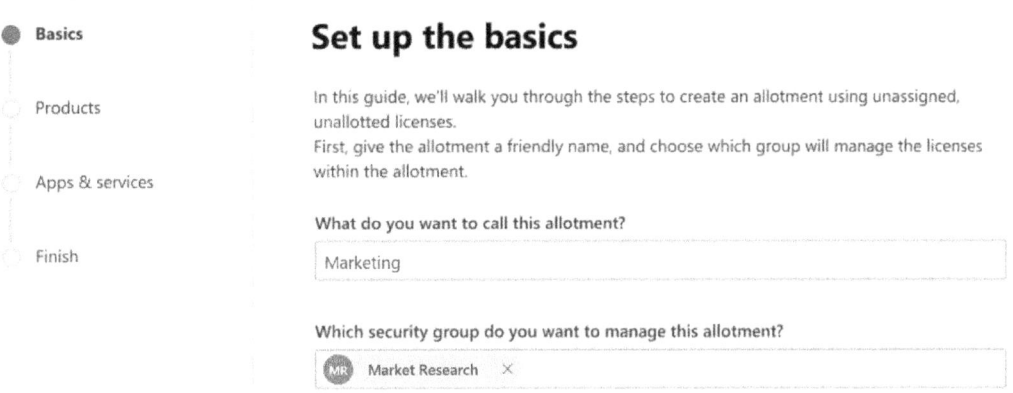

Figure 11.4 – Setting an allotment name and group ownership

3. Select **Dynamics 365 Customer Voice** in the product selection and type the number of licenses to assign to this allotment (*see Figure 11.5*). You can only assign up to the number of Customer Voice licenses your organization has purchased:

Create allotment

✔ Basics

● **Products**

○ Apps & services

○ Finish

Choose products

Select the products you'd like to include in this allotment, and set a limit on the number of licenses to be managed as part of the allotment.

If a product listed below doesn't have enough eligible licenses available, you can create an allotment using licenses already assigned to groups instead.

☑ Dynamics 365 Customer Voice

Licenses eligible for this allotment ⓘ
10

Set a license limit

| Enter a number up to 10 |

Figure 11.5 – Assigning the number of licenses to the allotment

4. Accept the default app settings on the next screen (see *Figure 11.6*). The allotment feature is designed across Microsoft products. This setting is not applicable to Customer Voice and so you can accept the default option:

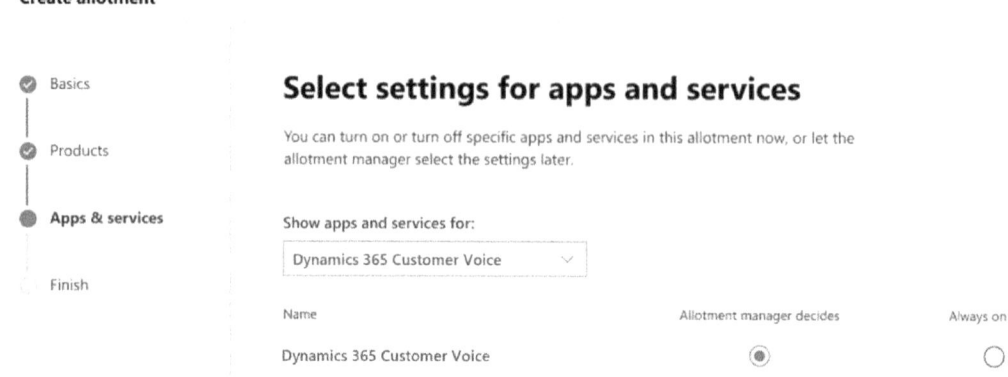

Figure 11.6 – Allotment app settings

5. The last step allows you to review and confirm the settings (see *Figure 11.7*). Click **Create allotment** to complete:

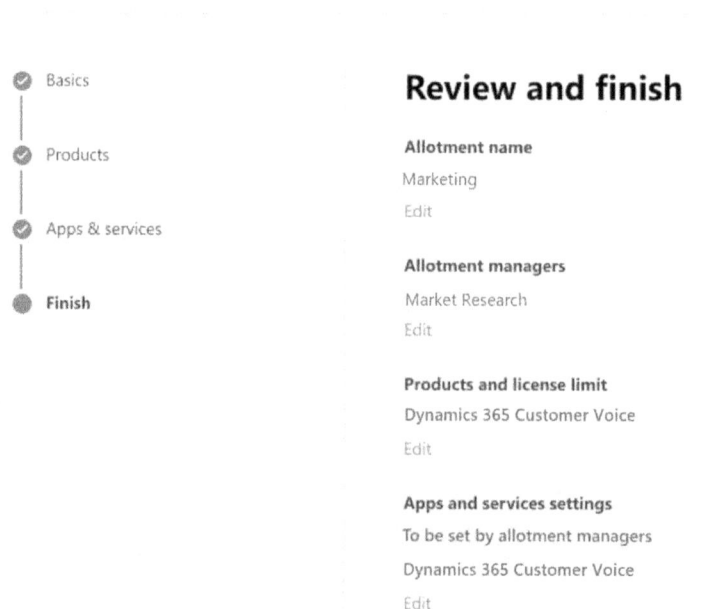

Figure 11.7 – The allotment confirmation page

After you create the allotment, members of the security group can select the allotment when creating a Customer Voice project.

Assigning a subscription to an allotment

A user who is a member of the specified security group can change the subscription associated with a project by opening the project and accessing the project action from the left panel (see *Figure 11.8*):

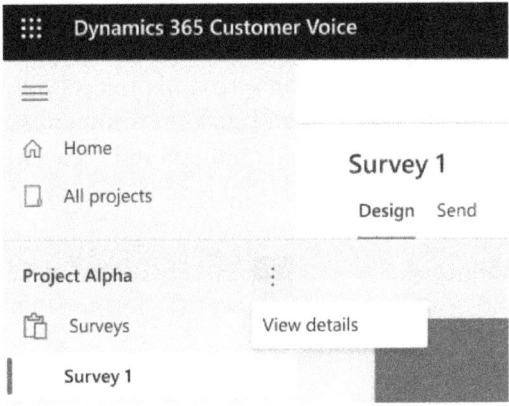

Figure 11.8 – Change subscription project action menu

Clicking the change subscription action opens a right-side panel where you can view the current subscription associated with the project, including how much has been used and the remaining capacity for the year. You can click the edit icon to open a drop-down menu with all the subscriptions available to you. If you are a member of the security group assigned by the administrator to the allotment, then the allotment will be available to you in the dropdown to select as your subscription (see *Figure 11.9*):

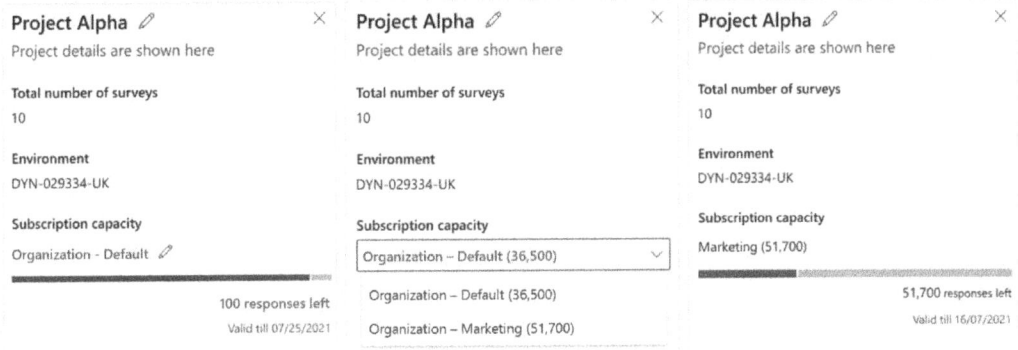

Figure 11.9 – Selecting a subscription panel

Selecting a subscription will change the usage and capacity chart accordingly. After you save the update to the subscription selection, any subsequent responses received from the survey will be counted against the assigned subscription and decrease the remaining capacity.

> **Important note**
>
> The remaining capacity is calculated daily, so any responses received would not be reflected in the subscription chart until the next day.

In addition to viewing the subscription usage and capacity on a specific project, you can also view the subscriptions' usage information across all projects you have access to. To access this, go to the **My projects** screen and click the **Show subscriptions** button at the top. A panel will open listing all the subscriptions and their usage information (see *Figure 11.10*):

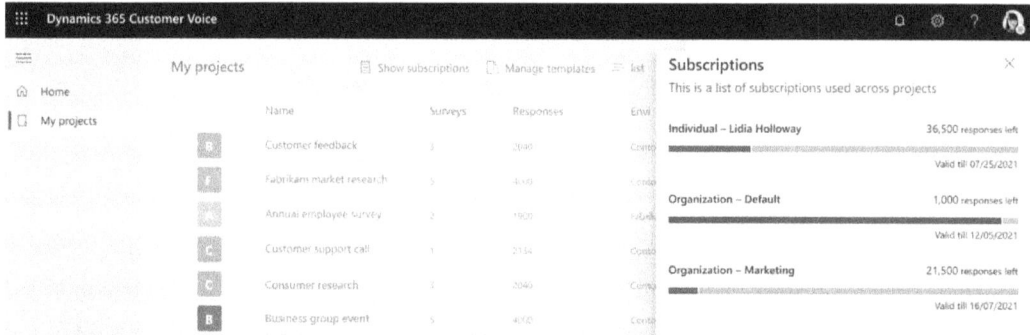

Figure 11.10 – Subscription information across all projects

Viewing all subscriptions enables you to monitor the usage capacity for all projects that you own or are shared with you. If any of the projects are nearing capacity, you can make an update to the project to change to another subscription or contact your administrator to purchase more licenses and assign the license to the allotment corresponding to the subscription.

Summary

In this chapter, we reviewed how Customer Voice measures survey responses and how you can monitor usage. Customer Voice has added a departmental allotment management functionality to enable you to divide Customer Voice licenses into multiple allotments and assign the allotments to a security group. Departmental allotment is available as a preview feature at the time of writing. You can check out `https://aka.ms/CustomerVoiceDoc` for the final documentation of the feature.

Using the capabilities we discussed in this chapter, you will now be able to manage the license capacity for Customer Voice and make sure different departments in your organization get the right capacity allocation for their survey needs.

James Phillips, president of Microsoft Digital Platform group said in the foreword that to deliver a great product experiences, organizations must learn from their customers. My team is actively listening and learning from you through our various feedback channels, whether that is through feedback surveys when you are using the product or through direct engagements from the community (`https://aka.ms/CustomerVoiceForum`) or by email (`customervoice@microsoft.com`). Please continue to provide your feedback – we will continue to improve our products to help collect feedback from your customers and take timely action to help you improve your product.

Packt.com

Subscribe to our online digital library for full access to over 7,000 books and videos, as well as industry leading tools to help you plan your personal development and advance your career. For more information, please visit our website.

Why subscribe?

- Spend less time learning and more time coding with practical eBooks and Videos from over 4,000 industry professionals

- Improve your learning with Skill Plans built especially for you

- Get a free eBook or video every month

- Fully searchable for easy access to vital information

- Copy and paste, print, and bookmark content

Did you know that Packt offers eBook versions of every book published, with PDF and ePub files available? You can upgrade to the eBook version at packt.com and as a print book customer, you are entitled to a discount on the eBook copy. Get in touch with us at customercare@packtpub.com for more details.

At www.packt.com, you can also read a collection of free technical articles, sign up for a range of free newsletters, and receive exclusive discounts and offers on Packt books and eBooks.

Other Books You May Enjoy

If you enjoyed this book, you may be interested in these other books by Packt:

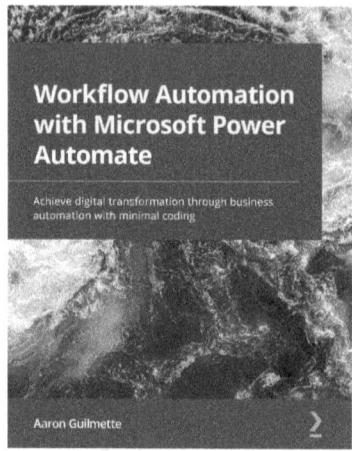

Workflow Automation with Microsoft Power Automate

Aaron Guilmette

ISBN: 978-1-83921-379-3

- Get to grips with the building blocks of Power Automate, its services, and core capabilities

- Explore connectors in Power Automate to automate email workflows

- Discover how to create a flow for copying files between two cloud services

- Understand the business process, connectors, and actions for creating approval flows

- Use flows to save responses submitted to a database through Microsoft Forms

- Find out how to integrate Power Automate with Microsoft Teams

Hands-On Microsoft Teams

João Ferreira

ISBN: 978-1-83921-398-4

- Create teams, channels, and tabs in Microsoft Teams
- Explore the Teams architecture and various Office 365 components included in Teams
- Perform scheduling, and managing meetings and live events in Teams
- Configure and manage apps in Teams
- Design automated scripts for managing a Teams environment using PowerShell
- Build your own Microsoft Teams app without writing code

Packt is searching for authors like you

If you're interested in becoming an author for Packt, please visit `authors.packtpub.com` and apply today. We have worked with thousands of developers and tech professionals, just like you, to help them share their insight with the global tech community. You can make a general application, apply for a specific hot topic that we are recruiting an author for, or submit your own idea.

Leave a review - let other readers know what you think

Please share your thoughts on this book with others by leaving a review on the site that you bought it from. If you purchased the book from Amazon, please leave us an honest review on this book's Amazon page. This is vital so that other potential readers can see and use your unbiased opinion to make purchasing decisions, we can understand what our customers think about our products, and our authors can see your feedback on the title that they have worked with Packt to create. It will only take a few minutes of your time, but is valuable to other potential customers, our authors, and Packt. Thank you!

Index

Lightning Source UK Ltd.
Milton Keynes UK
UKHW031835170522
403141UK00006B/1223